# Human
# Rights in
# International
# Politics

# Human Rights in International Politics

## AN INTRODUCTION

### Franke Wilmer

LYNNE
RIENNER
PUBLISHERS

BOULDER
LONDON

Published in the United States of America in 2015 by
Lynne Rienner Publishers, Inc.
1800 30th Street, Boulder, Colorado 80301
www.rienner.com

and in the United Kingdom by
Lynne Rienner Publishers, Inc.
3 Henrietta Street, Covent Garden, London WC2E 8LU

**Library of Congress Cataloging-in-Publication Data**
A Cataloging-in-Publication record for this book
is available from the Library of Congress.

ISBN 978-1-62637-148-4 (hc : alk. paper)
ISBN 978-1-62637-149-1 (pb : alk. paper)

**British Cataloguing in Publication Data**
A Cataloguing in Publication record for this book
is available from the British Library.

Printed and bound in the United States of America

 The paper used in this publication meets the requirements
of the American National Standard for Permanence of
Paper for Printed Library Materials Z39.48-1992.

5  4  3  2  1

# Contents

## Part 4  Where Do We Go from Here?

## 14  The Future of International Human Rights                    349

## 15  What Can I Do?                                             363

# Acknowledgments

WHO KNOWS HOW TO BEGIN OR END THE LIST OF PEOPLE WHO helped you to complete a project at least six years in the making? I first conceived of this book and proposed it to Lynne Rienner the same year that I decided to run for a seat in the Montana state legislature. Lynne liked the proposal, and I won the election. For the next seven years I played a firsthand role in a system of self-government created more than two centuries ago by people who were not only extraordinary, but also in many ways just like us. I wrote about civil liberties and fundamental freedoms while the Montana legislature debated abolishing the death penalty (we didn't), rejecting the Real ID Act (we did), and whether to restrict the distance between a funeral and Westboro Baptist Church–style protesters (we didn't). So I must thank my colleagues in the legislature on both sides of the aisle, as well as the voters who sent me there. I also thank the framers of our federal constitution and Montana state constitution, the latter being one of the most progressive in the country.

I thank Lynne Rienner not only for her initial enthusiasm, but for her perseverance and steadfast belief in the value of this book and its author through my four terms in the legislature (which without a doubt delayed progress several times) and as many rounds of reviews and revisions, and after all of that for being even more enthusiastic than she was when I first proposed the book. I thank my anonymous reviewers for taking so much time and care in responding to and suggesting improvements to the manuscript; it is absolutely a stronger work for all of their efforts. One person who must be thanked tremendously is Lillia Gajewski, the best, most knowledgeable, comprehensive, and insightful copyeditor I have ever worked with. No one has read this book more carefully and thoughtfully. Her expertise is indescribable and greatly valued.

I have taught human rights for decades and used versions of this text the past few years in classes large and small. My students have all contributed to its development and improvement—students from Montana and elsewhere in the United States, and from countries around the world. Their political views are diverse and conflicting. I thank them all. They are all coauthors, but all errors belong to me.

Not least, I thank my family and friends, with whom quality time was forfeited to the nights and weekends spent working on this project. In this regard, I especially thank my life partner, who patiently listened to every declaration of concern, frustration, and triumph that started with or included the phrase "the book." He must also be thanked for contributing substantively through numerous impassioned conversations on issues that strengthened our shared mistrust of government authority, though I have more hope than he does that it can also be used to relieve suffering, instead of causing it.

*—Franke Wilmer*

# Human Rights in International Politics

# 1

# Introduction

WHY, IN THE TWENTY-FIRST CENTURY, CAN WE STILL FIND SO MUCH needless and preventable human suffering, much of it caused by intentional human action? Don't we know a better way to be human? If the inherent dignity of any human being is impaired by conditions that can arise from and can be changed by human action—hunger, lack of access to clean water, torture, ethnic cleansing, genocide, discrimination—shouldn't we do everything we can to change those conditions, to stop and prevent suffering caused by human behavior and choices?

These questions, and others, lead people to want to know more about international human rights—and inspired me to write this book. The book is intended for those who have little specialized knowledge of the subject beyond familiarity with some of the more tragic and dramatic events reported in the media: genocides in Bosnia and Rwanda, mass human rights violations in Darfur, the growing problem of child soldiers, the long and brutal history of apartheid in South Africa, and rape in eastern Congo, to name a few. In this book, I address human rights concepts, theories, issues, and debates in an accessible way.

## The Framework and Structure of the Book

Two themes link the theories and subject matter of this text. One is the relationship between interests and values. In *A Framework for Political Analysis* (1965) David Easton famously defined *politics* as "the allocation of values." But where do values come from and how do they change over time? Values like economic freedom, political liberalism, social justice, nondiscrimination, cultural integrity, the inherent nature of human dignity, and the desire for greater security and prosperity give rise to interests and the con-

1

crete conditions and aspirations of material and social life. Interests—self-interests—are at the center of economic theory. They can be narrow and zero sum: that is, the more I get the less you have and vice versa. But political science takes a broader view of interests. They can be individual or collective, they can be self-centered or informed by shared values and a sense of shared fate, and they can change over time. We must always ask, "Whose values?" and "Whose interests?" when confronted with political actions and conditions that promote and protect or deprive people of human rights.

Constructivists provide some insight by claiming that interests are a product of identities and identities change over time. If interests are at least partly a product of values, and interests change, then values must also have changed. In the case of human rights, for example, why did they only emerge as international values in the twentieth century? The problems were not new; the arbitrary use of power to deprive people of their liberties and lives individually and collectively was not a twentieth-century phenomenon alone. Did human rights emerge at this historical moment because of a shift in how human beings understood what it meant to be human? Was the idea of inalienable human rights a product of Western thinking, a response to the institutional power of the modern state, an integral part of the identity of modern states, a culturally transcendent and universally good idea, or, to some extent, all of these? Interests and values are codetermined. From this perspective, human rights are asserted as values that transcend cultural and historical particularity to become common, human interests.

As a second theme, I highlight the dual role of the state as a perpetrator of human rights violations and as a protector of human rights. The relationship between contemporary international human rights and the formation of the modern state cuts at least two ways: as a limit on the authority of contemporary state institutions and as an expression of the liberal ideals of the Enlightenment. Human rights claims arose in response to centuries of abuses of power—the imprisonment of political enemies by despotic monarchs, torture, genocide, and extrajudicial execution, for example. Contemporary human rights are aimed at making government institutions more accountable and less abusive. In this view, the state is the problem, and respect for human rights is the solution. The other side of the balance sheet broadly implicates the role of the Enlightenment and spread of political liberalism in shaping the contemporary state as an institution of popular self-government, an expression of the authority that originates with the people and not from a divine or preordained source. Indeed, these two strands are connected by challenging the authority of the state and its excesses and are in many ways a consequence of shifting beliefs about the locus of authority from inherent in the state to inherent in the people.

Following this introduction, I begin Chapter 2 with an overview of the concept of human rights, the philosophies, theories, mechanisms, and documents that bear on and embody contemporary international human rights. This chapter serves as a broad introduction to the subject of international human rights. In Chapter 3, I explore the concept of human dignity across cultural traditions and then put the contemporary development of human rights into historical and cultural context. The thinkers of the Enlightenment articulated the idea that human beings, not institutional authority or power, ought to be the central concern of governance and source of authority. From this perspective, the state is an institutional expression of the Enlightenment's ideals. But are those ideals universal, or are they culturally specific to the experience of European societies? Contemporary international human rights emerged in the second half of the twentieth century as a central concern of world politics largely because of the unprecedented atrocities of the Holocaust as well as the predominant role of Western states in designing the postwar world order. But since then the number of states has quadrupled and non-Western voices have joined the dialogue, bringing new perspectives and challenging the emphasis on Western conceptions of international human rights.

The role of Western powers in this process raises questions about the universality of contemporary human rights, as discussed in Chapter 4. Are they universal or relative? Are they compatible with non-Western philosophical and religious traditions, or in fact, have non-Western traditions and actors already contributed to their modern conception and development? Does the prioritization of concerns differ across diverse historical experiences and cultural orientations? Do distinct Asian values exist, and if so, are they incompatible with prevailing conceptions of international human rights? Are Islamic beliefs inherently irreconcilable with international human rights norms? What role do human rights play in the recent Arab Spring revolutions against authoritarian governments?

In Part 2, I begin, in Chapter 5, with a critical examination of the relationship between human rights and the state by identifying a number of issues where this intersection has positive, negative, or ambiguous consequences for international human rights. These issues include the assertion of state sovereignty, its claim to a monopolization of legitimate force, constitutionalism, secularism, and state reliance on the construction of national identity in mobilizing internal support and legitimation. Of these, sovereignty is surely the most controversial and often regarded as a major roadblock to the enforcement of international human rights standards. The "dark side" of state sovereignty—the use of state autonomy as a shield against intervention—is, can, or ought to be mitigated by the rule of law. But the rule of law is weak to nonexistent in many states as well as at the international level. Furthermore, it can be severely weakened or undermined even in strong democracies when a climate of fear prevails under threats to national security, as happened in Britain during the "Troubles" in Northern Ireland and the United States in the aftermath of the 9/11 attacks.

How international human rights are implemented in national and international venues is the subject of Chapter 6. The range of mechanisms and strategies is broad, from national laws, foreign policies, and national reconciliation efforts to provisions linked directly to international treaties and conventions, international judicial institutions, and international commissions.

Nonstate actors play an increasingly important role in all aspects of international relations, and the area of human rights is no exception. In Chapter 7, I survey a variety of nonstate actors, including nongovernmental organizations (NGOs) and social movements, whose activities are undertaken to promote and protect human rights through advocacy, action, and publicity. I also include those nonstate actors whose activities are associated with the human rights violations, such as terrorist organizations, organized crime, and irregular armed forces. The role of multinational corporations is examined in this chapter as well.

In Part 3, I cover a range of human rights issues, beginning in Chapter 8 with genocide. I focus on the twentieth century when the definition and prohibition of genocide were raised to the level of a *jus cogens* norm—a norm from which no derogation is permitted. The horrors of the Holocaust propelled genocide to the top of the UN agenda in the aftermath of World War II, but the Holocaust was not the first or last genocide in the twentieth century. Political controversy still surrounds the Turkish government's unwillingness to acknowledge the Armenian genocide under Ottoman rule. The Armenian genocide, the Holocaust, and the atrocities committed in Bosnia and Rwanda seem to fit the criteria for genocide in a straightforward way. Two additional cases are raised that highlight weaknesses in the current definition of genocide and the application of that definition for the purposes of international law and action. Does a situation count as genocide when perpetrated by nonstate actors and the state fails to stop it or even tacitly approves? The International Criminal Court (ICC) in the case of Darfur must address this question in its investigations into the crimes in Darfur. The last case involves indigenous peoples, where state and nonstate actors have colluded to eliminate them as a group through direct and indirect violence over a long historical period and, in some cases, up into the present.

In Chapter 9, I continue examining the history, development, and current challenges to international human rights in the context of warfare. Arguably, the laws of warfare beginning in the middle of the nineteenth century, which attempted to "civilize" the conduct of war in Western societies, mark one of the earliest efforts to codify internationalized human rights. Provisions of and obligations under the Geneva Conventions have become controversial recently not only because of accusations that the United States violated treaty obligations by torturing prisoners in Guantanamo or creating a category of prisoners (unlawful enemy combatants), which the United States claims are not protected by the Geneva Conventions, but also because questions arise in conflicts involving nonstate actors, such as ethnic groups in the Yugoslav wars of secession, as well as those designated as terrorist groups, particularly when they use unconventional tactics and weapons.

In Chapter 10, I review the civil liberties and political rights that have coevolved with the liberal democratic states. These generally fall into the category of what many call "negative" rights, that is, rights protected by prohibitions on state conduct (versus "positive" rights that necessitate state action in order to be realized, such as providing clean water and sanitation). Civil liberties and political rights create a system of due process that restricts how governments may assert coercive authority by protecting individuals when subjected to it. Violations, such as torture, incommunicado detention, and extrajudicial and summary executions, implicate a failure or denial of due process.

In Chapter 11, I take up the question of civil rights and the related problem of discrimination, concluding with a brief look at some of the newer or emerging rights issues. Civil rights include freedom from discrimination, whether as a direct or indirect consequence of public policy or citizens' engagement in discriminatory practices in a private capacity. Discrimination can blur the distinction between positive and negative rights when the state acts to prohibit discriminatory practices by private citizens and provide legal remedy to those injured by discrimination, even when it occurs through the actions of private citizens. Discrimination also affects political rights when it is institutionalized and impairs an individual's ability to participate in civil and political life. States have historically been perpetrators of discriminatory practices that not only deny or deprive individuals of rights because of their identity as members of a particular group or class of people but also deny whole groups equal protection under the law and equal rights to political participation.

The issue of women's human rights is discussed in Chapter 12, which addresses a broad spectrum of political, legal, and social practices that diminish the status of women and deprive them of equality and basic human needs. In many cases, these conditions can result in direct injury and death. From a rights perspective, this issue is similar to other kinds of discrimination with an important distinction: discrimination and violence against women are deeply embedded within social and cultural practices involving the most intimate human relations and have been reproduced over a long historical period. Political and legal institutionalization of women's second-class citizenship is rooted in patriarchal beliefs about gender differences that, unlike racial or religious differences, are still rationalized on the grounds of biological difference. Arguments about cultural relativism are more often used to defend against changing laws and practices that marginalize and injure women.

In Chapter 13, I consider rights that, although not generally seen as basic freedoms, are necessary to achieve and maintain a healthy and secure lifestyle, as well as the social and political conditions necessary for the protection of cultural integrity. One question considered in that chapter is whether certain rights are inherently human rights that go beyond basic freedoms, equal opportunity for political and civil participation, and meeting basic human material needs. A number of issues in international human rights cut across the boundaries of civil, political, economic, social, and cultural rights.

In Chapter 14, I reflect on the future of human rights and return to a consideration of the relationship between human rights and the state. Do further realization and protection of human rights necessitate a reform of the state? What progress has been made in the development of an international human rights regime, and what needs to be done to make it more effective? What is the relationship between human rights and the democratization of world order? How useful are theories in explaining the causes of human rights violations and formulating solutions to prevent them?

In Chapter 15, I provide some ideas for further engagement or action on the part of the reader. The breadth of issues and the scale and severity of suffering caused by the failure to protect people against human rights abuses can be overwhelming and leave one with a sense of helplessness. In this short final chapter, I suggest ways in which readers who want to act on what they have learned but who have different amounts of time and interest can engage in activities to promote better respect for human rights.

## Advocacy and Human Rights

One of the questions inevitably raised as one teaches a course on international human rights is whether, where, and how to draw a boundary between scholarship and advocacy. International human rights as a subject proceeds from the premise that more respect for and protection of human rights would make the world a better, more humane place. Human rights are really also about human wrongs, and in this way, the subject itself constitutes a normative claim that rights are good and violations of or failure to respect rights are bad. Implicit in the subject is the normative directive that something should be done, by individuals acting privately as well as by governments as public actors, to reduce violations and increase respect for human rights. At the same time, many human rights issues should and do provoke debates among policymakers, among private citizens, and, certainly, in class. Writing an introductory textbook inserts the author into these debates. Students are encouraged to read critically and to challenge the normative claims made in this book. At times, in the text, I point out where these debates are taking place already and invite students to join them. But implicit normative claims are also made by way of choosing which topics to cover, deciding how much coverage to afford a particular issue, and suggesting explanations about the causes of certain human rights problems.

For example, many contemporary human rights violations—from genocide and ethnic cleansing to the dispossession and forced assimilation of indigenous peoples—indicate that a root cause of human rights problems is racial and ethnic discrimination and intolerance. By itself, this claim is not very controversial. But this text suggests that these factors are at the root and are so difficult to address because the structure and the narrative of the state as a natural expression of a national identity privilege one racial or ethnic identity over others, even without a malevolent intention to discriminate. Particular languages and cultural practices, as well as ethnic, communal, or religious identities, are marginalized by their minority status. This marginalization is inevitable in a world of just under 200 states and several thousand ethnic, identity, or communal groups given both the current role of identity in constructing narratives about the state and pragmatic issues such as the necessity of designating official languages to conduct civic discourse in the state.

One of the most pressing issues in contemporary debates about liberalism is its compatibility with multiculturalism. Can liberalism mitigate the tension between the quest for national unity and cohesiveness within states on the one hand and the fact of their multinational or multicultural demographic makeup on the other? Readers may disagree with the claim that racial and ethnic intolerance is a major cause of many human rights problems. They may disagree that the structure of the modern state exacerbates the problem and counter that liberalism has not yet clearly provided philosophical guidance that can resolve the issue. Alternatively, readers may agree with these claims and then proceed to think about ways to mitigate the tendency to privilege one identity over others in the state. Either way, they will have something to think about, and this text is spared from being a catalog or encyclopedia of human rights.

Finally, many of the worst human rights problems that directly and indirectly result in human suffering, for lack of a better way of putting it, occur because of the failure to understand them as preventable. The violence and killing in Darfur from 2003 to 2007, for instance, was simultaneously a civil war against the Sudanese government by a coalition of rebel groups, a ruthless counterinsurgency by said government, a conflict that implicates identity differences where Arab identity has been privileged and non-Arabs marginalized, and the site of widespread atrocities against unarmed and noncombatant civilians. The United Nations condemned the violence and authorized an intervention; however, only the African Union acted on that authority, sending a grossly inadequate force—only numbering several hundred troops—into the region. A UN arms embargo was undermined by Russia and China, while other permanent members of the Security Council remained focused on the ongoing wars in Iraq and Afghanistan and showed little political will to materially support an intervention in Sudan. Estimates of the number killed remain unsettled, but somewhere close to a half million people likely died in Darfur, with as many as 80 percent dying from diseases such as diarrhea resulting from deprivation of clean water and sanitation rather than from direct violence.

Virtually every issue involving human rights raises questions about justice and the ethical responsibility to act to prevent or intervene in human suffering whenever possible. As Henry Shue (1980) argues, starvation, disease, and the deprivation of basic needs like clean water kill human beings just as certainly as do torture, war, and genocide. To educate about human rights is to advocate their protection and to progress toward the elimination of the conditions and practices associated with the violation of these rights. This book was therefore also written as a call to action, a call to the reader to think about and do some things differently.

# Part 1
## What Are Human Rights?

# 2

# Human Rights: Concepts and Theories

Where, after all, do universal human rights begin? In small places, close to home—so close and so small that they cannot be seen on any maps of the world. Yet they are the world of the individual person; the neighborhood he lives in; the school or college he attends; the factory, farm, or office where he works. Such are the places where every man, woman, and child seeks equal justice, equal opportunity, equal dignity without discrimination. Unless these rights have meaning there, they have little meaning anywhere. Without concerted citizen action to uphold them close to home, we shall look in vain for progress in the larger world.
—Eleanor Roosevelt at the United Nations, March 27, 1958

POLITICS IS ABOUT BOTH INTERESTS AND VALUES. THE CONTENTIOUS-ness between these two often-conflicting features of political life is nowhere more evident than in the area of human rights. The idea of human rights has broad appeal, and most people would agree that all human beings should be afforded some basic rights. But disagreements quickly surface when the discussion turns to identifying specific rights that ought to be basic or the obligations that follow from those basic rights. Asserting human rights places obligations on governments, for example, to refrain from or engage in certain kinds of actions, follow the requirements of due process, and guarantee economic opportunities that enable people to meet their basic needs. Yet these kinds of discussions are exactly those that people and societies must have when they address issues of human rights. Discussions about human rights reveal many cleavages involving both interests and values, such as security versus civil liberties, collective versus individual welfare, or universal claims versus culturally relative practices.

The philosophical question "What rights should all humans have?" is intimately tied to what it means to be human. In that sense, virtually every

11

culture or tradition engages questions of human rights and the conditions necessary to maintain human dignity. Confucianism, for example, focuses on both the ethical obligations and duties humans have to one another within a complex network of familial and societal relationships to maintain the necessary social harmony and commitment to family (de Bary 1998; de Bary and Weiming 1998; Jacobsen and Bruun 2000; Angle 2002). Although this contrasts with the Western emphasis on rights asserted by individuals primarily as a limit on government, Confucius also advocated for achieving and maintaining a social harmony that does not rely on force and that places limits on government power (Little 2005).

Two things distinguish contemporary discussions of human rights. First, human rights are seen as truly international, transnational, global, and cross-cultural. They are international because they literally involve representatives of all states and are therefore a concern of all states in their relations with one another. But they are also transnational because violations, consequences, and interventions on behalf of human rights take place across national boundaries and are undertaken by people and states acting in concert across state boundaries. The protection and promotion of human rights are features of modern international relations, but the preservation of human rights also concerns nonstate actors like NGOs as well as ordinary people who do not represent states. These discussions are global not only because the scale of concern is worldwide, and actions and debates take place among people virtually everywhere in the world, but also because the issues raised by human rights are deeply embedded in global processes and structures. Discussions about human rights are also cross-cultural because they occur among people of diverse cultural and philosophical orientations.

Second, contemporary discussions about human rights engage people acting in both official and unofficial capacities and across the boundaries of cultural difference in seeking agreement about human rights. This aspect of human rights gives rise to debates about their universality. Do certain rights transcend differences of nationality, citizenship, or cultural orientation? On what basis can a claim about universality be made: consensus in the international community, natural law, or the inherent quality of human rights? Two features—the global scale of discussions about human rights and the cultural diversity of those engaged in them—are unprecedented in human history.

Notwithstanding the persistence of narrowly conceived national security and state interests, the tragedies of human-induced humanitarian crises, and the fragmentation of political will that often hinders the development of an effective and enforceable global human rights regime, some progress in the articulation and promotion of human rights norms over the past half century is evident. The creation of the International Criminal Tribunal for the Former Yugoslavia (ICTY), International Criminal Tribunal for Rwanda (ICTR), and International Criminal Court (ICC), humanitarian interventions authorized by the United Nations and the North Atlantic Treaty Organization (NATO), and the establishment of numerous truth commissions all attest to a growing consensus on the need to develop mechanisms and institutions to address and redress, if not prevent, human rights violations. Economic, social, and cultural rights are more problematic to secure because their realization depends on a complicated relationship between policies strongly influenced by politics, trade and development, debt, debt relief, and economic assistance, as well as the political conditions in countries where economic and social deprivations are most severe. Cultural rights are also problematic to secure because the boundaries of cultures and the boundaries of states are enormously incongruous.

## What Are Human Rights?

Human rights—those rights that inhere in all people by virtue of their simply being human—are inalienable, indivisible, interdependent, and not subject to derogation—or in legal terms, nonderogable (Morsnik 2009). They are considered inalienable because they are fundamental to being human and cannot be separated or alienated from our humanity. Any attempt to restrict or remove them must be undertaken only through due process of law and only with a just reason, such as conviction of criminal violation of the law. They are also indivisible because they are all necessary to live a fully dignified and decent life: that is, if any one of them is taken away or impaired, the fundamental dignity and decency of life is impaired. Their interdependence means that they are mutually dependent on one another: for example, the exercise of political rights is meaningless without the fulfillment of basic economic, social, and cultural rights.

Human rights are also legally not subject to derogation, meaning that they cannot be limited or taken away without extraordinary justification. For example, states may derogate rights like freedom of speech or assembly under declared states of emergency. Article 4, paragraph 2, of the International Covenant on Civil and Political Rights (ICCPR) explicitly states that no derogation may be made to the right to life; freedom from torture or cruel, inhuman, or degrading punishment; right to knowledgeable consent for medical or scientific experimentation; freedom from slavery or servitude; freedom from imprisonment because of inability to fulfill a contractual obligation; the principle of legality in the field of criminal law (one cannot be tried for offenses that were not offenses at the time of commission); right to recognition as a person before the law; and right to freedoms of thought, conscience, and religion as spelled out in the covenant.

If rights inhere in us because we are human, then our humanity is the source of human rights, which is a moral claim. Human rights are legal, political, and socially created, and they raise moral, legal, political, and social questions. They even raise economic questions like whether every human being who is born has a right to the essential necessities of physical existence—food, water, and shelter. Basic health care can also be added, but then what constitutes basic health care must be stipulated. This approach to defining human rights is one of focusing on basic human needs or basic rights. The question of whether human rights are culturally specific or universal, discussed more thoroughly in Chapter 4, raises one of the perennial questions in debates about human rights.

Regardless of how moral claims about human rights are philosophically grounded, they remain social facts, or nonphysical facts created by social processes that only have meaning within the context of those processes. Money, for example, is a social fact most people use every day, but it is really just paper (or metal) with certain pictures, words, and numbers imprinted on it. Without social agreement among its users about its value and how it can be used, it would remain a physical fact of a trivial nature—a piece of paper with things printed on it. Similarly, as a social fact, a right can be held by one person and asserted against someone else or against a social institution. Rights are intangible resources allocated by political institutions and secured by law. Who gets what rights, when, how, and where, and how they will be promoted, protected, and enforced are political and legal questions. Whether the moral basis of human rights is attributed to God, natural law, or our humanity, they are not observable until they are recognized politically and, arguably, enforced legally.

The question of how moral claims of human rights are grounded should not be dismissed as an inconsequential metaphysical discussion. The moral basis of human rights depends on how questions like "Where do human rights come from?" and "Why should we have human rights?" are answered, and those answers, in turn, compel people to support human rights, or not. These questions are foundational and normative to political and legal order, and changes in that order can be observed over time. Discussing the origin of the idea of human rights necessarily involves the philosophical assumptions of personal and particular moral claims. People tend to answer the question—"Where do human rights come from?"—in one of three basic ways.

First, some suggest that human rights are God given. In his 1963 "Letter from Birmingham Jail," Martin Luther King Jr. wrote, "We have waited for more than 340 years for our constitutional and God-given rights" (King 1990). While the allusion to God may strengthen and broaden the appeal of such arguments, such an appeal can be problematic because people have different conceptions of God and different religious frameworks for making rights claims, for example, opposition to legal abortion is often grounded in religious doctrine of "ensoulement," when a fetus becomes a human being endowed with the same rights as other human beings. However, different religions have different answers to this question.

The second answer comes from Thomas Jefferson and the US Declaration of Independence: "We hold these truths to be self evident, that all men are created equal." The self-evident argument is premised on natural law, the idea of an implicit moral order that underlies human society. The moral order of natural law derives from human nature, from the world in which humans live, and from the ability of humans to be reasonable and reflective. In addition to equality, the signatories regarded as self-evident the belief that humans are "endowed by their Creator with certain inalienable rights; that among these are life, liberty, and the pursuit of happiness." Those who favor a natural law orientation also often argue that law can never be entirely separated from morality and that some kinds of law ultimately rest on the authority of moral claims. The argument for human rights as based in natural law is similar to arguments that locate the moral authority for human rights in a concept of God because in both cases the authority on which the moral claim rests cannot be contested through logical debate. However, natural law does not rely on an appeal to God or divine authority. Rather, it derives from the Enlightenment notion that reason is a universal human capacity that leads people to certain moral conclusions. Holding "truths" as "self-evident" means that any reasonable person on reflection would come to the same conclusion that all human beings are created equal.

Third, human rights are the rights all people have by virtue of their being human. This answer also implicates natural law because rights are conceived as part of our nature or existence as humans. This argument derives both from the belief that being human involves something transcendent and that humans have widely recognized down through history: human beings in a global society cannot disregard the basic humanity of others without diminishing our own humanity. This is well known to psychologists who study the psychological impact of torture on perpetrators (Jayatunge 2010). This idea is elegantly captured by the African idea of *ubuntu,* which roughly translated means "my humanity is only fully realized through my relationship with and respect for your humanity" (Battle 1997:5).

Even though human rights may not exist as social facts until a consensus about their existence is expressed politically, and even though they are not enforceable without both laws and the political will to enforce them, one should still talk about human rights in the absence of political agreement, legal recognition, and a willingness to enforce the law. Indeed, politics—the authoritative allocation of values, as David Easton (1965) put it—is very much about discourse as well as decisionmaking. In democracies, decisionmaking is preceded by discourse that takes place in both formal and informal settings. An issue or a problem gets onto the decisionmaking agenda by being talked about in the media and civil society, as well as, eventually, in a legislative body, where it can be acted on.

A good example is genocide and the idea of genocide as a crime. The term *genocide* did not come into wide use until the second half of the twentieth century. However, that someone in the world today would not know what this word means seems unlikely, though it is sometimes used rather loosely to refer to mass atrocities. It was originated by Raphael Lemkin, a Jewish lawyer born in Poland in 1900, who was deeply disturbed by the Armenian genocide in Turkey that occurred between 1915 and 1917. He spearheaded a campaign against what he initially called barbarity and what others at the time called race murder. Lemkin eventually conceived the term *genocide* and fought to make genocide illegal under national and international law.

Human rights violations are physical, material facts. People are murdered, tortured, made to disappear, deprived of basic needs even to the point of death, and subjected to cruelty as a result of state action or failure to act. But when defining, seeking agreement, and acting to protect human rights, their social construction as social facts also soon becomes apparent. The adage that "one man's terrorist is another man's freedom fighter," the claim that the same act of violence can be regarded as an act of oppression or liberation depending on whose interests and values are being articulated, illustrates the importance of recognizing both the material and social dimensions of human rights facts.

## Protecting and Promoting Rights

Rights are asserted to protect individuals and groups against abusive and arbitrary actions by governments and private individuals as well as to protect individuals against a government's failure to act or intercede on their behalf when others are violating their rights. An acknowledgment of basic rights provides a shield of protection and a sphere of security. Through this acknowledgment, an individual's rights can be asserted, thereby restraining or limiting another's actions or obligating a third party to intervene. For example, recognizing a right to due process means that when a government uses coercive power against individuals, it must do so according to a legally proscribed process—the rule of law. Due process distinguishes arbitrary power from authoritative power. Most elements of due process are found in a state's constitution, but some have been progressively recognized over time through judicial precedent and generally recognized principles of law. Due process applies to making, enforcing, and adjudicating the law, so it affects the legislative, executive, and judicial functions of government. The right to a speedy and fair trial and protection against cruel and unusual punishment, for instance, are due process rights that place restrictions and obligations on the judicial branch. But a police officer arresting a criminal suspect must also observe the limits of due process, informing the accused of his or her rights, allowing the person to inform others of the arrest, allowing the accused to obtain legal representation before questioning, and refraining from coercion to extract a confession. Additionally, laws must be written so that people can understand what is legal and what is not, and a law cannot be applied retroactively. These are elements of due process, too.

Rights that result in a restriction of governmental behavior include not only the requirements of due process but also fundamental freedoms such as those enumerated in the First Amendment to the US Constitution—freedoms of speech, press, religion, petition, and assembly. The Canadian Charter of Rights and Freedoms is incorporated into the Canadian Constitution through the Constitution Act of 1982. The term *the bill of rights* derives from the English Bill of Rights—literally a bill passed by Parliament in 1689. A hundred years later, French revolutionaries issued the Declaration of the Rights of Man and of the Citizen.

Fundamental rights also extend more broadly to many civil and political freedoms. For example, no one, whether acting on behalf of a government or as a private individual, may obstruct someone from exercising a right to vote on an equal basis with all other voters and without discrimination. However, having such a right does not mean that if a polling location closes at 5 p.m. and a voter arrives at 5:15 p.m. to vote, he or she must be allowed to vote, so long as all voters arriving after 5 p.m. are not allowed to vote, and so long as all voters had an equal and reasonable chance to know what hours the polls would be open. Political rights are equal rights to participate in political processes. The rights to which people are entitled because they are citizens are civil rights, such as the basic or fundamental freedoms of speech and association or the right to be protected against discrimination.

The right to be free from discrimination places an obligation on private persons (or groups) as well as on governments and their representatives. An employer, for instance, is acting as a private person when making a decision to hire someone and is obligated by the establishment of civil rights to give all applicants equal and fair consideration based on their qualifications rather than on their race, sex, religion, ethnic identity, age, disability, or political affiliation. The same applies to other employment decisions such as promotions, raises, and working conditions. Even if particular democracies differ over the specific protected classes and the protected activities, such as employment, education, government services, and finance, all democracies are expected to recognize civil rights in concept and practice.

Basic individual rights and freedoms are those government cannot interfere with unless they are exercised in a way that creates a "clear and present danger," in the words of the US Supreme Court (restricting speech such as yelling "fire" in a crowded auditorium). Fundamental freedoms have a long and well-established tradition in Western democracies, but some rights also place expectations on governments to take action in order for rights to be enjoyed. The right to work, for instance, is widely recognized in many Western democracies other than the United States, and it obligates governments to pursue policies that maximize employment at wages that enable workers to meet their basic human needs. The Universal Declaration of Human Rights, passed by the United Nations in 1948, says that everyone has the right to work, to free choice of employment, to just and favorable conditions of work, and to protection against unemployment. These economic human rights are asserted on the basis of arguments both about economic justice and against exploitative labor practices. Most documents recognizing the right to work include an explicit recognition of the right of workers to organize. However, in the United States, antiunion forces advocate so-called right-to-work laws that generally work against the ability of workers to organize labor unions. Economic and social rights generally create obligations for governments to do something in order for those rights to be fulfilled.

Another example of an economic and social right—the subject of some controversy in the United States today—is the expectation that employers will undertake an affirmative action to remedy a history of discriminatory practices. In Europe, affirmative action is called positive action or positive discrimination. Although neither the United States nor the European Union has an official definition of affirmative action, a directive by the EU Council, the main decisionmaking body of the European Union, suggests that "the concept of positive action embraces all measures which aim to counter the effects of past discrimination, to eliminate existing discrimination and to promote equality of opportunity" (quoted in Defeis 1999:17). Several international agreements encourage positive action to remedy historical discrimination, including the International Convention on the Elimination of All Forms of Racial Discrimination and the Framework Convention for the Protection of National Minorities.

Developed as a corollary to equal opportunity civil rights law, particularly dealing with education and employment, affirmative action came about because stopping discrimination through enacting laws is not enough. Societies have a moral obligation to remedy historical patterns of discrimination and their effects. Even when all forms of discrimination cease to exist so that no child experiences discrimination from birth onward, theoretically a full generation would still have to come and go before a group began to realize all of the benefits of ending discrimination. Normally affirmative action means extending the recruitment area and process to include in the applicant pool a yield of applicants that proportionately represents a minority group (ethnic minority, women, etc.) according to the demographics of the area served by the employer or educational institution. Thus, if the population of South Carolina is 29.9 percent black, then according to the principle of affirmative action, a university there should attempt to recruit an applicant pool resulting in somewhere around 29.9 percent black students in the incoming class. An affirmative action plan would include recruitment strategies aimed at this result though it may be difficult to achieve.

Affirmative action policies were designed as aspirational goals, not numerical quotas, but because they have been implemented in ways that critics regard as having the effect of creating quotas, they have become the subject of much controversy in the past decade or so. Although quotas are actually illegal in the United States, except as a court-prescribed remedy in exceptional cases (Leporini 1998), critics argue that aiming to recruit applicants based on percentages defined by race or gender amounts to discriminating against those in the race or gender categories not targeted for affirmative action. The idea of taking positive or affirmative action, however, illustrates the principle of positive rights, which are more widely accepted in European democracies than in the United States (Mowbray 2004).

Whether or not a distinction is made between negative rights, which place limits on government action, and positive rights, which create expectations of government action, is often a matter of political orientation. Henry Shue (1980) argued that the obligations generated by a rights claim almost always entail both negative and positive duties, challenging the notion that civil liberties, civil rights, and political rights create only negative obligations, and economic, social, and cultural rights create only positive obligations. Although the concept of negative and positive rights is still widely used in legal philosophy and can be relevant in the context of ideological or philosophical discussions about the appropriate role for government and the collection and use of public resources, the distinction is not as widely accepted today as it once was.

## One Declaration, Two Covenants

The Universal Declaration of Human Rights together with the two covenants on civil and political rights and economic, social, and cultural rights are commonly referred to as the International Bill of Rights. The UN General Assembly passed the Universal Declaration unanimously on December 10, 1948, after the fifty-eight member states voted more than 1,400 times on the wording of the final document (Treaty Database Online 2006). Eleanor Roosevelt chaired the eight-member committee that drafted the original declaration. Its provisions cover a broad spectrum of civil, political, economic, social, and cultural rights. The discussion and rounds of voting revealed a number of concerns, for instance, that equal marriage rights and the right to choose one's religious belief threatened traditional Islamic cultures, or that the recognition of economic, social, and cultural rights created new litigable rights within Western states. Unanimity was achieved with eight abstentions, but the cleavages that eventually formed over civil and political rights, on the one hand, and economic, social, and cultural rights, on the other, had less to do with legal and philosophical disagreements than with Cold War politics that emerged shortly after the founding of the United Nations.

The Cold War was not only a conflict between adversarial superpowers seeking dominance in the world but also a struggle over normative claims, a conflict of ideas or visions of what the good society, on the global level, ought to look like and what underlying values and objectives ought to be pursued through international relations. Therefore, US leaders increasingly aligned US foreign policy with advocacy for human rights defined in terms of civil and political rights, while Soviet leaders identified their foreign policy with advocating for economic and social justice. Each criticized the other for failing to equally protect both kinds of rights, or specifically for being weak on the rights identified with the other. Thus the United States criticized the Soviet Union for denying or restricting political and civil rights like universal suffrage or freedoms of speech, religion, and press, while the Soviet Union was critical of poverty, hunger, and the very graphic civil strife associated with the civil rights movement in the 1960s.

Splitting the two sets of rights into two treaty documents or covenants therefore became politically expedient. General Assembly declarations do not constitute international law, although the customary practice of states, similar to domestic common law, is a primary source of international law, and to the extent that the UN General Assembly reflects a consensus in the international community, its resolutions can be regarded as strengthening (or weakening) certain international norms. In this case, the unanimous vote for the Universal Declaration strengthened norms pertaining to human rights and was a strong endorsement for their codification in international law. However, such norms would not become obligations unless they were codified in a treaty or convention and not until the requisite number of states signed and ratified the agreement. Even then, such agreements were, and are, only binding on signatories. Therefore, while the covenants were adopted as General Assembly resolutions in December 1966, neither of them entered into force until a decade later as the Cold War conflict and the normative and political cleavages created by the United States and Soviet Union deepened.

As of 2014, the International Covenant on Civil and Political Rights (ICCPR) had 168 parties and 74 signatories, and the International Covenant on Economic, Social, and Cultural Rights (ICESCR) had 162 parties and 70 signatories.

Two optional protocols lend further support to the ICCPR. An optional protocol is an addendum to a treaty that may or may not be signed and ratified along with the treaty to which it is attached. The first optional protocol to the ICCPR "recognizes the competence of the [Human Rights] Committee to receive and consider communications from individuals subject to its jurisdiction who claim to be victims of a violation by that State Party of any of the rights set forth in the Covenant (Article I)."

Without the protocol, individuals must rely on states to bring their complaints before the Human Rights Committee, and obviously, a state accused of violating the human rights of an individual has no incentive to bring complaints by individuals to the committee. Indeed, the state has an incentive not to do so. Thus, the first protocol substantially strengthens the capacity of the committee to bring pressure to bear on states to comply with their obligations under the covenant. As of 2014, 115 states were parties to the first protocol, and 35 were signatories. The first protocol was passed by the General Assembly and opened for signature and ratification as a treaty in 1966, but like the two covenants, it did not enter into force until much later, in 1976.

The second optional protocol opened for signature and ratification in 1989 and entered into force two years later. Parties to the second optional protocol agree not to execute persons in their jurisdictions and to "take all measures to abolish the death penalty" within their jurisdictions (Article 1, paragraph 2). The United States did not sign the second optional protocol and had previously registered reservations to Article 6, paragraph 5 of the ICCPR because, although it did not outlaw the death penalty, it limited the scope of application, including, among other things, the exemption of juveniles from execution for any conviction. A reservation, for treaties that allow them, means that the signatory agrees to the terms of the treaty overall but wants to clarify its position or register an exception to some part of it. The use of reservations enables more states to sign a treaty but can water down its provisions, according to critics of the practice. No other state has registered a reservation to this provision, and ten countries have formally objected to the US reservation.

Although the death penalty was legal in Europe and most of the UN member states at the time the covenants were adopted, the number of countries abolishing the death penalty since then has increased substantially, and today slightly more than half of all states have abolished capital punishment by law. However, only 80—fewer than half of the nearly 200 UN member states—have signed and ratified the second protocol. Support for abolition of the death penalty for all crimes has grown from just under 40 states in 1988 to nearly 100 today, and 140 states in total have either abolished the death penalty completely, at least in practice, or abolished it for all but a few exceptional crimes (Amnesty International 2014b).

The idea of economic, social, and cultural rights is more contentious in politically conservative societies. Economic and social rights are given more credence in European states and are regarded with more apprehension in the United States. Cultural rights are more problematic in general since the majority of states might be multicultural, but they are characterized demographically by the dominance of one identity group and the presence of multiple minority groups. Recognition of cultural rights can seem threatening to cultural majorities and critical to minorities. From the perspective of democratic theory, what holds people together as citizens within states is a shared sense of what constitutes the good society. In reality, religious, ethnic, cultural, or linguistic identity more often forms the basis for solidarity, and most states include a group that constitutes some kind of majority identity along with one or more minority groups whose language, religion, and cultural practices differ from those of the majority. Notably, many African states have large multiple pluralities and communal groups split by colonial/postcolonial boundaries.

People can easily be marginalized because of their identities, even in democracies. Furthermore, the histories that led various groups together to live now in a single state are often marked by violence, leaving contemporary intergroup relations vulnerable to conflict arising out of unreconciled historical injury, discrimination, marginalization, or policies aimed at the forcible or coercive assimilation of minorities in the past. Many majorities are not self-conscious of the ways they can be privileged in comparison with minorities. For example, minorities must often learn a second language in order to enjoy the full benefits and protections of citizenship. The African Charter on Human and Peoples' Rights, adopted in 1981 and coming into force in 1989, explicitly recognizes the rights of both individuals and peoples, and many commentators consider this a distinguishing feature of an emerging African approach to human rights (Umozurike 1997).

## Categories of Human Rights

Because efforts to universalize and internationalize human rights at the United Nations were led by representatives of the European and British settler states (Canada, the United States, Australia, and New Zealand), the discourse about international human rights has paralleled both the democratization of European societies since the eighteenth century and the emergence of a transnational normative order, led by Western states. The West's leadership role does not mean that other societies lacked a conception of human rights or human dignity, as is demonstrated in the next chapter. This fact also does not mean that Western societies have not committed serious human rights abuses, including through imperialist policies. Indeed the unprecedented horrors of the Holocaust—a European genocide—gave a great amount of initial momentum to mobilize the political will to develop international restrictions on the ability of those who control states to commit mass atrocities with impunity. The Convention for the Prevention and Punishment of the Crime of Genocide (Genocide Convention) was adopted by the UN General Assembly in December 1948 and entered into force two years and one month later with forty-two of the sixty members of the United Nations ratifying the convention. Most states are now party to the convention.

Human rights are often thought of as occurring in three generations, an idea first proposed by Czech-French jurist Karel Vasak in the late 1970s but that soon came into widespread general use, particularly in Europe. Vasak associated the idea of three generations with the French revolutionary principles of liberty, equality, and fraternity. These generational categories roughly correspond to the political or ideological and historical characteristics that distinguish civil and political rights of individuals (first generation), from rights predicated on social justice (second generation), and finally rights that are primarily collective or involve solidarity (third generation). This concept is not without its critics, however, as will be discussed later.

First-generation rights are those widely accepted in Western states and specifically recognized in their constitutional documents as civil liberties and political rights. Many Westerners associate civil and political rights with due process and ideas about human rights that developed within the framework of the political experiences of Western cultures. Not surprisingly, in light of the role imperialism and colonization played in internationalizing Western political ideas and institutions, many people in non-Western or formerly colonized parts of the world criticize these conceptions of human rights as culturally biased and view efforts to internationalize and universalize them as a continuation of Western imperialism. These contrasting attitudes have given rise to a debate about whether human rights are universal or culturally relative, a subject more thoroughly discussed in Chapter 4.

While the content of first-generation rights is straightforward and widely agreed upon, more confusion and controversy surround the question of second- and third-generation rights. Apart from the ideological polarization during the Cold War, democracies with stronger socialist constituencies or traditions advocate for more or equal attention to a second generation of human rights that include economic, social, and cultural rights. Focusing on individual liberties alone, they argue, does not take into account economic disparities and injustices, in this view. The aftermath of decolonization and a more critical view of the nation-state, with boundaries often produced by violence or imperialism, also opened space for non-Western and nonstate voices to join in struggles over an emerging international normative order. These voices challenge prevailing conceptions of international human rights that privileged civil and political rights or rights emerging out of conflicts within the core capitalist democracies. They also make claims regarding collective rights that sometimes overlap with the idea of second-generation rights and also break new ground by claiming "solidarity" rights. But the boundaries between these new third-generation rights and second-generation rights are far from settled. Formerly colonized peoples and others more critical of the state-centric world order bring additional concerns to the table, reflecting their own histories and political experiences and giving rise to discussions about a third generation of solidarity rights including rights to development, food, clean water, peace, and a healthful environment.

The first- and second-generation and some third-generation human rights are codified in the two covenants. The rights contained in the ICESCR, like freedom from hunger in Article 11 and those in Article 12 calling for improvements in "environmental hygiene and enjoyment of the highest attainable standard of physical and mental health," are sometimes viewed as aspirational objectives rather than legal claims individuals can make against states when they are violated. In joining the covenant, states are obligated to move toward the realization of these rights: that is, they aspire to achieve these rights within the limits of their own resources. In the words of the ICESCR, a state commits "to the maximum of its available resources" to achieve "progressively the full realization of the rights recognized in the present Covenant by all appropriate means" (Article 2, paragraph 1).

The aspirational view of human rights is controversial. Critics argue that a view of any right as aspirational weakens its claim, opening the door for political abuse and enabling states to easily dismiss their obligation to fulfill and protect a right out of political expedience. Hunger kills as surely as torture and execution, critics like Henry Shue (1980) point out; therefore, states must be as committed to eliminating hunger as to preventing torture and refraining from execution. Enforcement claims regarding economic and social rights can also be made: for example, individuals have a right to an education in order to understand and pursue the enforcement of other rights like those pertaining to due process or civil and political rights.

However, this ideal is just one way of thinking about human rights categorically, and perfect correspondence cannot be found either between the articulation of rights in the two covenants and these generational categories or between any consistent legal reasoning and the categorical distinction. For example, the first article in the ICCPR also recognizes the right of "peoples" to self-determination. The same article declares that "in no case may a people be deprived of its own means of subsistence," a declaration that can be viewed as an economic right and not a civil or political right. Similarly, reference is made to both self-determination and the right to participate in cultural life in the ICESCR.

Some rights seem to fall into two categories, for example, the right to form a trade union can be regarded as a second-generation right because it is associated with pursuit of economic well-being and fairness or justice in relations between employers and workers. It can also be regarded as a right exercised collectively. The right to clean water can be viewed as an economic right because clean water is essential to material or economic well-being, but it is also a collective right because people may be collectively deprived of clean water if the state fails to act to ensure that resource's availability and accessibility. Self-determination is perhaps the clearest example of a collective right because it attaches to groups who wish to control their collective destiny or express their collective identity, yet some writers refer to it as both a second- and third-generation right (Lynch and Maggio 1997).

The idea of generations has also been criticized as unnecessarily dichotomizing civil and political versus economic rights, encouraging an artificial association of civil and political rights with Western values and economic rights with non-Western values, fostering counterproductive debates about rights priorities, and even failing as an accurate historical or chronological account of rights development. The third generation often becomes a catchall for rights not included in the more sharply defined first- and second-generation categories. Bülent Algan (2004) asked perhaps the most important question: Does this categorization—specifically the identification of a third generation of rights—contribute to the goal of advancing protection of international human rights? He concluded that the categories are useful for educational purposes so long as one remains aware of the gray zones. He argued that wide agreement exists that first- and second-generation rights are equally important, indivisible, and interdependent, and that individuals are clearly the bearers of these rights. Third-generation rights, he said, are still in an early stage of development, and some, like the right to a clean environment, can be considered the right of an individual as well as a collective right.

The main obstacle to further development of third-generation rights is establishing who is the bearer of these rights and who has responsibility for their realization. This obstacle is most clearly illustrated by efforts to advance recognition of a group's right to self-determination. The International Court of Justice (ICJ) has recognized the right of self-determination as one that belongs to a people, but neither the court nor international political institutions have settled the question of how to define a people for the purpose of bearing the right of self-determination. This failing highlights the importance of political agreement among bearers of both rights and obligations in order to advance the protection of rights.

Henry Shue's (1980) approach took a different view of basic rights, beginning with the premise that rights create obligations; if someone has a right, then someone else has an obligation relative to that right. Claim rights, as he called them, have corresponding duties. In Shue's original formulation, three correlative duties can be found for every basic right asserted: (1) the duty to avoid violating the claim right or depriving the right-bearer of that right, (2) the duty to protect the right-bearer from deprivation or violation, and (3) the duty to aid the right-bearer when the right is violated or the right-bearer is deprived. Asbjorn Eide later reformulated this tripartite model of duties when he applied it to the case of a social right to adequate food as creating a duty to "respect, protect, and fulfill" (Eide et al. 1984). Both Shue and Eide were concerned more specifically with social rights.

Shue showed that security rights—the rights essential to the physical security of a person—cannot be held as a higher priority than subsistence rights, rights to a minimum level of physical and economic well-being. In his view, the basic needs for physical survival constitute the threshold for a minimum level of subsistence rights. Shue's notion of basic rights included those rights without which other rights are meaningless. If people do not have access to enough food and clean water to survive, then rights to free speech, assembly, religious practice, association, self-determination, work, equality, or a clean environment cannot be enjoyed either. The deprivation of basic subsistence needs is on par with torture and other practices that threaten physical integrity through direct violence. Furthermore, he argued, all rights are associated with both negative and positive duties. For example, Shue argues that the right to be physically protected against a violation of our physical integrity (a negative right) creates an obligation for the government both to refrain from violating that right (a negative duty) and an obligation to collect taxes to pay for police and other institutional protections of our physical security (a positive duty).

## IR Theory and the Study of Human Rights

Theory has a wide-ranging mission because it frames not only how one thinks about problems but also what is or is not to be considered a problem, and how the task of inquiry is formulated. In the case of investigating hypotheses, theories determine what empirical evidence is needed to evaluate a problem and suggest possible solutions. Political theory, however, also straddles the boundary between the social sciences and the humanities: Scholarship in the humanities engages in reflection on our humanity, in other words, what it means to be human. When human rights are violated, humanity is called into question, and political theory becomes a study of how to redeem our humanity. In the study of politics, theory functions sometimes as it does in the natural sciences, but it can also have a more humanistic purpose as a form of philosophy when the role of values or ethics is highlighted. Given the range of contexts in which discussions of human rights take place—from normative claims to policy directives—the scope of relevant theoretical tools referenced in this book is equally diverse.

Theories can also be lenses through which to interpret or assign meaning to events and experiences. While a discussion of the concept and role of a theory as compared with a paradigm or an approach is beyond the scope of this book, four macrolevel lenses are available through which many international relations scholars view their subject: liberalism, realism, economic structuralism, and constructivism. In addition, feminism highlights the general invisibility of women and patriarchy in all perspectives and looks at the differences between how men and women look at and are influenced by the world, particularly whether feminine and masculine experiences produce different epistemologies and psychological orientations.

Both scholars and policymakers have a tendency to view things through or favor one of these lenses. Throughout the twentieth century, realism and liberalism alternatively competed for favor among scholars and policymakers. The preeminence of one over the other at different historical points also reflects efforts by scholars and policymakers to make sense out of macrohistorical events and trends. Examples include the rise of technology and decline of war among the major powers in Europe in the late nineteenth and early twentieth centuries, the unprecedented atrocities of the Holocaust before and during World War II, and the occurrence of two global wars within the span of thirty years. Constructivism, the most recently articulated theoretical lens, in a way accounts for these shifting theoretical sands by arguing that subjectivity produces identities, and as subjectivities change, so do identities (Wendt 1987, 1999).

Economic structuralism is associated with Marxism, neo-Marxism, and critiques of capitalism more broadly. In terms of world politics and human rights, economic structuralism played a major role in superpower narratives during the Cold War as well as more recently in critical postcolonial perspectives and new social movements. Feminist theory and scholarship intersect with some elements of Marxism and postcolonial perspectives, particularly when an emphasis can be found on how and why certain identities are privileged and others marginalized and on the epistemic origins of hierarchical social and economic stratification. Feminist theory also points to hierarchy and exclusion, central to imperialism and postcolonial theory, as elements of patriarchy generally.

Liberalism, realism, constructivism, economic structuralism, and feminism are briefly discussed below so issues that raise theoretical questions throughout the text can be viewed from these different perspectives. Table 2.1 provides a summary of how each perspective views human rights and their role in foreign policy.

**Table 2.1 International Relations Theories and Human Rights Perspectives**

|  | Human Rights | Foreign Policy |
|---|---|---|
| Liberalism | The basis for democratic society and democratic world order | Should promote respect for human rights and democracy |
| Realism | The basis for democracy in states; inevitably violated by nondemocracies | Should not mix ethics with foreign policy |
| Constructivism | Social facts created by social agreement; can shape identities and interests | Will incorporate human rights when identities and interests include human rights |
| Economic Structuralism | Grounded in equality of opportunity and outcomes where all basic human needs are met | Should promote social justice and conditions that eliminate structural inequalities |
| Feminism | Economic, social, political, and legal equality for all regardless of gender or sexual identity | Should eliminate gender inequalities and discrimination; should promote peace and social welfare |

### International Liberalism

Liberalism captured the philosophical character of the Enlightenment and the populist revolutions of the seventeenth through nineteenth centuries. It emphasizes individual political freedom and freedoms of economic choice such as how to use one's labor and how to spend or invest one's material assets. Both economic and political liberalism initially focused on laissez-faire or limited government, but a growing awareness that unequal economic opportunities are often due to the circumstances of economic and social class prompted a modification of contemporary political liberalism. Contemporary liberalism includes a commitment to the gradual improvement of social justice and the mitigation, if not elimination, of social and economic inequalities of opportunity. The goals of contemporary liberalism evoke some controversy within Western liberal democracies, a controversy made evident in political parties that agree on a shared value of freedom but disagree over the extent to which government should act to eliminate structural and institutional barriers to equality of opportunity.

Contemporary human rights are directly linked to the philosophy of liberalism as it developed in Western societies. The major provisions of due process are aimed at restricting government authority. Fundamental freedoms including speech, association, religious practice, and the press are all essential to the foundation and maintenance of a liberal democracy. The English Bill of Rights was passed by Parliament in 1689. The French Declaration on the Rights of Man and of the Citizen was adopted in August of 1789. The first ten amendments of the US Constitution protecting fundamental freedoms, the right to bear arms (a restraint on government monopoly of force), due process of law, and limited state sovereignty, were introduced as a package in 1789 and ratified in 1791 and are popularly referred to as the US Bill of Rights, although they were ratified as individual clauses.

The internationalization of liberalism emphasizes two objectives. First, individual freedoms are to be elevated to the level of universality, as reflected in the views of Eleanor Roosevelt quoted at the beginning of this chapter. Many argue that US foreign policy should therefore focus on human rights because the United States should act as a beacon for these ideals in all of its international relations and foreign policies. Second, states should be free from international regulation and able to pursue their own self-interests to produce a world order of states acting on enlightened self-interest. International order ought to consist of a community of freely associated states with no suprastate authority. This perspective is particularly evident in policies promoting free trade between states and economic liberalism within states. These two objectives—individual freedoms and state freedom from international regulation—can obviously be in tension with one another. Should a state be free to structure its political institutions in undemocratic ways? An international human rights regime presses governments to democratize to the extent that respecting human rights creates a kind of international social capital, emboldening citizens to demand more openness, due process, and political participation. Liberals' mistrust of government stemming from the long experience with monarchies and arbitrary despotic rule in Europe was matched by their faith in the inherent capacity of free human beings to govern themselves and flourish socially and economically. Liberalism was prevalent at the beginning of the twentieth century following the long period of relative peace among European major powers whose conflicts had plagued the continent for most of the previous two centuries. It was embodied in the two Hague Conferences in 1899 and 1907, aptly called the Hague Peace Conferences. Liberals have confidence in the capacity of human reason to solve problems and make life better through the application of knowledge. Democracies are predicated on this confidence in progress through reason. The real question is whether this kind of progress can be extended to the worldwide community of states, particularly if some are undemocratic and antiliberal. The assertion of international human rights epitomizes the notion that human beings are capable of moral progress, even if such progress is not guaranteed.

### Realism

The "war to end all wars"—World War I—was followed twenty years later by World War II and atrocities exceeding anything that could have been imagined by people who just a few decades earlier at the Hague Conferences were celebrating the capacity of reason and progress to civilize, if not end, interstate war. For the first time in the history of modern warfare, civilians were the primary targets of violence, from the Holocaust to carpet bombing of areas primarily populated by noncombatants, to the war's conclusion with the first and so far only use of nuclear weapons targeting population centers in Japan. The violence itself was unprecedented in the scope of its inhumanity and cruelty. For many, World War II destroyed faith in the human capacity to reason and the inevitability of social progress. Realism, a view predominant during major power competition and imperialism in Europe in the nineteenth century, was revived to account for both the two world wars and the bipolar competition between the United States and Soviet Union during the Cold War that emerged after World War II.

From a realist perspective, reason, progress, and freedom are ideals that can only be realized within the institutional framework of a sovereign state by people committed to principles of democratic self-government. The development or maintenance of democratic institutions is in no way inevitable. The world of interstate relations is a world of uncertainty and risk with an ever-present potential for violence, aggression, inhumanity, and threats. In the realists' world, being prepared for threats and working to prevail over them are rational endeavors. In such a world, human rights violations are likely or even inevitable within nondemocratic states, and nothing should or can be done about that by democratic states. Military force and foreign policy must be guided by national interest and aimed at deterring or defeating potential threats (such as world communism or states that avow it). Foreign policy and military force should not be guided by ethical commitments to protect or promote the human rights of people in other countries.

Contemporary realists tend to be isolationists, like John Mearsheimer (2011), who argued that liberalism gives rise to interventions on behalf of ideals like human rights and democracy and, as Thanassis Cambanis (2011) argues, "creates more threats than it neutralizes." In their view, foreign policies can do nothing to promote democratization, including respect for human rights, and resources are wasted and national security weakened by efforts to do so. In the debate on interests versus values, realists are the ultimate champions of national interests. National interests are always focused on the survival of the state and preservation of its power vis-à-vis competitors that may arise to challenge it. In this view, instead of intervening in Iraq and Afghanistan, the United States should have conserved resources and focused on remaining the preeminent and sole superpower in light of China's growing power. Values are relevant domestically, and realists certainly value US democracy, but democratic values can, in their view, only be protected by wisely investing in security against those states that would undermine US power, the sole and ultimate protector of US values. Viewing the transatlantic relationship through the realist's lens, Robert Kagan (2004) argued that Europeans rightly emphasize a world order based on the rule of law, negotiation, and diplomacy because that is their most likely path to preserve influence, while the maintenance and protection of US interests necessitate unilateral action and the use of military force.

### Constructivism

Both sociologists and political scientists utilize constructivist perspectives with slightly different but compatible meanings. A sociological approach focuses on social facts—facts created by the agreement of social actors or agents. Human rights are a prime example. Social agreement expressed through treaties, conventions, speeches, articles and media reports, as a subject of education, and in the conversations and concerns of ordinary people has produced the social fact of human rights. In political science, and particularly in international relations, constructivism focuses more on the role of identities and interests, which are, arguably, also kinds of social facts. The important issue for scholars of international relations is that identities and interests change.

Both views of constructivism rest on the notion that social processes and interactions produce social facts. Social structures and political institutions are also social facts. The state is a social fact, sovereignty is a social fact, and treaties and conventions are social facts. Law is a social fact, and as I stated above, so are human rights. Social facts exist, as John Searle (1995) argued, because social agents agree to them. Some social facts are more widely agreed upon than others. In international relations, social processes (specifically, those that are political) exist through which agents articulate agreement to recognize new states, for example. At the time the United Nations was formed in the mid-1940s, the world was divided into approximately fifty states, twenty years later that number had tripled, and fifty years later it had quadrupled. States can also cease to exist, often but not always as a result of violence. The Soviet Union, Yugoslavia, and Czechoslovakia are examples.

Constructivism regards both social structures and social agents as important and codetermined or coconstituted. Agents act within, against, and for the purpose of shaping or changing structures. But the range of possible actions, including those that deliberately aim to change structures, is to a high degree determined by the structures in which agents act. The relationship between structures and agents is dialectic. Structures include states, norms, and philosophical or ideological narratives. The language used to constitute social facts, like states, is also a structure: that is, language structures how agents think about the social world. Patriarchal language, for example, structures how agents think about national security by privileging states over people and privileging militarized over diplomatic responses to conflict. Agents are people making choices and speaking, writing, justifying policies, formulating treaties, and passing laws about international relations and human rights.

Conceptually, widespread social agreement can be found on the existence of international human rights, but less agreement exists about what rights are included and even less on whether and how to enforce norms or prevent or stop violations. The identities of some states, notably Western democracies, are linked to narratives about human rights and freedom. Some states' interests focus their foreign policy on human rights violations in some places and not others, often because of strategic interests or specific political relationships: for example, the United States focuses on women's rights in Afghanistan, where the United States has committed to democratization in the aftermath of military intervention, while saying little about restrictions on women's rights in longtime ally Saudi Arabia. A constructivist might even note that to the extent that narratives produce or sustain social facts (identities and interests), both liberalism and realism are in play today as narratives through which identities, interests, and policies are produced.

European constructivism has given rise to the Copenhagen School and classical security complex theory (Waever, Buzan, and de Wilde 1998). This blend of constructivism with classical realism aims to explain or understand the "securitization" of actors and issues through social processes that articulate threats to a particular audience. Threats, in this view, are not objective facts; instead, they are social facts produced through a "self-referential practice" that makes an issue into a threat "not necessarily because a real existential threat exists but because the issue is presented as such a threat" (Wæver, Buzan, and de Wilde 1998:24). Classical security complex theory extends beyond militarized actions or threats of violence to economic, environmental, and identity threats.

## Economic Structuralism

Economic structuralism is grounded in the critique of liberalism for failing to address the inequalities and social injustices that both precede and are exacerbated by capitalism. Political liberalism may have aimed to over-throw a privileged ruling class that came to power by heredity, but it did lit-tle to create equalities of opportunity or to secure basic material needs for all members of a society. By the middle of the nineteenth century, it became apparent that capitalism does nothing to redistribute wealth or opportunities but, to the contrary, tends toward an increasing concentration of wealth in the hands of the few while the rest must make do on wages that are as low as possible in order to maximize profits.

Economic structuralism posits that the current structure of the interna-tional system is a product of the historical globalization of capitalism over the past three to four centuries. This school of thought is rooted in Karl Marx's observation and analysis of the inequalities and exploitation implicit in capitalist economies and was extended to international relations by social theorists including John A. Hobson (1902), Vladimir Lenin (2010 [1916]), and Immanuel Wallerstein (1980, 2004). Hobson and Lenin focused on the role of imperialism in globalizing capitalism while Wallerstein, more recently, laid out a theory of international stratification between core and periphery countries, a relationship between states that parallels the relation-ship between capitalists and workers or the exploiters and those exploited in Marxist theory. Like the capitalist class, the core countries will derive proportionately more of their wealth from finance and investment while the peripheral states provide cheap raw materials and labor, a pattern entrenched by the logic and functioning of capitalism that keeps the poor, poor, and the rich, rich.

The school of economic structuralism highlights several issues in the area of international human rights. First, according to this theory, rich core countries will sustain their privileged status by exploiting the people and resources in colonies and former colonies; indeed, their acquisition and expansion of wealth are predicated on such exploitation. This relationship can create a paradox of hypocrisy when the core countries are liberal democracies whose foreign policies, particularly when economic interests are involved, undermine or suppress the development of democratic institu-tions abroad. The US relationship with authoritarian and military dictator-ships, particularly in Latin America during the Cold War, illustrates this point. The term *banana republic* derives from the relationship between influential and wealthy fruit corporations in the United States (notably United Fruit Company, but also Dole, formerly Standard Fruit Company, for example) and the countries where their fruit was produced and har-vested under harsh working conditions and inadequate wages.

The exploitation of labor in underdeveloped countries by large multinational corporations based in wealthy developed countries points to the second human rights problem highlighted by economic structuralism. Even after independence, many postcolonial governments are dominated by cooperators, that is, a class of people sometimes sharing a common ethnic identity with which the former colonial government maintains a friendly relationship precisely because the postcolonial government perpetuates the same pattern of economic imperialism by proxy that existed under colonial rule. For example, the shah of Iran, Mohammad Reza Pahlavi, was a Western/US cooperator who maintained his power over the Iranian people through the use of secret police, torture, and a general reign of terror under the guise of modernizing his country. In 1953 when the democratically elected Prime Minister Mohammad Mosaddegh attempted to nationalize the Iranian oil industry, the shah cooperated with the Central Intelligence Agency (CIA) to oust the prime minister and return oil ownership to the private sector, and himself to power, at least for a few more decades. In another example, the colonial relationship between the British government and the Kikuyu ethnic group (or tribe) in Kenya, who were viewed as British "loyalists," had postcolonial consequences for how they were perceived domestically as agents or proxies for the former colonial power after independence. Tragically, a similar relationship between Belgian imperialists and the Tutsi minority in Rwanda figured prominently into the narrative of victimization used by Hutu Power to mobilize the 1994 genocide.

Third, the capitalist world system fosters tacit and direct collusion between multinational corporations, transnational banks, and the core states to perpetuate exploitation and deprivation in peripheral countries and classes. Thus oil development in Ecuador and Nigeria benefits Texaco, Chevron, and Shell corporations at the expense of local villagers, whose water is polluted due to a lack of regulation, and human rights activists, who are tortured, imprisoned, or assassinated for protesting the policies of their governments that allow these conditions to fester.

### Feminist Theory

Carole Pateman (1988) noted that liberal revolutions overthrew a patriarchy of fathers but replaced it with what she calls a fraternal patriarchy. This kind of insight is yielded by feminist perspectives on international relations. Where are the women and what are they doing? This question was raised by the so-called first wave of feminism. The second wave emphasized political and economic democratization: women must have equal opportunities, representation, and rights. Most recently, feminism has taken a more theoretical turn by asking, is there a feminine epistemology, or does feminist theoretical analysis reveal a gendered epistemology?

Does a perspective or way of knowing arise from the experiences that distinguish women or that construct the categories of feminine and masculine? Would a world of equally empowered men and women be more respectful of human rights? Do human beings socially produce and reproduce forms of masculinization that enable, if not inevitably produce, violent behavior (Wilmer Forthcoming)?

Of course women have always been present, however invisible to writers of history. Jean Bethke Elshtain (1987), for example, researched the role of women as the mothers and wives left at home but also defended and honored by the combatants in the Peloponnesian wars of ancient Greece. According to Elshtain, women enabled the violence of their soldier-husbands and soldier-sons by telling them, essentially, to come home victorious or come home dead but do not come home alive and defeated. Her point was that masculine warrior roles were interdependent with the feminine roles of their wives and mothers whose honor would be defiled should their defenders come home defeated and alive. Their husbands and sons were thereby encouraged to be brave and determined to fight to the death for victory or face unbearable shame. Times have changed, however, in some ways. Where were the women as the communist state collapsed in the Soviet Union? At least some of them were engaging in hunger strikes on behalf of their military husbands and sons and against the Soviet war in Afghanistan.

Most people today associate feminism with the issue of equality, and while democracies have developed legal rules that aim to ensure equality of educational and professional opportunities, in practice women overall in capitalist democracies still earn less than men with the same level of education. Some postcolonial or third world states have implemented gender quotas for representation in their governments as a means of fostering policies to promote equality, a practice that is more controversial in the United States. Contemporary debates on gender equality often focus on whether equality of outcomes must accompany equality of opportunity and to what extent the fact of women's reproductive role necessarily impinges on their opportunities for career and income advancement.

The question of a feminine epistemology gives rise to some of the most intriguing issues for international relations. For example, V. Spike Peterson in *Gendered States* (1992) and with Anne Sisson Runyan in *Global Gender Issues* (1993) elaborated feminist theories that reveal how power and states themselves are produced and reproduced by masculine epistemologies. The meaning of power and security and the purpose of the state in using power to provide security, they argued, have been socially constructed from a masculine-centric perspective. I (Wilmer 2002) explored how feminist theories of political psychology can help explain the dynamics of conflict and enemy making (and war crimes) when identity is invoked to mobilize violence. Feminist theory of the third wave also unmasks the proclivity of political analysts and others to view the social world as comprising hierarchical dualities where ideas associated with femininity are marginalized, submerged, or suppressed by masculine ideas. Some examples are war (masculine) and peace (feminine), military security (masculine) and diplomacy (feminine), realism (masculine) and idealism (feminine), rationality (masculine) and emotion (feminine). Third world and non-Western cultures are also feminized when they are portrayed as more motivated by emotion, passion, and sensuality in contrast with the intellectualism and institutionalization of their imperial conquerors.

Regarding the development of international human rights, one cannot imagine a world in which rights are fully respected but where half the population is marginalized. As Nicholas Kristof and Sheryl WuDunn (2009) have powerfully articulated in their book on ending the worldwide oppression of women, women hold up half the sky—a metaphor from a well-known quote by Mao Zedong, Chinese Communist revolutionary and founder of the People's Republic of China. Without their full and equal empowerment, the sky will surely fall. On the other hand, if the rights of women receive their due attention, human rights will be better for at least half the population and those whose welfare depends on them.

## Controversies Raised by Human Rights

Regardless of how the question "Where do rights come from?" is answered, human beings are the ones who must struggle and make claims for, defend, protect, respect, fulfill, enforce, articulate, and recognize them. The foundation of human rights only matters because those claims provide the moral justification for rights and the authoritative basis assigned to them. A right is like air—those who have it take it for granted, but deprived of it, a person finds that nothing else matters.

Undoubtedly, the Western emphasis on due process and negative rights is a product of the political experiences of Europeans who struggled to overthrow autocratic monarchs and to put in place a set of restrictions on government authority. Those restrictions include enforceable rights, checks and balances, and republican forms of government to remedy and prevent the worst abuses of authoritative power. This emphasis is also a product of the fact that men engineered these revolutions and, as Pateman (1988) pointed out, established in their place a fraternal patriarchy. As James Madison said in the Federalist Paper 51, "if men were angels, no government would be necessary." Nor would rights be needed. Neither humans nor governments are angels, and thus protection from abuses of power by both is required.

Many controversies are raised by recognizing human rights, and such issues have many intersections with other areas of political science. Below, in broad strokes, are some of these intersections. They can provide an excellent point of departure for discussion of the issues raised in Chapter 8 through Chapter 13.

*Rights and politics.* Rights are perhaps most controversial when governments are the perpetrators of violations. But states can be complicit without committing human rights violations by tolerating violations enacted by private citizens or by failing to intervene to stop ongoing violations inside or outside of their jurisdiction. Madison's wisdom and historical experience tell us that rights are also an answer to the enormous consolidation of power by the state. Rights, in other words, are a response to state formation, at least in the context of Western historical experience. The doctrine or belief in state sovereignty has shielded the state and made it possible for the state to use power arbitrarily. Law, in general, and legal rights, in particular, aim to reduce the arbitrariness with which states use power.

*Rights and law.* Law reduces the arbitrariness with which power is used in a variety of ways. Politics can be thought of as power: how power is constituted, how it is used, and how it structures relationships. The rule of law refers to the ability of law to assert a restraining influence on politics, one that reduces its arbitrariness by applying principles of fairness, equality, dignity, and so on. We often find some rights provisions in the main body of a constitution (habeas corpus, for example, in the US Constitution), though additional or elaborated rights may also be found in constitutional amendments or in documents incorporated into common law. The English Bill of Rights of 1689 was an act of Parliament, for instance. International human rights are secured both through recognition within domestic legal systems and in conjunction with the development and codification of international law. International legal rights include instruments that specifically address not only human rights but also humanitarian law, the laws of warfare, and crimes against humanity. International law, contrary to popular beliefs, is not a new development but rather has been a part of the history of the state and its development since the seventeenth century when Hugo Grotius, the "father" of international law, wrote *The Law of War and Peace* (1625). Indeed, as European imperialists began establishing permanent interests in the Western Hemisphere, influential sixteenth-century Spanish theologians and advisers to European monarchs, Bartolomé de Las Casas and Juan Ginés de Sepúlveda debated the moral merits of recognizing the human rights of indigenous peoples.

*Rights and morality.* Human rights raise normative, moral questions. Human rights aim to relieve or prevent human wrongs. Should politics be about reducing human suffering, about improving human well-being and infusing human social organization with justice? As a political ideology, liberalism advocates maximizing human freedom but balancing the freedom of the individual with principles of justice at the collective level. According to liberalism, governments are created by and to serve the individual and collective interests of people, not the profit and advancement of those controlling the government. If politics is also about preventing or relieving human suffering, particularly suffering caused by unjust treatment, then questions such as how to prevent or stop an ongoing genocide and when suffering rises to the level that requires action become relevant. Should genocides be preventable, as the promise of "never again" suggests? If so, why were the genocides in Bosnia and Rwanda not stopped? And can more ambiguous cases be identified that do not fit perfectly with the international definition of genocide, which nevertheless ought to be prevented or stopped, as in Cambodia or Darfur?

*Human rights and violence.* Human rights violations are a form of violence. They often but do not always occur in conjunction with wars. One might think that violence and restraint, or violence and law, are impossible conditions to reconcile. However, in just one example, authorities use violence to provide public subjects with agents to enforce the rule of law in democracies. Police officers often use violence to stop or prevent violence. When they do, however, they must face investigation and review to determine whether their use of violence was warranted, was used as a last resort, and was used consistent with rules and guidelines to prevent excessive force. Other than in times of war, states justify human rights violations as an exceptional practice warranted by threats to the security of the society—or, more often, threats to the security of the regime in power. Two examples of the latter are apartheid in South Africa and the brutal regime of Augusto Pinochet from 1973 to 1988 under which some 3,000 Chilean citizens were extrajudicially executed and another 27,000-plus made to disappear. The slippery slope of rationalizing extraordinary uses of power in the face of security threats is not only a problem for non-democracies. Great Britain during the Troubles in Northern Ireland and the United States in the aftermath of the September 11, 2001, attacks are both criticized for compromising human rights and due process in their efforts to combat terrorist threats.

Another issue raised by human rights abuses as a form of violence is the need for societal reconciliation in the aftermath of abuses. Whether the end of apartheid in South Africa, the end of the "dirty wars" in Central and South America, the end of communist governments in eastern and central Europe, or the end of slavery and, later, racial discrimination in the United States, an unreconciled society is vulnerable to subsequent conflict and cycles of violence rationalized and fueled by past injuries and victimization. The numerous "truth and reconciliation commissions" today represent a relatively new effort to address the injustices and suffering caused by human rights violations in postconflict societies.

*Implementation and enforcement.* At present, the international machinery for the implementation and enforcement of human rights appears very weak. Of course, a century ago, even a half century ago, such machinery was nonexistent. Still, more is expected, and while some remain skeptical of how effective the ICC can be in the near future, arguments bolstered by reference to international human rights standards often appear in domestic courts and national legislation. In a sense, all national courts of states that are parties to a human rights treaty are venues where international human rights can be litigated, though seldom are they the sole basis for litigation. Parties to a treaty undertake an obligation to promote appropriate national legislation to secure the rights contained in the treaty. In addition to the UN Human Rights Council, which replaced the UN Commission on Human Rights in 2006, a variety of regional venues, like the European Court of Human Rights or the Inter-American Commission for Human Rights, hear cases involving international human rights violations. Finally, nongovernmental actors like Amnesty International or Human Rights Watch play an important role not only in advocating for the implementation of human rights but also in enforcing human rights. They bring the glare of world public opinion to bear on the conduct of states or the failure of states to take action to prevent and stop human rights violations within their jurisdiction. In the end, however, the citizens of states who believe conditions would be improved for themselves or their compatriots by the enforcement of human rights are ultimately responsible for pressuring their own governments and thus create the political will to make a change. Citizens must also be willing to make sacrifices, take stands, and commit the resources necessary to enforce and uphold human rights standards.

*Rights and social evolution?* Do societies morally evolve over time? Were things like mass slaughter, slavery, mass rape during and after war, summary and mass executions for political purpose, torture, and arbitrary political imprisonment once considered normal or at least routinely left uncontested? Does a general contemporary opposition to these things reflect some measure of moral improvement in the human condition, even if little has been done to build a consensus among states to oppose, much less prevent, mass violations of human rights? Perhaps. One could also argue that moral improvement among humanity as a whole is neither inevitable nor entirely clear, and small-scale tribal societies (like indigenous communities) present an entirely different historical and social context. For some, climate change and its impact on human health and sustainability is one of the most pressing moral challenges of our time, yet many indigenous peoples and cultures were or are socially organized around the notion of an environmental ethic that regards all life forms and the material world they live in as connected. Certainly, no reason can be given to necessarily associate "modernity" with notions of social or moral progress. The Holocaust was European and, among other things, a high-tech and very modern genocide. In Chapter 3 I will argue that the Holocaust embodied the dark side of the Enlightenment, the separation of science and morality. One can also find plenty of human rights violations before and during the Enlightenment as well, but twentieth-century genocides suggest that the capability of humans to enact cruelty in some ways shows little or no improvement since ancient times. Still, the level of interdependence and interpenetration of human discourse and social interaction is also unprecedented, and therefore, however fitfully and however slowly, a degree of moral consensus about how power should be used and how it should be restrained is evident, even if the political will of the international community to restrain abuses of power often seems weak.

## Conclusion

In this introductory chapter, I surveyed the landscape of contemporary international human rights by, first, describing what they are, where they come from, and how they are protected and promoted and then, second, delving into some of the tools used analytically and theoretically by scholars, activists, and policymakers concerned with human rights. The question of values versus interests is apparent throughout—efforts to ground human rights in some foundation such as describing them as God given, part of natural law, or inherent in our humanity, are really attempts to elevate or transcend the thorny issue of human agency. If rights come from God, natural law, or our humanity, then humans have only discovered, not invented them. If human agents did not invent them, then they cannot be biased in favor of one historically and socially situated group of human beings. Are human rights universal? If so, then do they also give rise to universal values and, thus, universal interests? Do they transcend subjectivity, or are they just a good idea, a measure of the moral character of human societies?

Criticisms of categories, particularly the three generations of human rights and attempts to rank rights in a hierarchy privileging individual over collective rights present a straightforward moral question. What's the point of protecting the freedom to speak or the necessity that governments respect due process if the circumstances of an individual's life are so materially deprived that most of his or her energy every day is spent simply trying to obtain access to clean water, shelter, and adequate nutrition? What of individuals who must spend each day simply avoiding death or injury in an environment of armed conflict? Will freely speaking change his or her circumstances? Will voting change a person's situation if the political institutions and the economic conditions are inadequate to change these basic deprivations?

The tension between the state as perpetrator and protector is also evident throughout the issues raised in this overview. The unprecedented atrocities of the Holocaust were acts of state. Prosecutors at Nuremberg put individuals on trial, but individuals charged with criminal acts carried out in their capacity as agents of the state, a state that was also on trial by default. Sovereignty provided no shield of immunity. The very concept of crimes against humanity, as the prosecution argued, is that some acts are so heinous that not to be offended by them is not to be human; those acts are crimes not only against the individual victims but also against the humanity of all people. This argument is also one about transcendence and, indeed, natural law. States also came together—specifically, agents acting in their capacity representing states—to condemn the genocide, to affirm an anti-genocide norm, and to resolve to enter into agreements to prohibit and punish any state that violated that norm in the future. The extent to which they have made good on this commitment will be examined in other chapters.

# 3

# Human Rights
# in Context

Intercultural dialogue is the best guarantee of a more peaceful, just and sustainable world.
                    —Robert Alan Silverstein, US writer and social activist, 2000

The war we have to wage today has only one goal and that is to make the world safe for diversity.    —U Thant, former UN Secretary-General, 1968

THE HUMAN RIGHTS ENUMERATED IN THE "INTERNATIONAL BILL OF Rights"—the Universal Declaration of Human Rights plus the two covenants—primarily reflect rights discourses taking place within Western philosophical traditions over the past several centuries. But one would be mistaken to conclude that Western societies have a greater concern for human welfare or the protection of human dignity than other societies. Indeed, as I will show in Chapter 5, the emergence and internationalization of human rights over the last two centuries developed largely as a response to the assertion of sovereignty by the state, particularly when state sovereignty is used as a shield against accountability for excesses and arbitrariness. Human rights restrict the state's arbitrary use of authoritative power by subjecting it to the rule of law. Additionally, while the inclusion of social, economic, and cultural rights reflects a more collectivist and social welfare orientation toward rights favored by non-Western societies, these rights also find support in more recent European history. Contemporary ideas about international human rights have been more strongly influenced by the political history and philosophical traditions of Western societies and cultures, but non-Western voices, discourses, and traditions are also increasingly influential and important to their development.

In order to provide a better foundation for a multicultural dialogue about human rights, I briefly survey the ways various world religious and spiritual traditions approach the issue of respect for human dignity and social responsibility. While a human right is not the same as respect for human dignity or social responsibility, all three create obligations and responsibilities. In this chapter, I also aim to evoke more interest in cross-cultural dialogue as well as understanding. The discussions are necessarily brief, but hopefully they will spark an interest in knowing more. The more we know about each other's cultural orientation, the more likely we are to respect or even appreciate our differences.

Being comprehensive is impossible; however, the world's major religious traditions are included, along with the spiritual views of some indigenous peoples. In addition to engaging issues raised by cross-cultural human rights dialogue, I also raise issues about what distinguishes modern international human rights from the ethical prescriptions regarding respect for others in cultural practices and religious traditions with deep historical roots. The last section contains a review of human rights development in the context of recent European political history. Human rights may be universal, or a universally good idea (a controversy explored more thoroughly in the next chapter), but undoubtedly the articulation of contemporary international human rights in the aftermath of World War II is a product of not only the political ideals but also the atrocities and excesses of Western states.

## Human Rights and Religious Traditions

Canadian professor Rhoda Howard and US professor Jack Donnelly argued, "International human rights standards are based on a distinctive substantive concept of human dignity" (1986:801). Although professors Donnelly and Howard, both preeminent scholars of international human rights, went on to argue that only liberal regimes, in contrast to communitarian and communist regimes, can protect human rights, the point in this chapter is that many cultural and religious traditions have a concept of human dignity, and understanding that fact is important. Furthermore, the fact that many—but certainly not all—conceptions of human rights emerged in concert with liberalizing revolutions that overthrew autocratic regimes and with philosophical narratives of liberalism in Western societies does not mean that the protection of human rights is incompatible with non-Western cultures.

Both Western and non-Western societies have rich histories, sacred texts, and traditions that address questions of human dignity and limits on how power is used authoritatively. With some 4,000 distinct ethnic or communal groups (groups sharing a common identity and a history of cultural self-determination) living in just under 200 states, maintaining a cross-cultural dialogue about human rights values is both enormously complex and crucial to the development of widely shared norms and practices. Here the ideas of human rights and human dignity as well as obligations and responsibilities to respect them are viewed in relation to some of the most basic beliefs of seven major world religious traditions as well as the spirituality of indigenous peoples. With the exception of indigenous peoples' traditions at the end of the section, religious traditions are presented more or less in the chronological or historical order in which they developed.

### Confucianism and Taoism

As in pre-Christian Europe, religious practice in pre-Taoist and pre-Confucian China focused on nature, animism, divination, and household and fertility deities. Both Taoist and Confucian writings appeared around the 6th century B.C.E. Taoism and Confucianism were adapted within the context of ongoing Chinese cultural practices and beliefs—reverence for one's ancestors and for social class in Confucianism and the implicit order of the natural world in Taoism. Taoism was adopted as the official state religion in the middle of the 5th century B.C.E. and today is practiced primarily as a means of cultivating individual spiritual consciousness whereas Confucianism focuses on "right conduct" in social and political spheres. Both place responsibility for achieving consciousness or right conduct squarely on the shoulders of the individual practitioner, in contrast with Western philosophical traditions emphasizing restraints on public authority for the protection of human rights.

The Tao is the order of unity flowing through all things. Many verses of the Tao-te-ching text are aimed at revealing the paradoxes contained within oppositional thinking and point to the impermanence and unreliability of such thinking that, the Tao suggests, is implicit within a world describable only by language or categories. The best-known symbol of Taoism is the *yin-yang,* representing the unity and interdependence of opposites. In Taoism, no real or eternal opposites are recognized; rather all exist within a relationship. Therefore, unity is regarded as the underlying order of the natural world, and humans should strive to align themselves with that order through awareness. One of the ideals to which a Taoist practitioner aspires is consciousness of *wu-wei* or equilibrium derived from natural order.

Although scholars disagree as to whether Taoism aims to directly instruct humans in morality or ethical behavior, if one takes seriously the underlying unity of all things, including human beings, then one cannot harm another without harming oneself. The three aspirations, or "three treasures," of Taoist practice are compassion, moderation, and humility.

Seeing how human rights could be violated by anyone whose focus is on the cultivation of these qualities is difficult.

In contrast with Taoism, Confucianism prescribes specifically ethical conduct grounded in familial and social relationships. Cultivating character through right conduct in social relations is the central concern of Confucianism. The founder of Confucianism, K'ung Fu Tzu (Confucius), taught that human beings have a moral responsibility to engage in ethical behavior. By focusing on one's obligations to behave in a way that respects the dignity of others, the six basic values of Confucianism contrast with the Western notion that "rights" are necessary to protect human beings from one another (Sato 2003). The six values are tradition (*li*), the obligation of parents to love their children and of children to respect their parents (*hsiao*), righteousness (*yi*), honesty and trustworthiness (*xin*), humaneness (*ren* or *jen*), and loyalty to the state or society (*chung*).

Confucian scholars regard humaneness (*ren* or *jen*) as the basis for morality and ethical behavior. Confucian thought was further developed and interpreted by Chinese scholars over many centuries, including by Mengzi (Mencius), who taught that human-being-ness is grounded in our capacity for moral consciousness and based on four qualities: sympathy, self-restraint, reverence, and the ability to distinguish right from wrong or to make ethical judgments.

### Hinduism

As the oldest continuously practiced major world religion, Hinduism actually refers to the ongoing evolution of literally thousands of localized religions with roots extending backward 3,500 years or more and an estimated 950,000 practitioners today. One of the most prolific contemporary philosophers of comparative religion, Raimundo Panikkar, himself born to parents of a religiously mixed marriage (Catholic and Hindu), argued strenuously against drawing parallels between the contemporary Western notion of human rights and the teachings and beliefs of Hinduism. In fact, he argued against doing so across any religious or cultural divide, since philosophical concepts develop within particular cultural contexts: "It is wrong-headed methodology to begin by asking: Does another culture also have the notion of Human Rights?—assuming that such a notion is absolutely indispensable to guarantee human dignity" (quoted in Coward 2005:25–26). Instead, said Panikkar, the question that should be asked is whether and, if so, how a particular culture formulates the philosophical notion of social justice. From that position the issue of whether "the concept of human rights is an appropriate way of expressing this order" can be evaluated (quoted in Coward 2005:26).

The concept of dharma is the basis for a Hindu conception of a just social order and prescriptions for just social conduct. Dharma is a system of moral obligations rather than rights and refers to the broadest underlying metaphysical reality, having both universal and particular dimensions (Coward 2005). Obligations and rights are inseparable because dharma is reciprocal in nature. It is the present consequence of ever-balancing cosmic cause-and-effect forces, as well as the cause of future consequences resulting from present choices. In this way, given a belief in reincarnation, the caste system itself—and which caste one is born into in a particular life—is viewed as a product of dharma.

Dharma is both the cosmic order underlying and governing all earthly order and the force or law that determines at birth the place of each individual within the earthly social, economic, and political order. Justice is served when one's obligations are fulfilled within that order, and one's place in the social order is viewed as a consequence of the higher, universal justice of dharma. Obligations can vary across time, from youth to old age, as well as across the social space of caste (or class) and gender.

Dharmic Hinduism is praised for its ability to accommodate other cultural practices such as Islam, Sikhism, Buddhism, and Jainism. It is also sharply criticized for its adherence to the caste system. Mahatma Gandhi, who led the nonviolent Indian struggle for independence from Great Britain, was one of its most influential critics. Mahatma Gandhi (following the much earlier example of Buddha) undertook efforts to reform the cultural understanding and practice of dharma, particularly as it provided justification for discriminatory practices affecting women and "untouchables" (the caste name that includes Dalits and other tribal peoples). His commitment to reform led to the constitutional abolition of the untouchable caste, human trafficking, and forced labor and opened Hindu temples to Hindu Dalits. Inspired by Gandhi and continuing discrimination, the struggle for Dalit social justice and women's equality continues in India today.

## Buddhism

Prince Siddhartha Gautama, who became the Buddha, was born in India around the 5th century B.C.E. As a set of practices aimed at individual enlightenment, Buddhism can be practiced on its own or in conjunction with other religious beliefs, providing those beliefs are not exclusive of Buddhist practice. Three strains of Buddhism originated in India—Theravada, Mahayana, and Vajrayana—but other national forms of Buddhism exist, such as those in Thailand, Burma, Vietnam, Tibet, and Japan (known as Zen Buddhism). Asian trade routes introduced Buddhism into China, Korea, and Japan, where it intermingled with Confucianism and Taoism.

Buddha accepted the Hindu view that the universal framework within which humans experience and perceive the world is made up of dharma, karma, and maya. Dharma is the ultimate cause and effect of reality, karma is the process linking consequences to causes over time, and maya is the illusion of a reality that human beings see or perceive in the world as a result of projecting one's own ego. The objective of Buddhist meditation practice is to remove these illusions caused by ego and so become aware of things as they are. Buddhism shows how the illusions of maya can be overcome and individuals can be released from the "wheel" of karma by living a life of conscious awareness devoted entirely to relieving the suffering of others. Through the practice of *metta* or loving-kindness, one must know what constitutes an act that will relieve suffering, which in turn is predicated on awareness that is not distorted by self-delusion.

Two Nobel Peace Prize winners leading social justice campaigns today are internationally famous Buddhists—the Tibetan Dalai Lama and Burmese human rights activist Aung San Suu Kyi. Buddhism does not directly advocate for the rights of individuals but rather against the uncompassionate conduct of governments whose policies cause suffering. If political leaders actively sought enlightenment, they would cultivate compassion within themselves in conformity with the first and second principles of Buddhism: relieve suffering and do not cause it.

Thai Buddhist scholar Phra Payutto argued that contemporary human rights developed in response to historic conditions within Western societies. Government practices that cause suffering, however, have been reproduced within non-Western societies through the spread of modernity, a cultural framework made up of certain values and beliefs about power. Payutto described modern human rights in these terms: "It is a 'negative ethic': society is based on selfish interests—'the right of each and every person to pursue happiness'—and an ethic, such as 'human rights,' is needed to keep everybody from cutting each other's throats in the process" (quoted in Florida 2005:208–209).

What about Buddhism and social justice? Buddha himself altered centuries of Hindu discriminatory practice by ordaining both women and so-called outcasts. Addressing the UN World Conference on Human Rights, the Dalai Lama spoke of the need for all to develop compassion, refrain from violence and force, and respect universal human needs for freedom and dignity. Emphasizing the responsibility to act in accord with these principles, he spoke against totalitarian and authoritarian governments for failing to recognize either their responsibilities or the universality of human rights. Nobel laureate for 1991, Aung San Suu Kyi regarded her resistance to the authoritarian Burmese government as consistent with Buddhist practice and principles (Florida 2005). Founder of the Unified Buddhist Church of Vietnam, Thich Nhat Hanh is known for the practice of "engaged Buddhism" grounded in the application of Buddhist practices in daily life and focused on nonviolent social justice.

## Judaism

Written between the 9th and 2nd centuries B.C.E., the Torah, part of the Tanakh (Bible or Hebrew Bible) and the most basic and sacred text of Judaism, can be read both as a history of the Israelites and as the earliest written account of Jewish religious beliefs. The Talmud is the normative expression of the Torah and records the rabbinic discussions, legal opinions, and oral and written debates about Jewish law, ethics, customs, and history. Though focused on the responsible behavior of individuals in relations with one another, rabbinic law also prescribes behavior directed toward the fulfillment of one's relationship with God. Like earlier Asian philosophical systems, Judaism emphasizes individual obligations rather than rights protection, but it also asserts legal prescriptions about ethical behavior claimed to originate with a universal, if not divine, authority.

The Talmud lays out a vision of the just society and the behavior required to achieve and maintain it. Achievement of the just society is premised on the sacredness of human life, and the Talmud "makes it clear that the sacredness of human life means that each person, as a creature made in God's image, is due respect, justice, and fair treatment" (Haas 2005:201). Contemporary Jewish engagement with social justice is grounded in the idea of *tikkun olam*. Originating in the rabbinic tradition probably in connection with the development of mystical Judaism in the sixteenth century, *tikkun olam* has been specifically associated with social action since the 1950s. *Tikkun olam* obligates Jews to confront injustices and imperfections of the world through actions that contribute to repairing, healing, or making whole the broken and imperfect world.

Although Judaism is the religion of the Jewish people, the term *Jewish* also refers to ethnic, cultural, or religious identity. Israel is the secular state of the Jewish people. Though Jews and Arabs have lived in the area that now makes up the state of Israel since at least 1800 B.C.E., the horrors of the Holocaust that killed between 60 percent and 75 percent of European Jews under the German Nazi and other collaborationist regimes led to the creation of the modern state of Israel. As efforts to negotiate a mutually acceptable and peaceful transition to two-state independence got under way, the United Nations in 1948 declared the partition of Palestine into an Israeli and a Palestinian Arab state. The Arab League, acting on behalf of the Palestinians, rejected the partition, and military conflict between the Israel Defense Forces and Palestinian, Iraqi, Syrian, and Egyptian forces in the area continued until the Camp David Accords were signed in 1978. In 2012, polling indicated that a majority of Israelis and just over half of Palestinians supported a two-state solution (Weiniger 2012; Knell 2013). Unfortunately, a Zogby poll in 2014 showed support declining, and only about one-third of Israelis (34 percent) and Palestinians (36 percent) still believed that a two-state solution was feasible (Plitnick 2014).

No greater human rights controversy can be found within Judaism today than the troubled relationship between Jews and Palestinians. Palestinians make up about 20 percent of the population in Israel. Palestinian aspirations for self-determination and the creation of a Palestinian state out of the territories currently under Israeli occupation constitute a thorny issue bedeviled by the seemingly intractable violence between those Palestinians who reject the legitimacy of the Israeli state and the Israeli state's controversial occupation of the Palestinian territories.

### Christianity

Jesus of Nazareth was born during the rule of Caesar Augustus (27 B.C.E.–14 C.E.) during Rome's transformation from a republic to an empire. Christianity was at first regarded by the Romans as an anti-imperial sect of Judaism, and in many ways, it was. Unlike other religions practiced in the Roman Empire at the time, Christianity was free and open to women and men, rich and poor, Romans and Jews, and even slaves. Under Paul's influence, Christianity became an organized religion, and as Constantine came to power at the end of the 3rd century C.E. somewhere between 10 and 30 percent of Roman citizens had proclaimed Christian faith. By that time, the Roman Empire was well into the "Crisis of the Third Century" when civil wars were an almost constant feature of life in the empire and competition for military dominance was so intense and unsettled that this time span was known as the period of "military anarchy."

Historical accounts of the life and teachings of Jesus suggest that Christianity grew out of a messianic Jewish movement that hailed Jesus as the savior prophesied in Hebrew scriptures. The central tenets of Christian belief today—acknowledgment of the inevitably sinful condition of human beings, Jesus as the only Son of God and sole redeemer, and his resurrection as both proof of a nonphysical afterlife and absolution of sin through making amends (expiation) and appeasing God (propitiation)—were highly contested in the first three to four centuries following his death.

Finding support for the ethical mandates of contemporary human rights within these doctrinal teachings is more difficult than in the actual teachings of Jesus himself. How do the basic beliefs of Christianity relate to the contemporary idea of human rights? Jesus urged his followers to cultivate compassion and taught that all human beings were equal in the eyes of their creator. He demonstrated compassion and universal love by bringing relief from sickness, feeding the hungry, and showing respect and love for those reviled by others.

Contemporary Christians debate the authoritative basis of human rights—whether human rights derive from natural law, from a supreme being, or from humanity's ability to reflect on and morally improve human character—as well as how to balance rights with responsibilities regarding issues of social justice. Christian history includes many heroes inspired to act by moral obligations arising from or reinforced by their Christian beliefs. These heroes include Christians who put their lives at risk to save Jews during the Holocaust (Drinan 1980; Klempner 2006), Archbishop Oscar Romero and liberation theologians who led the poor in resisting authoritarian rule in Central and South America, Mother Teresa who was beatified as the Blessed Teresa of Calcutta, and civil rights leader Martin Luther King Jr.

The spectrum of contemporary Christian practices includes social activism on behalf of those marginalized or oppressed by economic and social injustices as well as some Christians who emphasize the proselytizing mission that distinguishes between the "saved" and "unsaved" and who view justice as ultimately dispensed by God. But as William Brackney noted in *The Christian Tradition,* volume 2 of *Human Rights and the World's Major Religions* (2005), modern human rights understood as a set of individual freedoms and rules of due process that limit state power emerged within societies that considered themselves essentially Christian, or at least Christian majority, in Europe and its settler states.

## Islam

Muhammad began his ministry in 610 C.E. at the age of 40, a time when the city of Mecca was completely inhabited by Arabs. Yahiya Emerick (2001) described the climate as "steeped in idolatry and tribal custom" and observed, "There was no police force or central authority governing the city. At best, a council of rich tribal heads dictated local policies, and these decisions were usually guided by self-interest. Public drunkenness, prostitution, infanticide, spousal abuse, the worst form of abject slavery, and robbery, and banditry were the order of the day" (193). During the next fifteen years, Islam spread from Medina to Mecca and across the Arabian Peninsula. The teachings of the Quran were introduced as the minority of monotheistic Islamic Arabs fought "idol-worshiping" Arabs in Mecca. The word *Islam* translates literally as "surrender," which is at the heart of Islamic faith. Like all religious precepts, the idea of "surrender" can have broad and varied meanings, as can the Islamic concept of jihad, or struggle. Surrender is a means of settling or learning to live with the jihad as an internal moral struggle endemic to the human condition. Islam emphasizes the ability of humans to choose between right and wrong. The tension created by the freedom to make moral choices can be viewed as the struggle of jihad, the struggle to make right choices as opposed to wrong ones. Islam teaches that human freedom is evidenced by our ability to make this distinction. Finally, while endowed by the creator Allah with freedom, human beings are also endowed with an impulse or inclination toward surrender to spiritual unity, known as the *fitrah*. Surrender to Allah enables us to follow the impulse of the *fitrah*.

The precepts of Islam are found in the Quran, a text composed of basic religious teachings transmitted to Muhammad by the angel Gabriel, and the Hadith, a guide to applying the teachings of the Quran to the practice of daily life. The Quran describes divine creation as including diversity—male and female, multiple tribes and nations—and thus in this sense encourages acceptance and respect of difference (Quran 5:8 and 49:13, for example). Followers of Islam believe that on the Day of Judgment, those who profess belief in Allah and recognize Muhammad as his messenger will be admitted to God's kingdom in the afterlife.

The Quran is sometimes criticized for taking a negative stance on Judaism; however, this perspective should be understood within the historical context of Muhammad's life and teaching. At the time of Muhammad's arrival in Medina, Jewish and Arabic clans were embroiled in very destructive blood feuds. Muhammad's early teaching seemed oriented toward Judaism and the incorporation of Judaic practice into his new religion. However, in Medina, he turned away from Judaism to establish a new religion among Arabic clans, strengthening the solidarity and unified purpose of Arab clans to establish themselves as the regional rulers.

The "five pillars" of Islam are (1) confession of faith, (2) daily prayer, (3) charity, (4) pilgrimage to Mecca, and (5) fasting during Ramadan. The obligation to perform these acts is conditioned on one's means and, in the case of fasting, on physical capability. Muslims are expected to practice charity, or *zakat*, by contributing 2.5 percent annually of the value of their wealth, including capital assets, either to a government-established institution, the purpose of which is to collect *zakat*, or to a local mosque or charitable organization. Like fasting, *zakat* is another way in which the theme of surrender and sacrifice undergird Islamic practice. Islam holds that "all true religions" are part of a single historical cycle revealed through a series of prophets whose single message runs through the thread of all prophets and all world religions. Religious practice is aimed at both providing moral guidance for human conduct and cultivating compassion.

## Indigenous Spirituality

Indigenous peoples are communities now living in areas where their ancestors lived prior to colonization and prior to state formation. Colonial or settler governments forcibly relocated many indigenous peoples. The term *settler states* refers to New Zealand (called Aotearoa by the Maori), Australia, Canada, and the United States as well as Central and South American states created in the aftermath or transition to independence of former colonial settlements. Many indigenous peoples live in states formed as a result of more recent decolonization. In contrast to indigenous people in settler states, since decolonization postcolonial states are governed by people indigenous to the area. However, the pattern of dominance and subjugation from colonial occupation is frequently reproduced (or perceived to be reproduced) in relationships between dominant and marginalized indigenous groups in the postcolonial state, like the Tutsi and Hutu in Rwanda. Some indigenous groups, such as the Maasai in Kenya or the Karen in Burma, continue to struggle to retain their primary communal identity, language, and culture, and can be subjected to policies of coerced assimilation by postcolonial governments.

There are more than 370 million indigenous persons worldwide. Since the 1970s, indigenous peoples have been networking on a global level in order to achieve international recognition and protection of their rights to remain culturally, politically, and economically distinct and self-determining, including retaining their rights not only to cultural practice and linguistic preservation but also to a land and resource base (Wilmer 1993). These actions are a resistance to essentially ideological assertions by settler states and advocates of modernity, such as manifest destiny or the so-called civilizing mission, made against a historical backdrop of long-standing and persistent discrimination. Indigenous peoples were cast as backward or primitive, even destined to become extinct, and always, therefore, as presenting an obstacle to progress and modernization. Through global mobilization and networking, indigenous peoples have become aware of commonalities not only in their political situations but also in their worldviews (Mohawk 1977). In an essay entitled "Spiritualism Is the Highest Form of Political Consciousness," John Mohawk (1977) described indigenous spirituality this way:

> We believe that all living things are spiritual beings. Spirits can be expressed as energy form manifested in matter—grass matter. The spirit of the grass is that unseen force which produces the species of grass, and it is manifest to us in the form of real grass.
>
> All things of the world are real, material things. The Creation is a true material phenomenon, and the Creation manifests itself to us through reality. The spiritual universe, then, is manifest to Man as the Creation, the Creation which supports life. We believe that man is real, a part of the Creation, and that his duty is to support Life in conjunction with the other beings. (49)

An indigenous concept of human rights should be understood within the worldview described above by John Mohawk. Rather than rights, indigenous peoples focus on the obligation or responsibility of human beings to other plant, animal, mineral, and climatic "beings" or forces with which they share an interconnected and interdependent physical existence.

The original instructions direct that we who walk about on the Earth are to express a great respect, an affection, and a gratitude toward all the spirits which create and support Life. We give a greeting and thanksgiving to the many supporters of our own lives—the corn, beans, squash, the winds, the sun. When people cease to respect and express gratitude for these many things, then all life will be destroyed, and human life on this planet will come to an end. (Mohawk 1977:49)

Attorney Robert T. Coulter, who has worked on the forefront of international indigenous rights advocacy since 1978, asserted, "Indian rights are human rights." The rights advocated by indigenous peoples, he said, are the same rights all people want—the right to cultural expression and perpetuation and the right to self-determination as well as the right to the resources necessary to exercise these rights, including land rights (Wilmer 1993). These claims have been the subject of decades of discussion, advocacy, and activism focused on the United Nations and culminating in the adoption of the Declaration on the Rights of Indigenous Peoples by the General Assembly in 2007.

## Overview

A summary of how these cultural and religious traditions view the issue of human dignity, where responsibility for respecting human rights rests, and the role of governmental authority in protecting human rights appears in Table 3.1.

## Human Rights in European History

The development of human rights as a legal concept and as a set of limits on the use of authoritative power through due process was concomitant with the establishment of the modern secular state as the primary unit of governance in Europe. Barrington Moore (1966) and Charles Tilly (2002) regarded rights within the context of European history as a product of social and political struggles. From this perspective, three historical developments converged between the seventeenth and nineteenth centuries to set the stage for the articulation of contemporary international human rights: (1) the consolidation and centralization of power that gave rise to European states, (2) a philosophical shift in thinking about the authoritative basis for the exercise of power (and the Age of Reason this shift gave rise to), and (3) the subsequent development of an imagined contractarian relationship between those governed and their leaders.

The idea of a contract can be traced to the feudal system, the predominant social, legal, and political order between the ninth and fourteenth cen-

**Table 3.1 Religious Traditions and Views of Human Rights**

|  | Source of Human Dignity | Responsibility for Respecting Human Rights | Role of Government |
|---|---|---|---|
| Taoism | Implicit in natural order | Individual enlightenment | Political action flows from natural order |
| Confucianism | Basic values and humaneness | Individual right conduct | Civil service carries out ideals of right conduct |
| Hinduism | Varies depending on caste | Dharma and karmic cause and consequence | Accommodate pluralism and class system |
| Buddhism | Inheres in all humans regardless of caste | Consciousness leads to self-restraint; relieve suffering | Political leaders should also seek enlightenment |
| Judaism | Humans are made in God's image | Individuals obligated to make world whole | Law and adjudication of disputes and justice |
| Christianity | Golden rule and compassion | Church doctrine and adherence to Christian ideal | Varied from Holy Roman Empire to secular state |
| Islam | Universal presence of *fitrah* in all individuals | Surrender to Allah leads to moral conduct | To make laws consistent with Quran |
| Indigenous spirituality | Creator endows all beings with inherent and equal dignity | Responsibility to respect all beings rests with individual | Spiritually grounded; reflects natural order |

turies, in which property owners granted land tenure to vassals in exchange for military service. The rule of monarchs was strengthened by their acquisition of large mercenary armies. The power of lesser feudal lords was weakened as vassals increasingly preferred payments to their masters in place of military service, and feudal tenures were finally outlawed in England in 1660. Well-armed heredity rulers consolidated and centralized power as the law of the crown, or in eighteenth-century legal philosopher John Austin's terminology, "the command of the sovereign" replaced customary law, feudal law, and Roman law. Bureaucracies loyal to the monarchs began to develop and expand to collect taxes and enforce laws. During the seventeenth century, rights emerged from a revolution against the "immunity of certain groups and persons from the power of the ruler," a revolution spawned by the notion that such action was justified when waged against unjust authority (B. Moore 1966:413). This altered the relationship between the governed and their rulers from one determined by divine providence of birth to one of a social contract, giving rise to a fundamental change in the conception of citizenship rights, an antecedent to human rights.

The most significant philosophical rupture was between the "divine right" norm that legitimated governing authority and the concept of natural rights emerging from the Enlightenment. The authority of divine right, bestowed by God at birth, was uncontestable, even if God's reasoning was, according to authorities, beyond the common man. In contrast, natural rights flowed from natural law, a moral imperative for a just social order that any reasonable person could, on reflection, discern. The foundation of authority shifted from religious faith to a belief in the human capacity to reason and reflect. The influence of natural law thinking is evident in the reference of the US Declaration of Independence to "inalienable" rights and "self-evident" truths.

By extolling the virtues of reason in human affairs, eighteenth- and nineteenth-century European intellectuals expanded the role of secularism in society, not only challenging the moral foundations of religious thought but also heralding a new faith in science and its capacity to foster human progress. Indeed, the Enlightenment's faith in science and the inevitability of progress continued well into the twentieth century. The emergence of citizenship rights, natural law, and separation of church and state thus gave rise to the modern secular state created and maintained by a social contract among citizens and between citizens and their rulers. The social contract is formed and renewed by consent (free, fair, and open elections) and is a key concept in understanding contemporary liberalism, which provides the ideological basis for the development of human rights and due process.

The transition from feudalism to monarchies and eventually to states altered the political landscape and the normative basis for exercising power authoritatively in Europe between the fifteenth and eighteenth centuries. This transition was accompanied by a philosophical shift putting reason, rather than religion, at the center of moral order, and liberalism emerged as the political expression of the Enlightenment. Divine right and sovereign absolutism gave way to a social contract based on citizenship and consent. The convergence of these political and philosophical developments provided the fertile soil in which contemporary international human rights would eventually take root.

## The Enlightenment

Understanding the intellectual revolution represented by the Enlightenment is important because two of the most profound moral issues of the twentieth century can be traced to its legacy. One is the centrality of reason and belief in the inevitability of progress resulting from the acquisition or production of knowledge through rational scientific methods. The other is the continuing debate arising out of Enlightenment thinking over the relativity versus universality of morality, specifically, the morality of international human rights.

The Enlightenment refers broadly to a set of intellectual, philosophical, and metaphysical shifts that produced a new metanarrative in European history and self-understanding. Metanarratives (sometimes called master or grand narratives) are the stories a society tells collectively about what being human means, how historical forces shape present social circumstances, and how the past and present project a shared vision of the future. Literary scholars John Stephens and Robyn McCallum defined a metanarrative as "a global or totalizing cultural narrative schema that orders and explains knowledge and experience" (1998:1298–1299).

As a metanarrative, the Enlightenment both placed reason at the core of social order and extended it broadly across science and philosophy. Many Enlightenment thinkers aimed to revive Aristotelian thinking about causality in the natural world but then went a step further in positing the perfectibility of the social world through knowledge produced by reason or rationality. Indeed, the idea of distinctly social sciences reflects this element of the Enlightenment metanarrative, an active element some refer to as "social engineering." Enlightenment philosophers viewed reason as independent or autonomous, as capable of producing or enabling human investigators to discover an objective truth independent of their agency as knowledge producers. In this view, knowledge is discovered rather than produced. Each question has only one answer when posed scientifically. When Enlightenment ideas are extended to the social world or questions of philosophy, there is then only one best political system, one best philosophy, one best economic system, and so on.

This kind of thinking, critics argue, is not productive in the social world because it silences criticism and shuts down opposition. The social world does not, critics posit, inevitably advance, and when it does, the progress is only the result of openness to and engagement with criticism (Marcuse 1964; Habermas 1984). This criticism was raised most poignantly following World War II and particularly in light of the Holocaust.

## Populist Revolutions in Western Europe

The political and military struggles that paralleled and embodied the philosophical revolution of the Enlightenment swept through Europe during the two centuries between 1640 and 1852. The decline of feudalism, the consolidation and centralization of power within a territorial state, challenges to the religious legitimation of political power, and the rise of capitalism and a commercial merchant class were all in play during the twenty years of the English Civil War (1640–1660). Rebellions in 1549, 1607, and 1631 that foreshadowed and climaxed in the Puritan Revolution ultimately brought Oliver Cromwell to power in 1650.

Thomas Hobbes, the earliest natural law philosopher, reflectively chronicled many of these changes. An acquaintance of Sir Francis Bacon,

Hobbes became an advocate for science, and his work is perhaps the first attempt to apply scientific thinking to social philosophy. He published a work entitled *Elements* just as the Puritan Revolution was brewing in Parliament and before it concluded with the beheading of King Charles I. His greatest work, *Leviathan* (subtitled *Or the Matter, Forme, and Power of Commonwealth*) was published in 1651, just as the Commonwealth was established and just before Oliver Cromwell was named lord protector in place of the monarchy.

The government of the Commonwealth established after the regicide of Charles I succeeded in ruling in place of the monarchy for a decade, but it also became oppressive and intolerant. The restoration of the monarchy under Charles II in 1660 reflected many of the aspirations of the Enlightenment including religious tolerance (which he tried but failed to establish) and very strong support for the arts and sciences. Charles II established the Royal Society, the independent academy of sciences, which was inspired by advocates of Francis Bacon's "new science" that aimed to understand the natural world through observation and experimentation.

Charles II died in 1685, but during his time and into the next century, the world saw an expansion in both the sciences and political freedoms. Sir Isaac Newton's *Mathematical Principles of Natural Philosophy* was published in 1687. By 1700, Europe was home to over 100 colleges and universities. The English Bill of Rights was passed in 1679, and in 1772, slavery was abolished in England. The peaceful "Glorious Revolution" overthrew James II and established the modern British parliamentary democracy in 1688. This period was also one of imperialist expansion beginning with two complementary legislative acts, known collectively as the Act of Union, by the parliaments of Scotland and England in 1706 and 1707 ratifying the Treaty of Union and creating Great Britain. British expansion through colonization in North America carried the ideals of the Enlightenment into the colonies. There colonial leaders struggled over the paradox (or hypocrisy) of dispossessing indigenous peoples from their land and resources on the grounds of bringing a superior social and economic order while also encountering indigenous societies that were in many ways already more politically liberal than any in Europe (Johansen 1982; Grinde and Johansen 1991; Johansen, Grinde, and Mann 1998).

Like England, France underwent a popular and regicidal revolution that ultimately brought to power a very undemocratic revolutionary dictatorship, though in the French case Napoleon lasted a bit longer (1799–1814) than Cromwell did in England (1653–1658). In its early stages, English as well as French philosophers welcomed the French Revolution as the final and full triumph of reason over superstition, but the extreme violence of the "Reign of Terror" in 1793 and 1794 dissolved many of these hopes. The

Reign of Terror characterization is not a historical exaggeration: on September 5, 1793, the constitutional convention passed a declaration that "terror is the order of the day," warning citizens that revolutionary armies would use force against French citizens who disobeyed its laws.

Despite the ugly outcome, the language of citizenship rights characterized the French Revolution, evident not only in the rally for "liberty, equality, fraternity" but also through several historical moves to implement equality of citizenship. This equality was aimed at ending the political exclusion of Protestants in the years before and during the revolution. Jews, while excluded from political participation in the life of the state, were granted the right to govern their own communities according to their own customs and practices. After petitioning the National Assembly in 1790, they were granted full rights as citizens in 1791, but in becoming citizens lost their local self-determination. Notably, the discourse about Jewish citizenship renounced specific prejudices and argued that they should be regarded as individuals equal to other French citizens upon swearing a civic oath, an act that also terminated their alleged privileged status.

In "The Petition of Women of the Third Estate to the King" written in January of 1789, women who worked in the paid labor sector also petitioned for the education and enlightenment that would make them better workers, better wives, and better mothers while reassuring King Louis XVI that they did not wish to overturn male privilege (Landes 1988). During the same period, English writer Mary Wollstonecraft, grounding her arguments in terms of natural rights, was advocating much more strongly for women's equal political and economic rights.

By any account, the natural rights movement that began in England was a major influence in mobilizing the French people to overthrow their own monarchy, eliminate class privileges, and end feudalism. Many of the French philosophers did not live to see Napoleon's undemocratic and imperialistic regime; Charles Montesquieu died in 1755, Voltaire and Jean-Jacques Rousseau both died in 1778, and Denis Diderot in 1784. The contributions of René Descartes are without question the most profound evidence of the influence of the early Enlightenment on the development of science in France. This legacy continued in mathematics, economics, and material philosophy. The main intellectual contributions during the postrevolutionary period were in the areas of political economy, socialist theory, and utopian writing.

The discourse of rights, including natural and citizens' rights, the overthrow of feudalism and privileged nobility, and nationalism as the basis for loyalty both among ordinary citizens and in the military were all part of the legacy of the English and French revolutions and the early influence of the Age of Reason or Enlightenment. What followed was the rise of capitalism and, with it, the commercial and landowning class. The ultimate winners in the aftermath of these revolutions, the businessmen and landowners wanted to institutionalize their gains by defining citizenship rights in terms that favored property, education, finance, and industrial interests. Thus, economic philosophies were implicated as much as political philosophies, and the roots of debates that continue today can be traced to this period in the early nineteenth century. Adam Smith's *Wealth of Nations* was published in 1776, and the physiocrats who espoused the doctrine of laissez-faire economics rejected the old mercantilism in favor of unregulated free markets. Political freedom and economic freedom were inseparable in their view. The American Revolution was also clearly inspired by Enlightenment philosophy, evident in the writings of Thomas Paine, Thomas Jefferson, and Benjamin Franklin, among others. Between 1848 and 1852, revolutions aimed at ending all vestiges of feudalism and installing popular governments controlled by the rising commercial class swept through most of Central and Western Europe except the Netherlands, Belgium, and Great Britain. Paris was the seat of the first workers' revolution, while nationalism and revolutionary change spread through Italy, Switzerland, Austria-Hungary, and Germany.

Finally, the roots of the Russian Revolution can also be traced to the earlier intellectual developments and populist reforms in Western Europe. With one face always turning west and the other turned inward, Russian history is rife with ambivalence about Russian leaders. Czar Alexander I abolished torture, granted amnesty to political prisoners, and made moves to abolish serfdom and to establish a constitutional basis for government. Upon his death, a short peasant uprising took place but was quickly defeated by his successor, Czar Nicholas II. Amidst numerous strikes and general civil unrest, Nicholas II established a parliamentary system in 1905, but his efforts came too late. The Bolsheviks, led by Vladimir Lenin, soon replaced the provisional government installed after the czar's overthrow in 1917. The communist government, put in power by the Bolsheviks and Lenin, would last until 1991. Whereas among Western Europeans the Enlightenment gave rise to a long ideological debate with roots in the Enlightenment about the structure of self-determined governments, Russian society was more distanced geographically and intellectually from the Enlightenment's influence. In the West the debate, which continues today, was between liberalism understood more in terms of economic (free-market) or physiocratic principles, and socialism, which emphasized the need for equality of economic opportunities and benefits and control of economic resources by the workers, whose labor creates wealth. Some argue that a position can be found in between—either democratic socialism or democratic liberalism. In both cases, the effects of political equality and freedom temper the extreme tendencies.

## The Dark Side of the Enlightenment:
## Imperialism and the Holocaust

In *The Origins of Totalitarianism* (1951), Hannah Arendt argued that imperialism and the Holocaust are linked by racism and what she called race thinking. The European roots of race thinking, she argued, are in the eighteenth century, and race thinking "entered the scene of active politics the moment the European peoples had prepared, and to a certain extent realized, the new body politic of the nation" (161). "Race thinking," she said, "was the ever-present shadow accompanying the development of the comity of European nations" (161), and "racism is the main ideological weapon of imperialistic politics" (160).

Before the Enlightenment, European identities were parochial and class based. Nationality, in the sense of an organic connection based on shared ancestry that connected citizens within the state, was much less important than links across class lines. Royal heritage crossed national boundaries. The effects can be seen today in the family tree of Queen Elizabeth II, which includes royalty from the Netherlands, Belgium, Sweden, Norway, Spain, Monaco, Germany, and, by marriage, France (Princess Charlotte of Monaco to Prince Pierre, Comte de Polignac in 1920). The Tudors' family tree extends to France, Denmark, and Spain, the Stuarts to France, Denmark, and Poland, and so on.

As nationalism rose and hereditary authority declined, loyalties were based on citizenship, and citizenship, in turn, was determined by blood (jus sanguinis) or birth (jus soli). One could eventually become a naturalized citizen upon swearing an oath of allegiance to one's new state and often, but not always, simultaneously renouncing any previous citizenship. The issue of refugees and human rights, the twentieth-century emergence of a right to a nationality, and the organization of the entire globe into a system of states are responses to the refugee problems created because state boundaries were carved out of empires, and civil and interstate wars often provoked a mass exodus from places of persecution.

Enlightenment thinking, emphasizing rational inquiry and objective knowledge, undermined hereditary privilege within European societies while simultaneously producing a kind of ethnocentric nationalism that was in many ways more insidious than the hereditary class system that preceded it. As Zygmunt Bauman argued in *Modernity and the Holocaust* (1989), "with the Enlightenment came the enthronement of the new deity, that of Nature, together with the legitimation of science as its only orthodox cult, and of scientists as its prophets and priests" (68).

Bauman went on to describe the moral implications of the so-called sciences of phrenology and physiognomy, which relied on measurable attributes of the skull and face that their practitioners believed were indicators of the moral character of individuals across racial lines. This scientific racism provided a justification for European superiority over non-Europeans, for the bloody imperialism of the "white man's burden," and, ultimately, for the attempt to exterminate and often to medically torture European Jews. In Bauman's view, racism combined with technology would still not be enough to produce the abomination of the Holocaust. The crucial ingredient was modernity enacted as an ideological project: "The murderous compound was made of a typically modern ambition of social design and engineering, mixed with the typically modern concentration of power, resources, and managerial skills" (77). The Holocaust was not the first politically rationalized mass murder in human history, nor would it be the last. But unique features like those above, Bauman argued, indicate that the Holocaust was as much a product, as it was a failure, of modern civilization. "Like everything else done in the modern—rational, planned, scientifically informed, expert, efficiently managed, coordinated—way, the Holocaust left behind and put to shame all its alleged pre-modern equivalents, exposing them as primitive, wasteful, and ineffective by comparison" (89).

Furthermore, he argued, while modernity always contained the possibility of the Holocaust, the unique connection between society and state made its implementation possible, primarily because of its bureaucratic logic and structure. This feature is at work in imperialism as well and is particularly apparent in the policies that carried out the so-called manifest destiny of European settler societies as they expanded in North America, Australia, and New Zealand. The indigenous peoples in these areas were regarded, as were European Jews, as a contaminant or obstacle to the future of the modernizing state. In the United States and elsewhere, indigenous children were forcibly placed into military-style boarding schools to be remade in the white man's image. In both cases, the logic of modernity combines with the logic of the state to produce what Bauman called a "dehumanization of the objects of bureaucratic operation" (102). A similar logic was evident in Rwanda in 1994 and in Cambodia when 20 percent of the population was killed between 1975 and 1979 by the Pol Pot regime.

## Conclusion

Although the contemporary notion of international human rights has developed within the context of state building in Western societies, many societies and the philosophical and religious traditions produced by and within them contain beliefs about human dignity, about the responsibility of human beings individually and collectively to respect human dignity, and about the characteristics that make power authoritative. The boundaries of societies, however, are porous, and people, ideas, and beliefs commingle across those boundaries—never more so than in our globalizing world today.

Discussions of globalization tend to focus on the economic implications, but humans are social beings and with the acceleration and proliferation of what sociologists call social exchanges come both the clashing and sharing of ideas. This interaction has the potential for both negative impacts and positive consequences. People need to have confidence in the ability of their worldviews to provide both an understanding of their experiences and a guide to actions that lead to the results they expect. They do not need a perfect or complete understanding and their actions do not always produce the results they expect. However, they need a certain amount of confidence that what they believe about the world they live in is more or less true in the sense that it is not generally contradicted by their experiences.

Psychiatrist Robert Jay Lifton (1993), who has studied the psychology of modernity through subjects ranging from Nazi doctors to the Japanese terrorist cult Aum Shinrikyo, argued that one of the most profound effects of modernity is to unsettle worldviews and thus require more adaptive approaches to evaluating and understanding our circumstances. The globalization of ideas and the globalization of vulnerability are presenting significant challenges to fixed, parochial, and impenetrable traditional worldviews. A few centuries ago, the number of people who encountered others whose worldview sharply differed from their own was much smaller than today. This globalization of ideas can provoke a backlash and lead to reactionary and revitalization movements and ideologies as a defense against these philosophical intrusions.

On the positive side is the possibility for globalizing norms including human rights norms that reduce human suffering and degradation. In this book, I am more concerned with the positive potential of globalization and the diffusion of human rights norms. I aim to provide a basic understanding of the kinds of things that constitute violations of those norms and the social context in which they have developed. The question of whether international human rights are universal may be less important than whether or not human beings are increasingly regarding them as if they were.

The tension and conflict between interests and values when evaluating cultural contexts for assertions of human rights seem straightforward, particularly in light of the constructivists' claim that interests follow from identities. Europeans acting to overthrow absolutist governments and liberate themselves through popular democracy were just as quick to find a rationale for violating the human rights of non-Europeans. Inhumane treatment was not limited to non-Europeans, as the Holocaust illustrates. Although Jews had a long history in Europe, they were regarded as outsiders on grounds of both ethnic and religious identity. The potential for such conflicts seems most likely when religious values are politicized and when religious values are posited as the foundation for political authority and action as they are today in Israel. Religion played this same role in the Crusades, when the Holy Roman Empire was aligned with the Roman Catholic Church, and in the Americas when Christian proselytizing provided justification for brutal and even genocidal conquest. Most religions have at some time been implicated in the legitimation of political authority, through aligning or partnering with governing institutions or individual rulers. This alignment is not always associated with abuses of power, and ample room certainly exists for more research on the relationship between religion and politics (Norris and Ingelhart 2004).

As for the dual and conflicting roles of the state as perpetrator and protector, the issues explored in this chapter emphasize the emergence of human rights in Europe as a form of resistance to the arbitrary exercise of power—the state as perpetrator of excesses and uses of power under the shield of sovereignty and divine right. These issues also point to the incompleteness of the liberal project of holding power accountable and challenge the notion that modernity makes such democratic accountability inevitable.

# 4

# Are Human Rights Universal?

The idea of cultural relativism is nothing but an excuse to violate human
rights.                                    —Shirin Ebadi, Iranian human rights activist
and Nobel Peace Prize winner, 2004

I know there is strength in the differences between us. I know there is comfort where we overlap.
—Ani DiFranco, US songwriter and women's rights activist, 1994

WHAT DO UNIVERSALITY AND RELATIVISM MEAN? UNIVERSALITY IS
often claimed in connection with religious beliefs—the universality of
divine right bestowed by God at birth, the universal presence of *fitrah* in
Islam, universal love in Christianity, the universal justice of Hindu beliefs
about dharma and karma, the universality of human needs addressed by the
Dalai Lama, the universality of ethics in Judaism, and even the Enlightenment's implicit belief in the universality of reason. Assertions of universality also often arise in connection with moral claims.

In debates about international human rights, the claim of universality is
challenged by arguments stressing the culturally relative nature of human
rights—that individuals can only make sense of rights claims from the perspective of their own culture. Anthropologist Franz Boas first outlined the
principle of cultural relativism in the 1940s. Boas and his students, like
Ruth Benedict, exposed the ethnocentrism of anthropology and the racism
and sexism of Western culture. They restructured anthropological inquiry in
a way that not only dignified the value of non-Western cultures but also
launched a radical critique that made Western culture a subject of critical
anthropological study (Benedict 1959).

Within contemporary human rights dialogue, cultural relativism has
come to mean that cultural practices regarded by some as violations of

**65**

human rights cannot be judged within the framework of human rights values that originate outside of that culture. As Fernando Tesón (1984) put it,

> Cultural relativism may be defined as the position according to which local cultural traditions (including religious, political, and legal practices) properly determine the existence and scope of civil and political rights enjoyed by individuals in a given society. A central tenet of relativism is that no transboundary legal or moral standards exist against which human rights practices may be judged acceptable or unacceptable. (870–871)

If culture is thought of as a socially produced system of meaning that includes language, norms, artistic and literary expression, and various ritual practices or observances, then clearly people do make sense out of rights claims through the lens of their own culturally grounded system of meaning. But *culture* is an imprecise term, even for anthropologists. At the very least, the boundaries between cultures are imprecise, and cultures are dynamic, porous, and, increasingly, multilayered, much as identity tends to be in an increasingly complex social world or, perhaps more accurately, worlds. Some scholars point to the fragmentation of identity under conditions of modernity (Giddens 1991). As more people interact and communicate formally and informally and articulate agreements on shared values, as states do in the United Nations, then perhaps a new layer of global culture is in the making. Just as Lifton's (1993) modern "protean individual" is made up of multiple identities in diverse and situated roles, modern and postmodern meanings can be intersecting, layered, and dynamic.

In discourses about human rights, universality may refer to the foundation of the moral claim that human rights transcend particularity and cultural relativism, for example, in the sense of deriving from natural law as discussed in earlier chapters. If human rights simply are universal, if possessing them is an intrinsic quality of being human, then their universality is an endowed characteristic. Universality may also be used to designate a right or norm about which such widespread agreement exists that it has achieved universal recognition. Universality may also refer to applicability, that is, a right that is applicable to all humans, no exclusions. International law recognizes universal jurisdiction in some cases, meaning that a particular crime, like genocide, can be tried in any national or international court. If the definition of human rights relies on their inherent nature, that they inhere in us because we are human, then in that sense they are universal. So universality can be a moral claim, the claim of an empirical fact (everyone does agree, and no one will be found who is in disagreement), a legal fact, or a social fact (agreement makes the fact social). Or universality can mean something more esoteric, that the very meaning of being human includes these rights.

Jack Donnelly (2013) suggested a continuum between radical cultural relativism and radical universalism, with individuals inclined toward relativism to the extent that they perceive a right to be more determined by internal than external (and therefore universal) influences. Rhoda Howard (1993) called the radical position "cultural absolutism" while Debra DeLaet (2005) preferred the less strident term *pure relativism*. On the extreme universal side, rights are asserted as a moral imperative that transcends cultural difference.

One must remember the underlying political issues that give rise to these debates. First, from a non-Western perspective, criticizing the universal assertion is a form of resistance against Western influence in the context of a history of domination through conquest and imperialism by Western empires and states. The claim of universality can be viewed from the perspective of those subjected to colonization as a mechanism for carrying out cultural imperialism, a point put forward in particular by indigenous intellectuals like John Mohawk (in Barreiro 2010). Mohawk criticized the "myth of progress" and called indigenous peoples victims of progress, saying that, at least for those species (of plants and animals) that have become extinct as a result of the expansion of capitalism, things have been getting worse and worse, not better and better (Mohawk 1997).

Another criticism is that non-Western influences on the development of international human rights are often invisible. Susan Waltz (2001), for example, noted that even during the formulation of the Universal Declaration of Human Rights, many non-Western participants contributed significantly to the articulation of standards later included in the final declaration. Representatives of Muslim states also participated, and she found that some non-Western representatives—from India, the Dominican Republic, and Pakistan—were especially instrumental in obtaining recognition for the inclusion of women's rights (Waltz 2004). Recognition of self-determination was also the result of primarily non-Western and non-European advocacy (Waltz 2001).

## Human Rights and Cultural Difference: Contemporary Issues

No individual formulates a worldview in isolation. Human beings are social, and from our earliest exposure to language, itself a product of social processes, ways of knowing ourselves and the world we live in are embedded within the structure of language and social practice. The theory behind contemporary international human rights claims is that all of us ought to be able to agree on some fundamental or, in Henry Shue's (1980) terminology, basic rights to which all human beings can lay claim. Some human rights, in this view, are universally accepted and respected regardless of cultural differences. This claim is underscored by the title of the original UN declaration—the *Universal* Declaration of Human Rights. A number of debates arise, however, on the tension between universality and cultural particularity, which is both a testament to the desire for universality and to the paradox of asserting universality while acknowledging the right of cultural self-determination. These debates raise several questions: (1) If the starting point for contemporary international human rights arises out of primarily Western philosophical traditions and historical experiences, is asserting them as universal an act of cultural imperialism? (2) Are there distinctly Asian values that fundamentally differ from Western conceptions of rights because they generally orient Asians toward regarding the well-being of the community or group as a higher good than the interests or well-being of the individual? (3) Is Islam compatible with the assertion of international standards of universal human rights, particularly in terms of the application of sharia as or in conjunction with state law? (4) What is the role of human rights in the Arab Spring? And (5) can human rights be asserted as universal moral claims or must they be evaluated in relation to specific cultural contexts?

## Human Rights and Western Imperialism

Political imperialism—the deliberate and forceful expansion by one society of control over one or more other societies—is both a form of violence and a violation of human rights. The present world political system is in many ways a product of Western imperialism as Britain, France, Spain, Holland, Belgium, Germany, and Italy extended control over most of Africa; Southeast Asia; the South Pacific; North, Central, and South America; the Indian subcontinent; and the Middle East into the twentieth century. Only Ethiopia and Thailand escaped the fate of colonization. Even though itself a settler state, the United States also asserted imperialistic control over Puerto Rico, the Philippines, Samoa, Guam, the Midway Islands, the Northern Mariana Islands, the Virgin Islands, the Marshall Islands, Micronesia (now the Federated States of Micronesia), Cuba (from 1898 until the revolution of 1959), and Hawaii. Certainly in this regard, Russia as the core of the Soviet Union also colonized Central Asia, the Baltic states, and the Soviet Republics that became independent following the collapse of the Soviet Union. Contemporary discourses of imperialism in general and the "Age of Imperialism" in particular refer mainly to the imperialism of Western European countries from the sixteenth to nineteenth centuries.

In the aftermath of political decolonization and with the rise of capitalist-led globalization, the term *imperialism* is also used to refer to economic and cultural domination; however, decoupling the economic and cultural effects of political imperialism is impossible, even after political decolonization. Thus in the past four decades or so, criticism of imperialism and its present effects as well as allegations of continued effective economic and cultural imperialism enter into discussions about international rights.

Native American psychologist Eduardo Duran (see Duran and Duran 1995) and Afro-Caribbean psychiatrist Frantz Fanon (1952, 1961) wrote about the psychological effects of internalizing the colonizer's image and construction of colonial identity. Sociologist Herbert Schiller (1976), whose work focused criticism on the cultural impact of imperialism, contributed to the movement for the New World Information and Communication Order in the 1970s. Edward Said (1977) was probably the most influential critic of Western cultural imperialism, specifically toward Islamic culture. The subject of economic imperialism dates to theories advanced by John Hobson (1902) and Vladimir Lenin (2010 [1916]) in the early twentieth century, citing economic motives for political imperialism. This criticism was prevalent during the 1960s and 1970s as postcolonial third world intellectuals and leaders identified neocolonialism as a continuing cause of deprivation and marginalization in the aftermath of political decolonization. The negative legacy of imperialism was the central theme in the mobilization of the nonaligned movement and the New International Economic Order advanced by new non-Western states in the United Nations. Much criticism has coalesced recently within the framework of the World Social Forum, which has organized annual meetings globally and regionally since 2001, advocating a polycentric, grassroots, "people-centered," democratic world order based on social justice. The forum describes its mission as providing

> an open meeting place where social movements, networks, NGOs and other civil society organizations opposed to neo-liberalism and a world dominated by capital or by any form of imperialism come together to pursue their thinking, to debate ideas democratically, formulate proposals, share their experiences freely and network for effective action. (World Social Forum 2014)

The UN Educational, Scientific, and Cultural Organization (UNESCO) has also been the site of debates over the extent to which efforts to internationalize human rights standards infringe on the cultural self-determination of member states. In 2005, concerns over threats to cultural integrity and diversity led to the adoption of the Convention on the Protection and Promotion of the Diversity of Cultural Expressions, which entered into force in 2007.

European imperialism beginning in the fifteenth and sixteenth centuries was both a material and religious project. The Christianizing of conquered peoples gave rise to the debate between the two most important theologians and royal advisers of the time, Bartolomé de Las Casas and Juan Ginés de Sepúlveda over the humanity of indigenous peoples. The

Christianizing mission soon became the "civilizing mission," later the "white man's burden," and, finally in the United States, manifest destiny. Indeed, international law well into the twentieth century still referred to the "law of civilized nations" in order to make a distinction between European and settler states, on the one hand, and colonized, non-Western "uncivilized" nations, on the other. The rhetoric of Western moral superiority is an impediment to garnering support for the internationalization of human rights today to the extent that they are framed within the discourse of international law. Unsurprisingly, when the impetus for internationalizing and universalizing human rights comes from those same countries that led the world through four centuries of imperialism, some non-Western leaders push back critically and regard such efforts as yet another case of ethnocentric cultural imperialism.

## Asian Values and International Human Rights

The political landscape of world politics changed significantly between the end of World War II, when efforts to internationalize human rights standards were initiated through the United Nations, and the end of the Cold War in 1990. The number of states nearly quadrupled with the largest number of newly independent states formed out of formerly colonized areas. The 1970s saw the rise of economic power in some non-Western areas, specifically the Middle East as the epicenter of the Organization of the Petroleum Exporting Countries (OPEC). The growing influence of non-Western postcolonial states was further underscored by two OPEC-led oil embargoes, the rapid rise of Japan as a world economic power, and the dramatic economic growth rates first in the Four Asian Tigers (South Korea, Taiwan, Hong Kong, and Singapore) and then less spectacularly in Thailand, Indonesia, and the Philippines. India and China have also undergone explosive economic growth since the 1990s. China is now the third-largest economy in the world when the European Union is aggregated (in first place), generating $9 trillion in gross domestic product in 2013 alone, about half that of the United States, according to the International Monetary Fund (2014).

Advocacy of distinctly Asian, non-Western values is closely associated with Malaysian prime minister Mahathir Mohamad (1981–2003) and the former Singapore prime minister Lee Kuan Yew (1959–1990). Chinese leaders echoed the assertion that Asian cultures are more oriented toward collective or community well-being than individual rights and place greater importance on order, harmony, and family loyalty than Western cultures. In China, however, the claim of "Asian values" appeared to be more politically expedient than genuine on the part of the communist government responding to international criticism of Chinese suppression of the prodemocracy movement, particularly after the massacre in Tiananmen Square in 1989.

The assertion of distinctly Asian values should be understood within the context of this shifting economic and political landscape. Meeting in Bangkok two months in advance of the World Conference on Human Rights held in Vienna in June 1993, thirty-four Asian and Middle Eastern states outlined objections to prevailing conceptions of international human rights, declaring that human rights "must be considered in the context of a dynamic and evolving process of international norm-setting, bearing in mind the significance of national and regional particularities and various historical, cultural and religious backgrounds" (Asia-Pacific Human Rights Information Center 2014). The Bangkok Declaration explicitly rejected the notion that human rights could legitimately be used as an "instrument of political pressure." It asserted the "interdependence and indivisibility of economic, social, cultural, civil and political rights, and the inherent inter-relationship between development, democracy, universal enjoyment of all human rights, and social justice, which must be addressed in an integrated and balanced manner" (Asia-Pacific Human Rights Information Center 2014).

The Bangkok Declaration set off political and philosophical debates about whether one can identify distinctly Asian values in contrast with Western values and, if so, whether they conflict with the assertion and implementation of international human rights, or, alternatively, whether the claim of Asian values was really aimed at shielding undemocratic governments from criticism and potential intervention. Setting aside the shield issue, which cannot be proven one way or the other, the central contention is that Asian cultures, traditions, and worldviews on the whole assign equal weight to or attempt to balance the welfare of the group with the welfare of the individual (Koh 1993; Zakaria 1994). Widespread agreement on the validity of this claim can be found among diverse and distinguished Asian thinkers and writers like Fareed Zakaria (2002) and Nobel Laureate Amartya Sen (1997).

However, this balance cannot be used as an excuse for Asian governments acting in a despotic manner or violating the basic rights of their citizens. Sen (1997) argued that authoritarian governments and the suppression of civil and political rights are not "really beneficial in encouraging economic development" (11), though developing Asian countries often defend the opposite claim—that strong government intervention and subsuming individual rights are necessary to economic growth. To the contrary, Sen said, the political practices of authoritarian governments not only fail to prevent but also often lead to crises that impair and injure human welfare. He then went on to examine Asian philosophical traditions and concluded that while diverse, they often advocate for freedom, tolerance, and rights, and thus these values cannot be rightly claimed as uniquely Western. While, in Sen's view, Asians should be engaged in a debate of their own about rights, values, and tradition, he questioned the "usefulness of a grand contrast between Asian and European values" (1997:30). He concluded that "authoritarian readings" aimed at defending Asian states that violate international human rights against criticism or even intervention "do not survive scrutiny" (31).

## Is Islam Compatible with International Human Rights?

The term *Muslim world* is used primarily to refer to the adherents of Islam and states with Muslim majorities in the Middle East, including Iran, though Iran is not an Arab state. Although when one thinks of the Muslim world one typically thinks of the Middle East, the state with the world's largest Muslim population is actually in Southeast Asia. Out of Indonesia's 240 million people, 207 million are Muslim, making that country the state with the largest Muslim population. Indonesia began its transition from an authoritarian military government to a civilian democracy in 1998. In spite of its substantial Muslim majority, Indonesia is also a secular state. According to the *CIA World Factbook*, only about 20 percent of all Muslims in the world live in Arab states.

   Cultural relativism aside, from a Western perspective, two relatively good examples of secular Muslim countries with good human rights track records exist: Turkey and Indonesia. However, even these countries face certain problems. Turkey continues to struggle with balancing Islam, democracy, modernity, and secularism, although in 2008 Turkey's chief prosecutor petitioned to ban the Islamist Justice and Development Party, which was working to make sharia the law of the land in Turkey (Vries 2009). In 2013 and 2014, concerns among those who credit Mustafa Kemal Atatürk with Turkey's commitment to a secular democracy led to apprehensions about a growing politicization of Islam (Reuters 2013). However, for the most part, Turkey has demonstrated that Islam and democracy are not incompatible. A history rich with intellectual creativity and freedom, a well-established civil society, and a nineteenth-century movement for representative and constitutional government all contribute to Turkey's success as a Muslim democracy.

   In Indonesia, the peace between Islam and issues of international human rights is less a case of compatibility and more one of coexistence. Indonesia's transition to democracy followed a thirty-two-year history of authoritarian rule. Extremes of economic inequality, ethnic tensions that focus resentment (and discriminatory legislation) on the commercially successful ethnic Chinese Indonesians, legal and political conflicts in Papua, restrictions affecting political and religious freedom, and failure to reconcile past human rights violations are still of concern to international NGOs that focus on human rights.

The particularly pressing issue in the Muslim world is the conflict between international human rights standards and sharia. About half of the fifty-seven Muslim states in the Organization of the Islamic Conference incorporate quranic sharia into the national legal system to some degree. The legal system in Saudi Arabia is based primarily on a strict interpretation of sharia. The Taliban government in Afghanistan also applied the most repressive interpretation of sharia during its rule from 1996 to 2003. Islamist political parties that promote Islam as the basis for political and legal order exist in twenty-eight countries. In 1990, the Organization of the Islamic Conference issued the Cairo Declaration on Human Rights and Islam, declaring that "all the rights and freedoms stipulated in this Declaration are subject to the Islamic Shari'ah" and that "the Islamic Shari'ah is the only source of reference for the explanation or clarification of any of the articles of this Declaration."

Some Islamic and Middle East scholars argue for and others against the notion that international human rights are incompatible with Islam on grounds of Western cultural imperialism. However, if one accepts the argument that human rights like gender equality; universal suffrage; democracy; political participation; nondiscrimination; freedoms of religion, speech, and association; and the basic provisions of due process are or ought to be universalized to apply to all states regardless of cultural or religious traditions, then Islamic states today do not fare very well. One must ask, however, if the oppression of human rights from a universalist perspective is a result of an inherent fault in Islam or in how its precepts are applied? Many scholars, both Muslim and non-Muslim, argue the latter.

When he wrote in the late 1970s, Abdul Aziz Said (1979) noted,

> About two-thirds of the governments of these states are military or quasi-military regimes, nearly one-third are absolute or near-absolute hereditary systems, and only two of them are politically viable. About two-thirds of the Islamic states lack workable machinery to conduct participation and legislation. Only fourteen Islamic states have universal suffrage. (70)

Said concluded that "a picture of human rights practices in the Islamic World . . . bears little resemblance to Islamic precepts" (75). Other than the democratization of Indonesia, things have not changed dramatically since then. By the year 2000, seventeen states had declared Islam as the religion of the state and others "state that Shari'ah is [a] major source of law" (Artz 1990:204). Azerbaijan (over 99 percent Muslim), Tajikistan (98 percent Muslim), Chad (55 percent Muslim), Somalia (over 98 percent Muslim), and Senegal (96 percent Muslim) have constitutionally declared themselves as secular states.

"Islam is not the problem," says 2003 Nobel Peace Prize recipient Shirin Ebadi. "It is the culture of patriarchy. Some clerics have interpreted Sharia law in a way that discriminates against women" (Ebadi 2004). So Ebadi's view, which comports with the view of many liberal Islamic scholars, was really that Islamic beliefs and sharia do not in themselves necessarily conflict with international human rights (see also Said 1979; Khadduri 1984; Esposito and Voll 2001; Handwerk 2003). Rather, the interpretation and cultural context in which certain interpretations are acted on account for the contradictions between Islam and human rights and Islam and democracy. The Center for the Study of Islam and Democracy, founded in 1999 by a consortium of Muslim and non-Muslim academics and professionals, specifically promotes such a dialogue.

Even regarding the application of sharia, some Muslims see no incompatibility. They see orthodox or fundamentalist interpretations as the root of the problem. Professor Abdullahi an-Na'im, the Charles Howard Candler Professor of Law at Emory University, has lectured widely on issues of human rights and sharia. He argued that sharia is divine law prescribed for personal conduct, and that the state by nature is secular. Therefore, he said, sharia cannot be the law of the state without losing its divine nature (an-Na'im 2011). He advocated for both a liberal understanding of Islam and the legitimacy of international human rights norms.

Louay Safi, a member of the board for the Center for the Study of Islam and Democracy, said, "I think that Islam as a set of norms and ideals that emphasizes the equality of people, the accountability of leaders to community, and the respect of diversity and other faiths, is fully compatible with democracy. I don't see how it could be compatible with a government that would take away those values" (quoted in Handwerk 2003).

Fundamentalist interpretations of Christianity and Judaism have come into conflict with international human rights, as certain historical events and even current examples demonstrate. In addition, Islam is not the only religion, nor the only non-Western religion, recognized as a state religion today. Four states—five if Tibet is counted as a government in exile—regard Buddhism in whole or part as the official state religion. The Anglican Church is the official Church of England. Scotland recognizes the Reformed Church as its official state religion. Three Swiss cantons recognize the Old Catholic Church as official. Lutheranism is the official state religion in four Scandinavian countries. Five states recognize official state Eastern Orthodox Churches, and ten countries plus the Vatican recognize Catholicism as their official state religion. All of these states are generally regarded as subject to the standards of international human rights, most have signed the major human rights instruments, and they do not claim exemptions based on state religious traditions. In other words, through the example of other state-sanctioned religions, Muslim and even sharia do not have to be at odds with international human rights standards.

John Esposito and John Voll (2001) made the point that the rectification of religious authority and human rights can also be seen in the history of other religious traditions. A similar shift occurred when divine right was replaced by reason and reflection as Europe transitioned from the "Dark Ages" to the "Age of Reason." Esposito and Voll claimed,

> The process in the Muslim world [today] is similar to that which has taken place within other major religious traditions. All of the great world faith traditions represent major bodies of ideas, visions, and concepts fundamental to understanding human life and destiny.
>
> Many of these significant concepts have been used in different ways in different periods of history. The Christian tradition, for example, in premodern times provided a conceptual foundation for divine right monarchy; in contemporary times, it fosters the concept that Christianity and democracy are truly compatible. In all traditions, there are intellectual and ideological resources that can provide the justification for absolute monarchy or for democracy. The controversies arise regarding how basic concepts are to be understood and implemented. (1–2)

## Human Rights and the Arab Spring Revolutions

Protests that broke out on December 18, 2010, in Tunisia following the shocking self-immolation by Mohamed Bouazizi are now widely recognized as the beginning of the Arab Spring uprisings. The term *Arab Spring* most likely derives from the anticommunist revolutions in eastern and central Europe that began in 1989, sometimes called the Autumn of Nations, a play on the Spring of Nations, a year of political upsets in 1848. Though many differences can be found between the two eras—the Arab Spring and the fall of communism—they share a similar pattern of beginning with a few relatively quick overthrows or restructuring of some authoritarian regimes, followed in some cases by sustained but low levels of conflict and protest and in other cases protracted and violent civil wars.

The Tunisian protests led quickly to the overthrow of President Zine El Abidine Ben Ali just two months later, along with the resignation of Prime Minister Mohamed Ghannouchi, disbanding of the state political police, dissolution of the ruling party, and release of political prisoners. In all, 338 people were killed, but democratic elections were held in October 2011 (Associated Press 2012). By 2013, however, the tensions between secular and Islamist sectors threatened to throw the country back into political and possibly violent turmoil. In the subsequent democratic elections, the moderate Islamist movement turned political party Ennahda won a substantial plurality of seats in the parliament. Party leaders negotiated an agreement to share the three highest positions—speaker of the parliament, president, and prime minister—with the next two parties that were runners-up in the election. They began the process of drafting a constitution and held the first elections under the new constitution in November 2014. Beji Caid Essebsi became the country's first democratically elected president.

After Tunisia, the protests spread. Calls for change in Algeria began soon after, where protests and riots, including a spate of self-immolations, met with government suppression under an ongoing twenty-year state of emergency. Although the state of emergency was ended to appease protesters, the authoritarian government managed to stay in power. Since the protests ended in 2012, there has been neither a transition to democracy nor a descent into civil war (*The Economist* 2014). Protests starting in January 2011 in Jordan led to some governmental changes, including the dissolution of Parliament and dismissal of Prime Minister Samir Rifai (followed by additional parliamentary and cabinet turnovers). Jordan has been stable or stabilizing since that time, but the flood of Syrian refugees as well as the Syrian civil war itself threaten the economically and politically fragile post–Arab Spring government. Protests began in Oman in mid-January 2011 and ended four months later when Sultan Qaboos, the leader of Oman, made economic concessions and granted lawmaking powers to the country's elected legislature.

The Arab Spring protests began to appear in earnest in Western headlines and receive extended major network TV coverage when over 100,000 people filled Tahrir Square in Cairo, Egypt, and called for the overthrow of President Hosni Mubarak and the election of a popular government. The protests looked more like an occupation and lasted three weeks before Mubarak's government was ousted, the prime minister resigned, and a thirty-one-year dictatorship ended. The constitution was suspended and the military assumed power while democratic elections were organized. About 850 people died in clashes with the government before it was successfully overthrown (*Detroit News* 2011). Egypt destabilized again when President Mohamed Morsi—the first democratically chosen president in Egypt's history—was deposed by the military only one year after his election. Morsi was elected as a candidate of the Freedom and Justice Party, the civic political arm of the popular Muslim Brotherhood. After the September 2013 military coup, the Muslim Brotherhood was outlawed and Morsi along with others of the group's leaders were arrested and imprisoned. More than 600 death sentences were pronounced on Morsi supporters in the spring of 2014, but nearly 500 of them were subsequently reversed and fewer than ten executions were actually carried out. The Muslim Brotherhood was declared a terrorist organization by the military-backed government.

The government of Yemen was also overthrown in February 2012 following protests that started in January 2011, but there protracted conflict between the government and armed rebels, including some al-Qaeda fighters, left 2,000 people dead. President Ali Abdullah Saleh was granted immunity from prosecution when he stepped down in November 2011, turning over power to President Abd Rabbuh Masur Hadi (Kasinof 2012). Djibouti, Somalia, and Sudan were also sites of some minor protests that started in January 2011, but no real changes took place except that Sudanese president Omar al-Bashir, under indictment by the ICC for crimes committed in Darfur, announced that he would not seek another term as president in 2015. Much the same took place in Iraq beginning at the end of December 2012, although the protests were more widespread and some provincial and local leaders resigned. Post–US occupied Iraq is, for all intents and purposes, now a failed state where those who oppose the Shiite majority government or are hostile to the West, or both, mobilize to carry out acts of terrorism.

Protests beginning in late February 2011 in Morocco led to greater protection for civil rights, a promise to end corruption, a constitutional referendum, and political concessions by King Mohammed VI, who remained in power. Ten months of protests in Lebanon in 2011 resulted in only minor changes. Ongoing protests in Bahrain, Kuwait, Mauritania, Saudi Arabia, and, of course, Palestine are all related to the Arab Spring movement at least in the timing of the protests. Economic concessions have been made in Bahrain and Saudi Arabia, in Kuwait the Parliament was dissolved and Prime Minister Nasser Al-Sabah resigned, and in Saudi Arabia women were granted the right to vote in municipal elections beginning in 2015.

Libya and Syria suffered much more violent civil wars. Although the war that overthrew dictator Muammar Qaddafi in Libya only lasted six months, the failure to establish a functional and legitimate democracy in the three years afterward enabled the rise of militarized conflict among rival militias, including some representing Islamist factions that failed to garner much support in parliamentary elections. The revolution that culminated in the death of Muammar Qaddafi and included a UN-mandated military intervention in Libya has left that country unstable, with its private sector completely dysfunctional and as many as 200,000 individuals in militia positions paid for by the government (*USA Today* 2013).

The Syrian civil war shows no sign of abatement in late 2014 and runs the risk of escalating into a regional conflict with fighting along the Jordanian border and across the border with Lebanon. In May 2013, the United States and Russia agreed to convene an international conference aimed at ending the violence in Syria. Evidence of human rights abuses, including the deaths of many children and the use of chemical weapons, compounds the violations of human rights and international law. According to a report released in early December 2013, United Nations inspectors and experts found that rebels had used chemical weapons but they were not able to determine whether the weapons used were government produced or not (Stea 2013). By the spring of 2014, more than 150,000 had been killed and more than 6 million people were internally displaced in Syria.

All speculation about the compatibility between Islam and democracy will face the ultimate test in the aftermath of the Arab Spring and once the hard work of nation building and democratization begins. The protests employed mostly nonviolent methods of resisting and demanding change from authoritarian governments as protesters shouted, "Ash-shab yurid isqat an-nizam" (The people want to bring down the regime), and indeed regime change of some kind occurred in six countries (Ertuna 2011). Although the revolutions appeared to be secular, Islamist parties or leaders came to power through elections in the aftermath of the Arab Spring, including in Tunisia, Egypt, and Morocco (Al-Jazeera 2012). In summarizing a 665-page report following the revolutions, Human Rights Watch warned that

> the creation of a rights-respecting state can be painstaking work that requires building effective institutions of governance, establishing independent courts, creating professional police, and resisting the temptation of majorities to disregard human rights and the rule of law. But the difficulty of building democracy does not justify seeking a return to the old order. (Human Rights Watch 2013b:1)

Executive Director Kenneth Roth added, "As the Islamist-dominated governments of the Arab Spring take root, perhaps no issue will better define their records than the treatment of women" (Human Rights Watch 2013b).

Democracy is not the same as human rights; democracy does not inhere in us because we are human. Nevertheless, democratic processes provide channels for people to make the case for particular rights and to express grievances in the absence or impairment of rights. Democracies are not always responsive, either, as the case of indigenous peoples in settler states indicates and as, for that matter, does the continuing economic marginalization of women even in rich democracies.

## Moral Relativity and Moral Universality

Are human rights universal, or should they be evaluated in relation to specific culturally produced understandings and practices? This question was introduced through the perspective of Raimundo Panikkar at the beginning of Chapter 3. The survey of different religious traditions in the previous chapter shows that all have a concept of human dignity and moral responsibility. But do they have common or universal beliefs about a set of rights that should be internationally respected and endorsed?

On one hand, when conceived of as rights that inhere within us because we are human, rights without which we would not be human, or rights that, when not respected, call our humanity into question, then one is asserting that indeed, they are universal. When confronted with the most offensive atrocities—the Holocaust or the Rwandan genocide in 1994—one has difficulty making an argument that cultural differences could either justify them or render them beyond the moral judgment and condemnation of "outsiders." However, most offenses are not so stark. Two cases illustrate this point, one involving a group of non-Western societies and the other a Western society. Both cases generate debate about the universality of human rights versus the right of a society to decide what constitutes a human rights violation.

Female genital mutilation (FGM), sometimes called genital cutting, is a practice that ranges from partially cutting to totally removing the external female genitalia. Usually performed on girls between the ages of four and ten, it is currently practiced in twenty-nine African and Asian countries on approximately 3 million girls a year (World Health Organization [WHO] 2014a). Is it a form of torture, or is the practice of genital cutting protected by the right to cultural self-determination? Does the claim of cultural self-determination shield those practicing FGM from criticism or pressure to end the practice? More detail on what constitutes the practice will be given in Chapter 12. Those who believe that FGM is no more injurious than male circumcision, or opponents of male circumcision who also want to draw attention to and condemn that practice, call FGM circumcision.

The second case sometimes defended on the grounds of cultural relativism interestingly involves the United States and its continuing practice of capital punishment. Is the death penalty inherently inhumane because in order to minimize the possibility of executing innocent persons, an elaborate and multileveled system of appeal and review must be in place? This process, in turn, means that following the issuance of a death sentence, the condemned individual must endure a long period of uncertainty as the appeal cases proceed. US Bureau of Justice Statistics reported that prisoners typically wait ten years on death row while the appeals process continues. Some are there over twenty years and spend most or all of that time in isolation. Additionally some 144 people waiting on death row since 1973 have subsequently been proven innocent and released, with the average time from sentencing to exoneration at just over ten years (Death Penalty Information Center 2014a). More than 100 countries worldwide have outlawed capital punishment, with the death penalty being completely abolished in all of Europe and, in practice, in most of Central and South America, with Belize, Guyana, and Guatemala the exceptions (Death Penalty

Information Center 2014b). Many US allies criticize the United States for its position, but the United States registered a reservation to Article 6 in signing the ICCPR, stating that "the United States reserves the right, subject to its Constitutional constraints, to impose capital punishment on any person (other than a pregnant woman) duly convicted under existing or future laws permitting the imposition of capital punishment, including such punishment for crimes committed by persons below eighteen years of age." (However, in 2005 in the case of *Roper v. Simmons* [543 US 551], the US Supreme Court upheld a decision by the Missouri Supreme Court that effectively abolished capital punishment for juveniles in the United States.)

The question that must be addressed is, how can any moral claim be defended as universal? That is, on what grounds does the universality of human rights rest? This conundrum brings us back to the issue of natural law or natural rights. Must one regard such a claim as issuing from a moral authority above the state? If so, does it rest on religious belief, or on faith in the capacity for human reflection? Are some acts so offensive that to have knowledge of them and *not be offended* calls into question our very humanity? In other words, is humanity a quality of our existence that presumes an underlying unity with all other humans? If so, how is that unity expressed, manifested, or known?

This question can be answered in several ways. One is to assert a belief in a moral authority that is greater than or beyond human reason. This moral authority may be conceived of in more or less concrete terms. Religious fundamentalists of all faiths who appeal to a narrow interpretation of sacred text would exemplify the latter. However, other religious leaders like Martin Luther King Jr. assert that one need only believe in the existence of some divine and ultimately incomprehensive moral order in order to acknowledge the limits of human reason as a guide to moral justice, the theme of King's "Letter from Birmingham Jail."

Another answer is that human rights are moral values and, as such, are relative to the human agents who articulate them. Since these agents do so within the limits of particular linguistic and cultural systems of meaning, no commensurability, much less universality, can be found across cultural values. Since all people live within such systems of meaning, the authority to judge the practices across cultures does not inhere in any of us. This argument does not preclude criticism by people in one culture of the practices of people in another. Rather, it means that the authority on which their claims rest can be no more or less than their own willingness to condemn and criticize practices they find offensive.

A third possible answer that may resonate more with natural rights, as understood by the framers of the US Constitution, is to assert that cultural differences are real but so is our common experience as human beings. The human capacity to reflect on our common humanity and to ascribe to it an underlying unity within a shared moral community is universal. Within that moral community of humanity, diverse perspectives on moral authority may be represented, but human beings also have the capacity to bring these claims into a field of common discourse and, in doing so, to be the architects of our own moral order.

In a sense, this last answer comes closest to the current reality of international human rights as reflected in the final documents of the World Conference on Human Rights held in Vienna in June of 1993. A total of 171 states (out of approximately 190 states that existed at the time) representing a full spectrum of cultural diversity on a global scale adopted by consensus the Vienna Declaration and Programme of Action. The declaration includes affirmations of equality and nondiscrimination based on linguistic, ethnic, and national identity; equality of women; the rights of children; freedom from torture; and the rights of the disabled. It asserts a need for greater cooperation within the UN framework for implementing human rights, for strengthening that framework, and for promoting human rights education. It affirms the need for cooperation between states and the United Nations, for monitoring human rights conditions, and for the General Assembly to implement the provisions and recommendations of the declaration.

## Conclusion

I began this chapter with a broad-ranging discussion of the relativity-versus-universality debate and then specifically considered the related issues of imperialism, Asian values, Islam, and the Arab Spring, and then revisited the debate. How are interests, values, and the role of the state implicated in these issues and this debate?

Western imperialism is a historical fact that left a legacy of mistrust and grievances among postcolonial states and peoples. It also literally shaped the political boundaries of many contemporary postcolonial states and had social-psychological as well as political consequences for the people living within those boundaries coming to terms with self-government. Imperialism was driven by material interests and rationalized by a claim that spreading Western values, from Christianity to capitalism, would benefit the colonized people. Interests in this case are very much linked to identity—the identity of Western leaders and societies as superior and "civilized" in contrast with the peoples they set out to dominate. Their encounter with those peoples has altered both their identities and interests, though critics might argue that the change has not been that great. Instead, they argue, the mind-set of imperialism is carried out through means other than direct domination through institutions like the International Monetary Fund. It is also evident in various forms of military intervention like the US interventions in Grenada and Panama, the US-led regime change in and occupation of Iraq, the protracted intervention in Afghanistan, and, more recently, drone strikes including in Yemen (Chomsky 2009; Greenwald 2012; Savage 2013).

The assertion of distinctly Asian values is not only about values but about identities and interests in the sense that it is a defense against perceived cultural imperialism coming from the West. In narratives of Western imperialism, non-Western peoples and cultures are depicted as backward. Asserting distinctly Asian values may be as much about resistance to imperialism and changing the identity of Asian peoples (as constructed by the West) as it is an assertion that Asian values are somehow in conflict with international human rights norms.

Exactly what gave rise to the Arab Spring at this particular moment in history is unclear. The governments opposed and overthrown were all undemocratic but they had been so for decades. Very wide income gaps had long existed within most of those states. Finally, in countries like Syria and Iraq, struggling, inefficient economies, in which the ruling elites often siphoned off any prosperity that did accrue and controlled the resources and economy, namely, oil, that generated wealth, had been the norm for generations, and the uprisings were not preceded by dramatic increases in inequality or deprivation. So the question of "Why now?" is difficult to answer. Demographic factors such as a large number of young people both unemployed and increasingly well educated may have reached a critical point. The global Great Recession of 2008–2009 exacerbated those conditions by driving food prices and unemployment even higher and increasing global food insecurity. Election protests in Iran in 2009–2010 may have sparked a more widespread willingness to oppose undemocratic governments, but Iran is neither an Arab state nor a secular state with a Muslim majority, as many affected by the Arab Spring are.

With autocrats out of power or with substantially reduced autocratic power, people in these post–Arab Spring states still face the question of "What holds us together, and what is our shared vision of the good society?" Most share a history of colonization followed by undemocratic rulers and regimes that held power by oppression for decades. However, they will have to find a shared vision on which to build democratic institutions, not just a shared history of oppression. What makes Islam so appealing is its potential as a unifying factor, and at some point these countries may look to the Turkish model, where a majority Muslim population lives in a state with increasingly democratic institutions and rights.

The question of interests versus values is also pertinent to decisions by Western states to intervene, not intervene, or intervene in a limited manner, on behalf of the antigovernment protesters, particularly when they became militarized as they did in Libya and have in Syria. Seeing Western-friendly governments come to power is definitely in the interest of Western powers, but democratization is not guaranteed to lead to that outcome. Many of the autocratic regimes were (and some, like Saudi Arabia, still are) historically very friendly with the United States, and this factor could have a negative effect on post–Arab Spring governments' relationships with the United States. Of course the United States had long viewed Qaddafi as an adversary, so intervening to assist in his overthrow was a convergence of interests and values. But the lesson of Iran still casts a large shadow over US relations with Islamist democracies following the overthrow of a government that might not have remained in power so long had it not been for US covert intervention and support. As far as the state in its dual capacity as the perpetrator and protector of human rights, the topics in this chapter focus on the former, with hope for improvement under conditions of democratization.

# Part 2

## Actors and Implementation

# 5

# Human Rights and the State

I am cognizant of the interrelatedness of all communities and states. I cannot sit idly by in Atlanta and not be concerned about what happens in Birmingham. Injustice anywhere is a threat to justice everywhere. We are caught in an inescapable network of mutuality, tied in a single garment of destiny. Whatever affects one directly, affects all indirectly. Never again can we afford to live with the narrow, provincial "outside agitator" idea. Anyone who lives inside the United States can never be considered an outsider anywhere within its bounds.
> —Martin Luther King Jr., "Letter from Birmingham Jail,"
> April 16, 1963

America did not invent human rights. In a very real sense, it is the other way around. Human rights invented America.
> —President Jimmy Carter, January 14, 1981

THE INTERNATIONAL SYSTEM IS COMPOSED OF STATES, AND NEW states are still being created, but the question of statehood is not always straightforward. In 2011, South Sudan was recognized as a state and became the 193rd member of the United Nations. Kosovo declared independence from Serbia in 2008, but widespread recognition did not immediately follow; in April 2013, Serbia and Kosovo came to an agreement mediated by the European Union, that Serbia would recognize Kosovo's statehood as long as Kosovo Serbs were granted broad autonomous powers within Kosovo. Taiwan's status as a state is controversial; since 1971, the People's Republic of China has represented Taiwan at the United Nations, though the latter is recognized by many states as having the capacity to enter into treaty obligations, one of the main legal attributes of a state. The

Holy See, or Vatican City, is an independent and sovereign papal state but chooses not to be a member of the United Nations. Virtually all people, territories, and resources in the world are under the jurisdiction of a state. States are implicated in international human rights both because they often perpetrate or enable the commission of human rights violations and because only states have the capacity to use force to stop and punish human rights violations, whether acting on their own, with others in a coalition, or through the mechanism of international organizations. Professor Abdullahi an-Na'im calls the combined power and responsibility of states the paradox of self-regulation: the state is the institution and actor most capable of violating human rights but also tasked with regulating itself not to violate said rights (an-Na'im 2011).

The state is a set of governing institutions sanctioned by international recognition. As discussed in Chapter 3, many of the norms that undergird international human rights today arose in connection with the aspirations of liberal democracy and the modern state. Given its importance to human rights, the contemporary state, along with the philosophical premises on which its authority rests, is analyzed in this chapter. I begin with a discussion of state sovereignty, the attribute that gives states the authority to use force and coercion over the people and resources within its territorial boundaries. Sovereignty, however, is not a static attribute. It is modified by international normative constraints.

Certain features of the contemporary state affect both its ability to promote human rights and any proclivity to violate or enable the violation of human rights. These features include a monopoly of force, equality with other sovereign states, secularism, a constitutional foundation, and nationalist narratives that contribute to its legitimation and internal solidarity. Not all states are equally committed to incorporating all of the features that would strengthen the protection of human rights, and having a constitutional foundation does not always mean that human rights will be adequately developed or upheld. But a normative expectation can be found within the international community, particularly by older Western and Western-style democracies, that these qualities are desirable. I conclude the chapter with a discussion of state sovereignty and human rights.

## Sovereignty and the State

The term *state*—in contrast with *country* or *nation*—has a specific meaning to political scientists. A state is essentially a set of governing institutions internationally recognized as having the capacity to exercise authority over people and resources within given territorial boundaries. The meaning of the term *sovereignty* is contestable and only recognized as an attribute of states recognized as sovereign by other states.

However, political will and international institutional authority remain weak when it comes to holding those who control governing institutions accountable for how they exercise the sovereign authority within their territorial boundaries (Weber 1994). States may be subject to criticism or condemnation for their human rights records. Leaders of states may consider the human rights records of other states in formulating foreign policies and attempt to punish states with poor human rights records and reward others for improvement. States may unilaterally or multilaterally employ sanctions in order to influence the conduct of other states on human rights (human rights issues are the most common rationale for sanctions). But these consequences are all mild at best. The only real exception is that state leaders may not perpetrate genocide, without expecting to face legal consequences afterward, as suggested by legal actions taken against those involved in the Yugoslav wars of succession and the Rwandan genocide. War crimes and crimes against humanity are often also cause for prosecution but mainly in conjunction with allegations of genocide or acts of genocide rather than on their own. War crimes trials in Sierra Leone offer hope of national enforcement. Otherwise, enforcement of international norms is weak and inconsistent for states that violate human rights other than, perhaps, straining their diplomatic (and possibly economic) relations with other states.

The international community has been willing to enforce very few limits on state power. States may not use force to engage in aggression against other states, so states that do use military force in relations with other states tend to offer justifications and rationalizations that refer to norms that would support their interventions. The US-led invasion and occupation of Iraq, for example, was presented as both a matter of US national security, on the grounds that Iraq's alleged nuclear program presented a threat to the United States that justified a preemptive act of self-defense, and as a violation of UN Security Council Resolution 687, which outlined the conditions for withdrawal of international forces in 1991. The war between Iraq and Iran in the 1980s was premised by Iraq as a dispute over contested territorial boundaries. Normally these rationalizations are enough to buy the country a pass with the international community as a whole, even if individual states condemn the actions. As an exception, in two cases involving four states, state sovereignty was restricted by the international community following aggressive uses of force: Germany, Italy, and Japan after World War II and Iraq after its invasion of Kuwait in 1990.

In other words, aggressive states are potentially subject to some international legal constraint in that their range of sovereignty, particularly exercised as military capability, can be restricted following their violation of international norms on the use of force, as in the case of World War II and the post–Gulf War enforcement regime. One might suggest that if these cases set a precedent for restricting state sovereignty as a punishment for violating the international nonaggression norm, conceivably the international community may develop the political will to impose restrictions on state sovereignty as a consequence for violating human rights. However, the difference is that reducing sovereignty following an illegal use of force, and not for violations of human rights, thus far has generally only been imposed by states following a military defeat of the violating state. The exception, a relatively recent development, has been the collapse of a state as a result of a civil war where war crimes, crimes against humanity, and acts of genocide have occurred, such as in the former Yugoslavia and Rwanda.

The international community is willing to enforce the prohibition on genocide through legal proceedings, conviction, and punishment in some cases. In Chapter 8, I will show that sovereignty does not, in theory even if not always in practice, permit a state, or individuals for that matter, to commit genocide. Sovereignty cannot be used as a shield against responsibility for genocide. In the opinion of some international lawyers and scholars, this constraint applies regardless of whether a state is party to the Genocide Convention mentioned in Chapter 2. Judge Elihu Lauterpacht wrote in the case *Bosnia and Herzegovina v. Yugoslavia (Serbia and Montenegro)* that "the prohibition of genocide . . . has generally been accepted as having the status not of an ordinary rule of international law, but of *jus cogens*. Indeed, the prohibition of genocide has long been regarded as one of the few undoubted examples of *jus cogens*" (ICJ 1993:1).

Sovereignty, in theory, does not endow a state with the ability to exercise power in a completely arbitrary and unaccountable way. As an attribute of statehood, sovereignty comes with some obligations such as refraining from aggressive uses of force against other states and seeking peaceful settlements of disputes. States accept these obligations by becoming members of the United Nations. Sovereignty also means that states may intervene in other states for humanitarian purposes or to enforce certain international norms pertaining not only to acts of aggression but also to ongoing human rights violations. The Genocide Convention obligates states not only to punish those guilty of genocide but also to prevent genocide. Thus far, however, the international community has acted more often to punish than prevent. They have only prosecuted and punished in the cases of Germany and Japan in World War II (for violations of Geneva Conventions, crimes against humanity, and the crime of planning and executing an aggressive war) and the genocides in former Yugoslavia and Rwanda. In 2005, Joseph Kony was indicted by the ICC for his role as commander of the Lord's Resistance Army and for crimes against humanity and war crimes in a guerrilla war against the Ugandan government. In

2009 and 2010, the ICC issued an indictment of Sudanese president Omar al-Bashir for war crimes, crimes against humanity, and genocide in connection with reports of atrocities and the deaths of an estimated 300,000 people in the region of Darfur.

In 1991, the UN Security Council authorized the use of force against Iraq for clearly violating an international norm. This intervention was notable for many things, including the unprecedented breadth of support from the international community. The nonaggression norm obligates states to refrain from violating the territorial integrity of other internationally recognized states. Although human rights violations provided some political justification, they were not the primary reason for the intervention. In this case, Iraq violated the territorial integrity of Kuwait, and the Security Council, led by the United States and supported very broadly in the UN General Assembly, undertook a military intervention to expel Iraqi forces from Kuwait. The Iraqi government's record of using chemical weapons against the Kurdish Iraqis was raised to underscore the moral authority for the intervention but not to justify it as an act of enforcement.

Three other cases involving the use of force authorized by international institutional actors and supported by a broad multilateral coalition should be mentioned. When the Allied Powers defeated the German-led Axis Powers during World War II, human rights were again not the primary justification for military action and the military action itself was not undertaken as an "authorized enforcement." This case is noteworthy, however, for its application of human rights norms to punish a state after the fact, setting a precedent followed half a century later in the former Yugoslavia and Rwanda. This issue will be taken up in more detail in Chapter 8.

The second case often included in discussions of UN-authorized international interventions is the Korean War in 1950. While similar to the UN-authorized Gulf War intervention of 1991, the conflict in Korea was still not a case of internationally authorized enforcement against a state for norm violation. First, the political interests on two sides of an essentially civil war—the dispute over the border and which country would govern a unified Korea—were well established before any international action was authorized. Second, the authorization for military action occurred only because the Soviet Union was absent, having boycotted UN proceedings, and with the Nationalist government in exile in Taiwan casting the Chinese vote.

The 1999 NATO intervention in Kosovo to stop the expulsion of Albanians by the Serbian government and demand the return of those driven out of the country also raised some of these issues and offers a clearer case of a humanitarian intervention. Kosovo had long been the site of violent conflict as the Serb minority felt increasingly threatened by a growing Albanian majority in the previously autonomous province before the wars of secession in the 1990s. Slobodan Milošević exploited anti-Albanian prejudices in speeches leading up to the war in Bosnia, and under Serbian rule, after the dissolution of the former Yugoslavia, the autonomy of the region was revoked. This chain of events led to the formation of an armed resistance among Albanians, and the Serbian government responded in kind. After Serbian soldiers killed forty-five Albanians in an attack in January of 1999, condemnation of the Serbian government came from NATO members and from the United Nations, followed by a threat of military intervention by NATO aimed at bringing the parties into discussion of a political solution. According to the International Criminal Tribunal for Former Yugoslavia (ICTY), about one-third of the Albanian population—740,000 people—was expelled by May 1999 (ICTY 1999). The ten-week military operation consisting of bombing campaigns was accompanied by three demands: (1) Serbian troop withdrawal from Kosovo, (2) the return of refugees and persons expelled from the region, and (3) the acceptance of peacekeeping forces under NATO command. These conditions were met in June 1999.

Other cases where the Security Council authorized limited interventions include Somalia, Bosnia, Sierra Leone, and Libya, but these were not as broadly supported. The initial UN mission in Somalia was aimed at providing humanitarian aid and monitoring a cease-fire in the 1990s civil war. The failure to achieve these goals led to an offer by the United States to lead an intervention more broadly authorized to use military force under UN Chapter VII Security Council powers. Thirty-six countries ultimately participated, sending troops and civilian staff into Somalia. Most of the mission consisted of efforts to disarm Somali warlords, chiefly Mohammed Farah Aidid. The failure to find Aidid, the death of eighteen US soldiers in what later became known as the Battle of Mogadishu (a battle immortalized in the book and film *Black Hawk Down*), and the failure of peacemaking led the Security Council to a unanimous vote for withdrawal in November 1994.

The Security Council's involvement in Bosnia was incremental, including economic sanctions, UN forces taking control of the Sarajevo airport, forces dispatched to secure the delivery of humanitarian aid (under Chapter VII authority), and finally the declaration of "safe areas" in Srebrenica, Žepa, and Goražde. Finally, the Security Council asked NATO to provide air support for a ground troop coalition between Bosnian Croat and Bosnian Muslim forces in 1995, ending the war.

The intervention in Sierra Leone began as an exclusively British operation, lasting between May and September 2000 during a civil war there. The British forces were evacuating foreign nationals when rebel forces attacked them, an event that led to an expansion of the mission in an effort to pressure the rebels to disarm. However, the rebels only did so under political pressure following the British intervention, and in 2001, an international force replaced the British forces. The intervention also led to the establishment of a special domestic court to prosecute war crimes committed during the civil war.

In 2011, the Security Council authorized an intervention in Libya, despite abstentions by Russia, China, Germany, India, and Brazil. An initial coalition of ten states expanded to nineteen with a mandate to end attacks against civilians and achieve a cease-fire. The operation involved a naval blockade, air strikes, a no-fly zone, and a NATO-enforced arms embargo. Following the death of Muammar Qaddafi during the fighting, the Security Council ended the military intervention in spite of requests by the new government that the mission be extended.

In assessing the history of the international community's willingness to use military force against states for violating international norms, one finds little evidence of actions undertaken to uphold human rights standards or to stop an ongoing injury. The criminal tribunals after World War II prosecuted German and Japanese leaders for war crimes and set a precedent for prosecuting genocides in Yugoslavia and Rwanda. The United Nations authorized the Gulf and Korean wars but neither were undertaken to enforce human rights norms. Kosovo offers the only example of an intervention that was authorized by an international organization for the primary purpose of responding to a humanitarian crisis, although undoubtedly strategic considerations were still in play, such as containing a conflict that might have spread to neighboring states, especially those where Albanians lived.

Alternatives to direct military intervention have met with limited success. Darfur and the Democratic Republic of Congo became sites of gross violations of human rights in the aftermath of the Rwandan genocide, as governments abetted, or at the very least turned a blind eye, to conflicts in which civilians suffered the greatest casualties and abuses. Condemnations and authorizations for limited intervention and observation by the Security Council did little to arrest the atrocities. In contrast, in 1999, the United Nations, through political pressure, stemmed the tide of violence when Indonesia invaded East Timor following a vote for independence. An Australian-led transition force and a UN transitional administration enabled the Timorese to establish a viable independent government within two years, although the occupation cost the lives of between 100,000 and 200,000 East Timorese out of a total population of 700,000.

## The Westphalian State

The contemporary state is frequently referred to as the Westphalian state because its normative and structural foundations are rooted in the European experience following the Peace of Westphalia, the collective name given to a series of peace treaties that ended the Thirty Years War and the

Eighty Years War in 1648 and created a political order in Europe based on sovereign states. Imperialism, decolonization, and then globalization led to the reproduction of European Westphalian-modeled states throughout the rest of the world. Contemporary states are patterned after the Westphalian state only in the sense that the norms and attributes associated with states and recognized by other states stem from the European state-making experience. Understanding the main features of the Westphalian state is important, particularly since they affect the capacity of states to commit, prevent, and punish human rights violations. These features include (1) a monopoly on legitimate uses of force, (2) sovereign equality, (3) secularism or separation of church and state, (4) foundational narratives that reference national identity and historical experiences, and (5) constitutionalism.

## Monopoly of Force

Not all state uses of force are regarded as legitimate, a fact that is at the heart of human rights as a legal issue. Despite the historical weakness of states to mobilize adequate political will in support of interventions to stop ongoing human rights violations, widespread agreement exists that a state does not have a right to use force to commit genocide. The international community has demonstrated the political will to punish, even if not prevent, genocides. International tribunals, such as the ICTY and the ICTR, have convicted individuals of genocide.

As discussed earlier, states also do not have the right to use force to violate the territorial integrity of other states. Although this restriction does not bear directly on the issue of preventing human rights violations, the regulation of state force has been and continues to be the subject of many treaties, conventions, and declarations within international law. Until the Armenian genocide in 1915 during World War I and the Holocaust during World War II, however, efforts to regulate the state use of force were limited to a state's external aggressiveness, in relations with other states. Indeed, the nonaggression norm prohibiting states from using force in their relations with other states was reinforced by the norm prohibiting states from intervening in the domestic affairs of other states. Both are recognized in the UN Charter in Article 2 of Chapter I:

> All Members shall refrain in their international relations from the threat or use of force against the territorial integrity or political independence of any state, or in any other manner inconsistent with the Purposes of the United Nations. . . .
>
> Nothing contained in the present Charter shall authorize the United Nations to intervene in matters which are essentially within the domestic jurisdiction of any state.

One of the most pressing normative conflicts in the area of human rights is the contradiction between an obligation to intervene to stop ongoing violations and an obligation to refrain from interfering in the domestic affairs of another state. The Genocide Convention specifically obligates states to prevent and punish the crime of genocide. The strengthening of human rights norms unquestionably weakens the nonintervention norm.

The state monopoly on legitimate force is important to the development of human rights for several reasons. First, if nonstate actors may not use force legitimately, then states are always advantaged in relation to nonstate actors and are subject to few internal restraints regarding how they use force, for example, to suppress rebellion or apprehend terrorists within their jurisdiction (and decide who is a terrorist and who is not). Thus, states with human rights records that come under international scrutiny often justify their actions by claiming that internal threats require such extraordinary measures. From the South American military dictatorships of the 1970s, to the junta ruling Myanmar, North Korea's Kim Jong-un and his predecessors, the United Kingdom's dealings with the Irish Republican Army, or the more recent US "war on terror"—all claim the necessity of violating international human rights in response to extraordinary threats to national security. The United States has suspended habeas corpus, tortured and detained prisoners without trial at Guantanamo Bay, and used drone strikes to execute US citizens without due process.

Second, the state monopoly of force is important because the enforcement of human rights norms must be left to states, and they often lack the political will to put at risk their own human and financial resources for purely humanitarian reasons.

### Sovereign Equality

While the concept of sovereignty has both philosophical and concrete implications and in both senses is unsettled and subject to political interpretation and application, the legal character of sovereign equality is much less ambiguous. Sovereign equality is akin to the notion of "equality before the law" within the domestic democratic legal systems. At the international level, sovereign equality is also found in the UN Charter, Chapter I, paragraph 1: "The Organization is based on the principle of the sovereign equality of all its Members."

Sovereign equality is a more meaningful legal concept than simple sovereignty, although states may use the claim of sovereignty to shield themselves from international condemnation. In this sense, being a sovereign state is still preferable to being a nonsovereign "entity." Tracing the history of the concept of sovereign equality, Robert Klein (1974) concluded that he could not find much evidence of broad support for the concept until the

Hague Conference in 1907. Klein also found that much of that support came from US leaders, though he admitted that this support could also have been a move to strengthen US prestige vis-à-vis its European friends at a time when Great Britain was still the hegemonic world power. Increasing acceptance of sovereign equality may also be viewed as a legal antidote to great power rivalry. Said Louis J. Halle, an influential scholar of international relations during the Cold War, "If it is true that the most basic changes in international relations are changes in the minds of men, then the rise to supremacy of the concept of sovereign equality is the most important development of modern times" (quoted in R. Klein 1974:xix).

If sovereignty means the freedom to act without restraint or accountability to any higher authority, then all states possess this attribute. However, more powerful states can and do interfere in the domestic affairs of other states, and weaker states are not as free of restraint as more powerful states. The concept of sovereign equality, however, means that when acting in a legal capacity, all states are equal. For example, states are equally capable of signing treaties, maintaining a military force, passing and enforcing laws, and so on. Nonstate entities cannot do any of these. In a practical and political sense, sovereignty may be impaired by relative weakness or enhanced by relative strength, but in a legal sense, all states are equal.

Why is distinguishing between the political realities that affect sovereignty as a quality of states and the legal reality that all states are equal important? Because although the development of international law is relatively weak compared to the law making, enforcing, and interpreting functions of the most well-developed and highly institutionalized domestic systems, international law does have consequence, and hope for progress rests in the potential for strengthening the rule of law in international relations as a means to creating a more secure future. Sovereign equality is a critical concept in laying the foundation for the development and strengthening of international law.

### Secularism

The Westphalian state is secular in the sense that it guarantees religious freedom by maintaining a separation between religious authority and political authority and by respecting the right of individuals to hold religious beliefs of their own choosing, or none at all. To some extent, human rights arose within the European experience to curb state power previously asserted under the absolutism of divine right during the pre-Westphalian era. This attempt to shake off the influence of the church initially took the form of separating religious and political authority, a self-serving move on the part of monarchies that were subject to the authority of the Roman Catholic Church as European states emerged from the Holy Roman Empire.

The secular quality of the modern state set the stage for assertions of religious freedom that would play out over the century following the Peace of Westphalia in 1648. Forty-two years later, John Locke (1690) wrote "Letter on Toleration," arguing that the right to choose one's own religion belonged to the individual, and not the state. Europe remained a site of continuing conflict over religious freedom versus state authority. Religion has historically been a very important marker of identity in Europe. Even recently, in the wars of Yugoslav secession during the 1990s, many people used the terms *Catholic* and *Croatian* or *Orthodox* and *Serbian* interchangeably (Wilmer 2002). Religious freedom was institutionally recognized in both the US Declaration of Independence in 1776 and the French Declaration of the Rights of Man in 1789. Both are still regarded as founding documents in the long struggle for religious freedom as a human right in Western democracies.

## Legitimation and Narratives of Identity

Until roughly the 1970s, scholars and policymakers frequently referred to the state as the *nation-state* without controversy. Although the term is still widely used, it needs qualification. The term *nation* has a broader use and more ambiguous meaning and is frequently appropriated for political purposes, for example, to bolster a claim to self-determination, as constituting the majority identity of a state's population, or to support outright secession and statehood. It comes closest to meaning *ethnic group,* though this term is also subject to controversy and ambiguity. Since most nations and ethnic groups, however, do not control states, many actually constitute minorities within states. A few states have made special provisions in an effort to share power across multiple groups. For example, South Africa's government recognizes eleven official languages and eight unofficial languages. To reflect its multinational character, Switzerland provides for a plural executive, called the Federal Council, consisting of seven members elected by the Federal Assembly. Although there is no requirement that its members correspond proportionately to the Swiss ethno-linguistic groups (German, French, Italian, and Romansh), it is very likely to result in ethno-linguistic plurality. Switzerland also recognizes four official languages. The only other plural executives are in the microstate San Marino and postwar Bosnia-Herzegovina. New Zealand reserves seven of sixty-nine seats in Parliament for Maori representatives, though critics say this only guarantees minority representation. Since the 1960s, many Western democracies, including the United States, have passed laws banning discrimination based on race, color, class, sex, religion, nationality, age, family and/or marital status, language, and disability.

A critical analysis of the term *nation-state* highlights its connection with a metanarrative about how the modern state came into existence. The term serves several purposes in the framework of this (mythical) metanarrative. First, it evokes a sense of "natural" order based on the relationship among and identity of citizens in the state. Citizens constitute a nation, and the nation finds its fullest expression as a state. Recalling eighteenth-century European nationalism, the narrative is liberating, at least for those who identify themselves as constituting the nation or, more accurately, a national majority within a state. However, it also legitimates domination by one communal group over others who then become "minorities." As a narrative of identity, a "nation" naturalizes the boundary of group identity marked by characteristics such as a shared historical narrative, kinship or ancestry, language, religious affiliation, and ethnic characteristics.

The relationship between national identity and state privileging of one group over others raises important questions because this privileging is implicated in many human rights violations, from racial or ethnic discrimination to ethnic cleansing and genocide. When one group is privileged, others are marginalized. Sometimes privileged groups experience efforts to alter an imbalance as a form of discrimination against them because they have not thought of their status as privileged. Their privilege is normalized or naturalized and reinforced by concepts like "nation-state" so that efforts to shift and balance power among groups and remedy the present effects of past discrimination are experienced by privileged groups as a loss of "rights."

When discrimination is based on long-standing historical patterns, the relationship between the cost of discriminatory practices to one group and benefits to another can be oblique. For example, when one group has been economically marginalized and subject to discrimination for several generations, then members of a privileged group have better access to and less competition for jobs, wealth, education, and other paths to personal material success by the simple fact of a generational accumulation of wealth and access, even with an otherwise "level" playing field. The fact that a substantial sector (usually but not always a numerical minority, as the South African case illustrates) of the population was excluded or marginalized creates an implicit advantage or privilege for the rest. If 15 percent of a state's population has less access to education, wealth for investing, and the highest-paying jobs, then the remaining 85 percent has less competition than if all had equal economic opportunities. This example is an accurate depiction of the historical pattern of black-white relations in the United States.

Zimbabwe is a reversed case, with the white population making up less than 1 percent of the population today after a transition to majority rule in 1979. Historically, under a 1961 constitutional provision that institutionalized white privilege, the white population (never over 2 percent) controlled about 70 percent of the land, including most of the best agricultural property. Measures undertaken by the black majority government to remedy this discrimination were equally harsh and led to very unstable and often violent conditions in the aftermath of postapartheid efforts to democratize. A political prisoner under the white supremacist regime, Robert Mugabe, who led Zimbabwe to independence, enjoyed significant respect during the early years of his presidency in the 1980s and into the 1990s. But his policies became increasingly destructive not only of the wealthier white population but also of political opponents, union leaders, and those living in the most dire poverty who were viewed as sympathetic to the opposition. In the face of internal and external pressure to moderate his policies or concede the office to someone who will, President Robert Mugabe has only become a more rabid nationalist, referring to Zimbabwe as the state of the "black nation." This illustrates both the ambiguity and the political appropriation of terms related to ethnicity and nationality.

The term *nation-state* intentionally evokes emotional sentiments about a presumed "natural" connection between the two, that nations find their fullest expression of self-determination when they control a state. Clearly, this situation is not possible given not only the number of potential "nations" but also the messiness of their territoriality, not to mention intermarriage and multinational genealogy. In spite of the fact that many political leaders of states throughout the world use the language of nationalism, most are very hesitant to recognize states created by nationalist secessionism.

Finally, while narratives of national (or ethnic) identity have been closely associated with the mobilization of emotional sentiments to evoke support for political movements in the founding of modern European states, narratives of religious identity have also been utilized this way. The political role of religious identity in Europe was weakened by changes in the relationship between the Catholic Church and the Westphalian state under the Holy Roman Empire, but the religion-politics nexus is far from settled. The conflict or "Troubles" in Northern Ireland were not driven by differences in religious belief but differences in identities as signified by religious affiliation. The conflict between Irish Protestants and Irish Catholics is not a disagreement about religious doctrine but about the historical marginalization of Catholics and identification of Protestants with Scots-English settlers. Irish Catholics in general identify as the original or indigenous Irish and regard Irish Protestants as descendants of British settlers (though many were Scottish) carrying out a British policy aimed at conquering Ireland. Irish Protestant identity, in contrast, is constructed around the idea of being British citizens of Irish nationality whose descendants can be traced to several Scottish migrations, including those sent by England in the sixteenth century specifically to colonize and exploit the resources and labor of the Irish. So in this case, both ethnicity (indigenous Irish versus Scots-Irish settlers) and religion serve as markers of identity and as the basis for historical relationships characterized by privilege and marginalization.

## Constitutionalism

Though the Peace of Westphalia marked the end of the Holy Roman Empire as an institution of European governance, it did not immediately lead to the development of constitutional forms of government in Europe. Instead, the development of constitutional monarchies and eventually representative constitutional democracies took place over a century in the aftermath of the French Revolution. The period of roughly 1648 to 1789 was one of rule by absolute monarchs, characterized by the struggle over secularism and the shift of economic and ultimately political power from feudal to commercial relations. The expansion of the commercial and middle class (industrialists, business owners, and professionals) led to the demand by those groups to have more influence in state affairs (Wallerstein 1980; Glassman 1995). Representative democracy has its roots in the direct democracy of the artisan guilds in the increasingly prosperous free-trade cities of northern European cities. Beginning in France in the second half of the eighteenth century and in England in the early nineteenth century, industrializing production created a very large and urban working class that further pressed for state policies to support the development of free markets.

These socioeconomic structural changes are reflected in the writings of the natural law theorists, physiocrats, and Enlightenment philosophers. The convergence of social change and philosophical shift was not coincidental and led directly to the development of literal and figurative social contracts in the form of constitutions. The first written national constitution was ratified in the United States in 1790. The second was the May Third Constitution of the Polish-Lithuanian Commonwealth in 1791. Though it dates to the Magna Carta in 1215, in Runnymede, England, the British constitution is characterized as unwritten because it is not contained in a single founding document but rather developed from Oliver Cromwell's time to the present through a series of petitions, acts of Parliament, conventions, and common law. Most European constitutions were developed in the aftermath of the revolutions of the nineteenth century, and some formalized basic laws outlining the powers and limits of government before codifying them in a constitutional document.

The purpose of a constitution is linked directly to human rights: to delineate what a government may and may not do and the rules by which it may use power authoritatively and not arbitrarily. Constitutions lay out how power is constituted as authoritative. Constitutions embody principles of governance, legitimate authority, and articulate a shared vision of the good society held by those it serves. Consequently, constitutions often contain language that is both aspirational and practical. Many contemporary constitutions are patterned after the US or French constitutions but also contain features unique to the history and cultural orientation of the particular state.

Constitutional language sometimes also underscores narratives of national identity. The Croatian Constitution, for example, opens with a statement on "historical foundations" and refers specifically to the Croatian "nation" or "national identity" six times in that opening section—a fact that potentially unsettles national minorities in Croatia, notably, Croatian Serbs. African constitutional development has focused on including reference to specifically African cultural values and self-determination (Mattei 1999; Deng 2003). These concerns are also reflected in the African Charter on Human Rights and Peoples' Rights that is distinguished from other regional human rights instruments by its emphasis on collective as well as individual rights (Ouguergouz 2003).

## Theories of the State

The international relations theories outlined in Chapter 2 take different views of the role and scope of the state in relation to human rights issues. Liberalism, for example, regards the state, when governed by a popular democracy, as an institutional expression of its citizens' freedom and will to be self-governed. Because a liberal government is chosen and consented to by its citizens while protecting dissenting minorities, it is a guarantor of human rights within its boundaries. The internationalization of liberalism, known as liberal or neoliberal institutionalism, seeks to promote the development of liberal democracies in other states as an end in itself and to promote friendly and interdependent relations among states, leading to an international order arising out of enlightened self-interest. In the view of some liberals—certainly the authors of the US Constitution—the state ought not have a monopoly on force. For this reason the framers of the US Constitution included the Second Amendment acknowledging the people's right to bear arms and form militias as a protection against the government's monopolizing of force. The sovereign equality of states is consistent with liberal ideas about a democratic world order and the rule of law requiring equality before the law. Liberals would also be committed to secularism and constitutionalism with checks and balances to prevent or mitigate the potential for arbitrary uses of power. Indeed, the modern state with these features is very much a product of liberalism as described earlier. Liberalism tends to overlook the role of legitimation narratives, including nationalism and its potential for exclusionary practices.

Realism focuses on the state as a unitary actor with unitary interests vis-à-vis its relations with other states and interests in maintaining state security within an international system that always includes potential enemies. From a realist's perspective, nothing compels other states to develop and sustain democratic institutions with constitutional checks and balances that restrain how leaders choose to use force. To the contrary, realists view the ability of the state, even the democratic states in which they live, to use force as needed for the protection or promotion of self-interests as paramount and certainly not to be constrained in any way by international law or obligations. Sovereign equality, from a realist perspective, is a fiction; states have unequal power and that's what matters to a realist. Realists will not be constrained by international obligations or international law. Having more power is better. Being more self-sufficient is better. Secularism is tolerated and valued if it strengthens the ability of the state to act solely on the basis of national interests—not the interests of particular groups within the state, such as religious groups. The same would be true for nationalism and legitimation narratives. Acting on and promoting the security interests of the state are central to realism.

For constructivists, the state is a social structure produced by the social processes of identity and interest formation. Sovereignty is also a social fact (Weber 1994), one that stands in opposition to intervention; that is, intervention is a violation of sovereignty. As a social fact, sovereignty cannot be settled or fixed, but rather it is variable in time (history) and space (political context). As Cynthia Weber (1994) said, "Not one but countless forms of state sovereignty co-exist in modern global political life" (2). Efforts to define, fix, or settle the concepts of sovereignty are really aimed at creating and maintaining "a particular state . . . with particular boundaries, competencies and legitimacies available to it" (Weber 1994:3). A monopoly on force would be one of those competencies and legitimacies while both constitutions and legitimation narratives are the social practices that produce and sustain the state as a social fact. Constructivists would not be surprised to find nationalist references in state constitutions, like this opening statement in the Croatian Constitution: "The millennial national identity of the Croatian nation and the continuity of its statehood, confirmed by the course of its entire historical experience in various political forms and by the perpetuation and growth of state-building ideas based on the historical right to full sovereignty of the Croatian nation, manifested itself." The document then goes on to list twelve "historical facts" that constitute the Croatian state in the opening section entitled "Historical Foundations."

For economic structuralists, the state is a product of capitalism and the globalization of capitalism. In their view, imperialism is the most advanced stage of capitalism, even if the imperialism itself is de facto: for example, the United States has over 700 military bases worldwide, with the country's widespread military presence often regarded as a form of imperialism (Wallerstein 2004). This view is unsurprising given that the state developed in the context of European capitalism, with a strong central government, an extensive bureaucracy, and mercenary armies (Wallerstein 1974). As states expanded into empires, their aim was to control and exploit the people and resources in colonies for the economic benefit of the imperial country. Under decolonization, states made every effort to ensure that the new governments in their former colonies would make continued cooperation with the capitalist world system a priority over the welfare of their own people. Many struggles in postcolonial states today reflect this conflict between those giving priority to the welfare of the people versus those giving priority to cooperation with the global capitalist system (Roy 2002, 2004).

In contrast with the Western states where capitalism developed and expanded (or "the core" of the world system), the governments of postcolonial states are weak and lack a well-trained bureaucracy and well-equipped military (Wallerstein 1974). The economies of core states produce wealth through finance, technology, and manufacturing, though increasingly manufacturing is outsourced or moved to postcolonial states where labor is cheap and regulations weak. The weak (and often corrupt) postcolonial states are the "periphery" of the system and rely heavily on exporting raw materials to the core. The periphery is also the site of the most exploitative and coercive labor conditions, such as sweatshops, child labor, human trafficking, and unsafe workplaces. In the economic structuralists' view, the system itself promotes human rights deprivations of all kinds, from torture and political imprisonment, when peripheral states' governments are corrupt, to child soldiers, child labor, sex trafficking, and economic deprivations such as a lack of clean water and high levels of exposure to airborne and waterborne diseases.

Feminists regard the state as an institutional manifestation of patriarchal social relations. Masculinized policies and concerns take priority over those considered more feminine: national security over health and human services, military capacity over diplomacy, fighting against external enemies instead of solving domestic issues such as violence in the family. Feminists also argue that knowledge produced predominantly by men, and extrapolated as knowledge about human experience more broadly, is really knowledge about men's experiences. Understanding or situating the state in nonfeminist perspectives requires a deconstruction of the way it is gendered (Peterson 1992). If the primary justification for the state is to provide national security or defense, then this purpose is a reflection of men's priorities, not women's, though the invisibility of the way the state is gendered and the male-as-norm ideal make this purpose appear to be a nongendered priority. Women's perspectives on security, for example, might emphasize access to basic material needs, an adequate income to provide basic needs, and the degree to which a society produces, values, and maintains peace rather than military capacity. The answer is not simply to have more women in public office: the structure of the state itself reflects and rewards primary attention to masculine perspectives or men's priorities, and men and women both are locked within a patriarchal social structure. Said Dale Spender in a book entitled *Men's Studies Modified: The Impact of Feminism on Academic Disciplines* (1981), "Most of the knowledge produced by our society has been produced by men; they have usually generated the explanations and the schemata and have then checked with each other and vouched for the accuracy and adequacy of their view of the world" (1).

Iris Marion Young (2003) offered a critique of the national security state claiming that, in what becomes a vicious circle, the national security state is the actual cause of the insecurity that gives rise to it. She compared international relations composed of militarized states to the "protection racket" created when mafias terrorize neighborhoods with violence and then extract tribute from local businesses to protect them against the mafias.

Feminists also point to the role of hierarchical dichotomies, including, in the case of the state, the distinction between public and private spheres. The public sphere, dominated by men and masculinity, is afforded more importance and includes politics, markets, and paid labor. The private sphere is the realm of the household and family, where, in patriarchies, women's roles are more central. This division does not mean that women have greater control over the private sphere, although such a balance of power may have been true historically (Peterson 1992). Today this division means, among other things, that women's work in the private, domestic sphere is unpaid within the family (but can be outsourced through day care or by hiring caregivers from outside of the family), while work in the public sphere is compensated financially.

In terms of human rights, the patriarchal structure of the state raises a host of problems, of which the following are just a few. The unpaid labor that women disproportionately perform and a gendered labor market mean women earn on average 25 percent less than men, for example (even less for women of color). Sex trafficking is an international criminal practice run by men for men and exploits mostly women. Women are often advocates for peace and nonviolence, while peace is marginalized by the emphasis (both in spending and policy) on militarized security. In the view of Nicholas Kristof and Sheryl WuDunn (2009), ending the worldwide oppression of women is the moral imperative of the twenty-first century just as ending totalitarianism was the moral imperative in the twentieth century and ending slavery was the moral imperative in the nineteenth century.

## Human Rights and State Sovereignty

In this chapter and the last, I have examined some of the socioeconomic, historical, and philosophical forces that gave rise to the contemporary state. The state in this sense is truly a social fact, that is, a fact produced by social

processes. It is not a fixed material fact. However, the state's lack of phys-
icality does not mean that the state isn't "real"; rather, it is a set of institutions recognized through social practice as having certain attributes. About
three-fourths of the states that exist today came into existence after World
War II. Many of the conflicts, political struggles, and civil strife associated
with human rights problems, undemocratic governance, and injustices due
to weak legal institutions can be traced to the processes, conditions, and
contexts that gave rise to the creation of these new states. Many new states
were formerly colonized, virtually all include multiple identity or communal groups, and in most cases, little relationship can be found between the
historical land occupancy of the groups who now live in them and the territorial boundaries of the new states. These circumstances mean that most
new (and old) states were created through some kind of violence characterized by historical injuries and injustice. Colonization, for example, contains
all of those characteristics. However, the fact of multiple communal groups
also creates problems as leaders attempt to mobilize a diverse population by
advocating "national" identities and loyalties, as discussed earlier. This
issue will be considered at greater length in Chapter 11, and to a lesser
extent in the discussion of genocide in Chapter 8.

One of the burning questions in the study of world politics is whether
the attribute of state sovereignty is eroding or in some other way undergo-
ing significant change today. Sovereignty is one of the most debated (and
debatable) concepts in world politics today (Weber 1994; Krasner 1999;
Philpott 2001; R. Jackson 2007). Sovereignty is a concern in two senses—
legal and political. Legally, sovereignty is no longer unlimited, nor is it a
license to use power arbitrarily. In addition to changes in the meaning of
the term *sovereignty,* a second trend has been at the heart of the development of rights and legal protections for people vis-à-vis governments that
are accountable to them modeled after the European experience since the
middle of the seventeenth century. Some restrictions on state sovereignty
are now codified in international law insofar as the UN Charter functions as
a legal document. The concept of sovereign equality replaced absolute sovereignty, and the Charter recognizes "matters which are essentially within
the domestic jurisdiction of any state." This statement, although appearing
to draw a boundary of sovereignty around "domestic jurisdiction," goes on
to qualify that jurisdiction by stipulating, in the same paragraph, that "this
principle shall not prejudice the application of enforcement measures under
Chapter VII." The same article also recognizes and protects "the territorial
integrity" and "political independence" of states. So at least for signatories
to the UN Charter, sovereignty has a more concrete and narrow meaning
that, even in the case of domestic jurisdiction, is still subject to conditions
that issue from the Security Council in measures undertaken according to
Chapter VII.

The political meaning of sovereignty becomes more elusive as differences in power reenter the picture. In all cases of strengthening, intervening in, or violating state sovereignty, the primary constraint in reality is the political will of the actors. If the Security Council lacks the political will for enforcement, then the violation of even a well-established norm will go unchecked, as was the case in the Rwandan genocide of 1994, for example. Similarly, if a state has the political will to violate the sovereignty of another state and it is unopposed by other states, then even the constraints of the UN Charter pertaining to domestic jurisdiction, political independence, or territorial integrity will not be enough on their own to prevent a violation of sovereignty. Some would argue that this describes the circumstances of the US occupation in Iraq.

The attribute of state sovereignty means that any discussion, criticism, and action pertaining to human rights conditions and violations should take place both within the state and at the international level. Violations occurring within states are a state responsibility, and therefore, to some extent, actions to oppose, end, or punish human rights violations must also take place at the level of interstate relations. These actions may be taken as a matter of foreign policy, as the 1976 amendments to the US Foreign Assistance Act of 1961 attempted to do. They may also occur through a military alliance outside of the framework of an international organization, which was the case in World War II; or they may be authorized by an international organization, as were the ICTY and ICTR. Again, this discussion highlights states in the contradictory position of being both violators and enforcers of human rights norms. States must regulate themselves, though they may create multilateral regimes to do so.

## Conclusion

Both the state and sovereignty are social facts produced and continuously reshaped through human agency. But the state is also a set of institutions, and sovereignty is a narrative used to legitimate certain social practices carried out by individuals acting authoritatively as agents of the state. Interrogating the historical and cultural context in which the state and sovereignty were produced illuminates some of the historical forces that gave rise to human rights norms and discourses, particularly in response to the use of state power to repress, injure, and otherwise cause suffering among human beings.

The state has a monopoly on force, but what this monopoly really means is that the norms that have developed in connection with the state require that force only be used legitimately when authorized by the state. This norm is not absolute; it is subject to certain constraints and conditions.

For example, states may not use force to take territory from other states, a norm upheld (however weakly and inconsistently) by events during and at the conclusion of World War II as well as by the 1991 UN-authorized Gulf War. States also may not use force to commit genocide and other crimes against humanity, a norm upheld by the creation of the Nuremberg, Tokyo, Yugoslav, and Rwandan tribunals. Norms may exist even when not enforced or not enforced consistently. From a broad historical perspective, norms pertaining to human rights have developed and strengthened steadily in conjunction with the state, both as rights of citizens and others within states and as international obligations.

# 6

# Implementation and Enforcement

There is no contradiction between effective law enforcement and respect for civil and human rights.      —Dorothy Height, US teacher, social activist, and 2003 Congressional Gold Medal recipient, 1963

International law is the law which the wicked do not obey and the righteous do not enforce.      —Abba Eban, former Israeli foreign minister, 1957

THE WEAK AND INCONSISTENT ENFORCEMENT OF EVEN THE MOST basic human rights norms is often the most troublesome aspect of international human rights. This gap between the articulation of norms on the one hand and compliance and enforcement on the other leads some, like Abba Eban, to take a cynical view of international law in general and international human rights in particular. Professor Christopher Joyner (2005), however, who has extensively researched the question of compliance, concluded most states take international law seriously and obey it most of the time.

International human rights norms are implemented and enforced through both national laws and policies and international and regional organizations. States have an obligation to respect human rights as members of international organizations, as signatories to human rights treaties, and under international law derived from the customary practice of states. Encouraging respect for human rights is among the four purposes found in Chapter I of the UN Charter. Under Article 56 in Chapter IX, members "pledge themselves to take joint and separate action" to promote "universal respect for, and observance of, human rights and fundamental freedoms for all without distinction as to race, sex, language, or religion." The ICCPR also obligates signatories to incorporate the provisions of the covenant through the development of national law.

The constitutions of more than half of states today contain provisions for human rights inspired by the Universal Declaration of Human Rights. About two-thirds of states established before 1948 already included in their constitutions references to rights outlined in the declaration (van Maarseveen and van der Tang 1978). Many postcolonial states becoming independent after World War II specifically incorporated into their constitutions norms articulated in and references to the declaration. The new postapartheid South African Constitution, one of the most progressive with thirty-two sections in its "bill of rights," includes not only civil and political participation but also rights to health care, food, water, social security, language, culture, and environmental protection. Failed or failing states are more prone to human rights problems. Unfortunately, many states have weak institutions, weak democracies, weak representation, and fewer resources to devote to law enforcement. The independent nonpartisan NGO Fund for Peace ranks 126 of 177 states it monitors as either on "alert" or "warning" status for failure (Fund for Peace 2014). Still, ratification shows support for core human rights treaties across a geographically, politically, and historically diverse list of states as shown in Table 6.1.

## National Laws and National Courts

Human rights law in European states and the United Kingdom has been profoundly affected by the formation of the European Union, especially since December 2009 when the EU Charter of Fundamental Rights became legally binding (Rozenberg 2013). Although a party to the charter, the United Kingdom and Poland submitted protocols declaring that the EU Court of Justice cannot trump national law when the two are in conflict. The primacy of EU human rights law and its ability to "disapply" (or overturn) acts of national parliaments was affirmed in a 2013 case involving employment discrimination (Rozenberg 2013). The legal protection of human rights in the European Union as codified in EU law is now regarded as much stronger than when such protection was found only in national laws. Although member states are still expected to address human rights first and foremost at the national level, and community-wide standards for national human rights institutions were adopted in 1993, a recent survey showing "low levels of reporting" and "low rights awareness" promoted renewed commitment to strengthening national mechanisms (EU Agency for Fundamental Rights 2010:1).

Under Canadian law, treaties must be explicitly incorporated into domestic law, although the doctrine of the "presumption of conformity" holds that domestic law ought to be understood as conforming with Canada's international obligations unless otherwise provided (Manirabona

**Table 6.1 Select Human Rights Treaties, Ratification Status by Select Countries, and Date Entered into Force**

| | 1 | 2 | 3 | 4 | 5 | 6 | 7 | 8 | 9 | 10 | 11 | 12 |
|---|---|---|---|---|---|---|---|---|---|---|---|---|
| Argentina | X | X | X | X | X | X | X | X | X | X | X | X |
| Brazil | X | X | X | X | X | X | X | X | X | X | X | X |
| China | X | X | | X | X | X | X | X | X | X | | X |
| Egypt | X | X | X | X | X | X | X | X | X | X | X | X |
| France | X | X | X | X | X | X | X | X | X | X | X | X |
| India | X | X | X | X | X | X | X[a] | X | X | X | X | |
| Japan | X | X | X | X | X | X | X | X | X | X | X | X |
| Philippines | X | X | X | X | X | X | | X | X | X | X | X |
| Russian Federation | X | X | X | X | X | X | X | X | X | X | X | X |
| South Africa | X | X[a] | | X | X | X | X | X | X | X | X | X |
| Tanzania | X | X | | X | X | X | | X | X | X | | X |
| Thailand | X | X | | | X | X | | X | X | X | X[a] | |
| Turkey | X | X | X | | X | X | X | X | X | X | X | X |
| United Kingdom | X | X | X | X | X | X | X | X | X | X | X | X |
| United States | X | X[a] | X | X | X | | X | X | X | X | X | X[a] |

*Notes:* a. Signed but not ratified.

**1** = International Covenant on Civil and Political Rights (1976); **2** = International Covenant on Economic, Social, and Cultural Rights (1976); **3** = Supplementary Convention on the Abolition of Slavery, the Slave Trade, and Institutions and Practices Similar to Slavery (1956); **4** = Convention on the Prevention and Punishment of the Crime of Genocide (1951); **5** = International Convention on Elimination of All Forms of Racial Discrimination (1969); **6** = International Convention on Elimination of All Forms of Discrimination Against Women (1981); **7** = Convention Against Torture and Other Cruel, Inhuman, or Degrading Treatment or Punishment (1987); **8** = Convention on the Rights of the Child (1990); **9** = Geneva Convention Relative to the Treatment of Prisoners of War (1949); **10** = Geneva Convention Relative to the Protection of Civilian Persons in Time of War (1949); **11** = Protocol to Prevent, Suppress, and Punish Trafficking in Persons Especially Women and Children (2003); **12** = Convention Relating to Status of Refugees (1951).

and Crépeau 2012). The Canadian Supreme Court also recognizes the relevance of the doctrine of legitimate expectation. This doctrine derives from a decision made by the High Court of Australia referenced by the Canadian Supreme Court, and holds that citizens may reasonably expect that agencies of the government will honor international obligations when the executive branch has ratified a treaty (Manirabona and Crépeau 2012).

Some US laws aim at strengthening the protection of international human rights within the US domestic legal system. Two examples are the Torture Victim Protection Act of 1991 and the Victims of Trafficking and Violence Protection Act of 2000. In 1996, Congress passed the Antiterrorism and Effective Death Penalty Act, which has been used in conjunction with the Torture Victim Protection Act by victims of torture where the offending state is designated as a state sponsor of terrorism by the United States.

The Convention Against Torture and Other Cruel, Inhuman, and Degrading Treatment or Punishment (or Convention Against Torture) was signed by President Ronald Reagan in 1988 and ratified by the US Senate in October of 1990. Two years later, President George H. W. Bush signed the Torture Victim Protection Act that grew out of a case that reached US courts under the Alien Tort Claims Act (ATCA), originally part of the Judiciary Act of 1789. The case of Joelito Filártiga utilized this provision to enable the family of a torture victim to sue the perpetrator in US court. In 1978, Dolly, the sister of Joelito Filártiga who was tortured to death in Asunción, Paraguay, at the hands of law enforcement official Inspector Americo Peña Irala, sued Peña Irala in US court for civil damages amounting to $10 million. The court eventually awarded the family $10.4 million, arguing that freedom from torture was well established under international law and that the complainant had standing to sue since both parties were in the United States at the time the complaint was filed (Claude 1983). The Filártiga case opened the door for human rights advocates to seek remedy by civil law when both victims (or their families) and perpetrators are in the United States. This precedent not only allows suits involving torture under US tort claims but also sends a "no safe haven" message to perpetrators and thus may have a deterrent effect.

Controversy soon arose around the use of the ATCA as a mechanism for prosecuting noncitizen human rights violators in US courts. In 1990, a

## The Case of Joelito Filártiga

*Filártiga v. Peña Irala* (630 F 2nd 876 [1980]) is a landmark case involving the 1976 death in custody of seventeen-year-old Joelito Filártiga in Paraguay. Joelito's father, Joel Filártiga, was a physician who offered free medical services to the poor at a time when Paraguay was governed by a repressive dictatorship. He was also an outspoken critic of the government. While his parents were away from home overnight, Dr. Filártiga's son Joelito was kidnapped, interrogated, and tortured by the local police inspector Americo Peña Irala. Joelito died from a heart attack as a result of the torture. Dr. Filártiga and his daughter Dolly discovered the evidence while performing a postmortem examination of Joelito's body.

After losing a fierce public opinion and legal campaign against Peña Irala and the Paraguayan government, Joel and Dolly Filártiga followed Peña Irala to the United States and filed suit in federal district court for civil damages to the family. The suit was brought under a provision of the 1789 Judiciary Act known as the Alien Tort Claims Act because it allowed noncitizens to sue one another in US courts. The Filártigas were awarded over $10 million, and the suit cited international customary and treaty law in support of human rights. The case led the US Congress to pass the Torture Victim Protection Act in 1991, making it clear that noncitizens had legal standing to sue other noncitizens acting in an official capacity for foreign governments for civil damages resulting from torture and extrajudicial killing.

California grand jury issued an indictment for a Mexican national alleged to have participated in the torture and murder of a US drug agent. When Mexico refused to extradite the defendant, the US Drug Enforcement Agency (DEA) hired Mexican nationals to kidnap the defendant and deliver him into US custody. After he was found not guilty for insufficient evidence, the defendant, Humberto Álvarez Machaín, filed suits under the ATCA (and the Federal Tort Claims Act) against both the US government and the Mexican agents who kidnapped him. The federal court sided with Álvarez Machaín, as did a federal appeals court later, prompting a Mexican citizen who assisted in the kidnapping, José Francisco Sosa, to appeal the case to the US Supreme Court. The Justice Department argued that private individuals could not file suit under ATCA. The court, however, while asserting "great caution when adapting the law of nations to private rights," still held that

> the First Congress understood that district courts would recognize private causes of action for certain torts in violation of the law of nations and that no development of law in the last two centuries has categorically precluded federal courts from recognizing a claim under the law of nations as an element of common law. (*Sosa v. Álvarez Machaín* 542 US 692 [2004] 331 F.3d 604, reversed)

Thus, the court both upheld the application of ATCA to human rights violations insofar as they are construed as settled international law and narrowed its application within the historical context at the time the 1789 act was passed by Congress. In the 1990s, this provision was increasingly used as the basis for filing over 100 suits against fifty-nine corporations. In 2012, a suit was filed charging Chiquita Bananas with complicity in incidents of torture in Colombia because the corporation provided funding to the military that committed the crimes (Chatterjee 2012). Although such suits are still brought under the ATCA, the US Supreme Court severely limited its scope in a 2013 decision holding that suits could not be filed in incidences where the injury occurred outside of the United States (Bowser-Soder 2013).

Since the attacks of 9/11, cases have also been filed under the Torture Victims Protection Act against individuals who allegedly tortured detainees when acting as agents of the United States, such as security contractors, and against states considered sponsors of terror. In a 2012 case against the Palestinian Authority (*Mohammed v. Palestinian Authority*, 11-88, DC Cir. April 28, 2012), the US Supreme Court unanimously ruled that the act applies to "natural persons" and cannot be applied to an organization such as a private contractor.

The administration of President George W. Bush argued against the use of the ATCA to prosecute alleged human rights violators because doing so could impede US foreign policy, particularly in the war on terror. A 2003 case invoked ATCA for human rights abuses in Myanmar, but the Justice Department argued that these kinds of cases could damage US relations with countries who were otherwise valuable allies in fighting terrorism. This position was consistent with the opinion issued in *Sosa v. Álvarez Machaín*, which cautioned that "the potential implications for the foreign relations of the United States of recognizing private causes of action for violating international law should make courts particularly wary of imping-ing on the discretion of the Legislative and Executive Branches in manag-ing foreign affairs."

On signing the Torture Victims Protection Act of 1991, President George H. W. Bush also called on Congress to pass legislation to imple-ment US obligations under the Convention Against Torture, leading to the enactment of the Extraterritorial Torture Statute in section 506 of the For-eign Relations Authorization Act. Section 506 allows for the prosecution of individuals charged with torture outside of the United States when they come into US territory, regardless of their citizenship. The first case brought under the statute was against Charles Taylor Jr., son of Charles Taylor, president of Liberia from 1997 to 2003, for crimes committed dur-ing his tenure as head of the Liberian Anti-Terrorist Unit as well as for war crimes committed during the armed conflict in Sierra Leone that ended in 2002 (Keppler, Jean, and Marshall 2008). Acts named in the 2006 indict-ment include "repeatedly burning a victim at gun-point, with scalding water and a hot iron; shocked various parts of the victim's body; and rubbed salt into the victim's wounds" (Keppler, Jean, and Marshall 2008:20). After numerous precedent-setting pretrial motions, the trial began in September of 2008 and concluded in March 2011, when he was sentenced to ninety-seven years in prison. On April 26, 2012, the Special Court for Sierra Leone also declared Taylor guilty of aiding and abetting the atrocities com-mitted in Sierra Leone.

The US Victims of Trafficking and Violence Protection Act of 2000 (Public Law 18-386) combines the Violence Against Women Act of 2000 and other antitrafficking legislation into one law requiring annual country reports and monitoring. It also creates an interagency task force, provides for both assistance to foreign governments to combat trafficking and actions against governments that fail to meet minimum standards as well as against the traffickers themselves, and strengthens prosecution and punish-ment of traffickers. In the first decade after the act was passed, 2,525 vic-tims of trafficking were issued eligibility letters enabling them to receive services, including refugee resettlement assistance. The act also allows immigration relief through "continued presence" for potential witnesses as well under nonimmigrant T-visas, which can lead to citizenship. Reducing the fear of deportation, and with the possibility of a path to citizenship, vic-tims are more likely to provide critical information that strengthens the capacity for enforcement. More than 200 of the 2,525 eligibility letters issued went to children from over fifty countries. Finally, the act provides assistance through a return, reintegration, and family reunification program administered by the US Department of State (Polaris Project 2010). Since 2003, between 5,000 and 7,000 individuals have been prosecuted for trafficking, with about half of the cases resulting in convictions (US Department of State 2013).

US courts are not alone in extending their reach to prosecute noncitizens for violations of internationally recognized human rights norms. In 1998, a Spanish magistrate issued a warrant for the arrest of former Chilean president Augusto Pinochet in connection with the torture, disappearances, and deaths of Spanish citizens in Chile under his rule. At the time of his arrest in London where he had traveled for medical treatment, he was still a sitting senator in the Chilean parliament having only recently resigned his position as head of the Chilean military. The House of Lords denied the former president sovereign immunity, although the British government appealed this decision, resulting in his release for medical reasons and his return to Chile. Between 1998 and his death in 2006, charges were considered or filed not only by Spain but also by France, Switzerland, Argentina, and five other countries as well as in Chile upon his return from Britain (Wilson 2010).

## Human Rights and Foreign Policies

An axiom in the study and practice of international relations has been that foreign policies serve national interests and that national security trumps other interests. However, changes in the social structure of international relations in the twentieth century have led to some rethinking of this assumption. The globalization of human rights, the globalization of security, and the globalization of conscience and public opinion have called the primacy of narrowly conceived national interests into question.

Boycotts and sanctions are foreign policy "sticks" or punishments, but states can also use the promise of improving economic or political relations as a reward, or "carrot," to influence other states' conduct. Countries have long used sanctions and embargoes unilaterally to signal disapproval of another state's policies on any number of issues. Western democracies have undertaken boycotts and sanctions related to human rights issues in a number of countries including Rhodesia (now Zimbabwe), South Africa, Poland, Myanmar, Haiti, Iraq, and the Soviet Union. In retaliation for the US boycott of the 1980 Moscow Olympics, the Soviet Union boycotted the 1984 Olympics in Los Angeles. The European Union collectively used sanctions against Belarus, the Democratic Republic of Congo, Côte d'Ivoire, Haiti, Myanmar, Sudan, and Zimbabwe (Baek 2008).

David Forsythe (2000) studied the role of human rights in foreign policies and concluded that although human rights seem to receive more attention in foreign policy discussions, most states, including liberal democracies, do not afford them equal or greater status than economic or security concerns. Putting human rights on the agenda of interests that inform the development of foreign policy can also lead to inconsistent and unpredictable policies. Forsythe also claimed that differences in the roles human rights play in the foreign policies of various countries arise not only from cultural and social factors but also from the orientation of states either toward international rights or toward national rights and sovereign rights' protection.

According to the "Memorandum of Understanding for the Implementation of a European Concerted Research Action," the result of a four-year research program prepared by British, European, and Scandinavian experts and institutes, a growing recognition for human rights is a key element of political stability and economic and social development (European Concerted Research Action 2004). Three strategies are employed to integrate human rights into foreign policies: mainstreaming human rights in existing peace and security activities like UN peacekeeping and enforcement operations; redesigning development aid programs to improve human rights conditions and restore or strengthen peace and security; and creating new instruments that contribute to the implementation of both human rights and peace.

In the United States, congressional hearings examining the role of human rights in US foreign policy between 1973 and 1976 led to legislative actions linking human rights to foreign assistance, including denial of military assistance to countries violating human rights. The hearings also recommended that the president deny economic and military assistance to governments known to incarcerate political prisoners, putting the political onus on the executive branch (Power and Allison 2000). The 1961 US Foreign Assistance Act was amended in 1976 to prevent countries engaging in a "consistent pattern of gross violations of internationally recognized human rights" from receiving security assistance from the United States. This piece of legislation placed the burden for exempting a country on its defenders and put debates about the human rights records of aid recipients on the agenda of the US Congress.

This conditionality of aid should be a key instrument in the toolbox of foreign policies for employing a carrot-and-stick approach to bringing pressure to bear on governments that have a history of violating human rights. However, reality does not always match theory. Since the 1976 amendment, human rights advocates have not found their high expectations met by the actual practice of policymaking, especially when subsequently elected policymakers lacked the same enthusiasm as those who authored and signed the 1976 amendment. The United States is criticized for exempting key allies from condemnation even with a record of abuses and for routinely subordinating human rights matters to other policy objectives like trade and strategic interests. It is also criticized because even well-documented abuses published in the Country Reports used to assess human rights conditions and improvements in states receiving US military aid, particularly in states in the Middle East, did not lead to decreased US military and economic aid and weapons sales (Stork 1999).

Several studies covering periods of aid during the 1980s show a mixed US record on using financial leverage in the face of human rights abuses in Latin America. In the 1970s and 1980s, the United States faced widespread criticism for providing assistance and training to repressive military dictators in Latin America, particularly after amendments to the Foreign Assistance Act called for linking such aid to improvement in human rights records. David Cingranelli and Thomas Pasquarello (1985) asked whether US aid to Latin America was conditioned on the human rights records of recipient countries and found that, with the exception of outliers like El Salvador, human rights concerns, particularly personal integrity rights (the term used in empirical research to refer to rights to bodily integrity), mattered when eligibility decisions were made but did not affect the level of aid. Research by Steven Poe (1992) also focused on US aid to Latin America during the 1980s and found similar results, as did Clair Apodaca and Michael Stohl (1999).

Eric Neumayer (2003a, 2003b) more recently expanded this kind of research to include a broader range of donor countries, collecting data into the 2000s. Applying statistical analysis to economic data, he evaluated the role of personal integrity or civil/political rights and, like Cingranelli and Pasquarello (1985), focused on two stages of decisionmaking: eligibility and aid levels. His results were also mixed, finding that better records on the part of recipient countries on issues of personal integrity rights correlated with more aid, but an improvement in a recipient country's record did not have the same effect (Neumayer 2003b). In another study using data from the Cold War era, he found that respect for civil/political rights is statistically significant for most donors at the aid eligibility stage, but again, El Salvador and Guatemala, where the United States remained committed to supporting repressive and undemocratic regimes, were outliers with some of the worst abuses occurring during this period (Neumayer 2003a).

A good record of respect for personal integrity rights in a recipient country under consideration can have a positive impact on aid eligibility from a few donors. However, once a recipient country jumps the hurdle of eligibility, most donors fail to promote respect for human rights in a consistent manner as indicated by level of donation and often give more aid to countries with a poor record on either civil/political or personal integrity rights. Neumayer

(2003b) also found no systematic difference between the like-minded countries commonly regarded as committed to human rights (Canada, Denmark, the Netherlands, Norway, and Sweden) and the other donors.

Alison Brysk (2009) asked why and how some states make promoting human rights a priority and whether states can be or become good global citizens. She concluded that norms can "guide national interest in more constructive directions than the traditional pursuit of military dominance and economic advantage" but that "the global demand for human rights constantly outstrips the supply [of human rights remedies] and that many states could do more to help" (220). Using a "report card approach" to assessment, she found six exemplary states with records of consistently incorporating human rights as a central concern of their foreign policies. These states have succeeded in persuading others to join them in developing interstate "coalitions of caring" in support of advancing human rights. These six exemplars are Canada, Sweden, Costa Rica, the Netherlands, Japan, and South Africa. She also concluded that the world's leading democracy—the United States—is suffering from a "democratic deficit," and that this obstacle is the single most significant one to the development and expansion of an effective international human rights regime. However, even countries with their own outstanding track records internationally can face problems domestically. Although Brysk's findings indicate successful incorporation of human rights into Canadian foreign policy, Canada's First Nations leaders as well as Amnesty International disagree with this assessment on the issue of indigenous peoples' human rights within Canada itself (Cross 2012).

### Truth Commissions

The best internationally known truth commission is undoubtedly the groundbreaking South African Truth and Reconciliation Commission created in the aftermath of the officially sanctioned apartheid state as black and white South Africans began the difficult task of constructing a democracy, deconstructing apartheid, and reconstructing every aspect of their society after ending four centuries of racism. Many other postconflict societies in Latin America, Africa, and Asia have also used truth commissions to facilitate transitional justice in the aftermath of conflicts or nondemocratic rule characterized by mass human rights violations (Hayner 2001). Truth commissions address the psychological and emotional scars of such violence suffered by both perpetrators and victims. Truth commissions attempt to facilitate societal reconciliation by encouraging confession, forgiveness, and healing on a very personal level. Thirty commissions have been established since 1974.

The Republic of Korea, or South Korea, created its own Truth and Reconciliation Commission in 2005 to deal with a variety of historical injuries and injustices, including the Japanese occupation of Korea between 1910 and 1945 and the killing of an estimated 100,000 to 200,000 political prisoners in 1950 who were alleged by the government of Syngman Rhee to be "communist sympathizers."

Canada opened the Indian Residential Schools Truth and Reconciliation Commission in June 2008 because of a 2007 negotiated court-approved agreement involving former students, churches, the government of Canada, and a number of organizations representing the First Nations of Canada. The commission's mandate is "to document the truth of survivors, their families, communities and anyone who has been personally affected by the Indian Residential Schools (IRS) legacy" (Indian Residential Schools 2008).

While these commissions focus primarily on acknowledgment of the past, they may also offer amnesty, reparations, remedial actions, educational programs, and an alternative to purely judicial proceedings (Hayner 2001). The sheer scope of commission proceedings gives some indication of both the daunting task they face as well as the ambitiousness of their missions. For example, the South African commission received testimony from more than 21,000 survivors and victims. Even in other countries, the numbers are striking. Somewhere between 10,000 and 30,000 Argentineans disappeared during the military dictatorship of Augusto Pinochet that terrorized the country between 1976 and 1983. The National Commission on the Disappearance of Persons reported on more than 7,000 statements, including 1,500 from prison camp survivors, on investigations into the disappearances of 8,960 people (Hayner 2001). In Chile, the National Commission on Truth and Reconciliation and the National Corporation for Reparation and Reconciliation received complaints on 3,400 cases (Hayner 2001). The Guatemalan commission considered 42,000 cases arising from twenty years of brutal repression in which an estimated 200,000 people were killed, 83 percent of them Mayans (Hayner 2001).

Truth commissions can serve two important functions. First, they enable a postconflict society to begin a process of public dialogue about the injustices, injuries, and trauma of a long and historically distant period of brutality and oppression in order to build a democratic political culture. Second, on a practical level, they expedite an impossible task of bringing tens of thousands and in some cases hundreds of thousands of perpetrators and victims into a relationship of conciliatory justice aimed at enabling them to live together as citizens in one society. These commissions do not and cannot bring either complete or comprehensive justice and closure, at least not in the short run. Nevertheless, they can open the door for personal, societal, and intergenerational reconciliation.

While truth commissions help states heal in one way, bringing individuals to justice provides another way to give closure to human rights abuses. In 2012, Guatemala became the first country to hold a trial against its own former president, General Efraín Ríos Montt, for genocide against the Mayan people and crimes against humanity during his rule from 1982 to 1983. Sadly, the May 2013 guilty verdict was overturned within weeks by Guatemala's highest court on a three-to-two vote, calling for a "reset" of the trial back to proceedings of April 19, in order to resolve a dispute over the recusal of judges. Taking a broader view, since the 1990s nearly seventy trials have been conducted by national or international tribunals for heads of state and high-ranking state officials for human rights violations (other than genocide, except for Slobodan Milošević) while in office. Some of the best known are Augusto Pinochet (Chile), Slobodan Milošević (former Yugoslavia), Alberto Fujimori (Peru), Charles Taylor (Liberia, for his role in the war with Sierra Leone), Saddam Hussein (Iraq), Augustin Bizimungu (Rwanda), Frederick Chiluba (Zambia), Joseph Estrada (Philippines), and Hosni Mubarak (Egypt). These trials are part of what is now called "transitional justice" processes central to a country's transition from authoritarian to democratic governance (Lutz and Reiger 2009).

## Regional Mechanisms

Regional organizations in Latin America, Europe, and Africa have developed both multilateral agreements on human rights and institutions to implement them. Similar developments have noticeably not occurred in the Middle East, among Arab states, or in South Asia, Southeast Asia, or East Asia. In spite of efforts to foster pan-European involvement both during and after the Cold War, the present and future status regarding regional protection and promotion of human rights in Russia, its former republics, and Central Asia remains uncertain.

### The Inter-American System

The idea of hemispheric cooperation across the Americas has roots in the early nineteenth century when, at a regional congress held in Panama in 1826, Simón Bolívar advocated the creation of a league of American states with common security interests, military, and a supranational assembly. The Organization of American States, founded in 1948, was preceded by the International Union of American Republics that met in Washington, DC, in 1889–90 and the Pan-American Union (previously known as the Commercial Bureau of American Republics) founded a few years later. The impetus for articulating agreement about human rights in 1948 stemmed from US dominance in the organization and its concern for preventing Soviet-backed communist governments from coming to power and thereby preventing communist ideology from spreading among the people in Central and South American countries. The Cold War continued to frame Latin American politics and simultaneously enable repressive undemocratic governments to establish and stay in power with US support. Therefore, the perpetration of gross violations of human rights was the norm for most countries in the southern hemisphere of the region for several decades. Thus, the promise of human rights protection was subverted by the political reality of Cold War politics. Political, economic, and social injustice became entrenched until democratic regimes came to power in the aftermath of the Cold War.

The American system is predicated on three regional agreements—the Charter of the Organization of American States and the American Declaration on the Rights and Duties of Man (both adopted in 1948 and coming into force with twenty-one signatories in 1951) and the American Convention on Human Rights adopted in 1969 and coming into force in 1978 with eleven signatories. The first investigation of human rights abuse by the Inter-American Commission on Human Rights, a commission established to implement the American Declaration on the Rights and Duties of Man, involved an on-site inspection of the human rights conditions in the Dominican Republic in 1961. In 1965, the commission was authorized to hear specific complaints expressed by individuals, NGOs, or governments. The commission's decisions are binding on all thirty-five members of the Organization of American States. The commission may also initiate investigations of particular countries with the permission or at the invitation of the country being investigated, and it regularly produces country reports. The commission's findings are publicized and include detailed analyses of a country's legal institutions and social conditions. As with other international and regional bodies, complainants must first exhaust domestic procedures for obtaining justice before filing a complaint with the regional commission.

In addition to conducting on-site visits, hearings, the collection of data, and documentation, the Inter-American Commission on Human Rights is also authorized to monitor situations of concern. It promotes public awareness by convening conferences and seminars and by working with NGOs and academic institutions. On the enforcement side, it can make recommendations to countries for specific actions to strengthen human rights protection or remedy deficiencies, refer cases to the Inter-American Court of Human Rights, and request that the court offer advisory opinions.

In just the three years from 1996 to 1999, the commission issued or continued fifty-two precautionary measures aimed at stopping and preventing further abuses in extreme cases. Nineteen were issued to the government of Colombia alone and undoubtedly reflect an increase in drug-war-related violence. Many incidences involved civilian massacres and attacks on indigenous villages. Since the end of the Cold War, the commission has averaged forty to fifty measures annually with an increasing number directed at the United States, and most of those involved capital punishment in cases of non-US nationals convicted of crimes in the United States (Inter-American Commission on Human Rights 2013).

The Inter-American Convention on Human Rights restated the objectives of the earlier convention and strengthened its call for the establishment of democratic national institutions and regional mechanisms for enforcement of its provisions. The Inter-American Court of Human Rights was created after the convention entered into force in 1978. The court only hears cases brought by the commission or by states that are signatories of the convention. It does not take individual complaints. The court has both an adjudicatory and an advisory function. Advisory opinions have jurisprudential influence, even though they are not legally binding. The court has issued about twenty advisory opinions. In contentious cases involving countries that have accepted the court's jurisdiction, the court's findings are legally binding, and it can order compensation and other fines or costs to be paid by the state. For example, in 2001, the court heard a case involving the Peruvian government of Alberto Fujimori and an army attack on civilians resulting in fifteen murders (Inter-American Court of Human Rights 2001). The court found in favor of the plaintiffs and against the state and ordered the state to pay $175,000 to the survivors of the attack and relatives of each of the victims and $250,000 to the family of one of the victims in a settlement that totaled more than $3 million. It also required the state to provide free health care and educational support to the victims' families. The court ordered that its decision be published in the media and ordered Peru to repeal two laws providing amnesty to the kinds of death squads who committed these murders, to declare extrajudicial killing a crime, and to ratify the International Convention on the Non-Applicability of Statutory Limitations to War Crimes and Crimes Against Humanity. The court also required that the Peruvian government publicly apologize for the murders and build a monument memorializing the victims.

The court's caseload reflects changes in the aftermath of the Cold War as many Central and South American states began the process of democratizing, bringing many longtime human rights advocates into power. Between 1987 and 1994 the court issued up to three opinions per year. In 1995, it issued five opinions, and from 1996 onward, opinions increased from six to twenty per year. The total number between 1995 and 2007 is 135, compared with before the end of the Cold War, when between 1987 and 1993 the court issued only 13 opinions.

## The European System

Three European regional international organizations deal with human rights: the Council of Europe, the Organization for Security and Cooperation in Europe (OSCE), and the European Union. The Council of Europe was formed in the immediate aftermath of World War II in 1949 by ten states—Belgium, Denmark, France, Ireland, Italy, Luxembourg, the Netherlands, Norway, Sweden, and the United Kingdom—and expanded to forty-seven members as of 2014. The council's broad objectives are to promote democracy, protect human rights, and promote the development of and respect for the rule of law. The European Convention on Human Rights, which is only open to council members, was signed by the members in 1950 and created the European Court of Human Rights. The court receives complaints from member states, NGOs, and individuals or groups of individuals claiming to be victims of violations of the convention.

The OSCE succeeded the Conference on Security and Cooperation in Europe, created in 1973 as a forum for developing second-track diplomacy and confidence-building measures to mitigate Cold War tensions on a continent otherwise divided between east and west. The 1973 conference led finally to the adoption of the Helsinki Final Act (or Helsinki Accords) in 1975. Signed by all European states except Albania, the accords declared ten guiding principles for relations among European states divided between the communist and Western blocs including equal rights, self-determination, and respect for human rights and fundamental freedoms, such as the freedom of thought, conscience, and religion or belief.

Following passage of the Helsinki Final Act, citizen groups formed in the Soviet Union and other communist-controlled states to monitor human rights as defined in the Helsinki document. These "Helsinki watch groups" contributed significantly to the eventual overthrow of totalitarian communist regimes and the democratization of Central and Eastern Europe. The watch groups increased the flow of information about human rights conditions in the communist states to their democratic neighbors. By shining the light of public awareness and opinion on conditions in communist states, they fostered accountability to the Helsinki principles on human rights. They enabled and strengthened the rise of dissidents like playwright and Czech Republic president Václav Havel in Czechoslovakia and physician Elena Bonner and physicist Andrei Sakharov in Russia.

After the Cold War ended, signatories met again in Helsinki in 1992 and decided to create a permanent organization, renaming it the Organization on Security and Cooperation in Europe (OSCE). The new organization was immediately challenged when wars of secession broke out in Yugoslavia in 1993. Although unable to avert or end the violence there, the

OSCE's first field mission was set up in Bosnia-Herzegovina to assist in the implementation of the General Framework Agreement for Peace in Bosnia and Herzegovina (Dayton Accords) ending the wars. Fifty-seven states participated, and in 2014, fifteen OSCE field missions, offices, and projects were still active in eastern and central Europe, including a monitoring mission in Ukraine. Working in cooperation with the United Nations, the European Union, and NATO, the OSCE promotes democratization by assisting in the establishment of independent media; independent judiciary; free, fair, and competitive elections; law enforcement training; development and understanding of due process; parliamentary capacity building; infrastructure and transportation development; and antitrafficking and anticorruption programs.

The European Community, officially called the European Economic Community, was created when Belgium, France, West Germany, Italy, Luxembourg, and the Netherlands signed the Treaty of Rome in 1958. Ratification of the Maastricht Treaty in 1993 created the European Union. In 1997, members signed the Treaty of Amsterdam to consolidate the founding documents of the European Economic Community and the European Union. While the Council of Europe focuses on the promotion of human rights, law, and democracy, and the OSCE is concerned with security, the European Union is developing as a set of governing institutions with jurisdictional and policy responsibilities that are both political and economic. The European Union has three goals for its member countries: economic integration, a common foreign policy, and a common security apparatus. The last two have been much more elusive than the first, evidenced already by the acceptance of the single currency, the euro, and the steady improvement in open borders among EU members. However, economic integration has not been without its challenges, the greatest of which have been how it has responded as an organization and worked with individual members to mitigate the economic impacts of the recession of 2008–2009 and increasing right-wing activism, including the rise of far-right political parties gaining electoral ground in some countries (Goodwin 2013; Efron 2014).

In 1999, EU members drafted the Charter of Fundamental Rights of the European Union, though the charter does not create binding legal obligations. The preamble says that the goal of the charter is "to strengthen the protection of fundamental rights in the light of changes in society, social progress and scientific and technological developments by making those rights more visible in a Charter." Six chapters describe the rights guaranteed to those living in the European Union: dignity, freedom, equality, solidarity, citizens' rights, and justice.

In addition to strengthening, promoting, and protecting human rights within current EU member states, admission to the union is conditional on the human rights standards both expressed and protected by applicant states. When a state applies for membership, its human rights record becomes the subject of scrutiny. Article 6 of the Maastricht Treaty stipulates that members must be committed to "respect for human rights and fundamental freedoms, and the rule of law, principles which are common to the Member States."

Once an application is submitted, the Council of Europe consults the European Commission, and with approval of the European Parliament, enters into negotiations with the applicant country. If the council concludes that the country is not yet meeting the conditions and standards required to be a member of the European Union, then it negotiates with the applicant state to remedy any problems while issuing periodic progress reports. The remedy may require amending state law, for example, on the state's treatment and protection of minorities or addressing an ongoing human rights issue, such as the status and treatment of Kurds in Turkey. The expansion of human rights is central to the process of EU enlargement.

Since Protocol 11 of the European Convention on Human Rights entered into force in 1998, the two-tiered system of a commission and court, which the inter-American system still has, was replaced by a single European Court of Human Rights. The court takes complaints from individuals or states, though states rarely file complaints against one another. The court receives tens of thousands of applications every year with about half arising from administrative reviews (European Court of Human Rights 2014a). Between 2002 and 2013, for instance, the number of applications more than doubled from around 28,000 to 65,000 (European Court of Human Rights 2014b). Every effort is made to resolve a complaint through direct communication with the government against which the complaint is made. In 2013, roughly 17 percent of all complaints were filed against Russia and about 14.4 percent against Italy. Ukraine accounted for 13.3 percent, Serbia 11.3 percent, and Turkey 11 percent. Romania, the United Kingdom, Georgia, Bulgaria, and Slovenia accounted for another 13 percent, and 18 percent were filed against the remaining thirty-seven members in total (European Court of Human Rights 2014b).

In addition to the European Convention on Human Rights, the European Social Charter was revised in 1996, with the changes entering into force in 1999. It addresses social and economic rights including housing, health care, education, employment, freedom of movement, and freedom from discrimination. An additional protocol allows workers' organizations and NGOs to file collective complaints. Complaints judged admissible can lead to a written response from the country against which the complaint is lodged, a public hearing, and a formal resolution recommending remedial action.

In 1989, all members of the Council of Europe ratified the European Convention for the Prevention of Torture and Inhuman or Degrading Treatment or Punishment. A protocol adopted in 2002 allows nonmember states to join the convention and established a committee permitted to visit any country where individuals are "deprived of their liberty by a public authority" (Article 2). All signatories agree to allow such visits. The committee uses site visits to investigate whether people being held are being protected against torture and other treatment prohibited by the convention. In order to facilitate compliance with the convention, the committee published standards addressing police custody, imprisonment, law enforcement training, prisoners' health care, the detention of foreign nationals, involuntary placement in psychiatric facilities, and the treatment of juveniles and women.

In 1993, the European Commission Against Racism and Intolerance was established to monitor and eliminate racism, xenophobia, anti-Semitism, and other kinds of intolerance in member states of the Council of Europe. The commission monitors and reports on conditions and developments through its regular country reports, holding conferences, promoting educational programs to combat racism and intolerance, and proposing actions that could be taken at the local, regional, and national levels based on its assessments.

A Framework Convention for the Protection of Minorities also entered into force in 1998. As the first legally binding international agreement on the protection of minorities, it promotes "the full and effective equality of national minorities by creating appropriate conditions enabling them to preserve and develop their culture and to retain their identity" (Council of Europe 2014). This convention grew out of earlier work on the European Charter for Regional or Minority Languages, adopted in 1992.

### The African System

Cold War politics and the struggle over apartheid in South Africa hindered the development of regional international organizations and a system of human rights protection in Africa. African states are poorer than states in Europe and the Western Hemisphere and support for national political institutions takes priority over supporting regional organizations. The transition from colonial rule to postcolonial democracies has given rise to violent struggles, and many African states remain in the grip of either autocratic governments or perpetual civil wars, or both. Governmental and societal corruption is widespread, and meeting basic needs for clean water and adequate food supply remains an ongoing battle for many Africans, exacerbated by intractable violence. One Oxfam report observed that achieving development goals of poverty reduction, improved health care, and education necessitates curbing arms transfers (Inter Press Service 2008). The report noted, "At least 22 of the 34 countries least likely to achieve the UN Millennium Development Goals are in the midst of, or emerging from conflict." The Oxfam report also noted that in the fifteen years between 1990 and 2005 a conservative estimate of $284 billion was spent on armed conflict for twenty-three countries (Oxfam 2007:8).

Historically, only South Africa had the resources to support the development of regional organizations, but four decades of brutal, undemocratic rule under apartheid and the gross violations of human rights by the South African government left the country paralyzed by its own status as a pariah within the international community. Thus, little progress was made by the Organization of African Unity or on the development of human rights until the Cold War ended and apartheid was replaced by democracy in South Africa.

The Organization of African Unity adopted the African Charter on Human and Peoples' Rights in 1981, which entered into force in 1986. Although patterned on the European and Latin American human rights instruments that preceded it, the charter is also distinguished and controversial for two features: recognition of the rights of "peoples" and its commitment to the elimination of Zionism. The first is not so much controversial as innovative and even progressive in light of the long-standing and still unresolved question of the rights of potentially thousands of state minorities. The second feature, however, found in the preamble, is problematic because it equates the aspiration for a Jewish state with "colonialism, neo-colonialism, apartheid . . . and all forms of discrimination, particularly those based on race, ethnic group, color, sex, language, religion or political opinions." The aim of "eliminating" Zionism is equivalent to eliminating Israel and caused South Africa to ratify with the reservation that the charter become compliant with UN resolutions "regarding the characterization of Zionism" (Ouguergouz 2003).

A year after the charter entered into force, the African Commission on Human and Peoples' Rights was established to oversee the implementation of the charter. Its headquarters are in Banjul, Gambia. The commission has quasi-judicial authority in that it interprets the charter and receives and considers complaints from individuals alleging charter violations. Six rapporteurs, who investigate complaints submitted to the commission, deal with specific kinds of human rights issues or have a special role: (1) extrajudicial, summary, or arbitrary executions; (2) freedom of expression and access to information; (3) human rights defenders; (4) prisoners and conditions of detention; (5) refugees, asylum, migrants, and internally displaced persons; and (6) the rights of women.

After the Cold War and apartheid ended, a protocol creating the African Court on Human and Peoples' Rights was adopted in 1998 and entered into force in 2004. In 2002, the African Union formed as the successor to the Organization of African Unity. Fifty-three states—all but Morocco—are members. The idea of an African court on human rights dates to the earliest days of postcolonialism, but concerns over whether or not the Western-style concept and system of jurisprudence resonate with African norms and social practice led to an abandonment of the idea during the time of the Organization of African Unity (Lyons 2006). The commission was regarded as an alternative and considered to be more compatible with African norms. However, the African Union formed the current African Court on Human and Peoples' Rights, which differs from the inter-American court in that it may take cases filed directly by individuals and NGOs, but only if they are recognized as having observer status. This requirement differs from the European court, which does not require such status for the filing of individual and NGO complaints.

Finally, the African court is unique not only because the African charter is the only international human rights instrument to recognize the collective peoples' rights but also because its jurisdiction covers any human rights instrument signed by any of its members, with the requirement that judges must be from member states and must recuse themselves from cases involving their own countries. Some of the worst human rights violations have occurred in Africa in the last few decades. No doubt mobilizing political will in support of the African Court on Human and Peoples' Rights was spurred on at least in part by these tragedies. The court is located in Arusha, Tanzania, which is also home to the ICTR.

## International Mechanisms

There are four purposes for the formation of the United Nations. The first is preventing another world war. The second is "to reaffirm faith in fundamental human rights, in the dignity and worth of the human person, in the equal rights of men and women and of nations large and small." The third purpose is to create conditions conducive to compliance with international law, and the last is "to promote social progress and better standards of life in larger freedom."

The United Nations pursues these objectives in a number of ways, and the Security Council, General Assembly, and Economic and Social Council all play roles. In addition to the United Nations, two other international organizations offer pathways to redress human rights issues. The World Bank now takes human rights and the human impacts of proposals into consideration when evaluating potential projects. The International Labour Organization (ILO) also has a mechanism for states to file complaints against one another for failing to comply with a convention to which those states are signatories.

## UN Human Rights Council

In 2006, the United Nations underwent a reorganization of its human rights bodies and mechanisms when the forty-six-member Human Rights Council, a subsidiary body of the General Assembly, replaced the fifty-three-member Commission on Human Rights. Membership is allocated on a regional basis with thirteen representatives each from Africa and Asia, six from Eastern Europe, eight from Latin America, and seven from Western Europe and other regions. The council was created under the UN Charter to promote human rights after the earlier commission was criticized for not linking criteria for respecting human rights standards to its members' records on human rights. Upon creating the new council, the General Assembly resolution declared, "Members elected to the Council shall uphold the highest standards in the promotion and protection of human rights" and provided for periodic review of its members' human rights records. In addition, the council has a formal complaint procedure, a procedure for conducting hearings about alleged violations in a less formal manner, special procedures that involve independent experts, thematic mandates such as arbitrary detention, mandates for specific countries, and procedures for conducting country visits as part of investigating a complaint.

The complaint procedure was established under the Commission on Human Rights by Resolution 1503 of the Economic and Social Council in May 1970. When the council replaced the Commission on Human Rights in March 2006, the complaint procedure put forth in Resolution 1503 was reviewed, and two working groups are now mandated with bringing communications before the council involving consistent patterns of gross violations of human rights. All communications are confidential, making it more likely that governments will cooperate without the immediate glare of world public opinion bearing down on them. The Working Group on Communications assesses the admissibility and credibility of communications regarding allegations of human rights violations and, if members agree, brings a confidential report to the Working Group on Situations. The Working Group on Situations then assesses these communications in its twice-yearly meetings and decides whether to make recommendations to the council and, if so, what. Assessments are intended to discourage the filing of complaints that are being brought for purely political purposes, lack factual support, rely solely on media reports, are not brought by the victims or victims groups, are already under consideration by the council or working groups, or are being brought even if domestic remedies have not been exhausted. Under the Paris Principles, adopted by the General Assembly in 1991, states are encouraged to establish national human rights institutions to protect and promote international human rights standards and work with the Human Rights Council.

## UN General Assembly

Besides the ICCPR and the ICESCR seven core international human rights treaties have been signed along with the Optional Protocol to the Convention Against Torture. All include monitoring bodies. The seven treaties are the International Convention on the Elimination of All Forms of Racial Discrimination (1965), Convention on the Elimination of All Forms of Discrimination Against Women (1979), Convention Against Torture and Other Cruel, Inhuman, or Degrading Treatment or Punishment (1984), Convention on the Rights of the Child (1989), International Convention on the Protection of the Rights of All Migrant Workers and Members of Their Families (1990), International Convention for the Protection of All Persons from Enforced Disappearance (2006), and Convention on the Rights of Persons with Disabilities (2006).

The development of all of these conventions has been facilitated by the General Assembly because although it does not have lawmaking authority, it provides a forum for all states to maintain ongoing multilateral diplomatic relations and communications. Its work often reflects the political climate in which it operates. During the Cold War for example, when the whole body of the United Nations was frequently paralyzed by the polarization of the superpowers, the General Assembly became more focused on social and economic issues. As decolonization dramatically increased the number of states—from around fifty at the inception of the organization to triple that number by the mid-1960s—the rhetorical climate and agenda in the General Assembly reflected the grievances of formerly colonized countries.

With the end of the Cold War, many anticipated a more cohesive and proactive United Nations, and in fact, the Security Council's authorization of the Gulf War in 1991 and a sharp increase in the number of peacekeeping missions suggested a move in this direction. However, the General Assembly's role remains limited to giving expression to the political will of the international community. By enabling states to achieve consensus on some issues, it facilitates the development of treaties and conventions that often make their first appearance as General Assembly resolutions outlining the draft principles that provide the starting point for treaty negotiations. One area where the General Assembly has remained consistently active is human rights. With the exception of the Supplementary Slavery Convention (1956), all of the core human rights treaties were either adopted by the General Assembly or by a conference convened pursuant to a General Assembly resolution.

Eight treaty-based bodies monitor the implementation of these core treaties. The Human Rights Committee was established pursuant to the ICCPR, and the Committee on Economic, Social, and Cultural Rights monitors the ICESCR. The Committee on the Elimination of Racial Discrimination monitors implementation of the Convention on the Elimination of All Forms of Racial Discrimination. The Committee on Torture and Subcommittee on Prevention of Torture monitor implementation of the antitorture convention and its protocol. The Committee on the Rights of the Child monitors compliance with the Convention on the Rights of the Child. In May 2008, the Convention on the Rights of Persons with Disabilities entered into force when it was signed by twenty states. The Committee on the Rights of Persons with Disabilities monitors its implementation. As of 2014, 145 states ratified or acceded to the convention and 80 to the optional protocol that enables the committee to receive and investigate the merits of communications (complaints). About two-thirds of UN members have signed at least six of the core treaties according to Srini Sitaraman (2009).

In 2005, the General Assembly adopted by consensus and opened for signature and ratification the International Convention for the Protection of All Persons from Enforced Disappearances. As of 2014, ninety-three states had signed the convention, which was introduced in the General Assembly by France. However, the United States and several of its closest allies in the Iraq War would not sign the treaty. French officials said that as of 2007, 51,000 people had disappeared at the hands of governments in over ninety countries since 1980 with 41,000 of those cases still unsolved in 2007 (*USA Today* 2007).

## UN Security Council

Article 24 in Chapter V of the UN Charter assigns the Security Council primary responsibility for maintaining peace and security in the international community. Additionally, Chapter VII, Article 39 charges the Security Council with determining whether or not a situation constitutes a threat to the peace, a breach of the peace, or an act of aggression. The Council has broad discretion to decide whether a particular situation warrants action, and many cases brought before the Council for consideration on the bases of threatening peace or constituting aggression also involve violations of human rights. The forty-three reports on missions authorized and undertaken by the Security Council from October 1992 to April 2013 illustrate this point. Missions to Congo, Central Africa, Sudan, the Great Lakes Region of Africa and Rwanda, Bosnia-Herzegovina, Kosovo, and Burundi, for example, all involved not only ongoing armed conflict but also massive human rights violations, including genocide (UN Security Council 2013).

The Security Council is involved in the enforcement of human rights standards in other ways as well. The ICTY and ICTR deal with not only war crimes but also crimes against humanity. The Security Council established both as subsidiary organs. The Security Council can also decide what measures to take short of military intervention, such as sanctions, in order to put pressure on regimes that violate human rights. More often, it "condemns" or "deplores" ongoing human rights violations, as it has in the case of Myanmar and the suppression of peaceful political demonstrations against the repressive government there. Under the Charter's Chapter VII authority to determine situations constituting threats to or breaches of the peace or acts of aggression, the Security Council has established fifteen working groups or sanctions committees, twelve dealing with specific countries. Two of the best-known sanctions cases were Rhodesia, which became Zimbabwe following the transition to majority black rule, and South Africa.

In 1966, the Security Council mandated an effort to encourage the overthrow of a government because of its human rights violations, namely, state-enforced apartheid in what at the time was the country of Rhodesia. Rhodesia declared independence from Great Britain in 1965 under the white supremacist government of Ian Smith. The Council voted eleven to zero with four abstentions to declare an embargo on 90 percent of Rhodesia's exports and to bar the 122 members of the United Nations from selling oil, arms, motor vehicles, or airplanes or providing any economic aid to Rhodesia in protest of its racial segregationist policies. The resolution did not provide penalties for noncompliance, which the African states had strongly advocated (*Time* 1966). The international community did not recognize Rhodesia, and an open civil war broke out in 1971.

One of the leaders of the black nationalist militant organization the Zimbabwe African National Union was Robert Mugabe, who had been a political prisoner before and after the white minority declared independence from Britain. The United Nations condemned the declaration of independence and called on member states not to recognize the apartheid government. In 1976, Mugabe left the country and joined the liberation struggle that carried out its war against Smith's government from bases in Mozambique. In 1979, Smith resigned and a biracial coalition government was established. In 1980, Mugabe was elected prime minister of the newly renamed Zimbabwe and called for racial and political reconciliation. UN sanctions and the failure of the international community to recognize the new white minority government no doubt played a role in weakening the segregationist regime and bringing a black majority government to power. Mugabe remains president of Zimbabwe and the civil strife following attempts at radical land reform in 2000 abated after controversial elections in 2008 led to a power-sharing agreement between Mugabe and Prime Minister Morgan Tsvangirai. The agreement also called for writing a new constitution, which was adopted by popular vote in March 2013. The power-sharing agreement ended with the first elections under the new constitution, and Mugabe was reelected with his party winning a two-thirds majority in the House of Assembly.

In contrast to Zimbabwe, the United Nations dealt with apartheid in South Africa more as an internal matter by creating a special committee for "peaceful change" in 1962 and sending observers to the 1994 elections. The difference in the two cases was most likely due to Rhodesia's unilateral declaration of independence from Great Britain, which brought Britain to the table in support of the mandatory sanctions supported by other major powers as an expression of opposition to Rhodesia's racial policies. South Africa was already independent, and British support for sanctions and opposition to the South African government was much less enthusiastic than in the case of Rhodesia. Condemnation of apartheid had been on the UN agenda nearly from its inception, but opposition was limited to criticism, condemnation, conferences, and discussions on apartheid. In 1963, the Security Council called for a voluntary arms embargo against South Africa supported by the United States and Britain.

Following the Sharpeville Massacre in 1960 when police fired into a crowd of unarmed protesters, killing and shooting many in the back as they fled, the United Nations stepped up pressure on the white supremacist government. The General Assembly commemorated the massacre by declaring its date the International Day for the Elimination of Racial Discrimination and in 1974 passed a motion to expel South Africa from the United Nations. The United States, Britain, and France—all of which had extensive trade relations with South Africa—vetoed the motion. A grassroots divestment movement gathered increasing support in the 1980s, and by the end of the decade, twenty-five states, including the United States and Britain, passed national laws imposing trade sanctions of some kind against South Africa. As a case of using sanctions to end human rights violations, South Africa is instructive because opposition to the apartheid government, starting in the early 1960s, had little effect until the major trading partners—the United States and Britain—joined the sanctions against the regime twenty years later. Within a few years, the weakened regime collapsed with the resignation of F. W. de Klerk and the democratic election of Nelson Mandela.

## World Bank

In 1986, the General Assembly passed the Declaration on the Right to Development, which in Article 3 elaborates a "right to development," declaring that "states have the primary responsibility for the creation of national and international conditions favourable to the realization of the right to development." Paragraph 3 of that article also declares that "states should realize their rights and fulfill their duties in such a manner as to promote a new international economic order based on sovereign equality, interdependence, mutual interest and co-operation among all States, as well as to encourage the observance and realization of human rights."

With the 1998 publication of *Human Rights and Development: The Role of the World Bank,* the World Bank announced that promoting conditions of respect for human rights was now a goal of development. A 2006 World Development Report entitled *Equity and Development* examined the link between inequalities of opportunity, deprivation of needs, and human rights (World Bank 2005a). This connection is supported by recent cross-country research (Barro 1991, 1997; Alston and Robinson 2005). The 1998 Report on Development described the relationship this way:

> Through its support of primary education, health care and nutrition, sanitation, housing, and the environment, the Bank has helped hundreds of millions of people attain crucial economic and social rights. In other areas, the Bank's contributions are necessarily less direct, but perhaps equally significant. By helping to fight corruption, improve transparency and accountability in governance, strengthen judicial systems, and modernize financial sectors, the Bank contributes to building environments in which people are better able to pursue a broader range of human rights. (World Bank 1998:3)

The Bank has also been criticized for not taking into account the negative impact of its projects on the rights of indigenous peoples, an understandable concern in light of the fact that most World Bank projects are undertaken in remote and rural areas of developing countries. They therefore often have great impact on communities of people living in these areas, many of whom are indigenous. India's scheduled tribes are disproportionately affected by that country's big dam projects. In Central and South America, dams, highways, and infrastructure projects displace indigenous communities. Prompted by the political activism of indigenous peoples, the Bank in 1982 adopted guidelines for the protection of indigenous peoples (at the time the Bank referred to them as "tribal" people). The intention of the Bank was to contribute to "the recuperation or restoration of tribal groups who have been, or are being or may in the future be affected by Bank-assisted development projects" (Goodland 1984:2). The Bank's rationale was that development projects ought to reduce rather than increase the gap between the well-being of tribal groups and that of the broader national population (Wilmer 1993).

This World Bank policy predates the agreement on draft principles for the protection of indigenous peoples' rights in the General Assembly by more than a decade. Some attribute the internationalization of human rights norms in part to the Bank's initiatives in creating social impact guidelines (Wilmer 1993; Sarfaty 2005; Martin and Wilmer 2008). Others believe that the World Bank needs to be more broadly and consistently accountable for the impact of its projects on human rights (Clark 2002). In 1991 the Bank adopted Operational Directive 4.20 on Indigenous Peoples, which aims either to ensure that indigenous peoples benefit from Bank projects or, if they do not, to mitigate adverse effects on indigenous peoples caused by Bank projects (World Bank 1991).

The directive calls for "culturally appropriate development" and for the participation of indigenous peoples in project planning and implementation. When the Bank undertook an evaluation of the implementation of the directive in 2003, 404 projects were reviewed and 183 of them were determined to have an impact on indigenous peoples. Of these projects, 77 percent were evaluated as having had satisfactory or highly satisfactory ratings in terms of protecting indigenous peoples (World Bank 2003). However, indigenous peoples' organizations and advocates do not always agree with the Bank's rather positive assessment (Treakle 1998; Institute for Indigenous Sciences and Cultures 2001).

### International Labour Organization

In addition to being the first international organization to address indigenous peoples' human rights in the Indigenous and Tribal Populations Convention (Convention No. 107, 1957) and updating Convention No. 169 in 1989, the ILO regards eight of the organization's agreements as forming the foundation of the way the ILO regards the basic rights of workers: the Freedom of Association and Protection of the Right to Organize Convention (1948), the Right to Organize and Collective Bargaining Convention (1949), the Forced Labour Convention (1930), the Abolition of Forced Labour Convention (1957), the Discrimination (Employment and Occupation) Convention (1958), the Equal Remuneration Convention (1951), the Minimum Age Convention (1973), and the Worst Forms of Child Labour Convention (1999).

The organization has passed and opened for ratification two conventions on migrant workers, but the ratification rate has been disappointing. The first convention, the Migration for Employment Convention (Convention No. 97, 1949), has been ratified by forty-nine states as of 2013. The second, No. 143 (1975), has been ratified by only nineteen states (International Migrants Rights Watch Committee 1999). Many states are still very protective of their ability to regulate immigration without being subjected to multilateral agreements that might restrict their ability to do so.

The ILO is involved in implementation of their conventions in a variety of ways. The ILO Constitution provides for a complaint procedure in Articles 26 to 34. Any member state can file a complaint for noncompliance against any other member if both members have ratified the convention in question. Complaints are referred to the Governing Body, which may then open discussion directly with the government against which the complaint was filed, or it may designate a commission of inquiry and begin an investigation, initiate fact-finding, and, if warranted, make recommendations on measures to resolve the complaint. As of 2013, the Governing Body had formed twelve commissions of inquiry (ILO 2013). Failure to carry out a commission's recommendations may trigger action under Article 33, which provides that "the Governing Body may recommend to the Conference such action as it may deem wise and expedient to secure compliance therewith."

An investigation into a 1996 complaint of violations of the Forced Labour Convention by Myanmar led the Governing Body to invoke Article 33 for the first time in 2000. The commission of inquiry in that case found "abundant evidence . . . showing the pervasive use of forced labour imposed on the civilian population throughout Myanmar" (ILO 1998). The report included witness accounts of the government sending women and porters to test for minefields resulting in death and injury, sick and injured laborers being beaten and abused, and "women performing compulsory labour . . . [and being] raped or otherwise sexually abused by soldiers" (ILO 1998).

The Committee of Experts on the Application of Conventions and Recommendations is a quasi-judicial body made up of jurists from member states and can intervene in the supervision of treaty obligations. It annually examines reports by governments and employers' and workers' organizations, monitors recommendations made by other supervisory bodies, and considers information resulting from various kinds of field missions including routine contact missions, study missions, fact-finding missions, technical assistance missions, and missions to promote the implementation of standards contained in specific conventions (Potobsky 1998). The Committee on the Application of Standards reviews the findings and concerns of the Committee of Experts and attempts to engage governments, employers, and workers in "direct dialogue" (Potobsky 1998).

Geraldo von Potobsky (1998) reviewed the record of the ILO in monitoring and implementing the standards contained in Convention No. 87, Freedom of Association and Protection of the Right to Organize. The ILO has engaged in reviews of its own activities aimed at incorporating convention standards into national law and policy since the 1920s. The Committee of Experts and the Conference Committee on the Application of Standards were involved in 119 cases in ninety-eight countries involving standards set in Convention No. 87 between 1970 and 1997. These two committees dealt with complaints arising in connection with the Freedom of Association and Protection of the Right to Organize. Furthermore, the Committee on Freedom of Association was established in 1951 specifically to deal with cases involving Convention No. 87. Potobsky contended that the sheer number of cases that particular committee has been involved in—over 2,000—indicates widespread acceptance of its mission and the convention's standards. Of 324 cases brought pursuant to the freedom of association and studied in detail, 24 percent dealt with human rights, many involving the sentencing or detention of trade union activists. Potobsky's conclusions lend strong support to the claim that the ILO implementation and enforcement machinery is effective: "A study carried out in 1982 maintained that over the four preceding years more than 500 trade unionists had been released following the direct or indirect intervention of the ILO. Since then, the Committee on Freedom of Association has continued to record the release of individual trade unionists in its reports" (Potobsky 1998:195).

## Is There an International Human Rights Regime?

Most students of international relations are familiar with the idea of international regimes. As first outlined in 1983 by Stephen Krasner and contributors to his edited book *International Regimes*, regimes are characterized by "implicit or explicit principles, norms, rules and decision-making procedures around which actors' expectations converge in a given area of international relations" (185).

One of the clearest examples of an international regime is in international trade. It includes regional free-trade and common market agreements, a set of international trade agreements known collectively as the General Agreement on Tariffs and Trade, and the creation of the International Trade Organization. Regimes give scholars of international relations a way of evaluating order in specific issue areas in spite of the absence of global governing institutions. Krasner identified three kinds of international relations theorists: realists, idealists (or Grotians), and modified structuralists (or neorealists). The first group views international relations as fundamentally anarchic, characterized by the inability to produce order given the diverse and zero-sum national interests of states. According to realists, even if regimes can be identified, they are only peripherally important and a secondary effect of the pursuit and assertion of power. Idealists or Grotians (named after the "father" of international law, Hugo Grotius) on the other hand, see regimes in every area where any cooperation appears among states. Neorealists regard regimes as a rational development arising from widespread agreement among states on norms to regulate their interactions and thus avoid costs associated with uncoordinated action (Donnelly 1986).

Jack Donnelly (1986) identified four types of regime norms or standards: (1) authoritative international norms, (2) international standards with self-selected national exemptions, (3) nonbinding international guidelines, and (4) national standards. He also outlined three categories of decisionmaking activities and further suggested that they can vary from weak to strong: promotional, implementational, and enforcement. Donnelly concluded that, as of 1986 and taken as a whole, the overall international human rights regime was heavily promotional. But a lot has happened since then. All three kinds of regimes can be observed in human rights today. For example, the ICESCR and the conventions on the Rights of the Child, Elimination of All Forms of Racial Discrimination, and Elimination of All Forms of Discrimination Against Women are primarily promotional. Assistance in developing national action plans, provided by the Office of the UN High Commissioner for Human Rights (OHCHR), which did not even exist in 1986, is clearly more implementational. The Nuremberg, Tokyo, Yugoslav, and Rwandan criminal tribunals, as well as the ICC itself, most definitely make up an enforcement regime. Since World War II, 179 people have been convicted of crimes against humanity, 183 convicted of war crimes, and 32 convicted of genocide, representing over twenty nationalities and conflicts or wars including those in Yugoslavia, Rwanda, Sierra Leone, and Ethiopia and the anticommunist revolution in Romania (Crowe 2014).

Some research on human rights regimes asks why states participate in them and what state characteristics (strong, midlevel, weak, democratic, nondemocratic, emerging democratic, for example) are associated with a greater likelihood of participating in international human rights regimes. Here are some of the findings:

- States were more likely to participate if their neighbors were members (Goodliffe and Hawkins 2006; Neumayer 2008; Wotipka and Tsutsui 2008; Simmons 2009).
- States with deep historic commitment to democracy, newly democratizing states, and states closely linked to Western cultural mores and practices have ratified some human rights treaties more readily (Simmons 2009).
- Most nondemocracies (99 percent according to Hafner-Burton, Mansfield, and Pevehouse 2008) have ratified human rights treaties although they may have taken longer to do so (Simmons 2009).
- Democratizing states were the most likely to join human rights treaties (Cole 2005) and joining human rights treaties had more benefit for democratizing states (Hafner-Burton, Mansfield, and Pevehouse 2008).
- The "sovereignty costs" varied across different regimes, with powerful democracies not needing to sign treaties in order to secure rights and autocracies avoiding joining treaties or regimes because they were unwilling to pay the sovereignty costs (Cole 2009; Hafner-Burton, Mansfield, and Pevehouse 2008).
- Democracies were more likely to ratify human rights treaties that protect civil, political, economic, social, and cultural rights and outlaw discrimination against women; on the other hand, new democracies were inclined to sign all treaties with fewer reservations and accept greater sovereignty costs (Landman 2005; Neumayer 2007).

- States with a strong commitment to rule of law, strong domestic judicial institutions, and a peaceful history were more likely to join the treaty recognizing the authority of the ICC (Chapman and Chaudoin 2012).
- States with poor human rights records are more likely today to join human rights treaties than they were thirty years ago (Hathaway 2002; Hafner-Burton and Tsutsui 2007).
- Treaty ratification often had little or no effect on compliance and in some cases may have led to a worsening human rights record (Keith 1999; Hathaway 2002; Smith-Cannoy 2012).

## Conclusion

Lamenting that little progress has been made in the implementation and enforcement of internationally recognized human rights norms is easy, particularly when national mechanisms and international courts are ignored. Exaggerating inadequacies is also a result of the simple fact that an averted human rights disaster does not make good "headline" material. Human rights disasters not prevented do. One has no way to know, for instance, how much more conflict, death, and suffering would have taken place in Libya had the United Nations not authorized a NATO intervention in 2011. A broad view of history suggests that mobilization around common human rights values has accelerated over the past several decades and is evident in both national and international mechanisms for implementation of policies that give those rights and values a high priority.

Two contradictory and conflicting opinions about the relationship between national and international institutions prevail. One is a fear that international institutions will erode state sovereignty and, in doing so, override the will and right of people within state boundaries to both control their own political destiny and express and pursue their own vision of the good society without direct interference from external actors, whether other states or international institutions. The other is an expectation that "someone ought to do something" to prevent, stop, or punish those responsible for the suffering caused by gross violations of human rights. That expectation is often directed at international institutions as if they were "suprastate" institutions. But they are not. Perhaps they never will be. Considering the record of the state as both a violator and protector of human rights, the lack of supremacy may be a good thing.

When dealing with the "interests versus values" question, national interests are at the center of the problem, and thus far, the most powerful states, even democracies, seem less willing to put human rights values first. Brysk (2009) noted that middle-range powers are more likely to cultivate their own national identity as a "global good citizen," including acting to promote and uphold international human rights norms. Having more power means being able to act beyond the scope of international norms, to bend or attempt to modify them to suit a foreign policy driven by national interests first and human rights second, or later. The second war in Iraq, largely a US war and occupation supported by Great Britain and a handful of small states, is a good example. Under Saddam Hussein, the Iraqi government's use of chemical weapons against Iraqi Kurds became a secondary justification for the military intervention; the primary purpose focused on the regime's alleged threat to the security not only of the United States but the "international community." President George W. Bush carved out a policy of national security exceptionalism with the United States reserving the right to act outside the norms of international law when its interests are threatened.

States can also be effective as agents of implementation, whether by linking human rights to their foreign policies, by enforcing human rights both territorially and extraterritorially in their national courts, by enacting national legislation, or by creating truth commissions and other programs to bring justice for human rights violations within their own societies. States can continue to work toward concerted interventionist responses when they fail to prevent human rights catastrophes that result from state action or inaction. Central to the last strategy is a normative shift away from the *right* to intervene toward an *obligation* to intervene. This shift more generally applies to the prevention of disasters when the emphasis on the rights of states more broadly is balanced with a responsibility to protect based on, as Kofi Annan has said, "our common humanity."

Israeli foreign minister Abba Eban once said, "International law is that law which the wicked do not obey and the righteous do not enforce" (quoted in von Glahn 2012:4). Many people today might agree, and this statement also probably reflects substantial public opinion about international law. Such a cynical view, however, also belies the deep hope many people have that humanity, acting through international law, can do more to relieve suffering, particularly the suffering caused by "man's inhumanity to man" in the name of exercising political authority or, in world politics, state sovereignty to protect (narrow) national interests.

Research thus far on regime theory applied to human rights indicates that states at the midlevel of power that are also already in compliance with human rights norms are more likely to join regimes and incorporate human rights into their foreign policies. More powerful states are apprehensive that the cost to their ability not only to act outside of those norms but perhaps also even to shape them will outweigh the benefits of joining regimes that restrict their choices. Interests seem to trump values at both the national and international levels of enforcement. The tragedies in Darfur and central

Africa also show that interests in the form of trade and exploitation of immense natural resources can easily preclude support from major powers for intervention on behalf of victims of human rights abuses.

In this chapter, I do not attempt to resolve these issues but instead provide an overview of the variety of international, regional, and national mechanisms that address the enforcement and implementation of international human rights standards. Many are remedial ex post facto—after the violations occur. More preventive diplomacy as well as decisive, widely supported interventions to stop ongoing human rights crises such as those occurring in Darfur and central Africa would be better. However, the institutional capacity building that is taking place internationally and regionally as well as the utilization of national courts and foreign policy making to promote respect for international human rights norms and standards should also be acknowledged. Substantial progress has been made toward creating institutions through which norms can be articulated, strengthened, promoted, implemented, and, in some cases, enforced. Those wishing to advance and accelerate this process need not wait for the emergence of sufficient political will at the international or global level but can work to strengthen national mechanisms and foreign policies in support of human rights.

# 7

# The Role of
# Nonstate Actors

The candle burns not for us, but for all those whom we failed to rescue from
prison, who were shot on the way to prison, who were tortured, who were
kidnapped, who "disappeared." That's what the candle is for.
                        —Peter Benenson, founder, Amnesty International, 1961

THE GROWING IMPORTANCE OF NONSTATE ACTORS IN INTERNA-
tional human rights challenges the state-centric view that remains at the
core of most international relations theories, especially realist thinking.
Neoliberalism and liberalism, although more global in their thinking, can
also be regarded as somewhat state-centric to the extent that they also
advocate the expansion of global capitalism, carried out by states, as an
end in itself, overlooking the short-term impact on ordinary people in
developing countries. Even constructivism tends to be state-centric
because the identities and interests it highlights are those of states (Barnett 2008). The increasing influence of nonstate actors became apparent
in the 1970s, when international relations theorists like Oran Young
(1972) began to suggest a "mixed actor" model of world politics and
Robert Keohane and Joseph Nye (1977) outlined a theory of complex
interdependence that included state and nonstate actors. In 1990 James
Rosenau's *Turbulence in World Politics* developed a full-blown paradigm
for analyzing change in a complex, multicentric, and pluralistic global
landscape in which modern technology profoundly influences politics,
and nonstate actors participate directly in shaping world political events
and conditions. Two worlds concurrently exist, according to Rosenau
(1990): one populated by sovereign states and another occupied by a mul-
titude of diverse "sovereignty-free" actors, simultaneously both existing
within the jurisdiction of states and acting outside of them.

The term *nonstate actor* refers to a broad range of diverse actors, with varied interests and motives. Nonstate actors include international intergovernmental organizations like the United Nations or European Community, international NGOs, transnational corporations (TNCs), transnational banks (TNBs), churches and religious organizations, international crime syndicates, cartels, military contractors, ethnopolitical and communal groups, armed nonstate actors, and social movements. In this chapter, I survey nonstate actors that can or do have a positive and promotional influence on international human rights. TNCs and TNBs are also included because although their purpose is to create wealth and generate profits, and they are often accused of doing so at the expense of human rights, they are increasingly under pressure to incorporate respect for internationally recognized human rights into their policies and business activities. They are also criticized for doing business with governments whose human rights records are poor, especially when they seem motivated to increase profits by overlooking substandard wages and working conditions, unsafe workplaces, and exposure to environmental risks.

While national governmental and international intergovernmental actors and institutions have been slow to respond when international human rights violations including genocide are in progress, private sector action to promote respect for human rights has exploded over the past several decades. Most of this increased activity is a result of the dramatic proliferation of NGOs—from 176 in 1909, to 1,255 by 1954, to nearly 8,000 today (Kegley and Blanton 2014). Individuals acting privately or getting involved in social movements and domestic human rights groups and centers have also had a profound impact on broadening and deepening awareness of international human rights. In some cases, individuals have spearheaded efforts to mobilize the shame of world public opinion, and in others, they have been instrumental in stopping ongoing violations and bringing violators to justice.

These activities also provide growing evidence of an emerging international civil society. The World Bank has adopted the following definition of civil society:

> The term civil society [refers] to the wide array of non-governmental and not-for-profit organizations that have a presence in public life, expressing the interests and values of their members or others, based on ethical, cultural, political, scientific, religious or philanthropic considerations. Civil Society Organizations (CSOs) therefore refer to a wide of array of organizations: community groups, non-governmental organizations (NGOs), labor unions, indigenous groups, charitable organizations, faith-based organizations, professional associations, and foundations. (World Bank 2013)

The development of a global civil society is evident in the articulation, development, and strengthening (or undermining) of certain norms.

Research on human rights norms focuses on how they are articulated and diffused throughout the system, for instance, from the top down (international to local), or bottom up, from the grassroots or from nonstate actors like NGOs (Klotz 1995; Finnemore 1996; Finnemore and Sikkink 1998; Risse, Ropp, and Sikkink 1999). Although international relations have long been viewed as a system of institutional relationships, the emergence of system-wide norms, particularly those grounded in values associated with human rights, suggests to some scholars the emergence of a society that is more than a system of relations (Albert, Brock, and Wolf 2000; Brown 2000). Human rights play a special role in mobilizing individuals as private citizens around common values and norms. Private sector activities that promote human rights may be more important today, in part because states have not lived up to the promise enshrined in the UN Charter and elsewhere of protecting human rights either within their borders or by holding one another accountable.

International NGOs have been particularly influential in determining the policies of and the projects funded by the World Bank (Glennie 2011). Under pressure from transnational environmental and indigenous rights groups in the mid-1990s, the Bank created a mechanism for public input and accountability called the World Bank's Inspection Panel. People in developing countries where World Bank projects are planned or under way can make complaints about negative environmental and social impacts directly to the panel. No other international organization provides such opportunities. Communities negatively impacted by Bank projects essentially have a voice and a seat at the table and often come away with concessions, including even stopping some projects until the damage is mitigated. For example, in 2011 the Bank suspended loans to Cambodia in the midst of a controversy over the eviction of thousands of people in order to build luxury apartments and a shopping area in downtown Phnom Penh (Tran 2011). The controversy arose after complaints were made to the World Bank's Inspection Panel.

Like states, the role of nonstate actors can also cut two ways. NGOs often act internationally much like domestic interest groups. However, they can also be part of a large social movement that challenges existing power relations rather than, as interest groups do, simply influencing them. NGOs acting on behalf of indigenous peoples challenge the state-centric view of sovereignty and world order, by, for example, advancing their concerns by working for the development of an international convention that would obligate states to respect the rights of indigenous peoples, including their inherent sovereignty (Wilmer 1993).

Other nonstate actors work to advance private interests rather than social welfare or economic justice. The activities of TNCs and TNBs raise the issue of legal liability and standing, a subject explored by Philip Alston and Mary Robinson (2005). International organizations—which are also nonstate actors—have long been recognized as having standing under international law (Nijman 2004). As subjects of international law, they have both rights and obligations, although what those are is still the subject of much debate.

As I proceed in this chapter, I survey a variety of private sector actors that influence or are influenced by the emergence of international human rights norms. NGOs and TNCs are the most recognizable nonstate private actors, but I also cover individuals, social movements, and national human rights groups and centers. I conclude with a brief look at international efforts to articulate and foster compliance with human rights norms and ethics aimed at TNCs and other private sector business enterprises.

## NGOs and the Promotion of Human Rights

NGOs play a prominent role in the implementation and enforcement of human rights norms. Citizen-based advocacy for human rights is not a modern phenomenon. The Society for the Mitigation and Gradual Abolition of Slavery Throughout the British Dominions was founded in 1823. It focused on the abolition of slavery within Great Britain and British dominions. Having succeeded in doing so by 1839, its work was extended to a worldwide abolition effort as the British and Foreign Anti-Slavery Society. The International Committee for the Red Cross was founded in Geneva, Switzerland, in 1865 after Swiss businessman Henry Dunant watched thousands of soldiers die on the battlefield at Solferino in 1859 during the Second Italian War for Independence. The proliferation of NGOs over the past sixty years, largely prompted in response to the horrors of the Holocaust, also reflects the rapid pace of transportation and communication technology and the shrinking world that puts everyone's backyard in everyone else's living room.

Amnesty International is probably the most high-profile international human rights NGO today. Founded in 1961 by British lawyer Peter Benenson, Amnesty International has more than 3 million supporters in more than 150 countries worldwide (Amnesty International 2013). Although initially the organization focused on political prisoners, today Amnesty International has offices in eighty countries and publishes country reports on violence against women, children's rights, disappearances, health, refugees and immigrants, indigenous peoples, and the role of business in promoting or depriving individuals of their inherent human rights. Amnesty International maintains a researchable database including more than 50,000 reports that date from the 1970s to the present.

Since 1961, a number of other NGOs have also become influential in bringing pressure to bear on governments that violate human rights. They act as consultants in treaty negotiations, organize direct action on behalf of individuals at risk in countries with a consistent record of gross violations, mobilize public opinion, and provide direct assistance to victims of human rights abuses. Some of the more prominent international human rights NGOs are Human Rights Watch, Freedom House, the International Commission of Jurists, and Human Rights First.

NGOs use a variety of strategies to promote respect for human rights and improvement in conditions where human rights violations are taking place. As Father Robert Drinan (2002), law professor at Georgetown University, argued, they shine the light of public opinion on governments that violate rights by engaging in fact-finding, monitoring, reporting, on-site visitations, and mobilizing public campaigns aimed at particular countries or situations. They also promote awareness through human rights education so that people know what their rights are and how to seek redress. NGOs can take direct action by providing technical training and assistance to in-country human rights groups and governments transitioning to democracy, by providing humanitarian assistance, by lobbying governments to incorporate protection of human rights into their foreign policies or to undertake enforcement action, and by instituting lawsuits against violators.

Focusing world public opinion on specific cases enables NGOs to exert pressure on government officials to be more accountable than they would be otherwise. This spotlight can literally save lives as political prisoners whose fate may never have been known become cases of interest beyond the borders of the countries that imprison or detain them. Torturing and killing someone is harder when the world is watching. Putting a spotlight on abuses is one of Amnesty International's most successful strategies—calls to urgent action can mobilize tens or hundreds of thousands of letters to in-country officials at both local and national levels when the lives of political prisoners hang in the balance.

Similar to Amnesty International, Human Rights Watch and its regional offices monitor and report on conditions in countries of concern, enabling a steady stream of information to flow out of the darkest corners of repressive states into the light of international attention. Although criticized by some as biased toward countries friendlier with the United States, Freedom House collects data that can be used by researchers and policymakers to evaluate progress toward democratization, which goes hand in hand with respect for human rights and due process (Steiner 2014). Other groups, like the International Commission of Jurists, work to support the rule of law and judicial process to enable people in countries with repressive governments to strengthen protection of human rights and the democratization of institutions.

## National Human Rights Groups and Centers

Although when one thinks of an NGO, international organizations like Amnesty International and the Red Cross usually come to mind, a majority of states also have national human rights centers, commissions, or national NGOs that deal exclusively or primarily with in-country concerns. Many of the older ones, like the Mothers of Plaza de Mayo in Argentina or the Helsinki watch groups in former Soviet republics and Eastern European communist states, have been instrumental in bringing about democratization and ending human rights violations. Other national NGOs have been established in the aftermath of human rights tragedies like the genocide in Rwanda, such as the Sphere Project that coordinates global human rights networks, or operate in political environments that repress fundamental civil liberties, such as the Foundation for Human Rights in Cuba.

In new states, postcolonial states, and states in transition from nondemocratic forms of government, national human rights groups and centers play a critical role in the development of due process, an independent judiciary, open political participation, and democratic institution building. They monitor and report on conditions in their own societies and hold new leaders and institutions accountable. Some groups receive technical and financial support from philanthropists and centers in older, more well-established democratic societies. The Open Society Institute, now called Open Society Foundations, founded by Hungarian multimillionaire businessman George Soros in 1993, initially focused primarily on making grants to groups and educational programs that foster knowledge of democracy and social science research in eastern and central Europe. The Open Society Foundations now have programs in Latin America, Africa, and Asia as well. However, Soros was involved in human rights philanthropy in South Africa and in communist bloc countries long before the end of the Cold War. *Time* magazine estimated that as of 2007 Soros had given away more than $6 billion. Many of his investments in democratization projects led to the creation of national human rights centers and leaders throughout the world.

Older democracies have longer histories of progressively reducing or eliminating discrimination and expanding political participation, usually in response to protests and social movements such as the civil rights movement in the United States and union activism in Europe. The US war on terror, however, has raised new concerns about violations of civil liberties and due process. Questionable governmental actions include the use of drones to execute targets without due process, the massive warrantless surveillance of private communications involving the United States and most of its major allies as revealed by Edward Snowden, and the use of torture and detentions without trial in the Guantanamo Bay detention camp.

Older democracies tend to have fewer broadly focused human rights centers and groups; instead, groups are more focused on specific issues mobilized in response to confrontations and working toward reforms. Women's rights activists and organizations, such as the National Organization for Women, have a long history of success leading to democratic reform, from suffragists in the late nineteenth century to equal rights advocates in the 1970s. Contemporary women's issues are focused on equal pay and remuneration for mostly unpaid child and family care work that reduces their lifetime wage and salary income earnings, retirement, and benefits. Other groups have worked tirelessly to safeguard minority rights in light of widespread discrimination against and marginalization of national, ethnic, linguistic, and cultural minorities, such as the more than eighty groups regularly active in Minority Rights Group International, a coalition of advocacy groups promoting minority rights.

Older democracies also often have nonpartisan civil liberties watchdog groups. The mission of the National Council for Civil Liberties—now known as Liberty—in England, founded in 1934, is to protect civil liberties and promote human rights through public awareness campaigns, litigation, lobbying members of Parliament, and publishing policy analyses. One of the earliest campaigns undertaken by the council was against film censorship in the 1930s. They have worked for reform in the treatment of the mentally ill, equal rights for women, and an end to discrimination. More recently, the council has challenged the policies and tactics used by the British government in connection with the US war on terror through a number of lawsuits filed under the 1998 British Human Rights Act.

Other former colonies of England have their own groups. The New Zealand Council for Civil Liberties was founded in 1952 after a conflict set off by a waterfront workers strike protesting their exclusion from court-ordered wage increases after World War II. Australia has two civil liberties watchdog organizations: the Australian Civil Liberties Union and Civil Liberties Australia. The Canadian Civil Liberties Association was formed in 1964 over concerns about expanded police powers.

The oldest is probably the American Civil Liberties Union (ACLU), founded in 1920 in response to US government repression of antiwar speech. The ACLU has championed some of the most celebrated victories in civil liberties in the United States. It secured legal representation for biology teacher John Scopes in 1925, who was prosecuted for violating a state ban on teaching evolution. The ACLU renounced the internment of over 100,000 Japanese Americans during World War II and joined the National Association for the Advancement of Colored People in its landmark *Brown v. Board of Education* case that overturned racial segregation in schools. It defended the free speech rights of Nazi demonstrators in Skokie, Illinois, and, as with their English counterpart, opposed torture, violations of privacy, and a variety of legislation and policies that compromise the right to due process and individual civil liberties in connection with the war on terror and revelations in the Snowden documents.

One can have little doubt that the creation of Helsinki watch groups helped undermine the capacity of repressive communist governments to remain in power in the Soviet Union and the eastern and central European countries under its influence. The Conference on Security and Cooperation in Europe, aimed at improving security through more open relations between the countries of the eastern and western blocs of Europe, met in Helsinki in 1973 and produced the Helsinki Final Act in 1975, which, among other things, called for respect for human rights and fundamental freedoms. The act was signed by the United States, Canada, and Western European states as well as states then under communist governments, including Bulgaria, Czechoslovakia, Finland, the German Democratic Republic (East Germany), Hungary, Poland, Romania, the Soviet Union, and Yugoslavia. Citizens in these states then set up citizen-based watch groups to monitor their own governments' compliance with the spirit of the Helsinki agreements. Individuals who believed their rights were being violated could bring those concerns to the citizen groups, who then attempted to pressure their governments through both internal and external public campaigns to remedy the complaints. After the fall of communist regimes, these Helsinki watch groups played critical roles in facilitating the transition to democratization. In the case of former Yugoslavia, watch groups in Serbia, Croatia, and Bosnia all tried to keep the light of national and world public opinion on those responsible for the wars, war crimes, and repression of dissent during the 1990s.

## Individuals and the Development of Human Rights

Any discussion of individuals' impact on the contemporary development of international human rights must begin with Eleanor Roosevelt, cofounder of Freedom House in 1940, founder of the UN Association of the United States of America in 1943, US representative to the UN General Assembly from 1945 to 1952, and, most famously, chair of the committee that drafted the Universal Declaration of Human Rights. "How wonderful it is that nobody need wait a single moment before starting to improve the world," wrote Anne Frank in her diary. So many individuals have improved the world by advocating for human rights and choosing the difficult path of resisting oppression and defending human rights that their names alone could fill a book. A discussion of some of the more historically well-known human rights leaders as well as more recent champions illustrates the range of individual actions and the scope of their impact.

Prominent individuals in the arts, media, and business can also use their role in the spotlight of public opinion to promote human rights advocacy. U2 musician Bono was recognized for his humanitarian work along with Bill and Melinda Gates as *Time* magazine's 2005 persons of the year. DATA, which stands for Debt, AIDS, Trade, Africa, is a nongovernmental organization founded by Bono that fights poverty and the spread of the human immunodeficiency virus (HIV) and the resultant acquired immune deficiency syndrome (AIDS) in developing countries. Bono was also one of the performers at the 1985 benefit concert called Live Aid, organized by musician-activist Bob Geldof. That same year, Steven Van Zandt, who plays with Bruce Springsteen's E Street Band, mobilized a number of performers to form Artists United Against Apartheid. A related British organization, Artists Against Apartheid, performed concerts to publicize and oppose the human rights abuses of the South African regime in 1986 and on Nelson Mandela's seventieth birthday in 1988. This group was an outgrowth of the Rock Against Racism movement that started in England in the 1970s (Treaty Database Online 2006). From the civil and political rights violations of apartheid to the social and economic issues of AIDS and poverty, as influential members of civil society, performing artists have long been engaged in raising consciousness through public discourse about human rights issues.

Many famous international human rights advocates have also been awarded the Nobel Peace Prize, legacy of Swedish industrialist Alfred Nobel. The prize was first awarded in 1901 to recognize those who, as Nobel stipulated in his will, "shall have done the most or the best work for fraternity between nations, for the abolition or reduction of standing armies and for the holding and promotion of peace congresses" (Nobel Peace Prize n.d.). From 1901 to 2009, the prize was awarded to ninety-seven individuals and twenty-three organizations, from Henry Dunant, founder of the International Committee of the Red Cross, in 1901 and Muhammad Yunus, microfinance Grameen Bank founder, in 2006 to UN Peacekeeping Forces in 1988 and the Intergovernmental Panel on Climate Change in 2007. Alfred Nobel must be certainly counted among the most influential historical figures whose actions created a legacy of consciousness raising on issues of peace and human rights.

While men hold most of the Nobel Prizes, women have fair representation. Wangari Maathai, 2004 Nobel Peace Prize recipient, biological scientist, and the first woman in east or central Africa to earn a doctoral degree, has promoted both women's rights and environmental action. Her work led to the mobilization of the Green Belt Movement, which has aided women in planting more than 20 million trees throughout East Africa. Shrin Ebadi was awarded the Nobel Peace Prize in 2003 for her advocacy of human rights and democracy in Iran. Ebadi was a judge who was removed from her position following the radical Islamic Iranian revolution because Islam, according to Iranian clerics, forbids women to be judges. Ebadi went on to write books, advocate for women's and children's rights, defend journalists targeted for exercising freedom of expression, and founded the Defenders of Human Rights Center, which provides legal representation to individual victims of human rights violations in Iran.

The most remarkable individuals not only influence the world in their own time but their example continues to shine for those who follow. Mahatma Gandhi led all of present-day India and Pakistan to independence through engaged, nonviolent resistance to British colonial rule. His example has had so much impact that in 2007, Gandhi's birthday, October 2, was declared by the United Nations to be the International Day of Non-Violence. His example inspired, among others, US civil rights leader Dr. Martin Luther King Jr. to persist in using only nonviolent civil disobedience to oppose US racial apartheid and discrimination in the 1960s. The combined examples of Gandhi and King inspired Kosovar Albanian president Ibrahim Rugova to maintain nonviolent resistance against the Serbian government of Slobodan Milošević. South African president Nelson Mandela said, in his speech accepting the Nobel Peace Prize, "Let the strivings of us all prove Martin Luther King Jr. to have been correct, when he said that humanity can no longer be tragically bound to the starless midnight of racism and war."

Nelson Mandela, a lifetime activist and the first black president of South Africa, was among several remarkable figures to emerge in the contest over apartheid in South Africa. Mandela, who died in 2013, received a Nobel Peace Prize along with President F. W. de Klerk in 1993 for working to end apartheid in South Africa. The following year Archbishop Desmond Tutu was awarded the prize. Tutu's commitment was not only to the promotion of and respect for human rights by opposing the apartheid regime but to restorative justice and reconciliation. Tutu's leadership on reconciliation and human rights extends well beyond South Africa. He is known for his work on HIV/AIDS prevention and treatment, alleviating poverty, promoting democracy throughout the postcolonial world, and advocating an end to the Israeli occupation of Palestinian territories. He served on the board of directors for the ICC's Trust Fund for Victims and on a UN advisory panel on genocide.

Aung San Suu Kyi, 1991 recipient of the Nobel Peace Prize, was the first general secretary of the National League of Democracy formed in Myanmar during a 1988 prodemocratization uprising. The party was openly committed to nonviolence and civil disobedience in its pursuit of popular democracy for Myanmar. The military government banned her from taking part in elections and, without charges, placed her under house arrest in 1989. Even with its leader in detention, the National League of Democracy won 82 percent of the votes in May 1990. Aung San Suu Kyi would actually have been the first democratically elected leader of Myanmar since the 1962 military takeover of the government, but the election results were not recognized by the so-called State Law and Order Restoration Council, which took over in 1988. She has been imprisoned, detained, allowed only restrictive movement, or under house arrest ever since. She was also restricted from participating in elections in 2010. Suu Kyi used her Nobel Peace Prize award of $1.3 million to create an educational and health trust fund for the people of Myanmar.

The fourteenth dalai lama (Tenzin Gyatso), a Nobel Peace Prize winner in 1989, has not only advocated tirelessly for the self-determination of the Tibetan people but, unlike previous dalai lamas, has cultivated numerous contacts with Western political and spiritual leaders in order to advance world peace and international respect for human rights of all people. He has written, coauthored, or been the subject of 134 books ranging from Buddhist teachings to the intersection between science and spirituality and cosmology and physics. Much of his time and attention is directed toward intercultural and interreligious dialogue, understanding, and appreciation. His message has been one of compassion across differences as a necessity in an irreversibly interdependent world. He teaches that compassion is an ethic: "Compassion and love are not mere luxuries. As the source of both inner and external peace, they are fundamental to the continued survival of our species" (Dalai Lama 1999:130).

Chico Mendes was not a Nobel Prize winner, but his leadership, commitment, and personal sacrifice nevertheless illustrate the impact an individual can have on raising awareness and promoting respect not only for civil and political human rights but also economic and social rights. Francisco Alves "Chico" Mendes was a Brazilian rubber tapper who helped found the Xapuri Rural Workers' Union and then the National Council of Rubber Tappers. He advocated for the creation of reserves of rubber trees to preserve both the livelihood of rubber tappers and the environmental integrity of the rainforest. He worked to maintain nonviolent tactics among his supporters in opposition to rainforest destruction. He drew international attention when he attended a meeting of the Inter-American Development Bank to stop a bank-funded road project through the rainforest. He succeeded in stopping the road and protecting the reserves and won several environmental awards as a result but was assassinated by cattle-ranching enemies of his efforts in 1988, just one year after his trip to protest the road project. His legacy includes not only the reserve he fought for and which is now named after him, but more than twenty other reserves protecting 8 million acres of rainforest.

## Social Movements and the Development of Human Rights

Social movements are broad-based, bottom-up collective actions characterized by the informal association of individuals or organizations or a combination of both. Many are focused on rights since social movements are aimed at values, and rights allocate values, for example, the right to form labor unions or prohibitions against that right or the right of women to make reproductive choices without government oversight or regulation. Social movements have been around at least since the rise of the secular, citizen-governed state that emerged from popular democratic revolutions in the seventeenth and eighteenth centuries. Today they are larger and more numerous and have broader reach and impact than ever. Social scientists today distinguish between popular uprisings, like those that gave rise to the populist revolutions in Europe, and various labor movements emerging from class conflict and contemporary or "new social movements" that focus on changing social and political values.

Many movements seek to influence national policies but do so both from within and from without, particularly if they believe that bringing external pressure from the international community to bear on human rights violations is likely to be more effective than strategies aimed solely on efforts to address such wrongs from within the state. Indigenous peoples' global activism reflects this approach. Although indigenous peoples can be

---

### Mothers of the Plaza de Mayo

On April 30, 1977, fourteen mothers whose sons and daughters went missing—presumed to have been abducted by the government—during Argentina's "dirty war" (1976–1983) demonstrated in front of the presidential palace on the Plaza de Mayo. The movement became known as the "Mothers of the Plaza de Mayo" or "Mothers of the Disappeared."

The authoritarian right-wing government that came to power in the aftermath of a coup that overthrew Isabel Martínez de Perón in March 1976 targeted union leaders, left-wing activists and journalists, Peronist guerrillas, and people suspected of sympathizing with those who opposed the military junta and the right-wing president Augusto Pinochet. Estimates of the number of people abducted and tortured range from 10,000 to 30,000, including hundreds born to mothers pregnant during their long detention as well as three of the movement's founders. The military admitted to 9,000 missing.

After the military government transitioned to civilian control in 1983, the group continued to press for answers as to the whereabouts and fates of their missing family members. The National Commission on the Disappeared was created to investigate and turn over to the courts the relevant evidence in cases where crimes were committed. In 1986, the Mothers of the Plaza de Mayo split into two groups—those who continued to press for closure by documenting the fates of the disappeared and those who formed a more politically radical group to pursue the restoration of a more "Peronist" style of socialist government.

found in virtually every part of the world, indigenous leaders, communities, and organizations from the Western Hemisphere have taken the lead in mobilizing international efforts to secure recognition and respect for their rights in the states in which they now live. Contemporary activism started in the early 1970s and led to the creation of a working group on indigenous peoples within the United Nations under the Sub-Commission on Prevention of Discrimination and Protection of Minorities. The working group's process brought hundreds of indigenous groups into a discussion that led to several reports and finally a draft of the Declaration on the Rights of Indigenous Peoples. When presented to the General Assembly in September of 2007, the declaration was opposed by the United States, Canada, New Zealand, Australia, and the United States; all have since said they will change their position and support the declaration. Since General Assembly declarations often become the basis for subsequent conventions, this particular document is very significant both as a signal that indigenous rights are so widely supported and that the four powerful settler states with substantial indigenous constituencies (but not with the largest percentage of indigenous populations) initially opposed but now seem clearly to support international recognition of indigenous rights.

## Transnational Advocacy Networks and the World Social Forum

A transnational advocacy network (TAN) is a coalition or network of advocates that work across national borders to bring about social change. According to Margaret Keck and Kathryn Sikkink (1998), three conditions make the rise of TANs likely: (1) the unresponsiveness of domestic political actors to a domestic group's concerns (usually related to legal inequality or violence against vulnerable people), (2) a belief by political leaders of domestic advocacy groups that transnational networking will help them achieve their objectives, and (3) opportunity to meet and network transnationally through conferences or other kinds of gatherings. Transnational social movements are most evident on issues related to women, environmental concerns, indigenous peoples, and opposition to neoliberal economic globalization. Examples include Women for Women International, started during the Yugoslav wars in 1993 by women in Bosnia and Herzegovina; the Women's International League for Peace and Freedom, founded in 1915; the World Council of Indigenous Peoples, founded in the 1970s, which now has NGO status at the United Nations; and the many environmental and antiglobalization groups that mobilized protests focused on the World Trade Organization, the most famous being the 1999 Seattle protests.

Perhaps the largest TAN is the World Social Forum, a network of civil society organizations and individuals sharing a common concern for reconstructing social, economic, and political relations around an alternative to neoliberal globalization. It is a network that advocates values across national boundaries. Organized around principles of "sustainable development," members work toward the idea that "social and economic justice lies in alternative models for people-centered and self-reliant progress" (World Social Forum India 2006). The movement began in 2001 when a coalition of groups and individuals critical of the neoliberal model of global capitalism in what is sometimes loosely referred to as an antiglobalization movement met in Porto Alegre, Brazil, to show solidarity for an alternative concept of globalization. They contrasted their agenda and vision of global economic order with that of the state-centered World Economic Forum meeting in Davos, Switzerland. Over 10,000 people attended this first World Social Forum, 140,000 people attended the Mumbai forum in 2004, and over 150,000 returned to Porto Alegre in 2005. The forum has moved to a more polycentric structure—multiple forums held simultaneously at several locations, initially in the Global South, but now in rich industrialized countries too. They are characterized by an open space organizational philosophy that gives voice to anyone who wishes to speak and they encourage bottom-up dialogue. These features of open space mean that it is anti- or nonhierarchical and anti-elite. The forum's aspirations are outlined in a set of fourteen principles approved by the organizing committee of the first forum. The overall vision is a radical democratization of world order centered on economic and social justice and equality of access. Principles 4, 10, and 11 elaborate this vision:

> 4. The alternatives proposed at the World Social Forum stand in opposition to a process of globalisation commanded by the large multinational corporations and by the governments and international institutions at the service of those corporations' interests, with the complicity of national governments. They are designed to ensure that globalisation in solidarity will prevail as a new stage in world history. This will respect universal human rights, and those of all citizens—men and women—of all nations and the environment and will rest on democratic international systems and institutions at the service of social justice, equality and the sovereignty of peoples. . . .
>
> 10. The World Social Forum is opposed to all totalitarian and reductionist views of economy, development and history and to the use of violence as a means of social control by the State. It upholds respect for Human Rights, the practices of real democracy, participatory democracy, peaceful relations, in equality and solidarity, among people, ethnicities, genders and peoples, and condemns all forms of domination and all subjection of one person by another.
>
> 11. As a forum for debate the World Social Forum is a movement of ideas that prompts reflection, and the transparent circulation of the results

of that reflection, on the mechanisms and instruments of domination by capital, on means and actions to resist and overcome that domination, and on the alternatives proposed to solve the problems of exclusion and social inequality that the process of capitalist globalisation with its racist, sexist and environmentally destructive dimensions is creating internationally and within countries.

Criticism of the World Social Forum ranges from the far left, which views it as weak on actionable ideas (reflected, for example, by the communist party protest against the 2004 meeting in Mumbai, India), to those complaining that it only represents ideological goals of the left. Some groups representing the poorest of the poor also complain that its nature as a forum requires expensive international travel and accommodation and therefore favors donor-funded NGOs and leaves the poorest grassroots groups underrepresented (Barnett 2008).

Despite the criticism, the United Nations has shown support for the World Social Forum both by participating and by making public its view of the importance of the forum for partnership between international intergovernmental organizations and NGOs within a broader global civil society framework. UNESCO has said that

> [its] presence at the WSF [World Social Forum] marks the will of the United Nations system both to recognize civil society as an important player in international cooperation and to work towards reconstituting links with political decision-makers and the State. It shows its determination to:
>  • Listen to the messages of civil society;
>  • Consolidate existing partnerships and identify new ones;
>  • Act as an intermediary in building bridges between civil society and political decision-makers;
>  • Reaffirm its commitment to support the emergence of a different globalization. (Wallerstein 2007)

UNESCO therefore sees the World Social Forum as creating an opportunity for dialogue and a laboratory of ideas for the renewal of public policies that guarantee the right to education for everyone, respect for diversity, and democracy (Rasheed 2008).

## Promoting Corporate Responsibility

As Surya Deva noted, "states no longer enjoy a monopoly as violators of human rights" (2004:493). TNCs and TNBs have dramatically expanded their reach and influence throughout the world over the past four to five decades. Jed Greer and Kavaljit Singh (2000) estimated that between 1970 and 2000 the number of TNC parent companies grew from 7,000 to 38,000, controlling 207,000 foreign subsidiaries with 90 percent of them based in industrialized countries. In spite of the large number of corporations, the top 100 companies account for about 30 percent of all foreign domestic investment (where controlling ownership, or investors, of an enterprise located in one country are citizens of a different country), indicating a highly concentrated structure of economic power (Greer and Singh 2000). Liberalization of international trade has led many companies to establish subsidiaries in or move their base of operations to countries where the costs of labor are much lower and governmental regulation is much looser than in the rich industrialized countries.

The growing number of TNCs has also spawned an increase in the number of TNBs (Kowalewski 1983). TNCs facilitate the global movement of capital that enables TNCs to expand operations, but they have less direct influence on the human rights conditions related to TNC activity than intergovernmental or multilateral TNBs. The World Bank, along with various regional international development banks like the Inter-American Development Bank, the Asian Development Bank, and the African Development Bank, have been the targets of human rights campaigns aimed at requiring them to formulate policies that promote and respect internationally recognized human rights. These banks have generally been responsive and have instituted rules requiring impact studies of funded projects on the people and communities in countries where the funded projects are undertaken.

## Exploitation of Developing Countries and Consequent Disasters

Liberalization of world trade has occurred in conjunction with a simultaneous reduction of government involvement in the private sector. Businesses maximize profits in part by holding down or reducing costs, and they have few incentives to self-regulate to protect human rights or the environment. Lower labor costs and fewer regulatory restrictions often mean that working and environmental conditions are well below the standards in rich countries, leaving more people in the workplace at higher risk of injury and even death. A well-known example—and perhaps the most tragic to date—was the 1984 explosion of the Union Carbide India Limited chemical plant in Bhopal, India, which left 2,000 dead immediately by the explosion and another 1,787 from related chemical exposure. According to the government of Madhya Pradesh, the Indian province in which the plant was housed, damages have been awarded in 574,366 cases for injuries related to the accident.

The collapse of the Rana Plaza garment factory complex in Bangladesh in 2013 is another horrifying example of the consequences brought on by unsafe working conditions. A total of 1,129 people were confirmed killed and several hundred missing when the search for survivors ended in May 2013. That tragedy followed several other deadly garment factory fires in Bangladesh. The building that collapsed included four stories constructed in violation of building codes, and a citation had already been issued for a substandard foundation. The factory produced clothing for major Western clothing brands, and Bangladesh is—or was—the second leading garment exporter after China (Manik and Yardley 2013). In June 2013, President Barack Obama announced a suspension of Bangladesh trade privileges with the United States because the Bangladesh government was "not taking steps to afford internationally recognized worker rights to workers in that country" (Greenhouse 2013).

Both Chevron and Shell oil companies have been implicated in some of the most egregious violations of human rights in the oil-rich Niger Delta region. Opposition to oil development on both human rights and environmental grounds gave rise to organized nonviolent protests in the 1990s, spearheaded by the Ogoni people, whose community and traditional land base received the most direct impact. Ken Saro-Wiwa, who was Ogoni and a member of the Movement for the Survival of the Ogoni People, emerged as the most visible leader of these efforts. Between 1992 and 1995, Saro-Wiwa was subjected to a series of arrests followed by imprisonment without trial. Eventually, he was brought to trial on charges that he murdered four Ogoni chiefs allegedly opposed to his activities. Found guilty, even though the evidence that he actually committed the crimes was suspicious at best, he was executed by hanging in 1995. His family and supporters filed lawsuits against Shell in relation to his death along with those of eight other protesters. In June 2009, Shell settled out of court for $15.5 million just before the trial was set to begin, but the company did not accept legal liability for the protesters' deaths. Chevron is also believed to be complicit in government repression and even murder of activists who oppose oil extraction in the Niger Delta, though no legal action has ever been brought.

Chevron has also been highly criticized for environmental and groundwater contamination, dumping toxic waste, and leaving 18.5 million gallons of waste in 600 unlined oil pits in an area of Amazonian Ecuador traditionally occupied by indigenous communities. The oil extraction took place between 1964 and 1990. The first lawsuit was filed in US District Court in 1993, but the court only dealt with the question of whether the United States was the proper venue to hear the case. In 2002, the court concluded that the case had to be heard in Ecuador, a decision upheld in an appeal. The judgment of the Ecuadorian court, however, could be enforceable in the United States. A new suit was filed in Ecuador in 2003. Relying heavily on written testimony and documentary evidence, in 2008, a court-appointed expert initially recommended a $16.3 billion award for damages, a figure subsequently revised upward to $27 billion (*San Francisco Sentinel* 2014). In March 2014, however, the US District Court in New York ruled that the Ecuadorian judgment was the product of fraud and racketeering activity and is thereby unenforceable in the United States. Controversy over the case arose when possible forgery and discrepancies in figures submitted by a scientific expert on behalf of the Ecuadorans were discovered (*San Francisco Sentinel* 2014).

Allegations of severe environmental contamination, serious health effects, and human rights violations were also made against Chevron in California and against Chevron's subsidiary, Unocal, in Myanmar. Human rights watchdog EarthRights accuses Chevron of involvement in human rights abuses in connection with its operations in Myanmar, including rape, extrajudicial executions, and forced labor (Erman 2008). Lawsuits were filed against Unocal in both California state court and federal district court under the ATCA, raising the question of corporate responsibility for human rights abuses. The US government opposed this argument because setting such a precedent could interfere with US foreign policy. Notably, the court rejected this view, finding that corporations are liable under the ATCA when they are involved with governments that violate human rights on their behalf. Both the federal and the state cases were settled out of court before they could go to trial in front of a jury.

### Promoting Human Rights Responsibility Among Corporations

For the past four decades or so, an emerging concern has been corporate social responsibility that is more broadly conceived as including working conditions, environmental impacts, and respect for internationally recognized human rights. Many of the issues discussed in this chapter and others in this book suggest a strong connection among these concerns. For example, environmentally damaging activities often adversely impact clean water and health, which are human rights issues. Working conditions and labor practices are also human rights concerns. Another factor contributing to the growing focus on corporate responsibility is the simultaneous expansion of corporate influence along with an ideological shift toward less government involvement in the private sector. Corporate social responsibility is the idea that businesses ought to be good citizens and self-regulate their conduct with an eye to its social impact.

Efforts aimed at promoting corporate responsibility for respecting human rights reflect not only the growth of corporations and their influence in general terms but also an emerging recognition of corporations as citizens or legal entities not only in the societies of their origin but in all the societies in which they operate. As was stated and shown above, corporations as well as states can violate human rights. The duty to respect human rights falls on all individuals, including when they associate collectively to constitute a corporation, as does an obligation not to engage in activities that hinder government efforts to protect human rights, such as passing legislation to protect workers, to allow workers to organize, and to establish safety regulations for the workplace.

A number of highly publicized advocacy campaigns have been directed toward specific TNCs for their labor practices, including the use of child labor and maintenance of sweatshops that exploit the impoverished conditions of many developing countries. The high-profile international campaign begun in the 1990s against Nike for such practices led Nike to make promises to improve working conditions and to implement a "corporate social responsibility policy." Nike was criticized for paying wages so low in its Vietnam factories that they would not even cover the cost of three meals a day. It was also criticized for exposing workers to chemical air pollution and toxic fumes up to 177 times the legal limit in the countries where the factories were located and exploiting child labor, which was graphically exposed in a 1996 edition of *Life* magazine. The company responded by promising to meet US Occupational Safety and Health Administration standards for air quality in all its factories, raise the minimum employment age to sixteen in thirty-four factories, allow NGOs to monitor and publicize factory conditions, make high school equivalency education available to all workers, expand a worker microfinance loan program, and fund research on responsible business practices (Global Exchange 2007). Despite these promises and a proactive publicity campaign to dispel criticisms, human rights and labor groups continued to find the company falling short of ending exploitative labor practices (Read 2008).

One of the earliest boycott campaigns started in 1977 against Nestlé for misleading the public about the benefits of substituting infant formula for breast milk. This marketing campaign had an even greater negative impact among the poor in developing countries where as much as half of a family's income might be spent on the formula, and the dry formula might be mixed with contaminated water or overdiluted to make it last longer. The boycott against Nestlé was eventually supported by some 200 groups in about 100 countries and led to the adoption of the World Health Organization (WHO) International Code of Marketing of Breast-Milk Substitutes in 1981. But Nestlé's troubles did not end there. Nestlé has also been criticized for obstructing labor union organizing efforts, allegedly in collaboration with governments that repress human rights. The company has also been accused of utilizing child, forced, and trafficked labor in the African cocoa industry (International Labor Rights Forum 2009).

Some transnational organizations act as watchdogs of the TNCs. The campaign to end apartheid in South Africa brought the issue of international corporate social responsibility to the forefront of public attention in the 1970s when groups and individuals began to call for divestiture of business holdings by foreign investors in South Africa. The Interfaith Center on Corporate Responsibility (ICCR), an association of 275 faith-based institutional investors, for example, has its roots in the divestiture movement to pressure the South African government to end its apartheid policies. Today the ICCR ranks companies for climate risk profiles; advocates for reform in the meat industry because of practices that put consumers and workers at risk and have a negative environmental impact; pressures particular sectors known to exploit child labor; and targets companies engaging in alleged excessive executive compensation.

Formed in 1996, CorpWatch played a critical role in exposing the human rights records of Nike, Enron, and Chevron and aims its campaigns at exposing "multinational corporations that profit from war, fraud, environmental, human rights and other abuses, and to provide critical information to foster a more informed public and an effective democracy" (Corp-Watch 2014).

Though it might seem only obvious, the ILO has long been involved in promoting responsibility for human rights, particularly workers' rights, across the globe. The ILO passed the Declaration of Principles Concerning Multinational Enterprises and Social Policy in 1977 and reaffirmed and revised the declaration in 2000. Notably, although not a legally binding document, the declaration acknowledges that its principles, directed to governments, could also be applied to businesses and other private sector entities. The United Nations has historically had limited involvement in promoting corporate responsibility. However, the United Nations convened the UN Commission on Transnational Corporations in 1974. This commission held its first session in 1975 and its last in 1993 when its responsibilities were transferred to the UN Conference on Trade and Development. During its two decades of existence, the commission never focused much of its attention on human rights beyond the issue of divestiture in response to apartheid in South Africa and Namibia, though it did conduct several studies on infant and child nutrition in Africa. It did make an effort to develop a code of conduct for TNCs but failed to produce a final document. Much of its attention focused more broadly on corruption and on offering training courses for political and business leaders from postcolonial and newly industrializing countries on topics like technology transfer, accessing bond markets, and negotiating with TNCs.

The effort to promote corporate social responsibility through international action was reinvigorated in 1999 when then secretary-general Kofi Annan announced the Global Compact endorsing socially responsible business practices based on principles originally proposed at the World Economic Forum in Davos, Switzerland. The United Nations used the original nine principles developed at Davos and then added the tenth:

1. Support for internationally recognized human rights.
2. Obligation not to engage in activities complicit in human rights violations.
3. Freedom of association.
4. Recognition of the right to collective bargaining.
5. Elimination of compulsory and child labor.
6. Elimination of discrimination.
7. Precautionary approach to environmental challenges.
8. Promotion of environmentally responsible conduct.
9. Development and dissemination of environmentally friendly technologies.
10. Commitment to counter corruption, including extortion and bribery.

In 2000 the Organisation for Economic Co-operation and Development (OECD) revised its *Guidelines for Multinational Enterprises* calling on multinational businesses to have "respect for the human rights of those affected by their activities consistent with the host government's international obligations and commitments" and "encourage, where practicable, business partners, including suppliers and subcontractors, to apply principles of corporate conduct compatible with the *Guidelines*." The same year, a number of NGOs and corporate social responsibility organizations worked with a group of resource extraction companies to develop voluntary principles on security and human rights with support from the US, British, Norwegian, and Dutch governments. World leaders also affirmed the Millennium Development Goals, as will be discussed in Chapter 13, with virtually unanimous support in the United Nations.

The Global Compact prompted renewed international efforts to delineate TNC norms of social responsibility in 2003 when the Sub-Commission on the Promotion and Protection of Human Rights approved a statement of "Norms on the Responsibilities of Transnational Corporations and Other Business Enterprises with Regard to Human Rights." Surya Deva (2004) believed that these norms have been generally overlooked by academic human rights scholars and argued that they represent an important departure (if not a turning point) from past efforts because

1. They address human rights more comprehensively than previous efforts that focused primarily on environment and labor.
2. The norms are linked to obligations arising out of the UN Charter, which is a stronger and more widely accepted basis of human rights responsibilities than the Universal Declaration of Human Rights.

3. They focus on positive as well as negative obligations; that is, not only are TNCs obligated not to violate human rights but also positively obligated to "use their influence to promote and ensure respect for human rights."
4. Though the norms are still not binding, they delineate the nature of obligation for both states and TNCs in terms of "shall" rather than "should."
5. The provisions for implementation ask states to create legal and administrative frameworks for implementation by TNCs and to monitor, verify, and allow victims to seek redress in national courts and international tribunals.
6. Finally, the norms cover not only TNCs but also "other business enterprises," specifically naming partnerships, contractors, subcontractors, suppliers, licensees, distributors, and subsidiaries as having the same obligations.

However, Deva pointed out, the norms contain two important shortcomings that limit their potential as a vehicle for further progress toward a regulatory regime. First, they make a circuitous reference to international treaties as sources of law as to what constitutes violations, so the norms themselves cannot be used to ascertain violations. Second, acknowledging the universality of human rights makes more difficult the operationalization of obligations within particular local contexts. Universality is generally aspirational rather than operational as a standard that can be measured and monitored. Deva urged the United Nations to engage in a serious discussion of these shortcomings before moving to adopt the norms in the UN Commission on Human Rights, making them a legally binding document.

The subcommission that originally put forth the norms was hit by criticism that the entire effort was "antibusiness," and the UN Human Rights Council, the successor of the UN Commission on Human Rights, did not adopt the norms. Negative attacks came from the International Chamber of Commerce, International Organisation of Employers, and the US Council for International Business, who argued that responsibility for enforcing human rights rested with governments, not corporations. In spite of passing unanimously in the subcommission, the statement faced clear defeat in the full council. Instead, the council asked the OHCHR to compile a report surveying and recommending ways to strengthen businesses' incorporation of the norms. The resulting report included input from more than ninety states, NGOs, labor and business interests, academic institutions, and individuals (Amnesty International 2010). Following the report and still without adequate support to pass the document in the Human Rights Council, Secretary-General Kofi Annan appointed a special representative on business and human rights in April 2005. The statement was finally adopted, even though the United States voted against it. The representative, John Ruggie, was given a three-year term to examine the relationship between business and human rights, leading to a report outlining a threefold policy framework and a renewal of the position of special representative for an additional three years. The framework includes the duty of states to protect against human rights abuses by third parties, responsibility of corporations to respect human rights, and the need for greater access by victims to effective remedies (OHCHR 2010). The renewed mandate instructs Special Representative Ruggie to operationalize and elaborate the policy framework along specific guidelines. Today, the office of the special representative tracks "the positive and negative impacts of over 5100 companies worldwide" (Business and Human Rights Resource Centre 2013).

## Conclusion

The interests versus values problem is exemplified by the activities of nonstate actors in several ways. In the case of NGOs, those active in the field of human rights are united by the common purpose of advancing, promoting, and protecting human rights values. Those values *are* the interests of these organizations. In the case of private sector businesses, their main purpose is not the advancement of human rights but the generation of profits, which often means lowering the costs of labor and regulation as much as possible in order to maximize profits. At least that has been the case for much of the history of modern capitalism. However, human rights are increasingly asserted as an area worthy of protection by all entities against arbitrary power, and increasingly agreed upon is the idea that at a minimum, all human beings should have access to the most fundamental necessities of material life. In the context of states governed by democratic institutions, demands for protection are articulated through unions, by the media, and at the ballot box. As a force for the advancement of human welfare, human rights are now asserted internationally in the face of many forms of public, governmental, and private commercial sector power. The spread of human rights norms transnationally means that companies that do business in India or Bangladesh, exploit the workers in those countries, and then export goods to wealthy democracies are at least subjected to negative publicity and criticism.

The force of norms is highlighted by the role of nonstate actors in the advancement of human rights. Democratic governance means that because they support the norms underlying the laws, most of those regulated by the law obey most of the laws most of the time. Coercion to comply ought to occur only on the margins, against those who do not regard the law, the legal process, or the system of governance as legitimate, believe that norm violations come at little cost, or feel no allegiance to the system that produces the norms. Clearly, in the area of private sector responsibility for adhering to human rights standards and, further, promoting their development and respect, TNCs and businesses are not very invested in respect for international norms. On the other hand, NGOs and individuals have been very effective in bringing shame and accountability to bear on businesses in the "court of world public opinion." National courts are also a venue where injured individuals and communities can pursue remedies, although remedy after the fact is less satisfactory than preventing the practices that cause injury in the first place. Both NGOs (and private individuals) and governments have roles to play in mobilizing support for international human rights norms. Consciousness raising, shaming, and litigation are important strategies for the former while governments can operationalize and implement a regulatory framework for the development of national and international institutional mechanisms for proactive policy and remedial relief.

# Part 3

## Contemporary Issues

# 8

# Genocide

Genocide, after all, is an exercise in community building. A vigorous totalitarian order requires that people be invested in the leaders' scheme, and while genocide may be the most perverse and ambitious means to this end, it is also the most comprehensive.
—Philip Gourevitch, *We Wish to Inform You That Tomorrow We Will Be Killed with Our Families,* 1998

The 20th century taught us how far unbridled evil can and will go when the world fails to confront it. It is time that we heed the lessons of the 20th century and stand up to these murderers. It is time that we end genocide in the 21st century. —US congresswoman Allyson Schwartz, 2007

GENOCIDE IS NOT NEW TO HUMAN HISTORY. WHAT IS NEW IS THE mobilization of international political will to renounce and punish individuals for carrying out genocidal policies. On the one hand, those seeking evidence of progress in the development of international human rights can take heart in this fact. Although the mass killing of Armenians by the Turkish government in 1915 and the Holocaust in Nazi Germany were genocides by today's definition, not until after World War II, after the trials at Nuremberg, and after the United Nations was formed in 1945 did a convention defining genocide as a crime enter into force. The tribunals for former Yugoslavia and Rwanda were the first courts to issue indictments for genocide, and in September 1998, the ICTR rendered the first genocide conviction. On the other hand, the will to intervene or stop ongoing genocides, however, remains weak. Too often political and strategic concerns override the obligation the genocide convention places on states not only to punish but also to prevent genocide.

The term *genocide* is sometimes thrown around loosely to mean "the worst imaginable human-caused humanitarian disaster." However, this casual definition is part of the problem, for indeed many horrible, unspeakable human-caused humanitarian disasters do not fit the definition of genocide. The torture-rapes in the eastern part of the Democratic Republic of Congo that leave women to suffer with irreparable traumatic fistula and related infections come to mind. Many horrific offenses to particular human beings and to our collective humanity occur throughout the world and warrant responses and interventions, though they do not fit the definition of genocide. Defining a problem or offense can help us mobilize the political will to respond to it, but the act of defining itself is not a solution.

What insights can be gained about the definition of *genocide* from learning about the history and circumstances of each of the cases of genocide or potential genocide in this chapter? Is it too narrow? Could expanding the definition through a protocol strengthen and clarify resolve among international leaders to oppose genocides and humanitarian disasters that are like genocides? The antislavery convention, for example, was expanded through the 1956 Supplementary Convention on the Abolition of Slavery to broaden the scope of prohibited practices to include "institutions and practices similar to slavery." A similar supplement could be developed on the prohibition of genocide. Conversely, does the narrowness of the present definition allow political leaders an easy excuse to deny a responsibility to act on their obligation to prevent or stop ongoing genocides, as suggested by the Rwandan case?

## What Is Genocide?

The Convention on the Prevention and Punishment of the Crime of Genocide, often referred to simply as the Genocide Convention, was adopted unanimously by the General Assembly of the United Nations on December 9, 1948. The description in that definition is the most useful. The UN General Assembly considers genocide to be "any of the following acts committed with intent to destroy, in whole or in part, a national, ethnical, racial or religious group." Taken verbatim, the acts are

   (a) Killing members of the group,
   (b) Causing serious bodily or mental harm to members of the group,
   (c) Deliberately inflicting on the group conditions of life calculated to bring about its physical destruction in whole or in part,
   (d) Imposing measures intended to prevent births within the group,
   (e) Forcibly transferring children of the group to another group.

So how does genocide differ from violation of other rights? Genocide, or large-scale deprivation of a people's very right to life, differs from the violation of other kinds of rights in two ways. First, genocide violates a collective right in that individuals have a right to exist as a people or, in the terminology of the Genocide Convention, "as a group." The antigenocide norm protects a group from being targeted for physical elimination as a group. Civil liberties, due process, and political rights are individual rights. They are also rights that for the most part are left to states to protect and guarantee. States may criticize one another for failing to protect or for violating these rights, but such criticism or violations rarely give rise to interventions. Second, in addition to being a collective right, the antigenocide norm also obligates other states to prevent and punish genocide as an international crime. In this way, the antigenocide norm stands apart from other human rights norms.

A *jus cogens* (or peremptory) norm is one that claims a higher status over competing norms when a conflict arises between two or more normative claims in international law. *Jus cogens* norms have universal standing: that is, they apply to all states regardless of whether or not they have explicitly agreed to accept the norm as binding by signing a treaty or convention. Debates about which norms have achieved a *jus cogens* status usually encompass norms representing prohibitions, such as those against slavery, maritime piracy, torture, and aggressive war. Among them, the antigenocide norm is generally the only one about which little or no disagreement comes up regarding its status as *jus cogens*.

A straightforward example of how *jus cogens* status affects a normative conflict is the case of intervening to stop an ongoing genocide. Here the conflict is between a nonintervention norm and the prohibition of genocide. A military intervention to stop an ongoing genocide, whether authorized by an international organization or not, would be legal. The state in which the genocide takes place would not be able to claim legal cover by invoking the nonintervention norm. Unfortunately, no cases exist where such an intervention has taken place for the purpose of preventing or stopping a genocide, although a few cases can be found where humanitarian interventions garnered some international support, albeit amid controversy, such as the NATO intervention following the Serbian government's expulsion of hundreds of thousands of Albanians from Kosovo in 1999 or the UN-authorized intervention in Libya in 2011, in response to reports of systematic violations of human rights following antigovernment protests (Wheeler 2001; Holzgrefe and Keohane 2003).

Genocide itself is not the only crime punishable under the Genocide Convention. Other crimes that would result in possible punishment under UN guidelines are conspiracy to commit genocide, direct and public incitement to commit genocide, attempt to commit genocide, and complicity in genocide. Although the United States was the first signatory and the convention was strongly supported by President Harry Truman, it was not ratified by the US Senate until 1986. Seventeen states today that are parties to the treaty creating the ICC, which identifies genocide as punishable, are not signatories to the Genocide Convention. Another sixteen states are parties to neither. When a norm has reached a level of universality and is recognized as a *jus cogens*, even states that have not signed the convention are bound by the norm and may not violate it, as has happened with genocide. However, since the problem is more one of political will than legal foundation, this premise has not really been tested. It could become more relevant if charges of genocide were brought to the ICC for events occurring in a nonsignatory state or if accused persons fled to a nonsignatory state to escape prosecution in the ICC or any other court. However, the ICC has charged Sudanese president Omar al-Bashir with genocide, and although Sudan is not a signatory to the treaty creating the ICC, it has acceded to the authority of the Genocide Convention.

About thirty individuals have been convicted of genocide in the case of former Yugoslavia and about twenty-five in the case of Rwanda, with more awaiting trial or a final ICC decision. The ICJ ruled in the 2007 Bosnian genocide case that the massacre at Srebrenica constituted genocide under international law. Early in the Yugoslav wars of secession, the term *ethnic cleansing* was devised specifically to create a term distinct from *genocide* (Wilmer 2002). According to Yugoslav officials, the policy of forcibly transferring ethnic populations within areas of Bosnia and around the Bosnian-Croatian border in order to create ethnic majorities was "ethnic cleansing," not genocide. This policy included removing people to what Yugoslav leaders called "collective centers," but the media called "concentration camps." "Ethnic cleansing" also included the destruction of homes and murder of people not moved into centers or camps, and the torture, rape, and murder of people both in and out of the camps (Wilmer 2002). One Serbian intellectual and collaborator with Slobodan Milošević described ethnic cleansing as similar to what the US government did to American Indians when they were forced onto reservations (Wilmer 2002).

Seven cases of mass killings or the deliberate annihilations of populations are examined in this chapter. The first four cases fit easily into the definitional framework of the Genocide Convention: the mass killing of Armenians in Turkey, the Holocaust, the mass killings in former Yugoslavia, and the mass killings in Rwanda—although the Armenian genocide occurred well before that convention was drafted (as did the Holocaust) and remains a politically contentious issue both within Turkey and in Turkish foreign relations. The least ambiguous of the remaining three cases is the Cambodian genocide that, while widely recognized as genocide, fits less well into the international definition because people were targeted as being too (Western) educated or "Westernized" in general rather than because they constituted a group as described in the convention. In other words, broad agreement exists that the killing of 1 million to 3 million Cambodians is genocide even if those targeted were not a "group" as contemplated by the international definition.

Much less consensus exists as to whether the last two cases constitute genocides, that is, policies aimed at destroying a group as a group. In the case of Darfur, no case has been tried as of 2014 to evaluate whether the events there—400,000 killed and 2.5 million displaced—fit the definition of genocide or just very gross and mass violations of human rights. The current case for which President al-Bashir is under indictment alleges five counts of crimes against humanity, two counts of war crimes, and three counts of genocide and may break new ground in the application of the antigenocide convention to "on the ground" acts for which genocide is alleged. In the case of indigenous peoples, ample evidence can be given of government policies intended to destroy indigenous peoples as a broadly understood group as well as specific tribes, communities, and nations. Nevertheless, claims of genocide in this case remain controversial primarily for political reasons. Except for those that involve indigenous peoples, the cases are presented in chronological order. But first, a look at the international community's reluctance to intervene in conflicts of genocide.

## The Failure of Intervention to Prevent or Stop Genocide

While disagreement may exist about when to apply the term *humanitarian intervention,* little disagreement exists as to whether interventions are a legitimate use of force (with or without UN authorization) in the case of genocides (Welsh 2004). Why, in the aftermath of the Holocaust with the resultant apparent high level of political resolve and consensus to outlaw genocide, have there been so few interventions and so many more genocides?

One answer is that the UN Security Council's decisionmaking process was designed to prevent the use of military force for intervention. Being mindful that the United Nations was created in the aftermath of not one but two world wars—globalized wars that started among European major powers—one can argue that its main purpose was to prevent a third. Rather than excluding or alienating any of the major powers, the United Nations requires nine votes on the Security Council including the consent (or abstention) of all major powers to authorize a use of force. As discussed in the last chapter, the UN Charter actually gives the Security Council broad discretion to define a particular situation as one that warrants intervention. However, the Council is still unlikely to use that discretion because of the deep differences in political interests among its major power members. For this reason, authority for intervention has only been granted twice with broad support from UN members, once in Korea and once in Iraq. However, several multinational interventions with limited support have been authorized recently in Africa.

In March 2013 a limited force was authorized for one year "to neutralize armed groups" in the Democratic Republic of Congo (Cammaert 2013). Some ambiguity still can be found about changes in the role of UN peacekeepers from keeping the peace during a cease-fire with the consent of the parties to a more interventionist role ranging from securing the delivery of humanitarian aid or ending civil wars. Only the mission to the Democratic Republic of Congo was designated as an "intervention brigade" authorized to carry out offensive military missions (UNSC Resolution 2098 [2013]).

Another answer as to why so few interventions are approved is that the political leaders of states are unwilling to ask their electorates to spend tax dollars and put citizens in harm's way for interventions in conflicts that do not directly affect them or seem remote from their own interests (Ritenauer 2009; Western 2009; Hildebrandt et al. 2013). This conflict has become particularly apparent in US foreign policy, which has also been more studied because of the greater expectation that, given its power and influence, the United States will provide leadership in mobilizing international support for humanitarian interventions. Samantha Power (2002) said that policymakers' avoidance of interventions against genocide is explained by two delicately balanced and competing objectives:

> First, they wanted to avoid engagement in conflicts that posed little threat to American interests, narrowly defined. Second, they hoped to contain the political costs and avoid the moral stigma associated with allowing genocide. Largely, they achieved both aims. In order to contain the political fallout, U.S. officials overemphasized the ambiguity of the facts. . . . And they took solace in the normal operations of the foreign policy bureaucracy, which permitted an illusion of continual deliberation, complex activity, and intense concern. (508)

Finally, these two answers suggest a third reason for reluctance to intervene: multilateral humanitarian intervention requires leadership, and both the United States and the European Union have lacked the political will to offer it. The United States and the European Union have shown the willpower to act in other kinds of intervention, as demonstrated by the Gulf War, Iraq War, and military operations in Afghanistan. The intervention in Kosovo might have offered some hope of US willingness to spend some leadership capital on a limited NATO-supported mission. However, this same will was so starkly lacking in Rwanda and Bosnia. Only one country, the Netherlands, stepped up in defense of the UN-declared safe areas of Srebrenica, Goražde, and Žepa in 1995. The disastrous aftermath—Bosnian Serbs forced Dutch peacekeepers to witness a genocide in Srebrenica—led the Dutch public and political leaders to renounce future unilateral interventions (Honig and Both 1997).

## The Armenian Genocide in 1915

When the Russians invaded Turkey in 1914, they encouraged Turkish Armenians to join them in overthrowing the Ottoman imperial government. Though most remained loyal to the empire, by June 1915 the Turkish government proclaimed Armenians a threat to the "peace and security of the Ottoman state" and ordered their forced exile along with their "movable" property (Power 2002:2). They were prohibited from selling real estate and anything else they could not carry with them, simply having to abandon those things they could not move. Such policies gave a green light to those who wished to rape and brutalize the departing Armenians. The *New York Times* reported 800,000 killed by October, and 1 million killed or exiled by December (*New York Times* 1915a; *New York Times* 1915b).

Under Muslim Ottoman rule, Christians (including Armenians) and Jews were second-class citizens with restrictions on their conduct, religious practices, and individual freedoms. Western European states pressured the empire to extend equal rights to Christians living in the empire, but the government only gave lip service to reform. As tensions grew, Britain, France, and Russia threatened intervention on behalf of Christian minorities under the auspices of the 1856 Treaty of Paris. The empire responded harshly to Christian uprisings in Bosnia. Serbia, Bulgaria, and the Armenians reported the "forced conversion of women and children, arson, protection extortion, rape, and murder" to the great powers of the day as those powers engaged in negotiations with the Ottomans (Akcam 2006:37). A clause granting Armenians autonomy within the empire was included in the 1878 Treaty of Berlin, but the promised reforms were never implemented. Instead, Sultan Abdul Hamid II created a paramilitary force to "deal" with the Armenian problem, and massacres of Armenians followed.

As Armenians were caught up in the chaos of a coup against the sultan and then a countercoup against the constitutional monarchy that replaced him, more massacres ensued. The Ottoman army in Adana killed an estimated 15,000 to 30,000 Armenians in 1909 (Vilayet 1909). When World War I broke out between the Allied Powers and the Austro-Hungarian and German empires, the Ottoman rulers joined the latter, and along with Bulgaria, the four were known as the Central Powers. Given the history of efforts by the great powers, especially Russia, to defend Armenians and even threats to intervene on their behalf, the Ottoman government viewed Armenians as enemies of the state. According to Vahakn Dadrian (1995), their German allies were well aware of the extermination policy being carried out. Dadrian reported the public comments of the acting military attaché and head of the German plenipotentiary in the Ottoman Empire:

> The Turks have embarked upon the "total extermination of the Armenians in Transcaucasia. . . . The aim of Turkish policy is, as I have reiterated, the taking of possession of Armenian districts and the extermination of the Armenians. Talaat's government wants to destroy all Armenians, not just in Turkey but also outside Turkey. On the basis of all the reports and news coming to me here in Tiflis there hardly can be any doubt that the Turks systematically are aiming at the extermination of the few hundred thousand Armenians whom they left alive until now. (349)

Like the Treaty of Versailles outlining the postwar terms of defeat for Germany in its relations with the Allied Powers, the 1920 Treaty of Sèvres did the same for the successor state of Turkey. The Treaty of Sèvres also called for holding the Ottoman government leaders legally responsible both for the war of aggression and for its "barbarous and illegitimate methods of warfare," including violations of the laws of war. However, these provisions were never carried out.

Mustafa Kemal Atatürk, founder of the modern, secular state of Turkey, served as its first president from 1923 to 1938. For all he did for Turkey, controversy continues over whether or not he played a role in the anti-Armenian policies that fueled the 1915 genocide (Ulgen 2010). Until the 1970s, little attention was paid to the denial of the genocide, a denial that still exists in official Turkish policy. The Turkish government position on the genocide is that violence occurred on both sides, and this dark historical episode is better forgotten a century later (Hovannisian 1998). Several factors explain the international community's long acquiescence to the Turkish view. One factor is a hesitancy to criticize Atatürk, whose legacy of modernization and democratization of the Turkish state is revered throughout Turkey and much of the West. Turkey is the largest democratic majority-Muslim state with close political and geographic ties to Western Europe. Many in Turkey would consider it blasphemous to stain Atatürk's reputation for modernizing and democratizing Turkey by associating him with any responsibility for genocide. Another motive for tolerating Turkey's denial is the important strategic relationship between Turkey and the West particularly during the Cold War, a relationship that played a critical role in resolving the Cuban missile crisis peacefully when the United States agreed to remove its missiles from Turkey in exchange for the Soviet Union's removing its missiles from Cuba.

So what explains the shift in the 1970s and 1980s? For one thing, Turkey developed a close association with the European Economic Community, which became the European Union in 1993 after the Maastrich Treaty entered into force. Turkey has been a member of the Council of

Europe since 1949 and the OECD since 1961. Turkey became an associate member of the European Community in 1963 and a member of the OSCE in 1973. Turkey applied for full membership in the European Community in 1987. Turkish leaders wanted better and closer relations with Western Europe, and the European Union placed demands and expectations on Turkey to meet higher human rights standards. In 2008, for example, responding to criticism from the European Union, Turkey amended its penal code, which had previously made it a crime to "insult Turkishness" (BBC Online 2008). Perhaps the former prime minister of Armenia sums up Turkey's predicament the best. In October of 2009, Tigran Sarkisian declared, "Our goal on moral-psychological and cultural levels is to achieve justice. . . . It is very difficult to go beyond this level when it comes to the Armenian genocide. We all feel this burden and we carry it. Naturally, Turkey's denialist policy creates problems in the normalization of our relations" (quoted in ARKA News Agency 2009).

Some in Turkey have taken up the cause of ending official denial, such as that country's intellectuals, including political scientist and former ambassador Kamuran Gürün. In 1985, Gürün published the first widely read and well-documented exposé of the events in *The Armenian File: The Myth of Innocence Exposed*. Since its publication, some fifteen states have passed laws or resolutions acknowledging the Armenian genocide and calling on the Turkish government to do the same. France and Switzerland have even made denial of the Armenian genocide a crime (Welch 2007). Even with the trend toward acknowledgment, the genocide and its denial continue to arouse controversy and violence. On January 19, 2007, a young "Turkish nationalist" assassinated Armenian journalist Hrant Dink, whose writing focused on the Armenian genocide (Balakian 2007).

In 1975, the US Congress passed a resolution declaring April 24 as the National Day of Remembrance of Man's Inhumanity to Man. The joint resolution says

> the President of the United States is authorized and requested to issue a proclamation calling upon the people of the United States to observe such day as a day of remembrance for all the victims of genocide, especially those of Armenian ancestry who succumbed to the genocide perpetrated in 1915, and in whose memory this date is commemorated by all Armenians and their friends throughout the world.

Congress has considered several pieces of legislation condemning the Turkish denial of the genocide, but no legislation has ever been passed. As of July 2014, a new congressional resolution had passed in the Senate Foreign Relations Committee in April but had not yet been voted on by the full chamber.

## The Holocaust

Most people have some knowledge of the Holocaust's atrocities, citing 6 million Jews directly murdered and the heinous crimes committed in concentration camps. Outside of the concentration camps, nearly 1 million people died of diseases and starvation in the ghettos alone (Chirot 1996). Estimates of the Roma killed vary between 250,000 and 800,000 (Rummel 1992). Also targeted and murdered by the Nazi regime were between 15,000 and 220,000 homosexuals, 275,000 disabled persons, and 70,000 who were mentally ill (Rummel 1992; Chirot 1996; Totten 2004). Adolf Hitler's most systematic and sustained effort, however, was aimed at the absolute annihilation of virtually all European Jews. The Nazi leadership finally named this project "the final solution" to the "Jewish problem" following the Wannsee Conference in January 1942.

Less well known are the events that transpired from the time Hitler came to power as German chancellor to the normalization of a murderous mass pathology that swept through not only Germany but collaborationist regimes in Austria, Albania, Belgium, Bosnia, Croatia, Denmark, Estonia, Greece, France, Hungary, Italy, Latvia, Lithuania, the Netherlands, Norway, Romania, parts of occupied Russia, Serbia, Slovakia, and Slovenia. How did so many people in so many countries become, as Daniel Goldhagen (1997) called them, "Hitler's willing executioners"?

Hitler lost the runoff election against President Paul von Hindenburg in April of 1932, but, with a Nazi majority in the Reichstag (the German parliament), became chancellor in January 1933. Amidst a climate of apparent domestic terrorism—anti-Nazi street demonstrations mobilized by the Social Democratic Party and joined by the Communist Party and the fire-bombing of the Reichstag in 1933—the chancellor convinced the president to grant him emergency authority to suspend all civil rights and arrest and execute persons suspected of involvement. Although Hitler's own minister of propaganda, Joseph Goebbels, was responsible for issuing an order to set fire to the building where the Reichstag met, the crime was blamed on a member of the Communist Party, unleashing a public campaign associating leftist parties and organizations with growing violence. All media except Nazi sources were soon outlawed, and by March of 1933, Hitler's party took a majority of seats in the Reichstag, which then gave Hitler the power to make laws. Before the month was out, the first concentration camp to house Hitler's political opponents was established outside of Dachau. On April 1, he declared a boycott of Jewish businesses.

By June 1933, the Nazi Party—the only remaining legal party in Germany—controlled all of the legal media and the labor unions and had burned hundreds of thousands of library books. In July, Hitler revoked the citizenship of anyone who threatened the state, including Jewish immigrants from Poland who had taken German citizenship. When President Hindenburg died in August 1934, Hitler took over the presidency as well as retaining the position of chancellor and military commander in chief. Hitler made a distinction between "the German people" and "Jews" early on when he declared a boycott of Jewish businesses (The Holocaust\Shoah Page 1997). Following the 1933 boycott, the Nazi-controlled Reichstag passed a decree delineating the distinction between Aryans and non-Aryans. Non-Aryans included anyone descended from a "non-Aryan, especially Jewish parents or grandparents," including those with only one Jewish grandparent. Between 1932 and 1935, official and unofficial anti-Semitism grew at a time when Jews made up only about 1 percent of the German population (around a half million people). In 1935, the Reichstag passed the Nuremberg Laws that completely stripped German Jews of their German citizenship. Laws banned Jews from marrying or having sexual relationships with German citizens and from raising the German flag and forced Jewish doctors to resign from private hospitals. Anti-Semitism was officially incorporated into the public education curriculum, though it had been widespread in schools unofficially since the early days of the Weimar Republic in the early 1920s (Goldhagen 1997).

Hitler's aggression turned outward as he invaded the Rhineland in 1936. The Buchenwald concentration camp was opened in August of 1937 and further restrictions were placed on Jews, but not only by Germany. Britain also began restricting Jewish immigration to Palestine in an effort to appease unrest among Palestinian Arabs, particularly after the 1936–1939 Arab Revolt in Palestine. After Berlin's Kristallnacht, on November 9, 1938, when Jews and their businesses were violently attacked, synagogues set on fire, and more than ninety people killed, Jews were ordered to pay reparations for the damages, subjected to strict curfews, forbidden to attend public cultural events, and banned from German public schools and universities. Anti-Semitic fervor even spread to the United States where tens of thousands of US Nazis rallied in New York City, railing against US Jews and defacing synagogues in the city. The French government revoked citizenship of naturalized Jews and sent thousands into labor and concentration camps. German Jews were relocated to Poland, first to ghettos and then concentration camps. Austrian Jews were also deported to Poland, Hungary passed laws calling for the deportation of 300,000 Jews living there, and Germany began the deportation of the 210,000 Jews who still lived there. Hitler wanted to purge German society of his political opponents, especially communists, homosexuals, and Roma, but he wanted to "exterminate" all Jews in all of Europe.

Approximately 9.5 million Jews lived in Europe at the time Hitler became chancellor of Germany with over half of them living in Poland and Russia—3 to 4 million in Russia alone (Holocaust Museum 2008a). After the German invasion of Russia in June of 1941, killings and deportations accelerated, and slave labor camps turned into death camps. Schutzstaffel (SS) leader Heinrich Himmler ordered Auschwitz enlarged for the specific purpose of carrying out the "final solution" ordered by Hitler (Holocaust Museum 2008b). Although the "experimental" mobile gas chambers could only hold fifty people at a time, four new permanent gas chambers were installed at the expanded facility with a collective capacity to kill 4,420 people at a time. Over 15,000 camps (including subcamps) were set up in fifteen countries (Châtel and Ferree 2001).

Information about the camps and the atrocities being perpetrated against Jews reached Britain in June of 1942 when the *New York Times* reported to the *London Telegraph* that over 1 million Jews had already been killed by the Nazis (The History Place 1997). By December, knowledge of the atrocities and mass murders was widespread. British foreign secretary Anthony Eden read aloud to the House of Commons a declaration signed by the governments of Belgium, Czechoslovakia, Greece, Luxembourg, the Netherlands, Norway, Poland, the United States, the United Kingdom, the Soviet Union, Yugoslavia, and the French National Committee condemning "this bestial policy of cold-blooded extermination" (BBC News 2008 [1942]). These "United Nations," the declaration said, resolved to punish those responsible. Not only were Jews being killed in death camps, but the remaining ghettos were also targeted for annihilation. Jews fought back in the Warsaw ghettos in the Warsaw Ghetto Uprising of 1943 as an act of Jewish resistance and in the Treblinka and Sobribór camps outside of Warsaw in eastern Poland. About half of all Jews killed died in gas chambers.

On the same day when a record number of Jews were killed at Auschwitz (46,000)—July 23, 1944—the Russian army entered and liberated the first death camp at Majdanek. The liberation of Warsaw and Auschwitz by Russian troops followed within six months, and US troops liberated Buchenwald in April 1945. By November of that year, the Nuremberg trials had begun.

### Politicide in Cambodia

As the last US marines left Vietnam in April of 1975 and South Vietnamese president Nguyen Van Thieu resigned under pressure from his US patrons, the Khmer Rouge (the name given to the Communist Party of Kampuchea, or Cambodia) moved into Cambodia's capital city of Phnom Penh as "conquerors," in the words of that group's leaders (Power 2002). Over the next three and a half years, 21 percent of the Cambodian people were killed by their own government, renamed, by cruel irony, the "Democratic Kampuchea." Although elements of Khmer Rouge ideology targeted ethnic groups like the Muslim Chams, the primary justification for the imprison-ment, torture, starvation, and execution of 1.7 million Cambodians was to remove those who had become "Westernized." The Khmer Rouge used communist ideological arguments to bolster an anti-imperialist brand of nationalism. People who were educated or owned small businesses or even simply wore eyeglasses were targeted by the regime. Since the Khmer Rouge chose its target population by using a kind of ideological profiling, the Cambodian genocide has also been called a "politicide," that is, geno-cide where the target group is identified by political belief or identity (Harff and Gurr 1988).

The communist Khmer Rouge in Cambodia and the Vietnamese com-munists in North Vietnam had allied to fight regimes in the two countries backed by the United States. Following the US withdrawal from Vietnam, the Khmer Rouge moved quickly to control the rest of the country while persecuting the Chams and other "bourgeois" enemies of their communist state. Westerners, including journalists, were quickly expelled along with most diplomatic missions. Representatives from some communist countries were allowed to remain, but their freedom to travel was severely restricted and "minders" accompanied them when they did travel (Power 2002). With witnesses removed or under control and US attention focused on the post-withdrawal conditions in Vietnam, Khmer Rouge repression then mush-roomed into a full-fledged genocide.

Estimates of the number of people killed under the rule of Khmer Rouge leader Pol Pot vary between 1.7 million and 3 million (Shawcross 1985). Stories told by escaping refugees included those of whole villages evacuated to labor camps where prisoners were slowly starved to death; revenge killings of anyone associated with the former regime; death marches; and organized and spontaneous mass murder of "class enemies" including intellectuals, artists, Buddhist monks, and all religious practition-ers. Detailed reports based on interviews with refugees escaping into Thai-land were published in *Le Monde* estimating that 800,000 Cambodians had been killed in the first nine months (Power 2002).

No condemnation came from the United States or the international community for three years. Political leaders and human rights groups argued about the extent of the brutality, the reliability of evidence and reports, and the value of international law and organizations in stemming the violence. A constellation of political leaders in the US Congress worked with President Jimmy Carter to incorporate consideration of states' human rights records into US foreign policy, although the United States had not yet ratified the Genocide Convention. The pullout and failure of the US mili-tary intervention in Vietnam wreaked havoc on the morale of the US public as well as political leadership. Although many in the United States regarded communism as a monolithic enemy and made no distinction between Vietnamese and Cambodian communist parties, the Khmer rise to power was to some a consequence of the US failure to defeat Vietnamese communists. The United States had also secretly bombed Cambodia between 1969 and 1973—secret because Cambodia was officially neutral. Controversy still surrounds the question of whether the devastation of the US bombing campaign was a major factor in mobilizing support for the anti-Western, anti-US Khmer Rouge.

The Cambodian military continually attacked Vietnam along their shared border until the Vietnamese, with Soviet support, sent 60,000 of its own troops into Cambodia in December of 1977. In April 1978, President Carter finally denounced the Khmer Rouge regime as "the worst violator of human rights in the world today," citing "genocidal policies," but his condemnation fell short of advocating a military intervention to stop the genocide (Carter 1978). The lone voice calling for intervention was also the most outspoken opponent of the Vietnam War—Senator George McGovern. For McGovern, intervention to stop an ongoing genocide was the right use of military force. Taking sides in a civil war with no clear objectives in Vietnam was not.

Supported by the People's Republic of China, the Khmer Rouge took the offensive while the Vietnamese army pushed the Cambodian forces back across the border until the Vietnamese launched a decisive offensive of their own in December 1978, capturing the capital in January 1979. The Vietnamese joined a Cambodian resistance force—the Kampuchean National United Front for National Salvation—and together they overthrew the Khmer Rouge and deposed Pol Pot. The Khmer Rouge retreated to the most remote areas and remained in control of only about 25 percent of the country.

As the Vietnamese gained control of the country, documentation confirming the scale of the genocide reached the rest of the world (Power 2002). Nearly one-third of the entire Cambodian population had been killed, including virtually all but a thousand of the 60,000 Buddhist monks (Power 2002). The Vietnamese overthrew the Khmer Rouge, put a pro-Vietnamese government in power, and occupied Cambodia for ten years until the economic effects of boycotts by Western states and the need for aid from the West moved them to offer an unconditional withdrawal, while still requesting (rather than demanding) that support for opposition groups be halted. The United Nations facilitated the negotiation of a cease-fire and the Security Council agreed on a plan that included keeping the peace, setting up a mechanism to oversee preparations for elections, and then supervising those elections. The UN Advance Mission in Cambodia supervised the cease-fire and withdrawal of Vietnamese troops and then set up the UN Transitional Authority in Cambodia to assist repatriation and resettlement of 360,000 refugees in preparation for the elections in 1993. Nearly 90 per-

cent of registered voters participated. The role of the United Nations in bro-
kering peace and supervising transition to normalization in Cambodia is
often and easily overlooked, but this program is one of the most successful
ever implemented with the support of all permanent members of the Security Council. Over 21,000 civilian and military personnel from more than
100 countries participated in the effort (United Nations 2008a). In 1999 the
UN Group of Experts for Cambodia reported that crimes committed by
Khmer Rouge leaders during the 1975–1979 period included crimes against
humanity, genocide, war crimes, forced labor, torture, and crimes against
internationally protected persons, as well as crimes under Cambodian law
(United Nations 1999).

The group recommended the creation of an international tribunal to
prosecute and punish those responsible for the genocide and the creation of
a truth commission to reconcile Cambodian society and "denazify" the government of the Khmer Rouge ideology. In August 2001, the Cabinet of
Cambodia (the executive body of the Cambodian government) approved the
Law on the Establishment of the Extraordinary Chambers in the Courts of
Cambodia as well as the agreement between the Cambodian government
and the United Nations about its role in the process. On July 18, 2007, the
coprosecutors of the tribunal filed the first Extraordinary Chambers in the
Courts of Cambodia. The court found preliminary evidence showing cause
for the indictment of individuals responsible for committing "crimes
against humanity, genocide, grave breaches of the Geneva Conventions,
homicide, torture and religious persecution" (Cambodian Tribunal Monitor
2012).

The first individual indicted by the court in 2007—Kang Kek Lew,
who ran the Khmer Rouge prison camps and was the head of internal security—is now serving a life sentence. Four more top-ranking Khmer Rouge
leaders were indicted in 2010: one died in 2013 and trial proceedings were
terminated, another was found to be suffering from Alzheimer's disease and
thereby to be unfit for trial, and the two remaining defendants' trials began
in 2011 and were ongoing in 2014.

## Ethnic Cleansing in the Former Yugoslavia

The Wars of Yugoslav Succession, as the four wars in former Yugoslavia
between 1991 and 1999 are often called, became the site of war crimes,
crimes against humanity, and genocide. The four wars occurred in Slovenia
(1991), Croatia (1991–1995), Bosnia and Herzegovina (1992–1995), and
Kosovo (1998–1999), where NATO undertook a bombing campaign in
response to the expulsion of more than 200,000 Kosovo Albanians by Slobodan Milošević's Serbian government. More than 100,000 were killed and

more than 2 million became refugees or internally displaced people. The worst single act of genocide occurred in Srebrenica in July 1995 where some 8,000 Bosnian Muslims (or Bosniaks), most of them men and boys, were killed. How did this happen?

The death of Josip Broz Tito in 1980 left a mixed legacy in Yugoslavia. Under his leadership, Slovenes, Croats, Serbs, Albanians, and Hungarians and other minorities lived in one state for thirty-five years and developed a civic "Yugoslav" identity that overlaid their national identities. The standard of living, accessibility of education, gender equality, and tensions extant from centuries-old imperial fault lines had steadily improved in the new Yugoslav state.

By many accounts, Tito engineered the building of a different kind of communist society, more open than other post–World War II communist states. The arts also flourished so long as they avoided strongly nationalist themes or demands for greater freedom of nationalist expression, and many Yugoslavs regularly traveled to Western Europe (Wilmer 2002). However, these achievements came at a price. Thousands were imprisoned for expressing political views regarded as threatening by the charismatic communist leader, particularly views sympathetic to religious and nationalist identities. The tenuousness of political stability under Tito's communist rule first surfaced in the 1970s as both Croatian and Muslim nationalist movements met with severe repression and imprisonment of their leaders, including the future presidents of Bosnia-Herzegovina and Croatia.

Tito's death in May 1980 exacerbated the most serious and ultimately fatal weakness of his long charismatic rule—the inability to make a peaceful and stable transition to the next generation of postrevolutionary leaders. Yugoslavia struggled with this situation throughout the 1980s without resolve. The leadership vacuum enabled the rise of strong nationalist movements and leaders in the two most unsettled republics, Serbia and Croatia. Each had ethnic majorities large enough to garner widespread support but with significant minority populations who became the target of xenophobic nationalist political rhetoric and policies.

Efforts by an alliance of states in Europe and the United States to avert war ultimately failed, in part because of their own inability to sustain a unified policy and offer a viable negotiated solution. They also failed because the various nationalist movements had already gathered substantial emotional and political momentum, especially in Serbia and Croatia, in spite of vocal and visible antiwar movements in all the republics (Wilmer 2002). The wars of Yugoslav secession began officially when the Yugoslav army, controlled by the government in Belgrade, attacked Slovenia two days after Slovenia and Croatia declared their independence.

With large pluralities of all three major ethnic groups, Bosnia-Herzegovina soon became the primary battleground, though Croats, Muslims, and Serbs had lived together without violent incident for decades or longer. In Sarajevo, the intellectual and artistic heart of multinational Yugoslavia, people still remembered the positive international attention brought by the 1984 Olympics. Many could not believe the reports of war and war crimes they heard (or were shown on television) were taking place nearby and certainly could not imagine those things taking place in their own cities and villages.

Yet they did. In August 1992, Ed Vulliamy broke the story of concentration camp–like conditions at Trnopolje and Omarska, and an Independent Television Network story was broadcast with photos of starving Omarska inmates behind barbed wire, causing a flurry of international commentators to draw parallels with Nazi death camps five decades earlier (Vulliamy 1994). As the violence progressed in Bosnia and in the border areas, the objective of the Bosnian Serbs, backed by the Serbian government in Belgrade, and the Bosnian Croats, backed by the Croatian government in Zagreb, became clear: to establish their own ethnic majorities in various areas of Bosnia and then annex them to their respective states.

The term *ethnic cleansing* was widely used to describe the forced removal of and targeted violence against specific ethnic populations. Human Rights Watch (1997) estimated that those "cleansed" were moved to nearly 700 camps between 1991 and 1995. The NGO's 1997 report "Bosnia-Herzegovina/The Unindicted: Reaping the Rewards of Ethnic Cleansing" described conditions in the camps near Prijedor in what would become Bosnia-Herzegovina:

> After the Serbs took power on April 30, 1992, they opened at least four detention camps in the Prijedor opstina. Two of the concentration camps, Omarska and Keraterm, were places where killings, torture, and brutal interrogations were carried out. The third, Trnopolje, had another purpose; it functioned as a staging area for massive deportations of mostly women, children, and elderly men, and killings and rapes occurred there. The fourth, Manjaca, was referred to by the Bosnian Serbs as a "prisoner of war camp," although most if not all detainees were civilians. (Human Rights Watch 1997)

Journalist Alexandra Stiglmayer (1994) estimated that of the approximately 65,000 non-Serbs in the area of Prijedor in 1993, "20,000 were murdered, 30,000 were driven away, and 3,000 were still living in Prijedor" (86). By the time the violence ended in the fall of 1995, a quarter of a million people had been killed (70 percent to 75 percent of them civilians), more than 35,000 women had been raped, and 2.3 million had become refugees out of a prewar population of 4.4 million (Wilmer 2002).

Security Council Resolution 827 established the ICTY, empowering it to prosecute crimes committed "in the territory of the former Yugoslavia since 1991." Overall charges included crimes against humanity; violations of the Geneva Conventions; extermination; torture; persecution on political, racial, and religious grounds; murder; deportation; taking of hostages; and inhumane acts (ICTY 2014). As of August 2014, thirteen of twenty-three individuals charged for crimes related to the events in Prijedor were convicted. Four were referred for trial in Bosnia-Herzegovina. Radovan Karadžić was charged and was currently on trial in 2014 for genocide. Slobodan Milošević, also charged with genocide for events in Prijedor and elsewhere, died in custody in 2006. Ratko Mladić, commander of the Bosnian Serb Army, was also charged with genocide in connection with Prijedor and other sites and was still on trial as of 2014. Bosnian Serb president Biljana Plavšić was charged with genocide, but after she pleaded guilty to other charges, the genocide charge was dropped.

In December 1999, Goran Jelisić, the Bosnian Serb commander at the Luka camp in Brčko, was charged with thirty-two individual counts of genocide, violations of the laws and customs of war, and crimes against humanity. The court concluded that sufficient evidence was not presented of his *intent* to commit genocide to find him guilty as a perpetrator of that crime. However, he was found guilty on sixteen charges relating to violations of the laws of war and fifteen counts of crimes against humanity including twelve for murder and three counts of cruel treatment. He was also convicted on one count of plunder and three acts of inhumanity. He was sentenced to forty years imprisonment. The court's rationale for a guilty finding focused on "joint criminal enterprises" stemming from the policy of "ethnic cleansing," including deportation, forced transfer, persecution, murder, and extermination.

The most widely publicized and worst single case of mass murder occurred in July of 1995 in and around Srebrenica that, along with Goražde and Žepa, had been declared by the United Nations as "safe areas" but without provision for securing their safety (Honig and Both 1997). Sixteen individuals, including Bosnian Serb president Radovan Karadžić, were charged with genocide. The prosecutor in the case against Zdravko Tolimir, a commander in the Bosnian Serb Army, said that "by 1 November 1995, the entire Muslim population had been either removed or fled from Srebrenica and Žepa and over 7,000 Muslim men and boys from Srebrenica had been murdered by VRS [Bosnian Serb Army] and MUP [Bosnian Serb Special Police] forces" (ICTY 2014).

As of 2014, the court had charged 175 individuals with war crimes, crimes against humanity, and violations of the Geneva Conventions, including nine charged with genocide or conspiracy to commit genocide. As partially indicated above, the genocide cases resulted in four convictions, one of them later overturned, and two trials were ongoing as of 2014, with the case against Plavšić being dropped after she pleaded guilty to other crimes.

## Genocide in Rwanda

Like many formerly colonized states, Rwanda's postcolonial legacy is characterized by a mismatch between territorial and identity boundaries. European favoritism of one communal group over others and a century of foreign occupation destroyed both the knowledge and practice of local self-government. Within the boundaries of the postcolonial state drawn by Europeans at the Berlin Conference in 1885 lived a Tutsi minority constituting about 15 percent of the population, a smaller Twa minority of about 1 percent, and an 84 percent Hutu majority. Although the cattle-rich Tutsis had established themselves as the governing class who dominated the Hutu agriculturalists, the two lived together more or less peacefully before becoming a German colony in the 1890s, a colony that was later transferred to Belgium after World War I.

The same three groups (including Twa) lived in neighboring Burundi in approximately the same proportions. Following independence in 1962, control of the Rwandan government alternated between Tutsis and Hutus. In Burundi, however, Tutsis maintained control by exercising a sustained bloody military repression against several failed Hutu revolts between 1962 and 1993, killing hundreds of thousands of Hutus over that period. Hutus took control of Rwanda after independence, facing a challenge from Tutsis supported by the Tutsi-controlled Burundian government. They responded by killing some 14,000 Tutsis. In other words, the Tutsi-Hutu conflict was never wholly contained within Rwanda.

Even before independence, an ideology of liberation from Tutsi domination had begun to develop among Hutus in Rwanda. During the rule of Rwanda's first president Grégoire Kayibanda and his Party of the Hutu Emancipation Movement, Hutus commonly referred to Tutsis as "cockroaches." That language was popularized through hate speech whenever the Hutu-dominated government wanted to whip up support for anti-Tutsi grassroots violence in response to invasions launched from or supported by Burundi and Uganda, where the Tutsi Rwandan Patriotic Front was based. The last invasion occurred in 1990, before the 1994 genocide.

Violence between the Tutsi Rwandan Patriot Front and the Hutu-controlled Rwandan government began in 1990, and in 1993 President Juvénal Habyarimana signed an agreement with the Tutsi group, known as the Arusha Accords. However, the accords were strongly opposed by the extremist Hutu Power movement that was his base of support. The Hutu Power movement recruited "youth militias." "In public these violent young men roar around on motorbikes, like any gang of hooligangs, and hold drunken rallies under portraits of President Habyarimana. In private they gather together to perfect the skills of wielding machetes, setting fire to houses, and drawing up lists of local Tutsis and Hutu sympathizers" (Gascoigne 2001).

These groups became death squads during the genocide following the assassinations of the Rwandan president Habyarimana and Burundi president Cyprien Ntaryamira, when their plane was shot down returning from peace talks in Arusha, Tanzania, on April 6, 1994 (Wafula 2008). On April 29, Rwandan state radio designated May 5 as "cleanup day"—the day by which all Tutsis should be "cleansed" from the capital, Kigali (Gascoigne 2001). By July, 900,000 Rwandans were dead. General Roméo Dallaire, Canadian head of the UN peacekeeping forces who went to Rwanda in 1993 to supervise the Arusha cease-fire, is an outspoken critic of the international community, citing the failure to intervene and stop the genocide. Dallaire claimed that many indicators could be found that the genocide was being planned months in advance (Raymont 2002). He believed, and military experts now agree, that with just 5,000 troops, he could very well have preempted genocide (Silver 2002).

He had half that many troops and no authority to confiscate the arms caches arriving and being distributed to the militias. With the resources he did have, Dallaire provided security that saved the lives of about 20,000 Rwandans (Silver 2002). The genocide ended when Tutsi troops in the Rwandan Patriotic Front advanced and took control of the capital, Kigali, in July, and the Hutu government and *génocidaires* fled into neighboring Zaire and Tanzania—about one and a half million refugees. Christian Davenport and Allan Stam (2009) published a controversial article on their research in Rwanda over the decade following the genocide. Their careful empirical investigation strongly indicated that the genocide was part of a larger strategic plan by the Rwandan Patriotic Front to invade and take over the Rwandan government, or, at the very least, the Rwandan Patriotic Front exploited the genocide, possibly provoking some genocidal events to gain a strategic advantage in their war to take over the Rwandan government. Davenport and Stam do not deny that the genocide occurred, nor do they suggest that it was intentionally engineered by the Rwandan Patriotic Front, but that an ethnically driven genocide is not the whole story of what took place in Rwanda in 1994.

The refugee camps where Hutus relocated in neighboring states then became recruiting grounds for the Hutu Power movement in exile as killing continued in Rwanda—revenge killing of Hutus by the now Tutsi-controlled Kigali government. Hutus outside of Rwanda also killed Tutsis who fled the genocide for refugee camps, like the one in Goma, Zaire (Block 1994). By November 1994, the UN Security Council authorized a war crimes tribunal and one year later the first indictments were issued. In 1996 the Rwandan courts also became involved in genocide trials, and by July 2000 some 125,000 people were arrested, about 3,000 tried, 400 sentenced to death, and 22 executed (CNN 2000). The Rwandan government could not, however, extradite any of the 44,204 suspects in the genocide who fled to countries that have abolished the death penalty, so in 2007, Rwanda also abolished capital punishment (Twahirwa 2007).

At the international level, as of 2014, seventy-five indictments were issued by the Office of the Prosecutor, with forty-five cases resulting in guilty charges, and twelve suspects receiving acquittals. Ten cases have been referred to national courts, and nine of those indicted remained at large (ICTR 2014). The highest profile case was prosecuted against the former prime minister of Rwanda, Jean Kambanda, who pleaded guilty to the charge of genocide in October 2000. In the Kambanda case, the court evaluated the argument of the tu quoque defense that a party may be absolved of a responsibility to conform to the limits of international humanitarian law when the opposing party has failed to do so. Writing for the *Human Rights Brief,* Cecile Meijer and Amardeep Singh reported the court concluded that the antigenocide norm has attained the status of a *jus cogens* norm (Meijer and Singh 2001).

## Unofficial Genocide in Darfur

Darfur is a region in western Sudan that has more recently come to epitomize international indifference to genocide or at least atrocities on a scale that evokes the moral depravity and imagery of genocidal violence. Gerard Prunier (2005) called the situation in Darfur the "ambiguous genocide" because it fails to fit within the definitional boundaries of the Genocide Convention. No clearly defined group of victims fits the convention's definition, and without a group, moving on to an assessment of whether a policy is aimed at destroying the group, as a group, is difficult. However, people who care more about conveying outrage at the mass murder and rape of innocent civilians than about the technicalities of a legal definition have referred to the ongoing tragedy in Darfur as genocide from the onset of the violence in 2003. An online CNN headline in 2005 read, "UN report: Darfur not genocide: But perpetrators of violence should be prosecuted" (CNN 2005).

Sudan, like Rwanda, is a new state carved out of an old empire. Its boundaries were determined not by the people in Sudan but by colonial authorities in London. In 1916, the British incorporated Darfur into Sudan. North-south cleavages are marked by religious and racialized identity differences, with Arab Sunni Muslims in the north and Africans who practice indigenous or Christian religions in the south and west, though about 20 percent of Africans in Sudan also practice Islam. This imperfect alignment between race, religious identity, and violence contributes to the "ambiguity" and debate about whether to apply the term *genocide* to the mass killing of black African civilians in southern villages by Arab militias while the Arab-controlled government turns a blind eye if not providing support.

The British, who focused on exploiting the resources of northern Sudan and Egypt during its colonial rule, neglected Darfur. The new postcolonial (and Arab-dominated) government in Khartoum similarly neglected the region following independence in 1956. The Muslim Brotherhood, founded in Egypt and one of the first contemporary radical Islamist groups in the region, had a strong presence in Sudan even before independence. In 1989, a military coup brought Sudan's leader, Colonel Omar al-Bashir, to power. Osama bin Laden set up operations there in 1991, but left for Afghanistan in 1996 under pressure from Egypt, Saudi Arabia, and the United States. The influence of Islamist extremism remained in Sudan even though the new government took action to suppress several key political parties and leaders associated with the Muslim Brotherhood.

Not only imperialism but geo- and ecopolitics also played a role in creating the crisis in Darfur. The famines of 1986–1988 and 1998, which many argue were man-made and politically motivated, were centered and most severe in the south (Keene 2008). According to the US Department of Energy, the majority of Sudan's proven oil reserves are also located in the south and estimates of the extent of those reserves have recently been revised from 563 million barrels to 5 billion barrels (US Information Administration 2008). Whether by neglect or intention, the failure of the Khartoum government to address the crises in Darfur was the rationale for the mobilization of rebel groups that launched attacks against government facilities in the region in 2003. Over the next year the rebels inflicted severe losses on the government's military, and in 2004 President Omar al-Bashir began actively recruiting, arming, and encouraging the primarily black Arab Janjaweed militias to fight the rebel forces from Darfur. Soon the militias were beyond the control of the government, and brutal attacks on villages, in which these militias raped women and girls and killed men and boys, spread throughout the region.

In April 2004, UN undersecretary for humanitarian affairs Jan Egeland denounced the killings, calling the situation "the worst humanitarian crisis in the world" and describing it as a "scorched earth policy" of "ethnic cleansing" (Egeland 2008:89–90). As hundreds of thousands of refugees poured into neighboring Chad, the African Union sent a small number of troops to monitor a cease-fire, though it did not hold. As the crisis continued, the African Union increased its presence to 7,000 troops sent mainly to protect civilians now that the cease-fire was clearly not going to be respected. By September of 2004 an estimated 50,000 people had been killed and 1.2 million made homeless by the violence. The Security Council called the situation a "threat to international peace and security and to stability in the region" and, under the authority of Chapter VII, threatened sanctions against Sudan's oil imports if it did not accept the presence of an expanded peacekeeping force made up of soldiers from member states of the African Union (UN Security Council Resolution 1564). The Security Council also called for an investigation into reports of violations of international humanitarian law, human rights, and acts of genocide and into the identity of the perpetrators. The resolution also demanded

> that the Government of Sudan submit to the African Union Mission for verification documentation, particularly the names of Janjaweed militiamen disarmed and names of those arrested for human rights abuses and violations of international humanitarian law, with regard to its performance relative to resolution 1556 (2004) and the 8 April 2004 N'djamena ceasefire agreement.

In September 2004, US president George W. Bush and Secretary of State Colin Powell called the situation genocide, but the State Department took the position that "the use of the word genocide does not legally oblige the US to act" (BBC News 2004). In January 2005, a UN investigation concluded that genocide was not occurring, but that the militias were perpetrating "systematic abuses" (Hoge 2004). By March 2006, with no effective international intervention in sight, the number of dead rose to 180,000, and by August 2008 the UN estimate of the death toll reached 300,000 with 2.5 million displaced (*St. Petersburg Times* 2006; CBC News 2008). In August 2006, the United Nations called for a greatly increased peacekeeping force of 23,000 but "invited" the consent of the Sudanese government, which President al-Bashir declined.

In May 2007, the ICC issued the first arrest warrants for perpetrators of crimes against humanity in Darfur. The warrants were for Ahmad Muhammad Harun, former minister of state for the interior and minister of state for humanitarian affairs but currently, in 2014, serving as governor of South Kordofan, and Ali Muhammad Al Abd-Al-Rahman, also known as Ali Kushayb, a Janjaweed militia leader. The court's chief prosecutor announced that the government of Sudan had a legal obligation to arrest the two men, and the warrant confirmed a connection between the high-level Sudanese government official and the Janjaweed militias carrying out the attacks on civilians, a connection that went all the way to the top. As a result, in 2009, Omar al-Bashir became the first sitting president of a country to be indicted by an international criminal court. Though still president, he is facing five counts of crimes against humanity, two counts for war crimes, and three counts of genocide.

## Systematic Violence Against the World's Indigenous Peoples

Government-sponsored violence against indigenous peoples within European colonies and settler states presents a unique set of circumstances and challenges to the contemporary legal definition of genocide. The definition in the Genocide Convention emphasizes intent, underscored by the legal application of the convention in the Rwandan and Yugoslav cases. A second key element is that the "intent to destroy" is aimed at a target group defined primarily in terms of national, ethnic, racial, or religious identities. Finally, the definition does not require that the intent be to destroy every member of the group but to "destroy, in whole or in part," the group as a group. In addition to the definitional language, the convention then lists acts that constitute genocide when enacted with the "intent to destroy." It does not require that all of the enumerated acts must occur, but that such acts together with intent constitute genocide. Beyond the direct violence of killing and causing serious mental or bodily harm, the convention also includes (unspecified) acts "calculated to bring about" the physical destruction of the group (again, in whole or in part) as well as acts "intended to prevent births" or "forcibly transfer children of the group to another group." Many of these apply to policies enacted by settler states regarding indigenous peoples as well as to postcolonial governments and their treatment of what are often called tribal peoples.

Indigenous peoples today live on virtually every continent and number around 370 million people worldwide (Wilmer 1993). In September 2007, the General Assembly adopted the Declaration on the Rights of Indigenous Peoples by a vote of 143 to 4. The four states voting against the declaration were, not surprisingly, the powerful British settler states: the United States, Canada, Australia, and New Zealand.

The UN Working Group on Indigenous Peoples adopted a working definition in 1982 that has two elements most often included in any definition. According to this definition, (1) indigenous people are descended from people who inhabited an area prior to a conquest or settlement that resulted in the domination or colonization of prior inhabitants, and (2) groups of those people still constitute culturally distinct groups vis-à-vis the dominant society created as a result of conquest or settlement. Taking control of the postcolonial state and pursuing modernization schemes, dominant groups often subordinated remote tribal people who clearly fit the second criteria of the definition but who were subordinated by other local ethnic or communal groups who reproduced the pattern of settler states by forcing the displacement and assimilation of culturally distinct tribal groups.

India provides an example. Indigenous peoples there are called "scheduled tribes." They make up about 24 percent of the population and are explicitly recognized in the Indian Constitution. These diverse tribal communities, who call themselves Dalits (referred to by upper castes as the "untouchable" lowest caste in the Indian caste system) and Adavasis (regarded as aboriginal), have been both economically marginalized by the modernizing Indian state and subjected to many of the same policies, including forced removal and assimilation, as indigenous peoples elsewhere. Dalits and Adavasis also experience discrimination in India, and they have been subjected to forced evictions as the Indian government proceeds with a large number of "big dam" projects aimed at increasing India's energy generation and accessible clean water. These projects come at the expense of the indigenous peoples living in those areas flooded by the big dam projects (Roy 1999, 2002). However, the Indian government has not really tried or intended to destroy indigenous Dalits and Adavasis as a group.

Similar conditions occur throughout Africa where an ethnic or communal group rises to power in the immediate aftermath of decolonization—usually a group favored or privileged under colonial rule—and carries out a modernization program aimed at building infrastructure, markets, and capital-intensive manufacturing. The rhetoric of modernization and development reveals an ideological bias that rationalizes the marginalization of indigenous peoples as primitive and backward, even casting them as "obstacles to progress," particularly when they occupy areas rich in raw materials or natural resources or areas that have the potential for hydroelectric power development. One example is the Saami in Norway and the hydroelectric power dam project on the Alta River; another is the indigenous Crees living in northern Quebec when the Canadian company Hydro-Québec proposed the Great Whale Project. The Canadian project was delayed through collaborative opposition between the Cree and environmental groups.

Making a case for genocide is difficult based on forced displacement and eviction alone. The issue of genocide is raised when, in the name of modernity and progress, a government engages in any of the five acts identified in Article 2 of the Genocide Convention with the intent to destroy a group as a distinct group. These are killing, causing mental or bodily harm, inflicting conditions aimed at the destruction of the group, forced sterilizations or measures intended to reduce births, and forcible transfer of children to another group. Policies involving these acts have occurred in virtually all of the four largest British settler states—the United States, Canada, Australia, and New Zealand (Wilmer 1993). The question of intent to destroy the group as a group may still be more difficult to evaluate, at least politically. Until recently, the ideology of modernization regarded indigenous peoples as vanishing in the face of the superior technology of modern societies (Wilmer 1993).

In the United States for example, by even the most conservative estimates, between 10 million and 12 million indigenous peoples lived in the lower forty-eight states at the onset of European settlement (Thornton 1987; Mann 2005). Higher estimates are common, ranging from 20 to 50 million. Using the conservative figure, however, the destruction of indigenous peoples between early settlement and the first census including indigenous peoples taken in 1890 is still astounding: the population dropped from even a conservative figure of 10 million to just under 250,000 (Dippie 1982). Between 75 percent and 90 percent of the indigenous population died from epidemic diseases such as smallpox (Crosby 2002). David Stannard (1993) argued that these deaths should also be included in what he calls the "American Holocaust" in the same way that Jews who died of starvation and diseases under Nazi imprisonment were included in the figure for that genocide.

The most dramatic decline in the population of indigenous peoples occurred between the early contact when they were viewed as "savage" in roughly the seventeenth and eighteenth centuries and the internment and assimilation period that began in the late nineteenth century. The nineteenth century was aptly and infamously called by Helen Hunt Jackson (1995 [1881]), a poet, writer, and activist of the time, "a century of dishonor." The worst of US policy and public attitudes toward indigenous peoples in the 1800s is captured by General Philip Sheridan's often-paraphrased comment to Comanche chief Toch-a-way that "the only good Indians I ever saw were dead" (quoted in Morris 1991:328).

## Conclusion

Of all the norms that could qualify as peremptory or *jus cogens*, genocide—acts intended to destroy in whole or in part a group as a group—seems to be the most straightforward. On closer examination and in applying the norm to particular cases, the issue becomes a little more complicated. The Holocaust remains the clearest and most extreme case, yet even here, with reliable information about the nature and scope of the Nazi government's activities (and those of collaborationist regimes) aimed at destroying Jews in Europe, no one intervened to stop the ongoing atrocities. In the case of the Holocaust, political motives and strategic interests played an equal if not greater role in determining who would act and when an adequate commitment would be made to stop the Nazi program. Indeed, the primary objection was to Nazi expansionism rather than the regime's genocidal policies.

Measured by the international community's responses to Cambodia, Rwanda, and Yugoslavia, much progress does not seem to have been made since the Holocaust. Indeed, the precedent set at Nuremberg led to the creation of the two criminal courts for the former Yugoslavia and Rwanda (which in turn contributed to mobilizing the political will in support of the ICC), and individuals have been convicted of genocide in both venues. But these are both after the fact. The political will to support an intervention remains weak, as evidenced by these cases as well as, more recently, Darfur. The greatest obstacle to intervention is not disagreement over whether or not the events in question constitute genocide. The disagreement is over whether (1) an international obligation exists to intervene to stop ongoing atrocities on the scale of a genocide even if the technical question of applying the term *genocide* has been resolved or not, and (2) sufficient international political will can be found to support such an intervention among states with the resources to do so. President Bill Clinton was sharply criticized for avoiding the use of the term *genocide* to describe events in Rwanda allegedly because using the term might have triggered an international responsibility to intervene. On the other hand, the willingness of President George W. Bush to use the term to describe events in Darfur did not lead to either an intervention or even a serious debate about whether condemnation of these events as genocide did entail a responsibility to intervene.

Genocide, acts of genocide, and acts similar to or bordering on genocide have all increasingly been incorporated into the strategic calculations of those who stand to benefit from the outcomes, the changes in power, that follow a conflict that is overshadowed by war crimes and crimes against humanity. In other words, genocide can be used as a smoke screen by those who benefit both from the change in power relations and perhaps even by generating a public image of themselves as rescuers or victims. This ruthless political calculation would surprise no one in former Yugoslavia. Davenport and Stam's (2009) research, however, leaves little doubt that genocide can be exploited for strategic purposes.

Finally, there is the case of indigenous peoples. In order to constitute genocide within the legal framework of the Genocide Convention, must a very large number of people be killed in a very short period? Must the violence be direct and overt? Indigenous peoples were (and may still be in some countries) targeted by state-sponsored, state-supported, or state-assisted violence intended to destroy indigenous "groups as groups" and intended to destroy indigenous peoples "on the whole as a group or category of groups," in the wording of the Genocide Convention. But the events and policies enacted to carry out this project in settler states took place over a century or more and accompanied the violent expansion of control by the postcolonial settler government and boundaries of the settler state. Surviving and descendant indigenous people have little doubt that these events and policies were intended to destroy, by violence or forced assimilation or a combination of the two, indigenous peoples as indigenous peoples. A similar case can be made for African slavery, particularly (but not exclusively) the slave trade conducted by the British and their counterparts in the United States, both before and after the War for Independence.

The arguments for humanitarian intervention, reparations, and postconflict justice and reconciliation are most compelling in connection with cases of genocide, but even in the extreme, mobilizing sufficient political will for interventions remains difficult. Yet returning to a point made earlier, most states are multiethnic, made up of people with a variety of identities. Thousands of communal or identity groups live within fewer than 200 states. The myth of the homogeneous nation-state coupled with the state's monopoly on the legitimate use of force has enabled states to carry out policies aimed at destroying those whose identity is perceived as a threat to the state. In the next chapter, this tension and its consequences short of genocide are examined in more detail.

# 9

# The Laws of War

With all my heart I believe that the world's present system of sovereign nations can only lead to barbarism, war and inhumanity, and that only world law can assure progress towards a civilized peaceful community.
—Albert Einstein, quoted in 1945 after the
US bombing of Nagasaki and Hiroshima

The world no longer has a choice between force and law; if civilization is to survive, it must choose the rule of law.
—President Dwight D. Eisenhower, 1958

EXAMINING THE LAWS OF WAR IS ESSENTIAL TO UNDERSTANDING contemporary international human rights for two reasons. First, every state that violates human rights claims to do so out of necessity—the necessity of national security. Second, the ultimate act in defense of national security is the conduct of war or armed conflict, and at present, most judicial enforcement of human rights takes place primarily through the prosecution of war crimes and crimes against humanity committed during armed conflicts, as several of the genocide cases in the previous chapter illustrate. Individuals fighting on behalf of nonstate actors and irregular forces have also been prosecuted for war crimes and crimes against humanity, particularly in the internal or civil wars in former Yugoslavia and Rwanda. In earlier chapters, I discussed the development of the contemporary state in relation to human rights and international enforcement in areas other than the laws of war. The earlier chapters provided a backdrop for the question addressed in this chapter: How has the development of legal restraints on state use of force strengthened international human rights norms, the protection of human rights, and the enforcement of those norms?

The modern state promises security for its citizens' rights and freedoms. In Chapter 5, I showed how alleged threats to national security can be used as a pretext for exempting the state from social contract obligations (like guarantees of habeas corpus) when threats to national security arise from internal sources. The normal condition of protecting citizens' rights is reversed when citizens are suspected of threatening to attack the state or overthrow its government, and the state responds by suspending, diminishing, or compromising due process and the rule of law that normally provide safeguards against the arbitrary use of state power. Threats to national security also arise from external sources, from nationals of other states, or from policies enacted by other states. Since the attacks of September 11, 2001, however, no problem has presented a greater challenge to democracies than the difficulty of distinguishing between internal and external, or domestic and foreign, threats in the case of terrorism.

Though the contemporary state claims a monopoly on the legitimate use of force, not all uses of force by states are regarded as legitimate. International norms restricting the way states use force in their relations with other states developed before norms restricting state use of force internally. These limits address both how and why force is used and are codified in the laws of war. They evolved from the long history of the laws and customs of war that parallel the development of the modern state. The earliest writing on the subject of war and the state was Hugo Grotius's *The Law of War and Peace*, published in 1625, twenty-three years before the Peace of Westphalia.

Human rights and humanitarian law are different but complementary. Both aim to protect the rights and dignity of human beings but in different ways and different contexts. Humanitarian law applies to people in areas of armed conflict—combatants, civilians, and prisoners of war. Human rights, alternatively, apply to people in zones of conflict and zones of peace. Many armed conflicts today are conducted in "gray zones" where war has not been declared. Individuals participating in the violence are irregulars or not members of a military at all. Weapons and forms of violence, from improvised explosive devices to unmanned combat air vehicles, or drones, often bear little resemblance to conventional arms. Finally, parties to a conflict are frequently nonstate actors. Similarly, states otherwise at peace have undertaken a war on terror that has no geographic or temporal limits and blurs the boundaries between internal and external threats.

Why are norms pertaining to the conduct of war relevant to contemporary human rights? One reason is that genocide, covered in Chapter 8, is often carried out in the context of war or of armed conflict not necessarily formally declared war, as the genocides in Rwanda and Cambodia demonstrate. As a human rights violation, genocide is now a punishable international crime for which individuals have been charged, found guilty, and sentenced in the twentieth century, as demonstrated by the ICTR, which rendered the first genocide conviction in 1998. Another reason for the relevance of war to human rights is that the national security argument is used not only to justify making an exception to the norms with a country's own citizens but also in the treatment of individuals captured, detained, and imprisoned during a war. National security exceptionalism, discussed further in Chapter 10, means that the state claims that protecting the citizens and the order of the state makes exceptions to the normal protection of citizens' rights necessary. Normally, due process is guaranteed to all, but threats to national security require that exceptions be made, so the argument goes. This argument is not new. For example, the right of habeas corpus was suspended during the US Civil War, ironically by the president best known for his defense of rights: Abraham Lincoln. Of great concern to human rights is the potential for abuse, for claiming a national security necessity as the basis for exceptional measures that derogate the normal protections based on questionable evidence and without checks and balances or accountability.

Claiming a national security exception creates an obvious potential for conflict between national security interests and democratic values. Democracy is grounded in values of due process, civil liberties, and fundamental freedoms including speech, association, and press. States generally do not provide exactly the same protections of due process and civil liberties to noncitizens as they do to citizens, but some do. On balance, at least prior to the attacks of 9/11, the United States has recognized constitutional protections for foreign nationals, although in some circumstances, the courts have ruled they can be treated differently, for example, they are entitled to due process in the court system and their first amendment freedoms are protected the same as US citizens, but they are denied the right to vote and hold office (Cole 2003). The difficulty of distinguishing internal and external enemies and the porousness of national boundaries combined with the perceived increase in threats from terrorist tactics create unprecedented pressures on democratic governments to compromise these values as the price for providing security against such threats. Examples of the consequences of this conflict in the US responses to post-9/11 security threats are abundant, beginning with the creation of a new category of detainees— unlawful enemy combatant—specifically for the purpose of placing them beyond the protection of both domestic and international law. Since 2002, the US war on terror has been used to justify practices internationally defined as torture (e.g., waterboarding), indefinite and incommunicado detentions at Guantanamo Bay without trial, and the extrajudicial execution (euphemistically called "targeted killing" to refer to killing specific individuals believed to be enemy combatants by the United States) of US citizens Anwar al-Awlaki and his teenage son in separate events in 2011. As David

Cole notes, since the September 11 attacks "thousands of foreign nationals have been detailed under terrorist-related initiatives, most conducted under the rubric of the immigration law. Foreign nationals have been subjected to selective interrogation, registration, detention, and deportation on the basis of their national identity" (Cole 2003:367).

Many provisions in the laws of war aim to clarify and protect the rights of prisoners of war and detainees, but some gray areas remain. For example, do the laws of war apply universally or only to state signatories to various treaties and conventions? The answer to this question is complicated by modern factors that could not have been contemplated by our forefathers. The laws of war contemplate interstate war, not war between states and nonstate actors, though they do address the limited situation where a belligerent party in a civil war is internationally recognized. Should these laws be applied to nonstate actors whose use of force is of questionable legitimacy in the first place? If so, how? These questions are also raised in connection with US policies as part of the war on terror and led the United States to create a special category of detainees known as "unlawful enemy combatants," a term that does not appear in either the Hague Conventions or the Geneva Conventions. What about crimes against humanity that take place in the context of a civil war in a state that has not signed any instrument subjecting it to international enforcement of prohibitions against crimes against humanity? This question arose when the UN Security Council referred allegations of war crimes and crimes against humanity taking place in the Darfur region of Sudan to the ICC, even though the government of Sudan is not a signatory to the statute that created the court.

Many ask, is it possible to civilize the conduct of war in the first place? Vietnam veteran and author William Broyles Jr. said poignantly that "there is a difference between killing and murder and every soldier knows what that is" (quoted in Keen, Jersey, and Friedman 1985). Broyles, who served in Vietnam as a first lieutenant in the US Marines, went on to say that "there is no greater gulf between men than the gulf of the battlefield" and then described his own experience encountering an "enemy" in the pitch-black darkness of an underground tunnel he was lining with explosives. He found denying his enemy's humanity impossible and so tried to warn him to evacuate the tunnel before it exploded and save his own life.

Broyles's experience is a testimony to the great difficulty in denying the humanity of another human being even when circumstances or the orders of a superior authority would have us do so (Grossman 1996). The experience of US soldiers in Vietnam also offers evidence of the opposite effect in the case of the My Lai Massacre when more than 500 defenseless South Vietnamese, including women, the elderly, children, and infants, were murdered by US soldiers (Cookman 2007). Most were civilians, and many were sexually assaulted, gang-raped, mutilated, and beaten before being killed. The victims included a Buddhist monk (Cookman 2007). Notably, although rape has been used throughout the history of war as a weapon to demoralize and terrorize local civilian populations, it was not prosecuted as a war crime until the ICTY. Why some people find disregarding and violating the humanity of others impossible and others seem willing to do so with impunity is a complex psychological question (Wilmer 2002). War normalizes behavior prohibited in times of peace, but where are the boundaries between war and peace? The laws of war, especially pertaining to the treatment of prisoners of war, attempt to delineate those boundaries.

## Just War Theory

The concept of a just war as a matter of international law originates with writings from St. Augustine on Christian theology during the fourth and fifth centuries, Thomas Aquinas in the thirteenth century, and, in more modern times, Christian realists like Reinhold Niebuhr in the early to mid-twentieth century. In this view, moral individuals are obligated to combat evil and even act as agents to punish sin and moral wrongdoing. Just war theory contrasts with the notion that "might makes right" still found in contemporary realist thinking. Augustine's criteria for just war begin by requiring a just or properly constituted authority, just cause, just intention, and an exhaustion of diplomacy and other peaceful efforts to resolve the situation. His view of the just conduct of war required proportionality (no more force than necessary to achieve victory), the necessity of discriminating between civilian and combatant individuals and property, and taking responsibility for achieving an outcome where the benefits outweighed the injury caused by the war.

In the thirteenth century, Aquinas elaborated on Augustine's theory by adding that not only must a just war be fought to remedy a moral wrong, but there should also be a reasonable expectation of winning. Dutch theologian Hugo de Groot—known publically by his Latin name Hugo Grotius—challenged the Christian foundations of just war theory by taking a more humanist or natural law perspective in his three-volume treatise *On the Laws of War and Peace* published in 1625. In the treatise, Grotius, who lived during a time of great political turmoil in Europe including the Dutch-Spanish Eighty Years War and the Thirty Years War of religious conflict between Catholics and Protestants throughout Europe, outlined three causes that could justify war: self-defense, reparation for injury, and punishment. From a human rights perspective, his third volume is the most relevant because it addresses the rules that govern a justly fought war, once begun. Grotius delineated what acts are unlawful in war, the status of property, the nature of reprisals, the right to kill an enemy, the "right way to lay waste an enemy's country," acquisition by conquest, and the "right" over prisoners of war. But he also called for tempering "with moderation and humanity" the "right of killing enemies, in just war," and "moderation in despoiling an enemy's country" as well as in "making captures during war."

Perhaps the most influential and widely read contemporary work on just war theory is Michael Walzer's *Just and Unjust Wars* (1977). Walzer segregated responsibility for choosing to fight a war—a responsibility that rests with the political leadership—from the soldier's responsibility to fight it in a moral manner. He disclosed in the preface that political activism and the Vietnam War motivated his inquiry into just and unjust wars. War, he argued, is a "moral condition" involving permissiveness among combatants to be morally equal because "without the equal right to kill, war as a rule-governed activity would disappear and be replaced by crime and punishment, by evil conspiracies and military law enforcement" (41). According to Walzer, two kinds of rules pertain to killing: rules prescribing how soldiers kill one another and rules protecting noncombatants from being targeted. The second set of rules, he argued, is the most important because it acknowledges a moral boundary between combatant and civilian, or between killing and murder in Lieutenant Broyles's terms. Prisoners of war acquire rights because they have surrendered but, in surrendering, give up their right to kill.

The case for having a just cause is always stronger when broad and diverse support is present as in the first Gulf War rather than resting on the overwhelming influence and power of a lone superpower, as was the case in the Iraq War. The war on terror brings several sets of problems relating to the conduct of war, and human rights come to the forefront of the discussion. The first is the straightforward problem of compliance by signatories of the conventions. The United States, for example, argues that since war crimes allegations against US military personnel are prosecuted adequately within the US system of military courts-marshal, the United States has no reason, nor should it be expected, to join the treaty giving the ICC jurisdiction over these crimes. This issue will be addressed a little more fully later in the chapter. Of course, all allegations of criminal conduct are not guaranteed to be dealt with by domestic military courts. The second set of problems centers on how one party to an armed conflict can prevail within the restraints of legal conduct when the opposing party is not so restrained because it is not a party to the convention. The authors anticipated this problem, and Article 2 of the Third Geneva Convention requires that parties to the convention respect its terms in conflicts with nonsignatories, although this convention was clearly only anticipated to apply to states because it refers to the "powers." So a third problem is how should the issue be handled when one of the parties to a conflict is a nonstate actor? In the case of the wars in former Yugoslavia and the genocide and war in Rwanda, the international tribunals created by the UN Security Council solved or averted this problem by establishing that the courts' competence and jurisdiction applied to "persons" who violated the Geneva Conventions and customary laws of war and "persons" who committed various war crimes and genocide.

The United States dealt with the problem differently following the attacks of September 11. Individuals fighting in the Taliban forces were treated as enemy combatants under the command of the State of Afghanistan. But members or individuals alleged to be members of the al-Qaeda terrorist network were designated as "illegal enemy combatants," a term thus far only used by the United States although Israel makes a distinction between legal and illegal combatants that is very similar. The term *illegal enemy combatant* should not be confused with the term *unlawful combatant*, which had previously been used by the United States in prosecuting war criminals in World War II. At that time, the relevant distinction was between individuals who deliberately attempt to conceal their military status and those who wear uniforms openly, affirmed in the US Supreme Court case *Ex parte Quirin,* where eight Germans faced a US military commission in 1942. The handling of the war on terror has raised a host of thorny legal issues in US government efforts to create a category of individuals that due to their real or alleged actions are deprived of the protections of the laws and rules of warfare and any rights under US domestic law.

Finally, the US Congress passed the Military Commissions Act of 2006 (Pub. L. No. 109-366, 120 Stat. 2600) amending Section 10 of the US Code to define unlawful enemy combatants as "(i) a person who has engaged in hostilities or who has purposefully and materially supported hostilities against the United States or its co-belligerents who is not a lawful enemy combatant (including a person who is part of the Taliban, al-Qaida, or associated forces); or (ii) a person who, before, on, or after the date of the enactment of the Military Commissions Act of 2006, has been determined to be an unlawful enemy combatant by a Combatant Status Review Tribunal or another competent tribunal established under the authority of the President or the Secretary of Defense." The act defined a lawful enemy combatant as "(A) a member of the regular forces of a State party engaged in hostilities against the United States; (B) a member of a militia, volunteer corps, or organized resistance movement belonging to a State party engaged in such hostilities, which are under responsible command, wear a fixed distinctive sign recognizable at a distance, carry their arms openly, and abide by the law of war; or (C) a member of a regular armed force who professes allegiance to a government engaged in such hostilities, but not recognized by the United States."

## Hague and Geneva Conventions on the Laws of War

*Hague Conference, July 29, 1899*
Hague I: Pacific Settlement of International Disputes
Hague II: Laws and Customs of War on Land
Hague III: Adaptation to Maritime Warfare of Principles of Geneva
    Convention of 1864
Hague IV: Prohibiting Launching of Projectiles and Explosives from Balloons
Declaration I on the Launching of Projectiles and Explosives from Balloons
Declaration II on the Use of Projectiles the Object of Which Is the Diffusion
    of Asphyxiating or Deleterious Gasses
Declaration III on the Use of Bullets Which Expand or Flatten Easily in the
    Human Body
Final Act of the International Peace Conference

*Hague Conference, October 18, 1907*
Hague I: Pacific Settlement of International Disputes
Hague II: Limitation of Employment of Force for Recovery of Contract Debts
Hague III: Opening of Hostilities
Hague IV: Laws and Customs of War on Land
Hague V: Rights and Duties of Neutral Powers and Persons in Case of War
    on Land
Hague VI: Status of Enemy Merchant Ships at the Outbreak of Hostilities
Hague VII: Conversion of Merchant Ships into War Ships
Hague VIII: Laying of Automatic Submarine Contact Mines
Hague IX: Bombardment by Naval Forces in Time of War
Hague X: Adaptation to Maritime War of the Principles of the Geneva
    Convention
Hague XI: Restrictions with Regard to the Exercise of the Right of Capture
    in Naval War
Hague XII: Relative to the Creation of an International Prize Court
Hague XIII: Rights and Duties of Neutral Powers in Naval War

*Geneva Conventions*
1864: Amelioration of the Condition of the Wounded on the Field of Battle,
    August 22
1906: Convention for the Amelioration of the Condition of the Wounded and
    Sick Armies in the Field, July 6
1906: Convention on the Amelioration of the Condition of the Wounded, Sick
    and Shipwrecked Members of the Armed Forces at Sea, October 18
1928: Protocol for the Prohibition of the Use in War of Asphyxiating Gas,
    and for Bacteriological Methods of Warfare, February 8
1929: Convention Between the United States of America and Other Powers,
    Relating to Prisoners of War, July 27
1949: Convention (I) for the Amelioration of the Condition of the Wounded
    and Sick in Armed Forces in the Field, August 12

*continues*

---

### Hague and Geneva Conventions on the Laws of War

1949: Convention (II) for the Amelioration of the Condition of Wounded, Sick and Shipwrecked Members of the Armed Forces at Sea, August 12

1949: Convention (III) Relative to the Treatment of Prisoners of War, August 12

1949: Convention (IV) Relative to the Protection of Civilian Persons in the Time of War, August 12

1975: Convention on the Prohibition of the Development, Production and Stockpiling of Bacteriological (Biological) and Toxic Weapons and on Their Destruction, March 26

1977: Protocol I, Relating to the Protection of Victims of International Armed Conflicts, June 8; Protocol II, Relating to the Protection of Victims of Non-International Armed Conflicts, June 8

2005: Protocol III, Relating to the Adoption of a Distinctive Emblem, December 8

---

All of these problems should be kept in mind when considering how the customary laws of war and the body of positive law in modern treaties and conventions are applied to regulate the use of force in a world increasingly characterized by conflicts between parties with asymmetrical capabilities, conflicts involving parties using terrorist tactics and primarily targeting civilians, and conflicts between state and nonstate actors. The treaties and conventions relevant to the laws of war and international humanitarian law are listed in the box.

## The Rules of Warfare

*Jus in bello* refers to the legality of how a war, once begun, is conducted. In contrast, *jus ad bellum* refers to the legality of the reasons for going to war, that is, the criteria used to evaluate whether war is permissible or whether the "right" to go to war can be exercised in particular circumstances. The problem of one party attempting to conduct a war in a just manner and an opponent that is not is not new. General George Washington told his troops in his letter "Charge to the Northern Expeditionary Force" on September 14, 1775,

> Should any American soldier be so base and infamous as to injure any [prisoner] . . . I do most earnestly enjoin you to bring him to such severe and exemplary punishment as the enormity of the crime may require. Should it extend to death itself, it will not be disproportional to its guilt at such a time and in such a cause . . . for by such conduct they bring shame, disgrace and ruin to themselves and their country.

The British, who regarded the US revolutionary forces as traitors, captured all thirty-one insurgent soldiers at Bunker Hill three months before the above order was issued. Those soldiers died in captivity. Nevertheless, the next year General George Washington instructed his army on the humane treatment of prisoners in the custody of the Continental Army, saying, "Treat them with humanity, and let them have no reason to complain of our copying the brutal example of the British Army in their treatment of our unfortunate brethren who have fallen into their hands" (quoted in Horton 2007). "While we are contending for our own liberty," Washington said, "we should be very cautious of violating the right of conscience in others, ever considering that God alone is the judge of the hearts of men, and to Him only in this case, are they answerable" (quoted in Novak and Novak 2006:230).

David Hackett Fischer (2004) wrote of Washington's determination to treat enemy prisoners with humanity as an extension of his deep commitment to the values that motivated the revolution as well as, in practical terms, a policy that was more likely to foster desertion by the British and Hessian soldiers he wished to defeat.

Before the US Civil War, the humane treatment of prisoners of war was primarily a matter of customary law. In 1863, Francis (formerly Franz) Lieber, a German-born US legal philosopher and jurist, codified these norms in *Code for the Government of Armies of the United States in the Field*, a text that came to be known by its more popular moniker, the Lieber Code. The US Army field manual made a distinction between soldiers and criminals and prohibited "intentional suffering and indignity, as well as mutilation, torture and other barbarity" (Mayer 2008:84).

The Lieber Code was incorporated into the final documents of the Hague Conferences in 1899 and 1907. The Annex to the 1899 Convention recognizes that armed forces may consist of both combatants and noncombatants and declares that both have a right be treated as prisoners of war. Article 4 of Chapter II entitled "Prisoners of War" states that "prisoners of war are in the power of the hostile Government, but not in that of the individuals or corps who captured them" and that "they must be humanely treated." It also guarantees their right to practice their own religion and requires that they receive the same maintenance provisions as the soldiers of the government that has captured them.

The Geneva Conventions are the core of international humanitarian law. Virtually all states today have acceded to the conventions and their protocols. Though neither the term *humanitarian law* nor the term *human rights* was widely used until after World War II, the concepts of humanitarian law and humanitarian intervention have been subjects of normative development since the earliest period of modern state development. The terms *humanitarian law* and *laws of war* are often used interchangeably.

However, until the mid-nineteenth century, these norms were not codified and thus were not part of the body of customary international law.

The First Geneva Convention, the Convention on the Amelioration of the Condition of the Wounded on the Field of Battle, was based on an earlier convention signed in 1864 also in Geneva, Switzerland, and ratified by the United States in 1882. This convention was adopted in conjunction with the establishment of the International Red Cross organization. Inspired by the Swiss global Red Cross network on a visit to Europe after the Civil War, Clara Barton, along with her supporters, founded the American Red Cross to bring medical treatment and protection to those injured in war. As indicated in Chapter 7, the Swiss initiative was undertaken by Henry Dunant, who was horrified by the conventional practice of leaving wounded soldiers on the battlefield to die. After a battle between Austria and Sardinia left 40,000 French and Austrian casualties, Dunant called a conference of sixteen countries, and the first of the Geneva Conventions was drafted in 1864 (Solis 2010). The Geneva Convention of 1864 was ultimately ratified by the United States and twelve other states, including three (Wurttemberg, Baden, and Hesse) that were not yet unified into the modern state of Germany. Other parties to the original convention were the Swiss Confederation, Belgium, Denmark, Italy, Spain, France, the Netherlands, Portugal, and Prussia, with Great Britain notably missing. The 1864 convention guaranteed the neutrality of medical personnel and those assisting them on the battlefield. The original convention was revised in 1907 and again 1929 and then finally adopted in its current form as the First Geneva Convention in 1949.

The Second Geneva Convention extends the treatment of battlefield casualties to those who are injured in war at sea. The original convention was signed in 1906 but was reworked and finalized in 1949.

The Third Geneva Convention specifically addresses the treatment of prisoners of war. The original convention was signed by the United States and forty-one other states in 1929 and ratified in 1932. It refers to the 1907 Hague Convention annex identifying persons covered by the new agreement. The 1929 version was significantly revised and then finalized in 1949. The convention requires humane treatment and protects those captured "against acts of violence, insults, and public curiosity." Article 3 (called "Common Article 3" because it appears in all of the Geneva Conventions) declares, "Prisoners of war have the right to have their person and their honor respected. Women shall be treated with all regard due their sex." Article 5 states that "no coercion may be used on prisoners to secure information" and that those who refuse cannot be "threatened, insulted, or exposed to unpleasant or disadvantageous treatment of any kind whatsoever." Other articles guarantee that "the food ration of prisoners of war shall be equal in quantity and quality to that of troops at base camps" and "sufficiency of potable water shall be furnished them." It requires they be kept in sanitary conditions and enabled to correspond with family, exercise, freely practice their religion, and receive monthly medical examinations.

Numerous articles deal with the potential use of prisoner-of-war labor, its compensation and conditions, and prohibitions. Provisions are made for a complaint process and for complainants' representation in dealing with military and camp authorities. The conventions prescribe the offenses and conditions of punishment not to exceed thirty days even in the case of punishment for multiple actions. Chapter 3, Articles 60–67 outline the judicial process for suits against individual prisoners, which can only be brought in the same military courts and by the same procedure as those involving cases against the armed forces of the detaining power. Seriously ill or injured prisoners are to be returned to their own country.

In addition to the categories described in the 1907 Hague Convention, Title VII, Article 81 of the 1929 Geneva Convention applies to "individuals who follow armed forces without directly belonging thereto, such as newspaper correspondents and reporters, sutlers, contractors, who fall into the enemy's hands and whom the latter think expedient to detain, shall be entitled to be treated as prisoners of war." Common Article 3 in the Third Geneva Convention notably addresses the issue of "conflicts not of an international character," proclaiming that "in the case of armed conflict not of an international character occurring in the territory of one of the High Contracting Parties, each Party to the conflict shall be bound to apply, as a minimum, the following provisions." Those provisions include protection of civilians or combatants who surrender and prohibitions against murder, cruelty or torture, humiliating and degrading treatment, and extrajudicial executions. The US Supreme Court ruled in 2006 in *Hamdan v. Rumsfeld* (548 US 557) that Common Article 3 does apply in actions taken by the United States in Iraq, Afghanistan, and the global war on terror. This case will be further discussed in the next chapter.

The Fourth Geneva Convention, formally entitled "Geneva Convention Relative to the Protection of Civilian Persons in Time of War," was signed in 1949 and specifically deals with the protection of civilians in enemy hands and under any foreign occupation. It covers international and internal armed conflicts and protects citizens as well as foreign nationals (those who find themselves "in the hands of a Party to the conflict or Occupying Power of which they are not nationals"). As does the third convention, it also prohibits (1) violence to life and person, in particular murder of all kinds, mutilation, cruel treatment, and torture, (2) taking of hostages, and (3) outrages upon personal dignity, in particular humiliating and degrading treatment.

Article 4 excludes protection of nationals of a state not party to the convention. It also stipulates that nationals of a neutral, belligerent, or cobelligerent state are not protected persons under the fourth convention so long as the state in which they are nationals has diplomatic relations with the state in which they find themselves. In other words, the convention only protects civilians who are not nationals of neutral, belligerent, or allied states, since each of those groups are protected by their own state and its diplomatic representatives. The treatment of civilians by a state with which one has diplomatic relations is a legal and diplomatic matter between the two states. But if diplomatic relations are severed, then civilians of those states are protected. Under international law, states protect or are held accountable for the conduct of their own citizens in another state's territory. Article 4 also excludes those covered by the other Geneva Conventions. The revised convention is extensive with 159 articles in the main body and 8 more in the annex. Article 148 calls upon parties to pass legislation and provide penal sanctions for persons committing grave breaches of the conventions' provisions. "Grave breaches" are spelled out in Article 149 as follows:

> Grave breaches to which the preceding Article relates shall be those involving any of the following acts, if committed against persons or property protected by the present Convention: willful killing, torture or inhuman treatment, including biological experiments, willfully causing great suffering or serious injury to body or health, unlawful deportation or transfer or unlawful confinement of a protected person, compelling a protected person to serve in the forces of a hostile Power, or willfully depriving a protected person of the rights of fair and regular trial prescribed in the present Convention, taking of hostages and extensive destruction and appropriation of property, not justified by military necessity and carried out unlawfully and wantonly.

Along with the Geneva Conventions originally signed in 1864 and 1906, the Geneva Convention of 1929, the one regarding prisoners of war, was also revised in 1949. The revised convention further elaborates on whom its provisions are binding—for example, a signatory is bound in a conflict with a nonsignatory until the nonsignatory no longer acts in conformity with the convention. It also stipulates what kinds of conflicts are covered (those of an "international character" and those "not of an international character") as well as the status of combatants and how that status is determined. The fourth convention stipulates that "should any doubt arise as to whether persons, having committed a belligerent act and having fallen into the hands of the enemy, belong to any of the categories enumerated in Article 4, such persons shall enjoy the protection of the present Convention until such time as their status has been determined by a competent tribunal."

This point, together with Article 5 of the fourth convention, is critical in the debate over the US designation and subsequent treatment of unlawful enemy combatants. Article 5 of the fourth convention allows some persons—"spies, saboteurs" and those "suspected of or engaged in activities hostile to the security of the State" to be exempted from the convention's full protection. Nevertheless, it requires that "in each case, such persons shall nevertheless be treated with humanity," regardless of their designation.

Finally, in 1977 two additional protocols were added to the Geneva Conventions. A protocol is a separate international agreement that usually strengthens or extends the obligations of the treaty to which it is attached. Signatories may sign the convention or treaty without signing a related protocol. In the case of the Geneva Conventions, the first protocol pertains to victims of international armed conflicts and the second to victims of noninternational armed conflicts. Protocol I, in the "general principles" article (Article 1, paragraph 2), further underscores the protection of all persons in any armed conflict by the principles of international law and humanity, even when not covered by international agreements: "In cases not covered by this Protocol or by other international agreements, civilians and combatants remain under the protection and authority of the principles of international law derived from established custom, from the principles of humanity and from dictates of public conscience."

In Protocol II, Article 4 outlines specific prohibitions on the treatment of civilians and combatants who have ceased taking part in the hostilities as well as provisions for the care of children in noninternational armed conflicts. Article 5 applies to those who have been "deprived of their liberty for reasons related to the armed conflict, whether they are interned or detained," and enumerates their rights while detained as well as restrictions placed on those detaining them. Like the other conventions and protocol, it also includes a statement about the treatment of persons not covered: "Persons who are not covered by paragraph 1 but whose liberty has been restricted in any way whatsoever for reasons related to the armed conflict shall be treated humanely in accordance with Article 4 and with paragraphs 1 (a), (c) and (d), and 2 (b) of this Article."

## Terrorism and the Laws of War

The question of whether irregular forces—armed forces not under the command of a state—should be held accountable under the laws of war was answered in the ICTY in the affirmative. However, the wars in Iraq and Afghanistan and the war on terror itself raise a new set of questions about what protections should be afforded to, and the legal responsibility of, nonstate actors who carry out violent acts against primarily civilian targets. Furthermore, as suggested at the beginning of this chapter, the distinction between combat and civilian targets is not the only water that terrorism muddies, but also the distinction between civilian and militarized perpetrators. For example, the Taliban recruits women who appear to be civilians or uses handicapped children as suicide bombers (Roggio 2013).

Similar problems have always been part and parcel in guerrilla warfare, but guerrilla warriors do not necessarily target civilians. The distinction they muddy is between civilian and military combatants. The term *guerrilla warfare* has generally been used to refer to nonstate actors who take matters into their own hands, usually to expel or resist an occupying force or to overthrow an autocratic government. Guerrilla warriors often deliberately adopt a civilian appearance, and the laws of war address at least this much—they are only entitled to the rights of soldiers if they display some "fixed distinctive sign visible at a distance" (Walzer 1977:182). Guerrilla warfare is also generally associated with a grassroots force that is widely supported by the nonguerrilla or general population who aids and abets them. The Vietcong may be the best-known example of guerrilla warriors. No doubt, the Vietcong committed war crimes, as did the US forces (I make this statement not to suggest moral equivalency, just to state the fact that war crimes were committed by both sides). However, the ability of the Vietcong to thwart the US soldiers' ability to distinguish enemy combatants from civilians combined with the widespread support for the Vietcong among the general population created an advantage for the guerrillas. Yet the blurred lines between civilians and combatants are only the tip of the iceberg regarding the issues involved in the war on terror when the uniformed military under the command of a state or alliance of states accountable to the Geneva Conventions confronts guerrilla-like insurgents who use both terrorist tactics and improvised explosive devices as their weapons of choice.

The deliberate use of terrorist tactics takes the problem of distinction to an entirely new level. The authors of the Geneva Conventions anticipated the involvement of civilians and combatants not under the command of a state or a signatory to the conventions, but when members of al-Qaeda turned huge hijacked passenger jets into weapons that targeted thousands of civilians, the laws of war and its advocates arguably faced their greatest challenge yet.

## Changing International Norms on State Use of Force

International norms on the use of force by states have several implications for contemporary human rights. One is that, as the previous discussion suggests, regulating state conduct during war has aimed at both protecting civilians and treating captive enemy combatants in a civil manner. Another way these norms impact human rights is that they not only distinguish between legitimate and illegitimate uses of force but also enable the development of norms pertaining to humanitarian interventions, discussed as an instrument of national foreign policy in Chapter 6. A third link between the normative framework in which state force is used and human rights is war crimes, a concern that has moved to center stage since World War II and has been addressed by subsequent tribunals and now the ICC.

The Geneva Conventions and subsequent protocols formulated and revised between 1864 and 1977 both reflect and parallel changes in international norms pertaining to the use of force over roughly that same period. The precursor of these changes was the defeat of Napoleon in 1814 and the Congress of Vienna that followed in 1815. The congress met from September 1814 to June 1815 and agreed to make an effort to utilize multilateral diplomacy to avoid armed conflict in post-Napoleonic Europe. They were not only concerned with returning to sovereign status those territories annexed by Napoleon but also consolidating Germany. Most importantly from the perspective of international norms, the Congress of Vienna negotiated an agreement to the free navigation of the Rhine River, creating a commission to oversee this agreement's implementation and to work toward the free navigation of other European rivers following the congress. From the perspective of human rights, also noteworthy is that the final documents include a condemnation of the slave trade by France and Great Britain, arguably the first time a human rights issue became a part of a state's foreign policy.

Following this historic meeting and its agreements, the notion that war was an acceptable instrument of foreign policy to be used for whatever reasons a state's leaders wished began to lose its appeal. European states continued to use force arbitrarily as imperial powers outside of Europe but showed restraint in their relations with one another. The Congress of Vienna, intended to restore a balance of power in Europe, marked the beginning of a long peace among European states. This "Concert of Europe" lasted until World War I, often credited with a century of peace in Europe, but this characterization downplays or overlooks the Crimean War of 1854–1856. The Crimean War was not a war between the major allied Western European states but was brought on by the decline of the Ottoman Empire and related territorial disputes. The decline of the Ottoman Empire, along with the decline of the Habsburg Empire, contributed to the outbreak of World War I.

The normative move from war as an acceptable tool of foreign policy to the illegality of aggression toward another state without provocation and the distinction between offensive and defensive war, began with the Congress of Vienna and was codified in the UN Charter in 1945. The shift is evident in the proceedings of the two Hague Conferences where delegates praised the success of their long peace and optimistically anticipated continued peace for centuries to come. When states did resort to force, delegates expected them to restrain themselves within the parameters set by the conventions. Even the outbreak of World War I—at the time thought to be the "war to end all wars"—did not convince them otherwise as they set about remedying what European leaders saw as the institutional deficiencies that gave states few alternatives to using force to resolve their differences and finding common interests that would compel them to do so. The Concert of Europe did attempt to maintain ongoing diplomatic relations, primarily to preserve the status quo. The 1899 Hague Conference established the Permanent Court of Arbitration. World War I renewed the commitment of Western states to create cooperative and adjudicatory institutions that would prevent or resolve conflicts short of using force. These aspirations were embodied in the League of Nations and the Permanent Court of International Justice.

Woodrow Wilson's "Fourteen Points" speech also anticipated the importance, if not the complexity and difficulty, of achieving self-determination as a principle of international order, driven by conflicts arising out of ethnic nationalism in the breakdown of the two empires in Europe. Efforts were also made to begin disarmament or at least arms control during the interwar period, along with an attempt to outlaw aggressive uses of force in the Kellogg-Briand Pact of 1928. All of these developments signaled a willingness to restrict state sovereignty in terms of the use of force in relations between states. However, a shift in states' attention toward restricting the use of force *within* states during peacetime would only come about as a result of the Armenian genocide and the Holocaust.

The UN Charter attempted to remedy some of the structural and political flaws that undermined the League of Nations, including the League's deliberate exclusion of a major power (Germany) capable of disrupting the order created by the League, the failure to persuade the United States to join, and the ease with which states could withdraw and then, with impudence, launch aggressive military campaigns against other states, such as Russia in Finland, Japan in Manchuria, and Italy in Ethiopia. If the success of the United Nations is measured solely by its ability to prevent direct war between or among major powers, then its record has exceeded the forty-year peace negotiated in Vienna in 1815. But perhaps as important from the perspective of international norms restricting the use of force is its delineation of the distinction between illegal force—aggression that violates the territorial integrity or political independence of other states—and legal force—self-defense against aggression exercised either individually or collectively and enforcement actions authorized by the Security Council.

Furthermore, the right of member states to use force for the purpose of self-defense can only be exercised until the Security Council acts on the matter. If the Security Council fails to act, then the state claiming legal exercise of self-defense may continue to use force until the belligerent parties cease hostilities on their own. The Iran-Iraq War (1980–1988) provides a recent example, as Iraqi forces invaded Iran in September of 1980. The UN Security Council repeatedly called for a cease-fire, but did not authorize any other action (such as an intervention) to bring the war to an end. It is not clear if the Security Council could have taken other actions to end the conflict sooner, but it did negotiate an end to the war with Resolution 598, which was accepted by both sides. The Security Council does have one major weapon in its arsenal, though weak political will and divergent interests among permanent members have thus far inhibited development of the Council's full authority. The Security Council may broaden the scope of its authority in any way its members see fit: "The Security Council shall determine the existence of any threat to the peace, breach of the peace, or act of aggression and shall make recommendations, or decide what measures shall be taken in accordance with Articles 41 and 42, to maintain or restore international peace and security."

The Security Council can authorize nonmilitary (Article 41) and military (Article 42) measures. In other words, the Security Council has wide latitude to decide what matters constitute threats or breaches of peace or acts of aggression so long as nine of its members agree and no permanent member vetoes the action. From the perspective of human rights, in addition to the fact that states engaging in aggression are also more likely to be engaged in human rights violations, the Security Council can determine that a situation involving human rights violations constitutes a threat or breach of the peace. However, as even recent humanitarian disasters demonstrate, the Security Council often lacks the will to exercise this authority, and either another international force intercedes or the genocide is brought to an end by domestic forces. NATO bypassed the Security Council when it authorized air strikes in Kosovo primarily on the grounds of human rights violations (expressed as a "humanitarian" crisis) as a result of the Serbian government's expulsion of hundreds of thousands of Kosovo Albanians and escalating violence by the Serbian government against Albanian irregular forces. However, neither did the Security Council condemn NATO's action, nor did the ICJ, when the rump Yugoslav (Serbia and Montenegro) government brought its complaints there (Simons 1999; UN News Center 2004). The Security Council had the authority to authorize a military intervention in Rwanda in 1994 to stop the genocide there but lacked the political will to do so for a number of reasons. Among them was the failed 1993 intervention in Somalia, where a US-UN assault on the government of President Aidid failed when Somali militia and civilian fighters shot down two US Black Hawk helicopters. The Rwandan genocide ended when the Rwandan Patriotic Front, invading from bases in neighboring Uganda, took control of the country in July.

## Humanitarian Intervention

*Humanitarian intervention* is a broad term referring to the use of military force to intervene in ongoing human rights violations or disasters. They may be undertaken unilaterally or multilaterally and can therefore be viewed as a form of international intervention or as a foreign policy decision. Humanitarian intervention has also been a concern of the United Nations, but states are cautious about treading on or diminishing their own sovereignty and their capacity to choose to undertake (or not) an intervention on humanitarian grounds. Since the UN Security Council under Chapter VII can essentially decide to intervene in any situation defined by the Council as a threat to or breach of international peace (or an act of aggression), the Council has considerable latitude in authorizing an intervention with or without clear humanitarian objectives.

The question of humanitarian intervention has always been politically thorny. It flies in the face of state sovereignty in general and the long-standing "nonintervention" norm affirmed by the customary practice of states and the UN Charter. Article 2, paragraph 4 of the UN Charter obligates member states to "refrain in their international relations from the threat or use of force against the territorial integrity or political independence of any state." At the same time, states that came together to form the United Nations were resolved to prevent both a third world war and another humanitarian catastrophe like the Holocaust. They were more committed to the first objective when it came to structuring the United Nations; as a result, the second tests the sacrosanct concept of sovereignty and thereby the ability of the member countries to cope with genocide's continued presence in the world. Secretary-General Kofi Annan posed the contemporary dilemma this way: "If humanitarian intervention is, indeed, an unacceptable assault on sovereignty, how should we respond to a Rwanda, to a Srebrenica—to gross and systematic violations of human rights that affect every precept of our common humanity?" (quoted in Evans and Sahnoun 2001:vii).

French political philosopher Jean Bodin argued, "Force may be used when the gates of justice have been shut for the good and honor of those unjustly oppressed" (quoted in Freeman 2004:1). Centuries later, Ayatollah Murtaza Mutahhari similarly asserted, "No one should have any doubts that the most sacred form of *jihad* is that which is fought in defense of humanity and of human rights" (quoted in Freeman 2004:1). The ethical and moral high ground is on the side of intervening to prevent or stop the ongoing injuries brought on by human rights violations, while narrowly defined strategic and self-interest are on the side of political expedience. Since any intervention diminishes, de facto, state sovereignty, the military enforcement of human rights norms returns the issue squarely to the assertion that state sovereignty is subject to certain constraints, namely, obligations arising from internationally recognized and secured human rights.

Situations where *only* humanitarian motives are present and political motives are entirely absent are difficult to find, though some interventions can be identified where motives are mixed and on balance lean toward the humanitarian. For example, the intervention of the 100,000-strong Tanzanian Defense Force to overthrow President Idi Amin in Uganda, who received some assistance from Libya's Muammar Qaddafi, and Vietnam's intervention against the Khmer Rouge in Cambodia both contain elements of humanitarianism. Operations frequently considered in analyses of humanitarian interventions are listed in the box. Humanitarian purposes may even be the overriding motives in these cases, and indeed, the examples are often debated and defended as good examples of humanitarian interventions. However, these operations were also conducted by neighbor-

---

### Humanitarian Interventions
### Most Frequently Cited by Researchers

Russian, British, and French anti-Ottoman intervention in the
  Greek War of Independence (1824)

French expedition in Syria (1860–1861)

Russian anti-Ottoman intervention in Bulgaria (1877)

Spanish-American War (1898)

US occupation of Haiti (1915)

UN Operation in the Congo (1964)

US intervention in Dominican Republic (1965)

Vietnamese intervention in Cambodia (1978)

Soviet intervention in Afghanistan (1979–1989)

Uganda-Tanzania War (1979)

Operation Provide Comfort in Iraq (1991)

Unified Task Force Somalia (1992)

Operation Uphold Democracy in Haiti (1994)

UN Assistance Mission in Rwanda (1994)

UN Transitional Administration in East Timor (1999)

NATO bombing of Yugoslavia (1999)

Coalition military intervention in Libya (2011)

*Sources:* Abiew 1999; Hilpold 2002; Chesterman 2011.

ing states with something to gain by a successful intervention and something to lose by a continuation of the status quo. As Michael Walzer (1977) argued, "the Indian invasion of East Pakistan (Bangladesh) in 1971 is a better example of humanitarian intervention—not because of the singularity or purity of the government's motives, but because its various motives converged on a single course of action that was also the course of action called for by the Bengalis" (105).

Michael Freeman (2004) examined five recent cases that elicited debates about humanitarian intervention: the British intervention in the Falkland Islands in 1982, the failure to intervene in Rwanda in 1994, the NATO air strikes in Bosnia in 1995, NATO intervention in Kosovo in 1999, and the overthrow of the Taliban in response to the attacks of September 11, 2001. He analyzed criteria that might be used to evaluate humanitarian interventions: the rule of law, communal integrity, just war theory, liberalism and natural law, utilitarianism, and the responsibility to protect. The last was affirmed by the International Commission on Intervention and State Sovereignty, discussed below, as a replacement for the customary "right of humanitarian intervention."

Freeman's study offers some lessons. Some crises, like Rwanda and Bosnia, arise so rapidly and reach such a scale that the case for intervention involving force seems more compelling. The NATO intervention in Kosovo had a clearly defined objective, authorization from a regional organization, and the objective of returning Albanians to their homes in Kosovo. When that was accomplished, the intervention ended. The 2003 intervention in Iraq, on the other hand, urges caution and shows the importance of UN authorization, in the absence of which the intervention is more likely to be viewed as politically motivated. He also noted that even if an intervention is driven by hegemonic or political interests it can still have the effect of improving human rights conditions. Finally, he warns that failing to resolve authorization issues puts the international community at risk for "another Rwanda," which may indeed be what is happening now in Darfur and the Democratic Republic of Congo.

In response to the challenge issued by former secretary-general Kofi Annan, the Canadian government initiated a project creating the International Commission on Intervention and State Sovereignty to evaluate the question of "intervention versus sovereignty." The study also aimed to "promote a comprehensive debate on the issues, and to foster global political consensus on how to move from polemics, and often paralysis, towards action within the international system" (Evans and Sahnoun 2001:81). The resulting report, "The Responsibility to Protect," completed before the September 11 attacks, resonates with Freeman's argument that the time has come to recognize a normative shift from states' rights to states' responsibilities. The commission was resolved to "reconcile two objectives: to strengthen, not weaken, the sovereignty of states, and to improve the capacity of the international community to react decisively when states are either unable or unwilling to protect their own people" (Evans and Sahnoun 2001:75). To that end it made a number of recommendations, among them adopting a resolution on principles of the responsibility to protect, including a definition of the conditions, such as large-scale loss of life or the presence of ethnic cleansing, under which nations should act to protect individuals and to possibly intervene militarily.

The commission also suggested identifying precautionary principles (right intention, last resort, proportional means, and reasonable prospects) that must be observed when military force is used for human protection purposes. The Security Council would have to agree on guidelines to govern responses to proposals for military intervention for human protection purposes. The commission asked the Security Council to seek agreement not to apply veto power to obstruct the passage of resolutions authorizing military intervention for humanitarian protection purposes for which the majority would otherwise give their support unless their vital state interests were threatened.

Whether adequate political will and leadership among states in the international community will match the work of the Canadian commission remains to be seen. If Darfur or the Democratic Republic of Congo is today's Rwanda or Bosnia, the answer seems to be "not yet." Thus, humanitarian intervention remains primarily a matter of unilateral action circumscribed by customary international law more than by contemporary and explicit agreements that include obligations and guidelines.

## International Tribunals

The development of norms in support of human rights and their protection is important, but such work is inadequate without the political will to take action against those who violate them, which is the grim task of the courts. In this section, I cover the Nuremberg and Tokyo tribunals after World War II, the ICTY, and the ICTR, all courts that were set up to hear cases involving war crimes. I will also look at the ICC, the first permanent court empowered to hear cases concerning not only war crimes but genocide along with crimes against humanity more broadly.

Before turning to a discussion of these criminal courts, a word is in order about the relationship between norms, laws, and enforcement. Since the mid-1990s, a growing number of international relations scholars have turned their attention to the role of norms and normative development in international relations, particularly regarding human rights (Klotz 1995; Risse, Ropp, and Sikkink 1999). On one hand, norms underlie the whole idea of state formation and interstate relations, such as sovereignty or sovereign equality, nonintervention, or the legal principle of *pacta sunt servanda* ("agreements must be kept," at the international level referring to the good faith performance of treaty obligations). Some norms also stem from complex social exchange at the international level, first theorized in terms of complex interdependence, with communicative and material transactions moving across national boundaries by both state and nonstate actors or agents. These exchanges enable actors or agents to articulate and find common values.

For the purpose of examining the development of international criminal courts, the questions relative to norms have to do with how norms become binding through law, and in turn, how the international community of states acts in relation to norm violations. Are they treated as legal violations? Do they meet with efforts to stop them while ongoing? Are they the basis for authoritative interventions? Are violators punished? Are most violators punished most of the time, or does politics impede enforcement and evenhandedness? Some of these important questions can be evaluated by taking a closer look at international criminal courts that have been created to prosecute and enforce crimes that violate the laws of war.

## The Nuremberg and Tokyo Tribunals

The 1919 Treaty of Versailles ending World War I required the Germans to admit responsibility for starting the war and, in Article 227 of the treaty, for committing "a supreme offence against international morality and the sanctity of treaties." The article further anticipated creating a tribunal with judges from the United States, the United Kingdom, France, Italy, and Japan. The tribunals, however, were national tribunals with judges representing the states whose nationals were the victims of the crimes of the accused. Kaiser Wilhelm II was never arrested, and of the hundreds of German officials who could have been tried, only thirteen soldiers were tried, convicted, and given light sentences (Foer 1997). Although these national tribunals were largely considered failures, they influenced the architects of the international tribunals following World War II (Harris 1954). Three categories of crimes were identified within the jurisdiction of the courts: (1) crimes against the peace, including planning, preparing, initiating, or waging a war of aggression; (2) war crimes, which primarily referred to violations of the laws or customs of war not justified by "military necessity"; and (3) crimes against humanity, which referred mainly to crimes against civilians not covered by war crimes and also discrimination on political, racial, or religious grounds in the execution of a crime.

The first category reflects changing norms pertaining to the use of force, especially in light of the Kellogg-Briand Pact and the intent of the

League of Nations to prevent aggressive war. The second was well-established customary international law and the least controversial, particularly since, as discussed previously, several efforts had already been made to codify the laws and customs of war in the early Geneva and Hague conventions. The new third category relied heavily on natural law arguments. For example, the crimes of the Holocaust did not fit within the other two categories and were not crimes within existing customary and positive (or written) law, but they were, nevertheless, so obviously criminal that they had to be recognized and thereby would fall within the new category. These crimes offended the totality of humanity to the degree that to know of them and not be offended called into question an individual's very own humanity. The idea that certain conduct is so offensive that not to be offended is not to be human is a remarkable assertion of the universality of the idea of "humanity"—that which sets humans apart from beasts. This idea also reveals another possibility: dehumanizing others erodes, diminishes, or at least calls into question everyone's humanity.

The German war crimes trials consisted of the International Military Tribunal at Nuremberg as well as regular military courts. Over 200 individuals were tried in the international tribunal and around 1,600 in the regular military tribunals. Twenty-four specific defendants were indicted and six organizations were named as criminal organizations including the Nazi Party, the SS, the Gestapo, Sicherheitsdienst (the intelligence division of the SS), the Sturmabteilung (perhaps more recognizable as the "stormtroopers"), and the Supreme Command of the German Forces. A distinction was made between criminal and noncriminal organizations because otherwise almost all German citizens could have been tried. For example, the Hitler Youth was not designated as criminal even though some members were suspected of having committed war crimes. Exempting certain organizations, or members of organizations, would set a precedent followed later in the case of Rwanda. Twelve of the twenty-four people indicted were found guilty and sentenced to death. Ten were executed (by hanging), one committed suicide the night before the scheduled execution, and another was convicted and sentenced in absentia (unbeknownst to the court, he had died while trying to escape Berlin). Three received life sentences, two received twenty years, one fifteen years, one ten years, and three were acquitted. Of the final two, one was tried on separate crimes of using slave labor and thereby escaped worse charges and a possible death sentence, and the other, Robert Ley, head of the German Labor Front, committed suicide before his trial even began. At the conclusion of the Nuremberg trials, Great Britain and France both held further war crimes trials under the authority of the order creating the original tribunal. The Moscow Declaration of October 30, 1943, allowed trials for war criminals and collaborators in the courts of countries "with sufficient legal interest to conduct the prosecutions" (Harris 1954:559).

The same three categories of crimes were the subject of prosecutions by the International Military Tribunal for the Far East, or the Tokyo War Crimes Tribunal. Twenty-five individuals were charged with crimes against the peace, and 5,600 with war crimes and crimes against humanity. Actions associated with the Japanese occupations in Korea and China were excluded. China later held thirteen tribunals resulting in over 500 convictions and 149 executions. One of the thirteen was the Nanjing War Crimes Tribunal in which crimes related to the Nanking (also spelled *Nanjing*) Massacre in the Second Sino-Japanese War (1937–1945) were heard and four of the accused high-ranking Japanese officers were sentenced to death and executed (Brook 2001).

The Tokyo War Crimes Tribunal is often criticized for allowing fifty or more accused persons to be released without trials, some who later served in the postwar Japanese government (Brackman 1987; Bix 2000). Details of biological and chemical weapons experiments and germ warfare were suppressed at the time of the trials (Barenblatt 2004). John Dower (1999) examined the reports on the indictments and outcomes of these trials, reporting that of 5,700 individuals charged, 984 received death sentences, 475 received life sentences, 2,944 were given shorter prison terms, 1,018 were acquitted, and 279 were never tried or sentenced. An additional 5,600 Japanese nationals were tried outside of Japan, resulting in 4,400 convictions and close to another 1,000 death sentences (World War II Database 2014). Another criticism, raised especially by the non-Western judges sitting on the tribunal, was that excluding colonialism and the use of the atomic bomb among the crimes was unfair and politically biased. Some observers argued that aggressive war was not clearly a crime before 1937 under either customary or treaty law (Onishe 2007). Non-Western jurists were not alone in criticizing the trials as kangaroo courts that carried out a completely biased and retributive "victor's justice," the term used by US senator Robert Taft, for example, to describe both the Nuremberg and Tokyo Tribunals (Kirk and McClellan 1967).

The most infamous post-Nuremberg trial was that of Adolf Eichmann, who was tried in Jerusalem after being found and captured in Argentina in 1960. Conflicting evidence pertaining to the correct identity of the person known during the war as Ivan the Terrible led the Israeli Supreme Court to overturn the conviction of John Demjanjuk, who was extradited from the United States to stand trial in Israel. Maurice Papon and Klaus Barbie were tried, convicted, and sentenced in French courts. However, many of the most infamous war criminals escaped judgment, including the notorious "doctor" Joseph Mengele, whose medical "experiments" were the most depraved, and Walter Rauff, who invented a "mobile" gas van. Both died after living more than three decades in South America. Death sentences resulting from convictions in the Nuremburg and Tokyo trials along with the tribunals in China and elsewhere across the world were carried out in seven countries: the Netherlands, Great Britain, Australia, China, the United States, France, and the Philippines.

### The International Criminal Tribunal for the Former Yugoslavia

UN Security Council Resolution 827 created the International Criminal Tribunal for the Former Yugoslavia (ICTY) in May of 1993 under the authority of Chapter VII of the UN Charter, which delineates the authority of the Security Council respecting "threats to the peace, breaches of the peace, and acts of aggression." The wars in Bosnia, Croatia, and parts of Serbia continued for another two years after the founding of the ICTY, which has jurisdiction to prosecute four categories of crimes: grave breaches of the 1949 Geneva Conventions, violations of the laws or customs of war, genocide, and crimes against humanity. The tribunal has concurrent jurisdiction with national courts, but the tribunal's jurisdiction takes precedence in case of a conflict. Sixteen judges serve four-year terms appointed by the UN General Assembly and can be reelected. The tribunal has three trial chambers and one appeals chamber. Translation equipment is available for English, Bosniak, Croatian, Serbian, French, Albanian, and Macedonian. Nearly 5,000 witnesses have given testimony or been interviewed by the prosecution. As of July 2014, 161 individuals had been indicted with 20 persons still in the custody of the ICTY, and 141 cases have been concluded with 74 individuals sentenced and 18 acquitted. Thirty-six indictments were withdrawn or the individuals died before a verdict could be rendered (true for both former Croatian president Franjo Tudjman and former Serbian president Slobodan Milošević). Thirteen cases were referred to national courts.

The ICTY is notable for including, for the first time, sexual assault and rape against both men and women not only as war crimes but also as crimes against humanity. The first conviction for sexual violence as a crime against humanity was in the case of Duško Tadić, whose conviction for inhumane acts included an incident where he ordered one prisoner to bite off the testicles of another (ICTY 2014). The next major case, Kunarac, Kovač, and Vuković involved three Bosnian Serbs—one member of the Bosnian Serb Army and two military police—who were charged with sexual slavery, rape as a form of torture, and rape as a crime against humanity, second only to genocide. Approximately 40 percent of the cases brought before the tribunal include charges of sexual violence (ICTY 2014).

The tribunal has considered as key elements of its mission strengthening the rule of law and judicial process in the Yugoslav successor states as well as generally facilitating postconflict reconciliation. The UN Security

Council passed two resolutions in 2003 and 2004 aimed at coordinating with national courts so that the court could close, and new cases could be tried in national courts. Accordingly, the tribunal is focusing on the prosecution of the most senior accused individuals and referring lower-profile and lower-rank accused to national courts. This move is also aimed at strengthening the capacity of national courts to hear war crimes cases. Several of the highest-ranking figures involved in perpetrating war crimes during the conflict were put on trial in July 2013: Bosnian Serb general Ratko Mladić, former president of the Republic of Serbia Krajina Goran Hadžić, and former president of the Republika Srpska Radovan Karadžić.

### The International Criminal Tribunal for Rwanda

The year after the ICTY was created, the Security Council created the International Criminal Tribunal for Rwanda (ICTR) to prosecute those responsible for genocide and violations of humanitarian law in Rwanda during the entire year of 1994. The worst of the Rwandan genocide occurred during the 100 days from April 6, following the likely assassination of Rwandan president Juvénal Habyarimana in a plane crash, through the middle of July. Nearly 1 million people were killed during this period. The Rwandan genocide was low tech compared to the Holocaust, but evidence shows that, by all accounts, it was just as meticulously planned and executed (Gourevitch 1999). As with the ICTY, the tribunal was authorized before the conclusion of violence.

The Security Council established the ICTR in Arusha, Tanzania. More than fifteen African countries have cooperated with the tribunal by facilitating the transfer of accused individuals. This level of cooperation will, it is hoped, have a more lasting impact on the development of and respect for international norms and judicial process in Africa beyond the borders of Rwanda or Tanzania. As of 2014, seventy-five trials were completed, of which twelve were acquitted. Of the sixty-three convicted, twenty-nine individuals were convicted of genocide, the act of aiding and abetting genocide, or conspiracy to commit genocide, and crimes against humanity. As in former Yugoslavia, the court had difficulty in some cases proving intent, a key element of the legal definition of genocide. Interestingly, the court also found, in *Prosecutor v. Ruggiu* (Case No. ICTR-97-32-I), that Georges Ruggiu, a Belgian journalist, was guilty of "public incitement to commit genocide" in connection with the use of incessant public broadcasts exhorting Hutus to kill and "exterminate" the "cockroaches." Ruggiu entered a guilty plea and admitted knowing that his broadcasts would incite mass violence. The court also took into account his expression of remorse, cooperation with the prosecution, and the fact that he was not involved in creating the editorial policy he carried out as mitigating factors in his sentencing. He was sentenced to a single concurrent sentence of twenty-five years for the two counts (Wisotsky 2001).

The magnitude of the genocide in Rwanda—more than 100,000 suspects have been named—renders it virtually impossible to complete all the trials within the framework of the international tribunal in a timely manner. Even with the international tribunal working in collaboration with Rwandan national courts, estimates are that 60 or even 150 years would be required to try all those accused of the worst crime, genocide (Wolters 2005). Therefore, in 2002 the government began a process aimed not only at achieving more timely justice but also at fostering national reconciliation. The process involved traditional courts called *gacaca* courts, which predate colonialism and are oriented toward conflict resolution and community restoration. They employed some 250,000 judges operating in 11,000 jurisdictions (Bamford 2002). The objectives, according to the Rwandan government, included justice, reconciliation, and eradicating the "culture of impunity" (Wolters 2005:67). The early phase of the program was limited to twelve pilot areas in 2002 and then expanded nationwide in 2005. Critics feared that the process was one sided and more divisive than healing. With recent estimates of the number of individuals involved in the genocide as high as 800,000, imagining how the success of any process could be measured within one generation is difficult. By the time the courts closed in May 2012, nearly 2 million people had been tried and two-thirds of them found guilty (BBC News 2012). Approximately 10,000 of the accused died in prison before being brought to trial. The link between the moral weight of the international community and the need for restorative justice and reconciliation within postgenocide societies is a common theme in both the Yugoslav and Rwandan cases.

## The International Criminal Court

The Rome Statute creating the International Criminal Court (ICC) entered into force in 2002. When delegates to the UN Conference of Plenipotentiaries on the Establishment of an International Criminal Court met in July 1998, the final document was adopted by a vote of 120 for and 7 against, with 21 abstentions. As of 2014, 122 states were parties to the statute, including 34 African states, 18 Asia Pacific states, 18 Eastern European states, 27 Latin American and Caribbean states, and 25 states from Western Europe and across the world (ICC 2014). The ICC only hears cases involving genocide, crimes against humanity, war crimes, and aggression. It is a court of last resort and as such, under Article 20, paragraph 3, does not hear cases that are under consideration or have been heard in national courts unless those proceedings "(a) Were for the purpose of shielding the person concerned from criminal responsibility for crimes within the jurisdiction of the Court; or (b) Otherwise were not conducted independently or impartially in accordance with the norms of due process recognized by international law and were conducted in a manner which, in the circumstances, was inconsistent with an intent to bring the person concerned to justice."

Twenty-one cases have been brought before the court. Eight cases are currently under investigation by the Office of the Prosecutor: the Democratic Republic of Congo, Côte d'Ivoire, Kenya, Uganda, Mali, Libya, the Central African Republic, and Darfur. Eleven warrants of arrest have been issued by the pretrial chambers. Treaty signatories are collectively called the Assembly of States Parties and constitute one of the major organs of the court. When the Rome Statute was adopted, the Assembly of States Parties also established the independent Trust Fund for Victims, recognizing that legal remedy is only one element of justice. Its motto is "Restoring Dignity, Rebuilding Communities, Ensuring Justice." The Trust Fund for Victims will provide support to victims and their families for basic needs like physical and psychological care and for community projects such as memorials, burials, educational needs of orphans, and peace education. Although the Trust Fund for Victims is independent of the ICC, it can only operate in areas where the ICC has jurisdiction, that is, in the territory of states party to the treaty or by special agreement.

Countries most likely to ratify the ICC treaty are democracies with low to no internal conflict in contrast with nondemocracies with weak legal systems that have more to fear from prosecution and are less likely to subject themselves to the jurisdiction of the court (Chapman and Chaudoin 2012). Of the 139 states that have signed the treaty, 31 have not ratified. Forty-one have not signed at all. Israel and the United States stand alone among democracies that have signed but not ratified and have announced that they do not intend to ratify the treaty.

The United States raised five objections to the Rome Statute in explaining its decision not to ratify the statute and give the ICC jurisdiction over its actions (Elsea 2007). The first objection is the US interpretation of the treaty claiming that the court is empowered by the statute to assert jurisdiction over nonsignatory states. This interpretation stems from the court's application of jurisdiction to individuals, regardless of citizenship, which is consistent with the customary laws of war and has led to the indictment of Sudanese president Omar al-Bashir, even though Sudan is not a signatory to the statute. The United States claims that asserting jurisdiction over individuals opens the door or is the equivalent to asserting jurisdiction over the state of an individual's citizenship. Congressional Research Service legislative attorney Jennifer Elsea (2007) explained, "The threat of prosecution, however, could inhibit the conduct of U.S. officials in implementing U.S. foreign policy. In this way, it is argued, the ICC may be seen to infringe on U.S. sovereignty" (86).

A second objection is that the court will be used to politicize prosecutions by states critical of other member states' foreign policies. Specifically, the United States is concerned that because its armed forces and foreign policies are more widely extended in more situations worldwide, the United States will be more vulnerable to this kind of manipulation of the court. A third related objection, in the US view, is inadequate accountability, or restraints on the Office of the Prosecutor where cases are initiated. This "unchecked discretion" further underscores the court's vulnerability to political manipulation (Elsea 2008:8).

The fourth objection is that the court usurps the Security Council's existing authority to determine whether an act of aggression in violation of the laws of war and the UN Charter has occurred. Furthermore, the General Assembly has been actively involved in developing a definition of aggression consistent with customary international law, so the court's assertion of jurisdiction to charge and try individuals for the crime of committing aggressive war undermines two of the main organs of the United Nations.

The final objection is that the court denies US citizens the full protections of due process provided in the US Constitution. However, the same procedural guarantees can be found in the Rome Statute and the US Constitution, except a jury trial, which is also the case with US military courts.

More than a decade after the Rome Statute entered into force and the ICC opened for business, a number of other criticisms have been raised. One is that it simply moves too slowly, though the court's sluggishness is largely attributed to states' dragging their feet on adopting obligations on enforcement and reforming their own criminal systems (*The Economist* 2013).

## Conclusion

Progress in regulating war and punishing violators of the rules of warfare may be difficult to see, but looking back at developments over the past century and a half offers some hope. Once an instrument of foreign policy, the use of force by a state is now categorized as an illegal act of aggression unless it is an act of individual or collective self-defense or arising from an intervention authorized by international organizations. The rule of law aims to reduce the arbitrariness with which power is used authoritatively, but law also depends on politics for implementation, to obtain compliance, and for enforcement when compliance fails. The abuse of human rights by states is usually, if not always, rationalized because those whose rights must be violated constitute a threat to the security of the state. In Chapter 8, I took a closer look at genocide, around which now can be found a rather strong prohibitionist consensus. Even when the political will to intervene to stop an ongoing genocide seems weak to absent, the will to punish *génocidaires* in the aftermath of their crimes is evident in both the criminal courts established for former Yugoslavia and Rwanda. With the creation of the ICC, taking legal action will be even easier even if the political will to stop or intervene militarily in ongoing human rights violations remains elusive.

# 10

# Civil Liberties
# and Political Rights

They that can give up essential liberty to obtain a little temporary safety deserve neither liberty nor safety.        —Benjamin Franklin, 1755

Those who make peaceful revolution impossible make violent revolution inevitable.        —President John F. Kennedy, 1962

ALTHOUGH CIVIL LIBERTIES, POLITICAL RIGHTS, DUE PROCESS, AND the rule of law are the four cornerstones of the foundation on which modern democracies rest, human rights rest on claims of inherent rights that belong to people everywhere, whether or not they live in democracies. The Universal Declaration passed the UN General Assembly unanimously in 1948—with abstentions by the Soviet Union, Ukrainian, and Byelorussian Soviet Socialist Republics, Yugoslavia, Poland, Czechoslovakia, South Africa, and Saudi Arabia—after each article was exhaustively debated. Non-Western supporters included Egypt, Myanmar, Iran, Iraq, Lebanon, Pakistan, Turkey, Syria, and Thailand. Citing "inalienable rights" as the foundation for freedom, justice, and peace in the preamble, the first two articles of the declaration underscore the universality of human rights without distinction "of any kind," including race, sex, nationality, political opinion, and, remarkably, the political status of any territory. Human rights are a birthright of all humans because of their humanity.

The next nineteen articles outline civil and political rights including fundamental freedoms and due process. These freedoms and rights include those of speech and opinion; thought, conscience, and religion; assembly and association; asylum as a refuge from political persecution; movement and a nationality that may not be taken away; privacy including correspondence; presumption of innocence; and protection from arbitrary arrest, detention, and exile. These articles also include the right to freely marry at the age of majority and the equal rights of men and women in marriage. The marriage article also proclaims the family as the fundamental unit of society. When the declaration was later split into the two covenants, these articles provided the basis for the International Covenant on Civil and Political Rights (ICCPR).

In this chapter, I consider how due process and the rule of law limit uses of state power in order to render uses of power less arbitrary and more accountable. Political rights and civil liberties protect citizens from arbitrary and abusive uses of power. Political rights and civil liberties include the right to due process; the fundamental freedoms of speech, press, religion, association, and conscience; negative rights such as the prohibition on cruel and unusual punishment or incommunicado detention; and the right to participate in the political process. Citizens hold their governments accountable through these checks and balances.

Before turning to the role of civil liberties, political rights, due process, and the rule of law in creating institutional safeguards for the protection of human rights, I first review research on the relationship between state repression and human rights. State repression, sometimes called political repression, refers to the use of state-sanctioned coercive power for the political purpose of restricting the ability of individuals or groups to participate in political life. It includes (but is not limited to) a variety of tactics that would otherwise be restrained by constitutional or international human rights, from surveillance and police brutality to stripping an individual or group of civil rights and the protections of due process, torture, extrajudicial and summary executions, forced disappearance, and forced resettlement and relocation without due process. When political repression is an official state policy, it may take the extreme forms of state-sponsored terrorism, genocide, or crimes against humanity. Why states engage in repression is a very important question for those advocating the protection of human rights.

I conclude the chapter with an examination of the problem of political prisoners and torture and then turn to a critical evaluation of current tensions between state assertions of sovereignty and the claims that political rights and civil liberties make against it. I also examine how the argument of national security necessity is used to justify derogations from the standards set by due process and the rule of law, in spite of the prohibitions laid out in the Universal Declaration and, later, the ICCPR. This defense is invariably invoked in cases involving torture used against those regarded by officials as enemies of the state, a trend that is now sadly true in democracies as well as nondemocracies.

## State Repression and Human Rights

On the other side of protecting human rights is the question of why states violate them in the first place. In other words, why do states repress their own citizens? One answer is "because they can," but this answer misses the point. Repression—the use of coercion to maintain order—is expensive. It costs resources, money, and manpower. And it is risky. Loyalty that is coerced or dependent on payoffs can always be undermined. Although it is common to talk about someone like Kim Jong-il or his son and successor, Kim Jong-un, as a dictator, even the most autocratic ruler maintaining himself (or herself) in power by coercion will need an armed force to do that. Autocrats need a loyal military and police force. Maintaining power is cheaper and more secure if most of the people most of the time support the government, or at least are not plotting to overthrow or undermine it. This conclusion is supported by the findings of Steven Poe, Neal Tate, and Linda Camp Keith (1999) that once a threat is diminished, human rights abuses decline.

The question "Why do states repress?" has been a subject of inquiry in political science and sociology for four to five decades. Early research on political or revolutionary violence focused mainly on the causes of rebellion rather than the causes of state repression (Gurr 1970; Snyder and Tilly 1972). Others analyzed the relationship between rebellion and instigation in response to repression, finding, for example, that repression did succeed in suppressing dissent up to a point but, beyond that point, instead provoked it (Davenport 2000). This pattern is called the "U-shaped" relationship between repression and dissent (Lichbach and Gurr 1981). Building on and sometimes challenging this research, others find that coercion and protest vary or oscillate over time, particularly when the threat stems from terrorism rather than protest (Francisco 1996; Lee, Maline, and Moore 2000).

In the research on state repression as a dependent variable, the hypothesis often is that states use repression as a regulatory mechanism aimed at reducing domestic threats. Many researchers come to the same conclusion: repression is employed to decrease dissent when it reaches a level that threatens state authority (Davenport 2000). Considerable agreement can also be found that the probability of repression correlates with regime type. Steven Poe and Neal Tate (1994) found that autocracies are more likely and democracies are less likely to engage in repression because of the absence or presence of the rule of law, respectively. Weak or failing states are, not surprisingly, less capable not only of providing economic security but also of protecting personal integrity rights, civil liberties, and rights to political participation (Englehart 2009).

Joseph Young (2009) asked perhaps the most important question, particularly in light of the challenges to civil liberties and due process presented by the notion that the most important enemy of democracies today is the use of terrorist tactics. Given that all democracies are grounded in the rule of law, making them less likely to engage in repression, Young asked why some democracies show more respect for and protection of human rights than others. Or conversely, why do some democracies seem more willing to violate personal integrity rights? He found that the degree to which leaders feel secure in their support from domestic constituents, incur lower costs in implementing their policies, and have more bargaining power with their critics influences how less likely they are to violate personal integrity rights. In other words, the more secure the leaders' positions and power, the less likely they are to repress the citizens' rights. These conclusions can be useful not only in understanding how to encourage the development of strong and legitimate regimes in postwar Iraq and Afghanistan but, paradoxically perhaps, in understanding the political dynamics of debates and criticisms over the diminishment of due process and civil liberties allegedly as the necessary price for greater security in post-9/11 United States.

## Civil Liberties and Political Rights

A variety of controversies arise in connection with civil and political rights. For example, is a government obligated to protect individuals from infringement on these rights by other private individuals, and if so, to what extent? Are corporations, as associations of individuals, entitled to these rights? Corporations, for instance, may contribute to political campaigns in the United States as an exercise of free speech, but given their vastly superior access to funds, this freedom is not without controversy. How can freedom be maximized and still balanced with protection against threats to public safety? This issue is often raised over the exercise of free speech. Can one freely speak words that are likely to result in injury, such as yelling "fire" in a crowded theater, or using "hate speech" intended to provoke a violent response? Finally, when may a government have a legitimate interest in curbing these rights because national security is at risk? Frequently, when governments abuse civil liberties and political rights, they do so on the grounds that extraordinary measures are necessary in order to protect citizens against threats.

Civil liberties protect individuals from abuses of government power and from restricting the exercise of rights and freedoms essential to democratic governance. They include procedural fairness, or due process, which is discussed separately in the next section, along with the broader conceptual framework of the rule of law as a check on abuses of political authority. Civil liberties, including fundamental freedoms, prohibit government interference in the private lives, practices, association, and expression of citizens. Civil liberties can secure fundamental freedoms, for example, by prohibiting invasions of privacy without probable cause ascertained by an open and politically independent judiciary or judicial officer. Many of these fundamental freedoms are not only essential to citizens' political participation but they also provide another check and balance on government accountability. They include freedoms of speech, expression, thought, conscience, association, religious practice, and movement. The right to privacy is sometimes inferred and other times specifically articulated in constitutions and covenants, as it is in the Universal Declaration and the ICCPR.

No sharp distinction can be found between civil liberties and political rights. However, in addition to these "freedoms to act" without government interference, other rights serve the political objective of guaranteeing citizen participation in political processes and holding governments accountable. To be effective, civil liberties and political rights must be embedded in an interlocking system of checks and balances. Governments don't have rights. Citizens do. All government authority derives from the people in a democracy, which is why democracies do a better job of protecting human rights. Political rights are fundamental to the functioning of a democratic society and include the right to freely assemble, to petition a government for redress of grievances, to vote, and to participate in civil society.

Civil liberties and political rights were among the first to be codified in contemporary Western legal systems and, as discussed in Chapter 2, often appear as guarantees in state constitutions or as a separate "bill of rights." Not all state constitutions or laws necessarily reference every one of these rights and liberties. In some cases, constitutional interpretation of a right such as free speech includes a very broad category of activities, like symbolic expression (flag burning, for example) and financial contributions to political campaigns.

Several international NGOs document and report annually on the status of civil liberties and political rights in the world. Amnesty International reported on eighty-nine countries restricting freedom of expression in 2011 (Amnesty International 2011). In 2013, ninety countries were classified in the "free" category, fifty-eight countries were classified as "partly free," and forty-seven were "not free." Freedom House reported 118 "electoral democracies" in 2013 based on a seven-point scale of assessment of political rights and civil liberties, giving the following explanation:

> Political rights enable people to participate freely in the political process, including the right to vote freely for distinct alternatives in legitimate elections, compete for public office, join political parties and organizations, and elect representatives who have a decisive impact on public policies and are accountable to the electorate. Civil liberties allow for the freedoms of expression and belief, associational and organizational rights, rule of law, and personal autonomy without interference from the state. (Freedom House 2014)

Voting rights are essential rights to direct political participation, and most contemporary democracies have a history of steadily expanding the franchise.

Such expansion was necessary because of initial exclusions, such as minorities and women. Edmund Burke is the best known of the eighteenth-century Enlightenment political philosophers who argued for restricted or qualified voting rights on the grounds that the natural order of a civilized society placed wiser, more educated, and knowledgeable people in a propertied upper class and a majority of that class ought to make the laws (Burke 1756, 1790). This idea has been steadily eroded and ultimately rejected by modern democracies where the franchise has become mostly universal.

Controversies persist, however. A particularly relevant one in a society with a large prison population is whether voting rights may be temporarily (while in prison) or permanently impaired for persons who criminally violate the law, for instance (Ispahani 2009). Other controversies raised by voting and voter registration regulations and requirements include closing registration before election day or requiring qualified voters to vote or pay a penalty for not voting (called compulsory voting). Imposing qualifications on voters is always suspect; examples include the so-called literacy tests in the United States that were used to exclude black voters from voting in general elections or from membership in a political party and, therefore, from voting in primary elections. Registration rules can make voting easier or more difficult: for example, a system may register all citizens when they become of age to vote, require more or less identification in order to register, allow registration up to and on election day, or allow provisional voting for individuals whose registration is in question at the time they vote. The rules governing political parties and voting may also impair or enhance voting rights. Requiring individuals to be registered as members of a political party restricts voting to those willing to register as a partisan, or it can exclude individuals from voting in primary elections. Disallowing or discouraging independent nonpartisan or minor party participation can also have an adverse impact on turnout and participation.

### Freedom of Movement

A relatively new right is that of movement. Before World War II, only about fifty states and most of the territory of the world was under colonial rule. By the mid-1960s, the world was divided into about three times as many states—about 150—and by the end of the twentieth century, nearly 200 states had come into existence. Both world wars, but particularly the second, created tremendous refugee problems. In a rapidly changing jurisdictional landscape, former colonies became independent states, then Soviet republics became independent, and, finally in some cases, postcommunist states broke up into several successor states. These changes meant that both citizenship and the movement of people across boundaries were subject to dramatic shifts. Recognizing both the right to a nationality and to freedom of movement became much more important within this political environment.

Some governments today restrict the freedom of movement in order to sustain a repressive regime. The South African government during the era of apartheid used restrictions on the movement of black South Africans as a mechanism to maintain the apartheid system of racial segregation and to control those who opposed it. Under the Soviet communist government, people were restricted internally as well as in their attempts to leave the country, whether permanently or temporarily. Similar policies exist in China today. Australia was criticized for restricting the movement of Aboriginal people, particularly by denying them passports or by requiring Aboriginal people to carry passports for movement within the country, all practices that ended with the passage of the Australian Passports Act of 2005.

Provisions establishing a right of movement both within and across national boundaries are outlined in Article 12 of the ICCPR: "(1) Everyone lawfully within the territory of a State shall, within that territory, have the right to liberty of movement and freedom to choose his residence. (2) Everyone shall be free to leave any country, including his own. (3) No person shall be arbitrarily deprived of the right to enter his own country."

Designating freedom of movement as a fundamental civil liberty can also raise controversy. At the very least, governments should not restrict freedom of movement within a state and should not prevent people from leaving and returning to their home state; however, recognizing this right does raise the issue related to refugees and migrant workers. People may have a right to leave their home state, but do they have a right to enter another state? Do other states have an obligation to accept them? States claim the right to regulate the flow of nonnationals across their borders since this potentially brings with it a demand for services, jobs, or asylum that can stress the resources of the host state or even create security risks. Individuals wanted for war crimes or human rights violations or those who are ordinary nonpolitical criminals may attempt to evade justice by fleeing to another state. At this time, while individuals may have a right to leave their home state, other states do not have a corresponding obligation to receive migrants, though some provision has been made for asylum-seekers—people fleeing persecution—and refugees. The international protection and status of refugees and migrants are emerging issues in international human rights and will be taken up in more detail in Chapter 13. The primary international agreement on refugees was written in 1951 and aimed specifically at the huge number of mostly European refugees resulting from World War II. A protocol to the 1951 convention removing previous geographic and chronological restrictions was ratified in 1967.

The freedom or right of movement is often more important to people who live in nondemocracies or who wish to escape living in nondemocracies like China or Cuba. Australia, however, also effectively restricted the movement of Aboriginal Australians who were unable to obtain passports because doing so required providing a birth certificate at a time when the births of many Aboriginal Australians were not recorded. In the case of Cuba, the United States also restricted the movement of its citizens by banning travel to Cuba. Two recent cases involving individuals who publicized information that the US government considered classified or at least protected against disclosure by the necessities of national security also underscore the fact that Western democracies can also be guilty of restricting people's freedom of movement. Some people regard their efforts as heroic attempts to hold governments accountable, while others view them as traitors. The first was Julian Assange, the editor in chief of WikiLeaks, a website that openly published information and videos considered to be news leaks or classified information provided by anonymous sources. The purpose of the nonprofit web-based organization is, according to its website, to bring raw news and information directly to the public to be judged alongside mainstream media stories and to ensure that independent journalists and whistleblowers are protected against prosecution and incarceration for submitting sensitive documents to the website.

Much of the information publicized through WikiLeaks calls into question the conduct of the US-led invasion and military occupation of Iraq. In 2010, in a move Assange supporters regard as using fabricated charges to harass an individual whose disclosures exposed hypocrisies and possible war crimes by the United States and its allies in the Iraq War, Assange was served an arrest warrant for sex charges unrelated to his work with Wiki-Leaks. He eventually sought asylum in the Ecuadoran embassy in London. The warrant for his arrest was issued simultaneously with revelations about source materials publicized on WikiLeaks linking Assange to whistleblower Private First Class Bradley Manning. Manning went on trial in 2013 for violating US law and US Army regulations related to the release of classified information, espionage, and aiding the enemy—the last carrying the death penalty. Manning initially faced thirty-four charges and, in August 2013, was convicted of most of them, but not the most serious—aiding the enemy. Manning, who changed his name to Chelsea just after the trial, publicizing his transgender identity, was sentenced to thirty-five years in prison. Assange, an Australian citizen, has been unable to leave the Ecuadoran embassy in London since 2012.

The second individual is Edward Snowden, a former employee of technology national security contracting firm Booz Allen Hamilton. On June 6, 2013, Snowden broke an international story through *Guardian* journalist Glenn Greenwald about the scope of US surveillance programs over telephone and Internet communications. Snowden, viewed as a whistleblower by some and a traitor by others, said that he thought the US public ought to know and debate whether the scope of their government's surveillance was acceptable and legal. According to Snowden, virtually all US citizens are subject to some kind of surveillance without specific warrants or probable cause, as required by the Fourth Amendment to the US Constitution. Snowden also revealed surveillance by the United States of its European allies through the offices of the EU member embassies in Washington, DC, and EU offices in Europe. The story broke in an interview by Greenwald of Snowden taped in Hong Kong, where Snowden deliberately fled before publicizing his claims. After it became apparent that the Chinese government was likely to turn Snowden over to US authorities, who brought charges of espionage and theft of government property against him, he left Hong Kong and ended up in the transit area of the Moscow airport where he began his applications for political asylum to escape extradition to the United States. The case for espionage seems weak since the law refers to making information available to a foreign government to the detriment of the United States. Snowden made the information available to the world. Freedom of movement in this case pertains to the United States' invalidating his passport and essentially cornering him in the transit area of the Moscow airport. He was later granted a year of asylum in Russia.

The Snowden and Assange cases also raise important questions about whether civil liberties should ever be compromised in the interest of national security, and whether doing so always impairs civil liberties in ways that destroy the checks and balances on which democracy and protection of human rights rest. In an interview in July 2014, Snowden contrasted national security with "state security," that is, that the governments employing warrantless surveillance and other violations of civil liberties are doing so not to protect citizens but to protect the government against citizens, turning national security on its head (Rusbridger and MacAskill 2014).

## The Rule of Law and Due Process

The discussion of constitutionalism in Chapter 5 raised the key question of the relationship between law and politics. Law can never be entirely separated from politics because law is produced by political processes and relies on political power or "political will" for enforcement. *Politics* can be defined as "the authoritative use of power to allocate tangible and intangible resources and values." This slightly revised version of David Easton's (1965) widely accepted definition of politics as "the authoritative allocation of values" focuses on the link between power, resources, values, and rights, which are intangible resources. In this definition, power becomes political when it is used to allocate resources and values authoritatively, and it is the rule of law that makes it authoritative. Law can be positive or common law and its role in bestowing authority on uses of power stems from its reliance on process (in the case of positive law) or normative notion of consent (in the case of common law).

The purpose of law is to reduce or, ideally, to eliminate the arbitrariness with which power is used. When the use of power follows from the whims and wishes of those who wield it without procedural constraints imposed by the rule of law or the checks and balances of political participation, it may be used arbitrarily, differentially, and inconsistently. A legal system prescribes the purposes for and means by which power may be used for the collective good, including for the achievement of shared values like justice, fairness, equity, and fulfillment of basic human needs within the means available. In *The Province of Jurisprudence Determined* (1832), legal philosopher John Austin famously defined law as "the command of the sovereign backed by sanctions" in order to distinguish law from morality (Austin 1995). Austin's definition points to the link between law and politics and the impossibility of severing it insofar as law needs enforcement. His views also reflect the times in which he lived, coming out of an age of absolutism and on the cusp of emerging representative and constitutional democracies. Democracy and constitutionalism make all the difference since they are the means by which sovereign authority is constituted. In the seventeenth through early nineteenth centuries, sovereign authority generally referred to a hereditary monarch who faced little or no accountability to his or her subjects. In the later nineteenth and twentieth centuries, constitutional and representative democracies developed in which citizens choose and empower their leaders.

A central problematic of liberalism is how to neutralize the political consequences of differences in power and, indeed, which kinds of differences ought to be neutralized. For example, being born to wealth, an individual will be more likely to have certain advantages over others right from the start, such as easier access to more resources, which in turn lead to, in general, reaching a high level of academic achievement. Couple greater education with inherited resources that can be invested in the commercial sector, along with the advantages of networking with similarly endowed individuals, and such people are already far ahead of the vast majority of their compatriots. Individuals with greater material privilege will also have more resources to influence the political process where campaigns are not publicly financed and may be able to afford better legal representation and therefore have better access to justice. For example, in regard to capital punishment in the United States, the socioeconomic class of the defendant and race of the victim strongly correlate to predict which capital cases will be more likely to result in the death penalty.

Thomas Jefferson saw public education as the backbone of democracy and a mechanism for equalizing opportunity, claiming that it would replace an "aristocracy of wealth" with an "aristocracy of virtue and talent" and "avail the State of those talents which Nature has sewn as liberally among the poor as the rich" (Jefferson 1782). Some contemporary political theorists, like Jürgen Habermas (1984), suggest mitigating the problem of power inequalities by equalizing the access of all citizens to public discourse or "communicative action" consisting of democratic deliberation in an environment free of domination (or in terms of this discussion, power used to dominate). In a practical sense, this argument favors restricting the influence of inequalities like money in campaign funding. Eliminating power differences and their effects is an ideal. As long as inequalities of power are present, some will have more access to and influence over law-making and law enforcing than others. Law requires political will for enforcement; inequalities of power render the law imperfect in terms of nonarbitrariness.

For this reason, due process is such an important concept when evaluating human rights. Due process ensures that when a government uses its monopoly on legitimate force over individuals within its jurisdiction that it will do so within the limits of a prescribed legal or "due" process. To say that governments monopolize the legitimate use of force does not mean that individuals are not authorized to use force or possess firearms, but rather that they do so because their governments or constitutions recognize their right to do so. Virtually all governments provide for the use of force as self-defense, and the US Constitution recognizes the right of citizens to "bear arms." The Magna Carta, written in 1215, may be the earliest source of due process in a Western legal system. It states, "No free man shall be seized or imprisoned, or stripped of his rights or possessions, or outlawed or exiled, or deprived of his standing in any other way, nor will we proceed with force against him, or send others to do so, except by the lawful judgment of his equals or by the law of the land."

The most basic element of due process is habeas corpus, a provision preventing unlawful detentions by allowing the detainee to petition the court to review the legal authority and the cause for the detention. If just cause cannot be shown in court, the detainee must be released. First codified in England in 1679, habeas corpus is one of the oldest common law rights and evidence of the necessity of showing cause for deprivation of liberty through detention can be found as far back as the twelfth century.

Elements of due process include informing accused persons of the crimes with which they are charged when arrested and detained; informing them of their rights when charged; holding a fair, timely, and public trial with an impartial jury; affording them the opportunity to confront their accusers; and allowing them to speak in their own defense but not requiring them to do so. In addition, due process is usually applied to a government's exercise of eminent domain, defined simply as the taking of private property for public purpose. The exercise of eminent domain also reveals the extent to which the system of sovereign states really functions to allocate property rights. It is based on the notion that the state is the ultimate holder of property rights, and citizens' own property only by permission of the state in the form of a title. In exercising eminent domain the state is really revoking the citizen's property title, but due process means that this revocation can only occur if the state follows the process prescribed by law (usually the constitution).

## Political Prisoners and the Problem of Torture

Political prisoners became a central concern of international human rights advocates following the founding of Amnesty International in 1961. British lawyer Peter Benenson started the organization to work on behalf of what he called "prisoners of conscience," or persons imprisoned for political activity. In 1977 the organization was awarded a Nobel Peace Prize for its efforts. Many recipients have been dissidents in their own societies, including Czech Republic president Václav Havel, Soviet dissidents Andrei Sakharov and Elena Bonner, former South African president Nelson Mandela, Mahatma Gandhi in India, and Martin Luther King Jr. in the United States. Many deliberately engaged in acts of nonviolence for which they expected to be arrested. Benazir Bhutto and her father Zulfikar Ali Bhutto both served as president of Pakistan and were imprisoned by their political enemies. Zulfikar was eventually executed as his daughter fought desperately to free him, and Benazir herself was assassinated. Burmese democracy activist Aung San Suu Kyi was imprisoned and is now under house arrest following winning the election that would have made her prime minister in 1990. Those individuals above are just a few one could name.

Provisions for due process or procedural fairness are critical to the protection of human rights as they create a shield against the arbitrary use of government power by ensuring that the same process in all cases and over all citizens limits coercive government power. Many democracies also require that the same rights and protections apply to noncitizens and citizens alike. Human rights violations such as arbitrary arrest and detention, incommunicado detentions, extrajudicial executions, summary executions, and torture are human rights violations that stem from the failure of governments to provide for or follow due process.

Arbitrary arrest and detention occur when an individual is arrested and detained without adequate evidence of probable cause that they have committed or abetted the commission of a crime. Procedural provisions such as those listed in the last section are aimed at reducing the likelihood of arbitrary arrests and detentions. Temporary detention is usually allowed when a person suspected of criminal activity or having knowledge of criminal activity is held for questioning. However, a limit on the length of time individuals can be held without being charged is necessary. Within that period, adequate evidence must be produced to charge the detainee, or, in general, he or she is released. A detainee is also safeguarded from being compelled to "be a witness against himself or herself." Without this right, an individual could be detained and coercively interrogated into providing a false confession, leading to the conviction of an innocent person.

The maximum period a person can be detained without being charged varies in older democracies from one day in Canada to twenty-eight days in the United Kingdom. The longer detention period in the United Kingdom is limited to cases involving suspected terrorist acts. Herein lies one of the most serious challenges to human rights. When a state, even an institutionally well-developed democracy, perceives an extraordinary increase in threats to national security arising from terrorist activities, virtually all provisions for due process can come under attack, a phenomenon that will be discussed at greater length under the topic of "national security exceptionalism" later in this chapter. Invariably, both democratic and undemocratic governments claim that extraordinary measures, including many that weaken or even suspend due process for detainees, are warranted in cases involving "enemies of the state." These extraordinary measures can range from imprisoning people because of their political activities, especially those that challenge the existing authority and oppressive conduct of undemocratic governments, to requiring individuals to surrender their passports. The suspension of rights can come from either repression in reaction to legitimate protest or well-documented cases of terrorism against a legitimate government.

Incommunicado detentions are a related problem. Once a detainee is placed in detention, possibly only the detainee and law enforcement officials will be present to witness the treatment of the detainee. Giving the detainee the right to contact someone outside of that setting is key to holding law enforcement accountable for respecting due process during detention. If suspects can be detained without anyone on the "outside" knowing of their detention, then the opportunity for mistreatment—coerced confessions, torture, self-incrimination, and so on—increases. The same is true of holding a public trial. Many military and authoritarian governments, particularly in the climate of the Cold War, engaged in such practices, employing "secret police" and holding detainees incommunicado indefinitely. In South America, these became known as "disappearances," and in the aftermath of transitions to democracy, many governments have tried to redress these injustices and bring closure to the many cases of disappeared persons during the long reign of undemocratic regimes. Amnesty International reported that in 2008, 57 percent of all countries detained people unjustly or "for prolonged periods without charge or trial" and in 32 percent of countries, individuals did not receive a fair trial (Amnesty International 2009a).

As discussed in Chapter 2, international support is growing for the abolition of the death penalty. Historically, capital punishment has been widely used everywhere in the world. Both the Nuremberg and Tokyo tribunals following World War II issued and carried out death sentences. As of 2013, eighty-one countries have ratified (and thirty-seven more have signed but not yet ratified) the Second Optional Protocol to the ICCPR abolishing capital punishment. Ninety-six countries have abolished the death penalty entirely. Ten have abolished it for all but extraordinary circumstances such as in a time of war. Thirty-five countries do not practice capital punishment or have a moratorium in effect even if the law remains on the books. However, fifty-eight countries retain the death penalty in law and practice (Amnesty International 2014b).

For those countries that still execute individuals convicted of crimes, due process remains the largest concern. Recently, the dubiousness of the "humaneness" of executions in the United States has added even further concerns where "botched" lethal injections prolong suffering for hours, cause the convict's vein to "explode," or are stopped in process because there is an inadequate supply of drugs to complete an execution. Furthermore, opponents of the death penalty argue that no amount of due process can guarantee that an innocent person will not be executed. Even in countries with more highly developed norms and practices of due process, such as the United States, cases of innocent persons being wrongly executed have been confirmed (Radelet, Bedau, and Putnam 1992). The terms *summary execution*, *extrajudicial execution*, and *extralegal execution* refer to the officially sanctioned killing of an individual by the state without judicial due process. Such executions are illegal under the ICCPR, which says in Article 6.2, "Every human being has the inherent right to life. This right shall be protected by law. No one shall be arbitrarily deprived of his life." They are also illegal under the Second Additional Protocol of the Geneva Conventions (1977): "No sentence shall be passed and no penalty shall be executed on a person found guilty of an offence except pursuant to a conviction pronounced by a court offering the essential guarantees of independence and impartiality." In 1982, the UN Human Rights Commission requested the appointment of a special rapporteur on summary or arbitrary executions to report to the commission (now council) annually. Despite all these prohibitions, in 2008 over a third of 157 countries surveyed by Amnesty International executed individuals extrajudicially (Amnesty International 2009b). In 2013, the UN special rapporteur issued a press release expressing "serious concern" about US use of lethal, armed drone strikes resulting in civilian casualties in Yemen and organized and participated in a conference on the legal issues raised by drone strikes and targeted killings. The rapporteur's 2014 report estimated that 2,836 people had been killed by drone strikes in Pakistan, Yemen, and Somalia (UN Human Rights Council 2014).

From a human rights perspective, political prisoners are individuals imprisoned solely because of their political beliefs. The reality is that individuals also act on those beliefs in ways that challenge the authority of the state, very often in response to a state's abuse of power, failure to provide due process, or failure to be restrained by the rule of law. In a nondemocracy, prodemocracy activists are viewed as a threat to the state. However, even in democracies with marginalized religious, ethnic, or cultural minority groups, individuals from such groups can become targets regarded by the government as constituting a threat to national or state security (Gurr 1970). Claims of threats to national security, in turn, frequently lead to what are called "extraordinary," "coercive," or "exceptional" interrogation techniques (Hersh 2004; Greenberg and Dratel 2005).

Such euphemistic terms are viewed with suspicion by human rights advocates because they are often used as a legal ploy to avoid charges of torture that would violate due process. Thus, the issues of political prisoners and torture are related. The UN Convention Against Torture defines torture as

> any act by which severe pain or suffering, whether physical or mental, is intentionally inflicted on a person for such purposes as obtaining from him or a third person information or a confession, punishing him for an act he or a third person has committed or is suspected of having committed, or intimidating or coercing him or a third person, or for any reason based on discrimination of any kind, when such pain or suffering is inflicted by or at the instigation of or with the consent or acquiescence of a public official or other person acting in an official capacity. (Part I, Article I, paragraph 1)

A 2009 Amnesty International report found that at least 50 out of 157 countries held prisoners of conscience in 2008 and that twenty-seven countries returned individuals seeking asylum to countries where they "faced detention, torture, and even death" (Amnesty International 2009b). More recently, Amnesty International reported that between January 2009 and May 2013, incidents of torture and other inhuman and ill treatment were documented in 141 countries (Amnesty International 2014a).

While 155 out of 196 states are parties to the Convention Against Torture, Amnesty International estimated that half of all countries in 2013 still engage in torture. Although no one questions that torture by anyone, whether acting in an official capacity or not, has powerful psychological implications regarding the motives of perpetrators (Alford 1997), the question here is with how its use is politically rationalized. Virtually no government tortures (or admits to practices regarded by others as torture) as a policy without offering some official explanation, which in itself may be an indicator of the extent to which human rights norms are internationally accepted even when flagrantly transgressed.

The Soviet Union until 1990, as well as other communist states today, rationalized torture as both necessary for the security of the state and, in turn, necessary for the future good of the communist society, which by the logic of Marxism is only temporarily undemocratic until the masses are so enlightened that the state "withers away." The Soviet Union engaged in policies critics call "punitive psychiatry" or "psychiatric terror," in which psychiatrists colluded with political authorities to fabricate diagnoses of mental illness in political prisoners. Prisoners sometimes had to confess to having a mental illness in order to obtain release (Bloch and Reddaway 1977). The communist government of China is perhaps the most high-profile state that engages in the torture of political prisoners today. The two most publicized Chinese cases involve the imprisonment of Tibetan activists and practitioners of the Falun Gong spiritual movement. The government regards the movement's philosophical views as hostile to the official ideology and, therefore, authority of the Chinese communist government. A report was issued in 2007 by two Canadian lawyers who investigated charges that the Chinese government engaged in "organ harvesting" of executed prisoners, most of whom followed Falun Gong. They found direct evidence supporting the allegations, concluding that organ harvesting targeting Falun Gong followers is systematic (Matas and Kilgour 2007).

Torture and inhumane treatment are obviously not limited to communist states. Many right-wing nondemocracies, especially during the Cold War, were notorious for their practice of torture, and democratic countries turned a blind eye if politically expedient. For example, US ambassador to the United Nations and foreign policy adviser to President Ronald Reagan Jeane Kirkpatrick (1981–1985) argued for making a distinction between "totalitarian" governments, which were nondemocratic for ideological reasons with no commitment to a transition to democracy, and "authoritarian" governments, which were only temporarily nondemocratic out of necessity to create conditions of law and order for the purpose of transitioning to democracy. Communist states, in her view, were in the former category while military dictatorships belonged in the latter, many of which were supported by the United States in the 1970s and 1980s because of their willingness to "crack down" on alleged communist revolutionaries (Kirkpatrick 1982). Critics regarded the distinction as politically expedient in light of the Reagan administration's support for many of the worst right-wing military dictatorships and opposition to communist governments. The governments of the Philippines, South Korea, Chile, Argentina, Nicaragua (before the Sandinista takeover in 1982), and Paraguay were some of the more notorious. Torture was also used to sustain the South African apartheid government as it was in Zimbabwe when that country was still called Rhodesia and controlled by a small white minority.

## National Security and "Exceptionalism"

Why do governments engage in practices that violate civil liberties and political rights? Why do they arbitrarily arrest, detain, torture, and execute people? Why do they oppress fundamental freedoms and political participation? The obvious answer is because they are fundamentally undemocratic to begin with and must rely on coercive and oppressive tactics to remain in power. But this answer is too simple. Even democracies do not have a perfect record on respecting civil liberties and political rights, two examples being Great Britain during the Troubles in Northern Ireland and the United States in the war on terror. In democracies as well as in nondemocracies, citizens often resist and criticize these deprivations. However, in a democracy, their resistance and criticism are more likely to both bring violations to light and see justice for victims and the society.

Regimes that violate human rights, or are accused by other states or the international community of violating human rights, most often claim that such measures are exceptions and not the rule, taken by necessity to safeguard national security, including incarcerating "political" prisoners. The term *exceptionalism* means that something is atypical or unprecedented, usually in a positive way. When applied to a country, as those in the United States often apply the term to this country, either the country itself or its historical circumstances are extraordinary or exceptional in some way that justifies its exclusion from responsibility to conform to rules other countries are bound by. When applied to the argument of national security as a justification for nonconformity with international standards of human rights, it can be thought of as "national security exceptionalism."

People, particularly those in the popular media, often refer to nondemocracies as "dictatorships," and indeed, some are associated with the strong personality of a particular autocratic ruler, such as Saddam Hussein in Iraq, Fidel Castro in Cuba, or Kim Jong-il in North Korea. But even these individuals cannot rely entirely on coercion to remain in power. At a minimum, they must have a security or military force willing to carry out coercive policies. In poorer countries, it is not hard to understand how people can be recruited into police and military service. Often too few jobs are available, leading to extremely high unemployment and poverty rates.

Undemocratic regimes can also look to three other potential sources of support. First, a regime may receive ideological support. Former US ambassador to the United Nations Jeane Kirkpatrick is well known for making a distinction between totalitarian and authoritarian regimes, the former relying on an ideology that justified repression (Kirkpatrick 1982). Some people, in and out of the coercive apparatus, will be loyal supporters of an undemocratic regime because of their commitment to the regime's ideology, a situation that is certainly true in Cuba and was true in the former Yugoslavia under communist rule. However, this support may not be adequate to support the regime under conditions of open democracy and with respect for civil liberties and political rights. Such regimes also typically utilize strong influence or even outright control over the media and educational institutions in order to foster or maintain support for an ideology supportive of the regime. Second, authoritarian regimes may basically "buy" their support through putting in place policies that enrich a certain group of powerful individuals. Those individuals have a vested interest in the status quo remaining the status quo because their fortunes depend on the regime's being in power, such as the Republican Guard under Saddam Hussein or many of the military dictatorships in Latin America from the 1950s to the 1980s. Third, a regime may find support in sharp cleavages of identity as certain groups identify with those in power, often involving ethnic or religious identity. The rise of Hutu Power in Rwanda in the 1990s (and at other times minority Tutsi rule) is an example of the former and Saudi Arabia and Iran are examples of the latter.

In virtually all of these cases as well as when democracies engage in practices or policies that systematically violate human rights, the regime in question will make a claim of necessity by reason of threats to national security. Clearly, the government's rationalization can become a self-fulfilling prophecy as well, since the claim of national security provides the rationale for human rights violations, which in turn may provoke increased criticism and resistance.

The argument that national security may require extraordinary measures that diminish or even suspend due process and the protection of civil liberties and political rights is acknowledged in international human rights treaties. Article 12 of the ICCPR, for example, provides that "the above-mentioned rights shall not be subject to any restrictions except those which are provided by law, are necessary to protect national security, public order (ordre public), public health or morals or the rights and freedoms of others, and are consistent with the other rights recognized in the present Covenant." In Article 4, the ICCPR explicitly addresses the conflict between national security and rights that otherwise would never be subject to derogation:

> 1. In time of public emergency which threatens the life of the nation and the existence of which is officially proclaimed, the States Parties to the present Covenant may take measures derogating from their obligations under the

present Covenant to the extent strictly required by the exigencies of the situation, provided that such measures are not inconsistent with their other obligations under international law and do not involve discrimination solely on the ground of race, colour, sex, language, religion or social origin. . . .

3. Any State Party to the present Covenant availing itself of the right of derogation shall immediately inform the other States Parties to the present Covenant, through the intermediary of the Secretary-General of the United Nations, of the provisions from which it has derogated and of the reasons by which it was actuated. A further communication shall be made, through the same intermediary, on the date on which it terminates such derogation.

Paragraph 2 of Article 4 quoted above explicitly prohibits derogation from the rights enumerated in seven of the covenant's articles. These include the inherent right to life and freedom not to be arbitrarily deprived of life; protection against torture, cruel, inhumane, or degrading treatment; protection against slavery and imprisonment for abrogation of contract; freedom from prosecution for ex post facto laws; and freedom of conscience and religion and from coercion regarding either.

The United States has recently come under criticism at home and in the international community for its treatment of prisoners held in Guantanamo Bay, Cuba; Iraq; and Afghanistan in connection with the war on terror. The largest number of reports of torture and inhumane treatment come from the now-notorious Abu Ghraib prison in Iraq. Following the attacks of September 11, 2001, President George W. Bush outlined a policy that would become known as the war on terror, consisting of, first, attacking and overthrowing the Taliban, who controlled the government of Afghanistan and harbored Osama bin Laden and, second, broadly declaring war on "thousands of terrorists in more than 60 countries" calling them "enemies of freedom," who, he said, "committed an act of war" against the United States (Bush 2001).

The first move to exclude detainees from legal protection occurred on November 13, 2001, when, by military order, the president authorized the detention and subsequent military trials of alleged terrorists and opined that they should not be subject to the same principles of law and rules of evidence that apply in US criminal courts (Greenberg and Dratel 2005). Next, the president and his advisers, specifically Justice Department attorney John C. Yoo and special counsel Robert Delahunty, in a memorandum dated January 9, 2002, initially argued that the Geneva Conventions did not protect either members of al-Qaeda or the Taliban militia. Assistant attorney general John Yoo asserted that US federal courts did not have jurisdiction to hear pleadings of habeas corpus, and in 2006 Congress passed a law prohibiting detainees from filing such pleadings. A series of memos generated by attorneys in the office of White House counsel, the State Department, and the office of the US attorney general contain conflicting opinions about the applicability of Geneva Conventions to members of both the Taliban and al-Qaeda. Some of the issues raised pertained to their status, or lack thereof, particularly of al-Qaeda agents as "legal combatants," as nonstate actors, and, if captured, as "prisoners of war" as anticipated by the Geneva Conventions. These conflicting opinions would set the stage for subsequent policies regarding not only suspending detainees' right to habeas corpus but treatment that has been characterized by critics as torture or otherwise cruel, inhuman, or degrading. Their treatment has been the subject of debate precisely because of the efforts of the administration to exclude detainees from both national and international legal status and protection.

Following an opinion by White House counsel Alberto Gonzalez that the Geneva Conventions did apply to detainees in the Afghanistan conflict but not more broadly to al-Qaeda and the war on terror, President Bush declared, "I accept the legal conclusion of the Attorney General and the Department of Justice that I have the authority under the Constitution to suspend Geneva (Conventions) as between the United States and Afghanistan, but I decline to exercise that authority at this time" (Greenberg and Dratel 2005:xxvi).

Notably, the State Department was the source of most of the concerns about excluding the detainees from Geneva Convention protections. State Department legal adviser William H. Taft IV argued that the Geneva Conventions did apply to the war in Afghanistan. Secretary of State Colin Powell cautioned that excluding any prisoners, Taliban or al-Qaeda, from Geneva Convention protection could both jeopardize US military personnel in the future and negatively affect US efforts to gain international cooperation (Greenberg and Dratel 2005:xxvi).

Testifying before the House Judiciary Subcommittee on the Constitution, Civil Rights and Civil Liberties in July 2008, constitutional law scholar Deborah Pearlstein (2008) told the committee,

> As of 2006, there had been more than 330 cases in which the U.S. military and civilian personnel have incredibly alleged to have abused or killed detainees. . . . These cases involved more than 600 U.S. personnel and more than 460 detainees held at U.S. facilities throughout Afghanistan, Iraq, and Guantanamo Bay. They include some 100 plus detainees who died in U.S. custody, including 34 whose deaths the defense department reports as homicides. At least eight of these detainees were, by any definition of the term, tortured to death.

According to the Center for Constitutional Rights (2014), UN special rapporteurs, the International Committee of the Red Cross, and US military investigators found numerous instances of torture techniques being used in the Guantanamo Bay facilities, at Abu Ghraib in Iraq and Bagram Theater

Internment Facility, and other US-operated facilities in Afghanistan. In the 2006 case *Hamdan v. Rumsfeld* (548 US 557), the US Supreme Court held that Guantanamo Bay detainees are protected by Article 3 of the Third Geneva Convention of 1949 (the Geneva Convention Relative to the Treatment of Prisoners of War that replaced the 1929 convention) pertaining to conflicts that are not international and protecting prisoners against torture. In fact, the court went so far as to say that the administration lacked the authority to try detainees because the government was in violation of not only the Uniform Military Code of Justice but also the four Geneva Conventions. Several months after the decision, Congress passed and President Bush signed the Military Commissions Act that narrowed the definition of torture and interrogation abuses. Although President Barack Obama issued an executive order in 2009 to halt abuses stemming from the Military Commissions Act, a Guantanamo military commission judge immediately overturned the order.

The issues raised by this policy are not unique to the United States. Indeed, short of offering no rationale at all, most states criticized for denial of due process and, more specifically, for the use of torture, claim that such extraordinary measures are necessitated by extraordinary threats to national security. These threats are typically internal or of ambiguous origin and characterized by violence that is often preceded by nonviolent efforts to change government policies or to overthrow a repressive regime or, in some cases, by secessionist movements. Thus, not surprisingly, nondemocracies have greater problems in this area, including such examples as the disappearances and routine use of torture in Argentina and Chile during those countries' rule by military dictatorships or juntas, the democracy movement in China and the "crackdown" in Tiananmen Square in 1989, the Philippines under the twenty-year dictatorship of Ferdinand Marcos, and South Africa under apartheid. All claimed to be acting under extraordinary threats to national security, such as threats to the stability and functioning of the institutions of the state from internal attacks.

During the approximately thirty-year period known as the Troubles in Northern Ireland, paramilitary forces mobilized on both sides and the Irish Republican Army openly claimed responsibility for terrorist attacks in London and elsewhere. When the security of a generally peaceful and democratic society is unsettled by the surprise and uncertainty of terrorist attacks, the rule of law and guarantees of due process will be strained to their limits under political pressure for the government to restore civil security. The most famous injustice under British law during this time involved the wrongful convictions of the Guildford Four and Maguire Seven including Gerry Conlon and his father, Patrick "Giuseppe" Conlon, who died in prison for a crime he did not commit. The civil rights movement in the United States also created special challenges from the 1950s to the 1970s. The Israeli government has struggled with these conditions virtually since its inception. In the aftermath of open military conflict with neighboring states that refused to recognize Israel or its right to exist as a state, Palestinians and their supporters increasingly resorted to terrorist attacks to undermine Israeli security in an effort to end occupation of the territories.

## Conclusion

Exceptionalism is the argument that extraordinary circumstances necessitate extraordinary tactics. Both sides often make exceptionalist arguments when an organized opposition challenges a government charged with human rights violations. Those who oppose governments are groups aggrieved by policies of the state who claim that nonviolent or ordinary means of political participation (voting, free speech, justice in the courts) either are inaccessible or have failed to effect responsiveness or change. Faced with the state's monopoly on force and overwhelming military advantage, they argue that they have no choice other than resorting to extraordinary violence themselves.

On the progovernment side are officials who claim that, faced with violent attacks that undermine their ability to fulfill the most basic function of government—providing security through law and order—they also have no choice but to use force to restore the peace. The government does not want to be repressive, they claim, but they have no other choice in light of the "exceptional" threat to national security. Antigovernment groups do not want to engage in violent opposition, they say, but the repression cannot be ended any other way. The clashing of these two perspectives can create a vicious cycle of repression and resistance, each one fueling the other.

A difference exists between national security and state security. *National security* aims at the protection of the nation, understood as the body of citizens who, under the best of democratic circumstances, are governed by consent and whose government is accountable to them. In contrast, *state security* aims at the protection of state, that is, protection of the institutions and bureaucracy of government and makes no claims of accountability. Indeed, state security often turns the security apparatus of the state, including law enforcement and intelligence gathering, against citizens and noncitizens alike. Although examples of political leaders enacting state security under the guise of national security abound, the most chilling current examples come from the ideas and practices associated with the war on terror. The blurring of internal and external enemies obliterates the idea that states can maintain a commitment to democratic principles internally while engaging in undemocratic practices to fight an enemy they regard as fundamentally antidemocratic, and, in the end, this impossible balancing act will destroy the democracies themselves.

In the fall of 2014, the ACLU and Human Rights Watch issued a joint report entitled *With Liberty to Monitor All: How Large-Scale US Surveillance Is Harming Journalism, Law, and American Democracy* (2014). In assessing the damage to internationally recognized human rights, the authors of the report concluded,

> In order for a democratic society to function, and in order for healthy debate over government policies to flourish, people must enjoy the fundamental rights to speak and associate freely, and to acquire information about matters of public concern. Without these, it becomes extremely difficult for the public to have an informed discussion about government policies and practices. (78)

The ACLU and Human Rights Watch noted that the United States is a party to the ICCPR, which includes protections for freedoms of speech, association, press, and equality before the law without regard to citizenship. These rights, along with the freedom of privacy and "the freedom to seek, receive and impart information of all kinds, regardless of frontiers" are central to the guarantees in the US Constitution (78). The organizations then sharply criticized US practices stemming from the war on terror, including overuse of authority to classify and withhold information on grounds of national security, stifling the speech of government employees, and disregarding internationally recognized standards for mitigating "the apparent tension between access to information and the protection of national security" (82).

Reflecting on the My Lai Massacre, William Broyles Jr. said of fighting the Vietcong that war crimes were the result of making the dubious leap from "anyone could be the enemy" to "everyone is the enemy." Yet this attitude is precisely the mentality justifying many of the practices and policies of the war on terror, including those cited in the ACLU–Human Rights Watch report as well as global, universal, and warrantless surveillance.

# 11

# Civil Rights and Identity Politics

I regard it as a duty which I owed, not just to my people, but also to my profession, to the practice of law, and to justice for all mankind, to cry out against this discrimination which is essentially unjust and opposed to the whole basis of the attitude towards justice which is part of the tradition of legal training in this country.

—Nelson Mandela, former president of South Africa
and Nobel Peace Prize winner, 1962

Affirming further that all doctrines, policies and practices based on or advocating superiority of peoples or individuals on the basis of national origin or racial, religious, ethnic or cultural differences are racist, scientifically false, legally invalid, morally condemnable and socially unjust.

—UN Declaration on the Rights of Indigenous Peoples

Difference is of the essence of humanity. Difference is an accident of birth and it should therefore never be the source of hatred or conflict. The answer to difference is to respect it. Therein lies a most fundamental principle of peace: respect for diversity.

—John Hume, Irish politician and Nobel Peace Prize winner, 1998

SEVERAL ASPECTS OF RACIAL AND RELIGIOUS DISCRIMINATION HAVE already surfaced in the topics discussed in earlier chapters, including, for example, the ethnocentric perspective, examined in Chapter 3, that Western societies invented the idea of human rights and human dignity and the idea that the contemporary state developed in connection with narratives of national identity in spite of the fact that virtually all states are multicultural, multicommunal, or multiethnic, as discussed in Chapter 5. The entire subject of genocide is predicated on taking a stand against policies directed specifically at the destruction of certain people because of their identity as "national, ethnical, racial, or religious groups" as Article 2 of the Genocide Convention puts it. In this chapter, I primarily address human rights problems rooted in discriminatory practices in the context of intergroup relations enacted through the politics of imperialism, state formation, and contemporary international relations. I also examine the social, psychological, and political motives for discrimination and how human rights violations stem from discriminatory practices. Thinking about discrimination when it takes the form of political violence is difficult without wondering, "Why do people behave this way?"

Civil and political rights are often bundled together, with some overlap. As discussed in the previous chapter, civil liberties and due process protect citizens against the arbitrary exercise of power in liberal democracies. Beyond that, political rights ensure freedom of participation in the democratic process, and democracies do a better job of protecting civil liberties. Movements challenging laws and practices that discriminated against particular groups or classes of citizens by denying them equal entitlement to participate in the political, economic, social, and cultural life of the state gave rise to the widespread use of the term *civil rights*. Civil rights guarantee that everyone will receive the same protection and enjoyment of civil liberties and political rights.

After briefly discussing social and psychological perspectives on the phenomenon of discrimination, I place the issues of civil rights, discrimination, and identity politics in an international context. I address basic questions of group identity and how it interfaces with the development of the contemporary state. In this chapter, I also consider how imperialism implicates discrimination and shapes the postcolonial experience. This discussion is followed by an assessment of the incorporation of nondiscrimination norms into international human rights and a review of efforts to address discrimination through international means. Finally, I identify new or emerging rights issues that have in some cases arisen in opposition to state policies and in other cases resulted from a call on states to take action to end discrimination and promote greater social justice in the private as well as public sectors.

Although women have been and are subjected to discrimination, their situation differs from other groups because they do not constitute a distinct identity group or community in the same way ethnic or religious groups do. Like racism and other discriminatory ideologies, discrimination against women is also deeply rooted within social structures across a wide range of cultural identities and practices, but inequalities and inequities affecting women also differ because they are not only perpetrated by public practices but are also embedded in women's most intimate personal relationships. Because they are unique, women's human rights are taken up separately in Chapter 12.

## Why Discriminate? Insights from Social Psychology

A range of human rights violations, from denial of equal political, legal, and economic opportunities to torture and genocide, implicate the question of "difference." Denying rights and dehumanizing those who are perceived by the perpetrator as "different" are simply "easier," in a psychological sense, than getting to know an individual as a unique human being and making judgments that take into account the full complexity of an individual and his or her circumstances. But why? Many human rights claims aim directly at preventing the kind of violence that dehumanization, often based on perceived identity differences, rationalizes. So why are human beings prejudiced toward those perceived as "different," what are the political implications, and how does this affect the development and implementation of international human rights norms? Since difference is primarily an issue of identity, answering these questions necessitates a critical examination of the relationship between identity and intergroup relations within states and how antagonistic intergroup relations become entrenched in the political practices of state institutions and struggles to control them. I therefore begin by exploring psychological and sociological theories of identity development and group behavior.

According to psychologists, a sense of self (identity) develops as an individual learns to distinguish his or her own agency, that is, the ability to feel specific emotions, understand himself or herself as the source of those emotions, and act with awareness of the consequences (Zahavi, Grünbaum, and Parnas 2004). The self is defined through the language of pronouns, not only associating *I* with agency, or the ability to "make things happen," but also simultaneously associating *you*, *he*, and *she* with the agency of others. The "identified self" thus associates with others who are similar while distinguishing itself from those who are different (Brewer 1991). Language teaches us who is the same and who is different.

The boundaries of identity develop within an increasingly complex web of selves, relationships, and multiple identities, for example, identities of gender, sexuality, ethnicity, nationality, religion, or neighborhood or community. (Gender and sexuality are not the same thing: "I am a woman and I am straight" or "I am a woman and I am a lesbian" are statements about gender *and* sexuality.) The development of the self as a moral agent emerges from the early association of "goodness" with others who gratify our needs and "badness" with others who frustrate them (Klein 1975; H. Segal 1981; Masterson 1988; Alford 1989). An individual also begins to understand his or her capacity to evoke affection and, at other times, frustration or anger in others. These realizations lead to a psychological process known as projection, that is, projecting one's own capacity for negativity onto others by demonizing them as "bad" and, conversely, projecting one's own capacity for good onto others by idealizing them. Negative projections are referred to as scapegoating when negative attributes such as blame or guilt are assigned to others, particularly when enabling the rationalization of injuries done to them as being justified by their own wrongdoing.

From a psychological perspective, these processes of early identity development are universal to all human beings irrespective of culture, although cultures make a difference in how the social categories, processes, and meanings are constructed. As a child matures and acquires the capacity for complex moral reasoning and an ability to appropriately assign agency or responsibility for the moral consequences of behavior, he or she learns that both the self and others are capable of both good and bad behavior and of both caring about and wishing harm to other human beings. The psychological capacity for projecting and scapegoating, however, remains and can be aggravated and collectively mobilized under conditions of stress and trauma (Wilmer 2002). Recent studies of patriarchy suggest that rupturing the capacity for connection and relationality early in identity formation is a prerequisite for the reproduction of a patriarchal psyche in both men and women. Men are generally more vulnerable to such ruptures because their sense of independent self-hood occurs at an early age while they are often in the care of and dependent upon women. Because the vulnerability to rupture—the development of a sense of independent self-hood—occurs later in women (adolescence), they are better positioned to resist and less prone to experience it as traumatically as men (Gilligan and Richards 2009).

From a sociological perspective, groups are the basic unit of society. The family is a group, as are clans, tribes, labor unions, religious communities, and political parties. Groups in this social sense are self-identified; that is, the people who make up a group identify themselves as members of that group. However, is something as broadly conceived as a "society" also a group? Is a "nation" a group? Is a "race" a group, a political category, a socially constructed attribute, both, or neither? How is the category of "ethnicity" socially constructed and with what consequences? Do adherents of the same religion constitute a group? More importantly, why does identification with a group evoke or lead to prejudices, negative stereotypes, targeted violence, and conflict? In Chapter 8, seven cases were examined of genocidal violence targeting people because of their identification with particular groups. Genocide is the most extreme violence targeted at specific groups, but various kinds of discriminatory practices and deprivations short of policies aimed at destroying a group as a group are also widespread.

Even though the psychological processes of identity formation and the sociological dynamics of identity group formation and behavior are common human experiences, this fact does not mean that intergroup violence or hostility, inhumane treatment, and discrimination are inevitable. After all, most societies or groups do not commit genocide, and while antagonistic intergroup relations and discrimination are pervasive, many societies make an effort to address and ameliorate these conditions, especially liberal democracies and particularly since civil rights movements arose in many democracies in the 1960s and 1970s.

Social psychologists Philip Zimbardo (1972, 2007) and Stanley Milgram (1963, 1974) conducted two of the best-known experiments on obedience and human cruelty in an effort to better understand how ordinary people can be induced to comply with orders to physically and psychologically cause harm to others. Studies by both support the conclusion that the ability to perpetrate cruelty is not exceptional. Zimbardo was recently asked to provide expert testimony in defense of a US sergeant court-martialed for prisoner abuse at Abu Ghraib prison in Iraq. His research led him to conclude that the ability to resist the psychological and situational inducements to cruel and inhumane treatment of prisoners in those circumstances was exceptional (Zimbardo 2007, 2008). According to Zimbardo (2008), his work as well as other studies

> demonstrated the relative ease with which ordinary people can be led to behave in ways that qualify as evil. We have put research participants in experiments where powerful situational forces—anonymity, group pressures, or diffusion of personal responsibility—led them blindly to obey authority and to aggress against innocent others after dehumanizing them.

Securing human rights means protecting individuals and groups not only from inhumane treatment but also from marginalization and discrimination insofar as these practices subject people to arbitrary, unequal, and injurious treatment because of their identities. In order to understand the link between political behavior and the problem of discrimination in the context of international human rights, the question of identity and the state is taken up in the next section.

## Identity and the State

The terms *country*, *state*, and *nation* are often used interchangeably and confusingly. Terms like *country* and *nation* obscure several key features of contemporary world politics because they suggest an image of the political and legal space of a state as fixed, natural, and coincidental with national identities. In fact, the world is divided into just fewer than 200 states with thousands of communal groups—groups whose identities are grounded in or defined by ethnicity, nationality, or religion. Virtually all states are multiethnic, multicommunal, or multinational. Understanding how and why state power is used in ways that violate human rights by discriminating against groups requires a more critical view of what the state is, how it came to be the basic political unit of world order today, and what the implications are of the tendencies of most states to privilege the identity of one communal group over others.

Using national language as an example, even without intentionally creating inequalities among citizens, for practical reasons states often designate an official language or simply use one language without a legal designation. Although some states recognize more than one language in order to equalize the language rights of multiple groups living in the state, the use of one language for legal and political discourse ensures citizens' equal protection of the law and enables full participation in the economic and political life of the state, providing all citizens are literate in that language. Nevertheless, those for whom the official language is a first language will be privileged over those for whom it is not. Speakers of other languages become language minorities.

No one wants to be a minority that must be granted rights by a majority. South Africa under apartheid privileged the white minority, including those of English and Dutch descent, until 1994 when Nelson Mandela became the first president of South Africa elected under the postapartheid constitution and the first black leader of the nation. In states like Bolivia and Guatemala, diverse indigenous peoples within the state constitute a majority under the broader category of "indigenous" but have still been the subject of historical discrimination by a nonindigenous minority identified with generations of European settlers. The point is that granting rights is always easier than seeking them, and the majority will always be in a position of power in this regard.

## Self-Determination

In Chapter 4, I argued that identity and state formation are connected because foundational narratives attempt to naturalize a connection between the identity and the ability of a group to control their own political destiny. Self-determination is a principle whereby a people can determine their own destiny, control the use of their resources, and pursue common values according to their own vision of the good society. In international law, the term *people* has a specific meaning as a self-identified and cohesive non-state group entitled to the right of self-determination. If a state is made up of a single "people," or identity group, then state sovereignty allows them also to be self-determining. However, due to the disparity between the number of peoples and the number of actual states, most groups cannot and do not enjoy the right of self-determination as a group when it is understood as controlling state institutions and possessing the attribute of state sovereignty. Since sovereignty does not belong to a group but to the state, when one group establishes itself as a majority, it can use its majority, de facto, to control political institutions, make its language the official one, recognize its own cultural practices as more valid, and privilege certain values over those of other groups who then constitute minorities.

Some states pursue policies to attempt to accommodate the identities of multiple nationalities. Switzerland, with its German, French, Italian, and Romansh peoples and languages, is one example; another is South Africa with eleven official languages, eight of them corresponding to groups as small as 4 percent of the population or as large as 23 percent of the population. Belgium has three official languages—Dutch, French, and German. Two of them correspond to the largest ethnic groups, French (40 percent) and Dutch (60 percent) with fewer than 1 percent speaking German. Canadians struggled for many years with the cleavage between *les Québécois*, the French language and identity advocacy movement centered in Quebec, and the English-speaking Canadians in the rest of the provinces. The movement extended throughout the provinces to all Canadians for whom French is a first language.

So why is identity important to state building, and by extension, how and why do some groups become marginalized and subjected to discrimination? The case of the bloody wars of secession in former Yugoslavia is instructive. Official languages are used in public education, courts, and campaigns and elections and even on street signs. One of the early warnings of growing intolerance in the republics of former Yugoslavia as they descended into violence was the official renaming of streets in the capital cities after well-known (and sometimes notorious) nationalist historical figures. Overnight, Serbo-Croatian language, an amalgamated language used for official purposes, was replaced by the separate and pure Serbian and Croatian languages. Bosnian Muslims began to refer to their language as "Bosniak." Streets were renamed commemorating pre-Tito nationalists, even collaborationists or nationalist resistance leaders from the World War II period. Asked about her identity during the war, one woman replied, "Well you see I am a Yugoslav, but there is no Yugoslavia" (Wilmer 2002:87). Serbs living in Croatia for generations, who were, along with their Croatian neighbors, simply Yugoslavs, became overnight a minority in the new state of Croatia. The same was true for Croats living in Serbia.

Bosnia-Herzegovina had no national ethnic majority, with a prewar ethnic distribution of 43 percent Bosniaks (Bosnian Muslims), 31 percent Serbs (Bosnian Serbs), and 17 percent Croats (Bosnian Croats). Sarajevo was arguably the artistic heart of former Yugoslavia, in part because of its multiethnic composition. Only 30 percent of its residents today are prewar Sarajevans (Ernst et al. 2003). Muslims, who were less than half the prewar population, now make up 78.3 percent of the city. Sarajevans are trying to reconstruct their cultural life in art and with reopened museums. "One of our problems is that we are trying to change history and the past and make it better than it was, especially each for their own ethnic group," said Jacob Finci, an elder statesman in Sarajevo in charge of developing a new civil service for Bosnia (quoted in Wilkinson 2007:A5).

Identity is important in state building because it enables the (highly emotional) mobilization of citizens around a sense of connection and belonging. The state makes the strongest claim on the loyalty of citizens whose national identity becomes synonymous with the state. Loyalty arising from national identity creates a reciprocal obligation between citizen and state. Citizens are obligated to abide by the law, pay taxes, and support the military. In return, the state provides practical order, security, and a mechanism for solving problems and channeling conflicting views of the good society.

The relationship between nationality and citizenship was elaborated in 1955 in the Nottebohm case (*Liechtenstein v. Guatemala*) heard by the ICJ. Friedrich Nottebohm was a naturalized legal citizen of Liechtenstein, born in Germany, and therefore a citizen of Germany by virtue of jus soli. However, he was also a businessman and resident of Guatemala from 1905 to 1943. A dispute between Liechtenstein and Guatemala regarding Nottebohm's citizenship arose when Nottebohm applied to become a naturalized citizen of Liechtenstein. Although born in Germany and having lived thirty-eight years in Guatemala, he had never applied for Guatemalan citizenship. And as the United States entered the war against Germany, he did not want to be a legal citizen of Germany and thus an enemy of the United States and Guatemala, its ally. He was extradited to the United States, held in an internment camp, and his property in Guatemala was confiscated. The dispute was raised by Liechtenstein, claiming its sovereign right to determine to whom the state would grant citizenship. The court was asked to resolve the question of the "bond of nationality between the State and the individual" insofar as it conferred upon the state of one's citizenship the rights and obligation of diplomatic protection. The court described the relationship this way: "Nationality is a legal bond having as its basis a social fact of attachment, a genuine connection of existence, interests and sentiments, together with the existence of reciprocal rights and duties."

To the extent that nationality constitutes a narrative of identity on which political rights and legal claims rest, the stakes are high for ethnic or communal groups to establish themselves as a majority population within the state and to use that numerical advantage to obtain and maintain control of the institutions of the state.

Cognizant of the role of European imperialism in contributing to the grievances and events that precipitated World War I, President Woodrow

Wilson advocated the affirmation of national self-determination as a right of a "people." It was directed toward the ethnic minorities in Eastern Europe where the end of Habsburg rule meant that numerous peoples would become minorities in new states under the new map of Europe. Even thought they recognized the need to balance self-determination with state sovereignty, European advocates of self-determination doubtfully understood the broader global context of minorities, where thousands of ethnic groups lived within the jurisdictional territories of about fifty states and empires.

Although the rights of minorities had been recognized in previous treaties, in 1919 the Allied Powers and those aligned with them assigned responsibility for implementing minority protections in postwar central and eastern Europe to the League of Nations at the Paris Peace Conference. Pablo de Azcarate, director of the Minorities Question Section of the League of Nations, defined minorities as groups having a "national consciousness" (de Azcarate 1945). He viewed the primary purpose of the protection system as averting future wars rather than protecting the rights of minorities. Recognizing that neither population transfers nor territorial rectifications could resolve the "minorities question," he advocated a more comprehensive human rights charter that would secure equality of rights between majorities and minorities. He also recommended the creation of a permanent commission for minorities' protection but did not believe the assertion of rights alone would be adequate to obtain state compliance. The system hardly had a chance to succeed before the crises setting the stage for World War II began to mount. Carole Fink's (1995) evaluation of the effect of the system within that historical context offers some insight into the link between the assertion of a self-determination norm and push back from sovereign states:

> By raising expectations among the subjugated Irish, Poles, Czechs, Romanians, South Slavs, Italians, Jews, Arabs, Africans, and Armenians to resist, oust their overlords, work for their own state, or join their brethren, the chancelleries and military chiefs of Europe sparked a series of volatile and competing aspirations that would erupt at war's end. The unprecedented and almost simultaneous collapse of the Romanov, Ottoman, Habsburg, and Hohenzollern empires together with the compelling Wilsonian and Leninist rhetoric of self-determination set the stage for the creation of a new configuration of nation states between the Baltic and the Black and Adriatic seas— and for new minority problems as well. (xx)

An enduring minorities issue in Europe is the status of the Roma or Romani, often pejoratively called Gypsies, believed to have left India in the eleventh century in the midst of unrelenting invasions by Emperor Mahmud of Ghazni of the Ghaznavid Empire, located in much of present-day Iran, Pakistan, and Afghanistan (Crowe 1995). They fled to the

Byzantine Empire, where, over the next five centuries, they became outcasts and often slaves in eastern and central Europe. Visibly distinct, they became the subject of discriminatory laws that aimed to expel or banish them, often under threat of death. Their nomadic life on the margins of European society has made them one of the most vulnerable European minorities. For example, Christians could legally kill Roma under the Diet of Augsburg, and in 1721 the Austro-Hungarian emperor Charles VI ordered the execution of all Roma in the empire. Between the fourteenth and nineteenth centuries, as many as half of the Roma population in Europe may have been enslaved (Robinson 2009). "Gypsy Hunts" became a "sport" in Germany in the sixteenth century (Center for Holocaust and Genocide Studies 2010). Even in modern times, the Roma are one of the most persecuted groups. Amnesty International (2014c) did not paint a flattering picture of the situation of the 10 million Roma living in Europe today:

> The Roma community suffers massive discrimination in access to housing, employment, and education. In some countries, they are prevented from obtaining citizenship and personal documents required for social insurance, health care, and other benefits. Roma are often victims of police ill treatment and their complaints are seldom investigated. Frequently Romani children are unjustifiably placed in "special" schools where curtailed curricula limit their possibilities for fulfilling their potential. Romani children and women are among the communities most vulnerable to traffickers.

Europe also had a long history of anti-Semitism even before World War II. Daniel Jonah Goldhagen (1997) traced European and US anti-Semitism to medieval Christendom, "with its uncompromising, non-pluralistic, and intolerant view of the moral basis of society" that "held the Jews to violate the moral order of the world" (37). Jews were denied citizenship in the Roman Empire. Once Constantine converted to and made Christianity the official religion of the empire, Jews stood alone in rejecting the claim that Jesus was the Messiah. They were massacred during the Crusades, often forced to live in ghettos, and legally restricted from property ownership and business activities. In Western Europe, the Enlightenment led to some loosening of these restrictions, particularly when accompanied by provisions for greater assimilation, which meant a diminishment in Jewish cultural and political expression or distinctiveness. Eastern Europe was marked by pogroms—violent rampages against Jews, their homes, and businesses— that claimed the lives of tens of thousands of Jews, from the 1880s through the Russian Revolution and beyond.

In addition to the long-standing historical pattern of discrimination against Jews and Roma, Western European states have struggled with, on the one hand, the formation of states based on national majorities and, on

## Minorities at Risk

The Minorities at Risk Project at the University of Maryland, founded by Ted Robert Gurr in the 1980s, collects data on the status and vulnerability of 283 minority ethnic groups worldwide. It contains information on minorities in 115 countries and makes use of 449 variables. The criteria used by the project in determining the inclusion of groups in the study are that the group collectively suffers, or benefits from, systematic discriminatory treatment vis-à-vis other groups in a society, and that the group is the basis for political mobilization and collective action in defense or promotion of its self-defined interests (Minorities at Risk Project 2008).

The Minorities at Risk Project is the most comprehensive effort to catalog groups vulnerable to or suffering from discrimination or its historical effects. It is designed for use by students, researchers, educators, journalists, and policymakers, and it includes political, economic, and cultural dimensions of discrimination. (For more information see http://www.cidcm.umd.edu/mar/.)

the other, numerous minority nationalities coexisting, or not, in a single state. Some examples are the Flemish and Walloons in Belgium; the French, German, Italian, and Romansh in Switzerland; the Basque and Catalan independence movements in the borderland between Spain and France; and anti-British backlash in Wales, Scotland, and Ireland. In addition to the tragic civil wars brought on by the dissolution of Yugoslavia, Europe today struggles with the status of Russians in many former Soviet republics as well as the continuing civil strife and violence in multiethnic former Soviet republics in Eastern Europe and Central Asia. In 2008, a new international security crisis emerged over the status of South Ossetia and Abkhazia, when independence movements in the two regions in Georgia in areas bordered by Russia led to violence between Georgia and the ethnic groups, and also between Georgia and Russia. Violent conflict erupted in 2014 between Russian- and Ukrainian-speaking Ukrainian citizens in the aftermath of a pro-Western coup. The Russian annexation of Crimea and the 2014 crisis in Ukraine do not bode well for stability in multilinguistic and multiethnic democracies in states now free of Russian domination. Newer minorities are also being recognized in the rest of Europe, like the Turks in Germany who came as guest workers in the 1970s and the many immigrants to Europe from former colonies, such as Indonesians in the Netherlands, Algerians and other Arabs in France, and Indians and Pakistanis in Great Britain. Many social scientists today view ethnic conflict and aggrieved minorities within states as the most potentially explosive source of conflict for the twenty-first century (Harff and Gurr 1994).

## Communal Groups

The term *ethnicity* is often used as if the meaning were self-evident when in fact many identities are multiethnic, layered, or even cosmopolitan. A group's most distinguishing feature may have a religious basis, or it may be embedded within complex historical narratives. The case of Northern Ireland is illustrative. Are Irish Catholics and Irish Protestants ethnically distinct? Are their conflicts over differences in religious beliefs? Historical narratives are central to the articulation and maintenance of ethnic identities. In the case of Northern Ireland, Catholic identity is structured primarily as "native" or "ethnic Irish," and many hold mixed views of what it means to be British (Moxon-Browne 1991). After more than two centuries in Ireland, many Protestants, in contrast, regard themselves primarily as British and secondarily as Irish. The case for an ethnic, religious, or cultural distinction between Protestant and Catholic Irish is not very clear. What is clear is that the Catholic Irish regard the Protestants as affiliated or identified with British settlers and antagonistically as agents of British imperialism. The Catholics in Northern Ireland identify with the Republic of Ireland that once overthrew British imperialism to establish an independent state. Catholics have also long been targets of discrimination and marginalization in Northern Ireland. Northern Ireland was severely plagued by civil strife, low-intensity conflict, and violence during the Troubles between 1968 and 1998. The situation in Ireland illustrates the elusive character of group identity and why the historical experience of a group and the interpretation of that experience are critical to understanding how group identity is constructed in relation to conflict. Identity is not the problem; the problem is discrimination based on identity.

Sociologist Anthony Smith (1991) elaborated the notion of nationality as the most politically powerful form of collective identity, anchored in enduring ethnic communities. Ethnic communities, Smith argued, have six characteristics: (1) a collective proper name, (2) a myth of common ancestry, (3) shared historical memories, (4) one or more differentiating elements of common culture, (5) an association with a specific "homeland," and (6) a sense of solidarity for significant sectors of the population. These characteristics need not be shared evenly or equally among all members and, he argued, will be found in greater intensity in the ethnic core of the group. Benedict Anderson (1991) regarded nations as "imagined communities," arguing that they are not based on face-to-face encounters the way local communities are. Members of a national community share a sense of horizontal belonging and believe that the national community ought to control its own political destiny as sovereign, having to answer to no higher authority.

Historical narratives contain and sustain certain perceptions of other groups, as researchers in former Yugoslavia discovered in a study of enemy imaging in Serbian schoolbooks (Rosandić and Pešić 1994). Homi Bhabha (1990) and Ernest Renan (1990) also wrote of the "nation as narrative." In a critique of "race," Renan argued that social scientists confuse the methodologies of biologists who categorize living things according to certain physical attributes with the methodologies of social science, where the subjects themselves produce the categories. Neither plants nor atoms talk to one another about what it means to be a plant or an atom, nor do they tell stories of their origins and the experiences they believe made them who and what they are today. They do not tell of obstacles overcome, of defeats and revitalization, of tragedy and triumph, and of historical injury and injustice. People do.

Viewing the contemporary state as both a set of authoritative institutions governing people and resources within a territorial space and a product of social processes reveals the powerful role historical and ethnic narratives play in mobilizing support for the legitimation of claims over territorial domain. French sociologist Pierre Bourdieu (1984 [1974]) brilliantly exposed the relationship between power relations and the construction of worldviews. Power elites, he argued, use all forms of capital, not only political and economic but also cultural and symbolic, to create and sustain institutions and social practices that preserve their privileges in a system of social domination and social subordination.

Bourdieu (1991) applied these theoretical arguments to a historical analysis of the role of language in the production of the French state. Language is one of the most powerful tools of symbolic capital and can be used to impose boundaries between speakers and nonspeakers or to marginalize second-language speakers. Language differences are significant in Europe because European state formation was linked to narratives of nationalism. Language is the most apparent national distinction. The French in France speak French, though French speakers can be found in a variety of countries including Switzerland, Belgium, and Canada. The English speak English in England, but the English deliberately displaced other first languages spoken in conquered areas as they consolidated control into the United Kingdom of Great Britain and Northern Ireland, linguistically subjugating Scottish Gaelic (or Gàidhlig), Gaelic (Irish or Gaeilge), Cornish, and Celtic Welsh (called Cymraeg). When Hitler made the irredentist claim that all German-speaking people should live in one German state and then invaded the German-speaking area of Poland and annexed Austria, this claim did not seem to be outrageous viewed within the context of European state-making narratives grounded in imagined national communities.

People can also be emotionally mobilized around feelings of solidarity, loyalty, and belonging by rhetoric that plays to perceptions of race and ethnicity (Ignatieff 1993). States did not "emerge" in a social and historical vacuum. Modern states are a product of the convergence, interplay, and conflicts arising from complex social, economic, philosophical, and historical forces. At the core of the matrix is the thorny issue of political identity, the link between the self and a set of governing institutions that make claims to loyalty on the basis of identity constructed or imagined as natural, like ethnicity, race, or nationality, or, alternatively, as a moral community made up of believers. Identity creates connections as well as boundaries, and boundaries include and exclude.

The role of religion as a signifier of identity is also illustrated in the case of former Yugoslavia. When asked about his identity, one young man in Serbia replied, "My mother was Catholic, my father was Orthodox, my grandmother was Jewish, and they gave me a Muslim first name." He referenced religious identity to mean that he had a Croatian/Catholic mother and a Serb/Orthodox father. With their mixed marriage, his grandmother's Jewish identity, and his own name considered "Muslim" even though he had no Muslim relatives, what should his identity be? He concluded with "I am going to Los Angeles and I don't want to meet anybody from Yugoslavia when I get there" (Wilmer 2002:110).

Referring to these groups as "ethnic" groups not only is misleading but also points to the socially constructed, rather than genetically predetermined, nature of ethnic identities. Jews were targeted by Hitler, the Nazi Party, and collaborationist regimes because of their perceived "difference" or, in psychoanalytic terms, their otherness. Different religious beliefs and practices were part of that difference, as were cultural practices. However, difference itself is not the cause of the problem; rather, the perception that group difference is threatening is what is problematic. This conclusion means we have to look at the narratives about difference to understand how the "fact" of difference is implicated in rationalizing discrimination, marginalization, and even violence.

In the Cambodian genocide, "difference" was not constituted in ethnic terms but rather predicated on the claim that people who were too "Westernized" had abandoned their Asian identity. The Khmer Rouge targeted business owners because capitalism was a Western value; they attacked intellectuals because they received a Western education; they attacked people who wore glasses because they were using their glasses to read Western literature; and they attacked and nearly annihilated the Muslim Chams because Islam came to Southeast Asia from the West. In Cambodia, violence was justified by not only difference but the abandonment of one's "true" or "authentic" Asian or Cambodian identity, a perception that made those targeted into a kind of "race traitor." Narratives of identity determine what difference, difference makes. Prize-winning novelist Amin Maalouf, a native Arab-speaking Christian born in Lebanon and now living in Paris, issued this challenge to readers of his book *In the Name of Identity: Violence and the Need to Belong* (2012):

We must act in such a way as to bring about a situation in which no one feels excluded from the common civilization that is coming into existence; in which everyone may be able to find the language of his own identity and some symbols of his own culture; and in which everyone can identify to some degree with what he sees emerging in the world about him, instead of seeking refuge in an idealized past. (163)

## Imperialism, Slavery, and Postcolonial Perspectives

Imperialism is the extension of state control over people and territories beyond its borders. Imperialism is also a form of direct violence because imperial control is established and maintained by force. Structurally violent and inherently discriminatory, imperialism results in the displacement of local societal and economic structures and practices and the appropriation of resources for the use and profit of the imperial power. Imperialist regimes also often press the conquered people into exploited labor and economic marginalization. European imperialism was directly linked to the African slave trade that peaked in the eighteenth century. Christopher Columbus, upon "discovering" the new land, infamously looked to establish a lucrative slave trade by capturing indigenous people in the Americas and selling them in Europe. Howard Zinn (1980), noted for his extraordinary history of European imperialism in the Americas, shared excerpts from the journals of the Catholic priest Bartolomé de Las Casas, who eventually became an ardent critic of the inhumanity of the Spanish conquistadors. Las Casas's account is chilling:

> After each six or eight months' work in the mines, which was the time required of each crew to dig enough gold for melting, up to a third of the men died. While the men were sent many miles away to the mines, the wives remained to work the soil, forced into the excruciating job of digging and making thousands of hills for cassava plants.
> Thus, husbands and wives were together only once every eight or ten months and when they met they were so exhausted and depressed on both sides . . . they ceased to procreate. As for the newly born, they died early because their mothers, overworked and famished, had no milk to nurse them, and for this reason, while I was in Cuba, 7000 children died in three months. Some mothers even drowned their babies from sheer desperation. . . . In this way, husbands died in the mines, wives died at work, and children died from lack of milk . . . and in a short time this land which was so great, so powerful and fertile . . . was depopulated. . . . My eyes have seen these acts so foreign to human nature, and now I tremble as I write. (quoted in Zinn 1980:6)

Although today the term *slavery* is synonymous with European trade in African slaves between the seventeenth and nineteenth centuries, slavery is not unique to European imperialism and was practiced by many societies from ancient Greeks to Barbary pirates. Muslims in North Africa and the Ottoman Empire took European Christians as slaves from the sixteenth to nineteenth centuries (Davis 2003). The East African Arab slave trade, much of it going through the ports on the island of Zanzibar, moved black African slaves into the Middle East and Asia (Segal 2001). However, the European slave trade in the Americas had the most profound effect on the economic history and the development of racial discrimination in the United States, itself a product of imperialism and a revolution for independence by the settler population that had become dominant by the end of the eighteenth century. The mentality of imperialism and ideology of Euro-centrism remained a powerful force within the newly independent settler state and was turned in full force on the indigenous peoples who still outnumbered settlers west of the Mississippi River at the time of independence. The "white man's burden" of European imperialism took on a new life as the settler state's "manifest destiny."

The European transatlantic slave trade and the subjugation of the black African diaspora in the Western Hemisphere; the displacement, decimation, and forced assimilation of indigenous peoples; and the creation of settler states where nonwhites were marginalized and subjected to discrimination are not the only troublesome legacies of imperialism. As in Rwanda, the postcolonial states carved out of areas formerly controlled by imperial powers created new or exacerbated old intergroup cleavages resulting in a variety of political conflicts that festered in the aftermath of decolonization. Imperialism split communal groups like the Tutsis and Hutus across new state boundaries; disrupted social systems, intergroup relations, and economic practices; and altered patterns of resource use and labor, replacing village-level and crop-diversified agricultural practices with plantation-style monoculture cash crops. As Philip Gourevitch (1999) showed, many things determined the status and identity of precolonial Hutus and Tutsis, and "the line between Hutu and Tutsi remained porous" (49). "Hutu and Tutsi identities took definition only in relationship to state power," said Gourevitch (1999:50).

Racial and religious discrimination today are a product of not only sociopsychological factors inherent in becoming a "self" in a social world but also structural conditions created by historical struggles for power and dominance. These are reinforced by norms underlying structures like the state, the system of state relations, international law, and postcolonialism. Boundaries of selfhood create boundaries of otherness and difference. Identity is implicitly a product of social relations as the individual identifies with one group as distinct from other groups. Group dynamics lead to favoring one's group more and other groups less. The social construction of the contemporary state, rooted in the experience, history, and normative discourses emanating from Europe and "the West" over the past three to four centuries, privileges majority nationalities as forms of civic identity, with few exceptions. Thus, one of the challenges to the development of international standards of human rights is to mitigate the effects of a state system that privileges majorities and marginalizes minorities in favor of an aspiration toward pluralism and social justice in the future and reconciliation of the past.

## Nondiscrimination and International Human Rights

Intergroup prejudices and discrimination are not new problems in human history. However, the development of the liberal state created the possibility, and eventually the expectation, that the ideal of equality could and should prevail over discrimination. Movements to combat ethnic, racial, and religious discrimination are among the earliest efforts to internationalize respect for civil human rights. The world antislavery movement dates to the early nineteenth century, and later the minorities protection system was instituted by the League of Nations in order to address the underlying problems associated with the quest of European nationalities for self-determination as the Habsburg and Ottoman empires collapsed. Another international organization, the ILO, also attempted to eliminate employment discrimination in the 1950s and frequently weighed in on the rights of other groups besides workers. However, attempts to resolve discrimination and racial issues at the international level have been hampered by the self-interest of states, whose leaders prefer to resolve discrimination issues without pressure from the international community.

### Abolishing Slavery

By 1789 the French colony of Saint-Domingue produced 40 percent of the world's sugar and was home to 500,000 African slaves, about 60,000 white colonists and plantation owners, and about 10,000 free blacks or mulattoes. After the French Revolution, free black Haitians began pressing for equal rights, but their discontent soon drew the far more numerous and aggrieved African slaves into a much-feared but surprising full-blown slave rebellion that led to Haitian independence and black majority control. In conjunction with the ideological fervor of postrevolutionary France, this successful slave revolt fostered a strong antislavery sentiment in France, in part because the movement had the added political attraction of being directed primarily toward the British. By 1807, British abolitionists saw their cause as a moral obligation arising out of their Christian religious beliefs. The movement succeeded in outlawing slavery in Great Britain, but the ban was not extended throughout the British Empire for another twenty-six years. Abolition across the empire was achieved primarily through the efforts of the Society for the Mitigation and Gradual Abolition of Slavery Throughout the British Dominions, commonly known as the Anti-Slavery Society. It was arguably the first modern international human rights NGO.

Founding the Anti-Slavery Society in 1823, early members disagreed over whether to take a gradual or radical abolition stance. Many believed that once slavery had been outlawed throughout the empire with the Slavery Abolition Act of 1833, the mission of the society was fulfilled. However, at that point, some members then redefined its objective as the worldwide abolition of slavery and formed a new organization, the British and Foreign Anti-Slavery Society, focused on the elimination of slavery and slave trading in the French colonies, the United States, Zanzibar, and elsewhere. The society held the World Anti-Slavery Convention in 1840. (Its infamous exclusion of women abolitionists, including Lucretia Mott and Elizabeth Cady Stanton, led directly to the mobilization of US suffragists who held their own convention on women's rights in Seneca Falls, New York, in 1848.) A total of 409 delegates, including forty from the United States, met in London. Excluded from the main floor of the convention, the women had to watch the proceedings from the gallery (Maynard 1960). In addition to condemning slavery in the United States and the slave trade throughout the British Empire, the convention called for an investigation into conditions in Sierra Leone, a major locus of slave trade activity, and the "Red Indian" slavery of the Hudson's Bay Company, which openly subjected captured indigenous people to slavery in the northwestern region of the United States and Canada. The convention also called for banning sugar produced by slave labor from entering the British market (Maynard 1960). In 1909, the society merged with the Aborigines' Protection Society and adopted the name the Anti-Slavery and Aborigines Protection Society until 1990 when it became simply Anti-Slavery International.

Between 1823 and 1888, eight newly independent countries in Central and South America abolished slavery. Fourteen states with holdings or interests in the colonization of Africa met in Berlin in 1885: Great Britain, Austria-Hungary, France, Germany, Russia, the United States, Portugal, Denmark, Spain, Italy, the Netherlands, Sweden, Belgium, and Turkey. The conference carved up European colonies into what later became independent decolonized states in the 1960s and 1970s and resulted in the first international antislavery agreement. Chapter 2, Article 9 of its final act bound those signatories exercising "sovereign rights or influence" in the Congo basin to "declare that these territories may not serve as a market or means of transit for the trade in slaves, of whatever race they may be. Each of the Powers binds itself to employ all the means at its disposal for putting an end to this trade and for punishing those who engage in it" (The Berlin Conference: The General Act of February 26, 1885).

Five years later, eighteen states signed the final act of the Brussels conference. It aimed to end the slave trade not only in Africa, particularly in the region of the Congo, but in the Middle East. The antislavery momentum continued into the twentieth century, and suppression of the slave trade was affirmed again in the Treaty of Saint-Germain-en-Laye in 1919. The League of Nations appointed the Temporary Slavery Commission in June 1924, leading to the first modern antislavery convention in 1926. It affirmed the work of the previous treaties, aiming to "prevent and suppress the slave trade" and bring about the progressive and "complete abolition of slavery in all its forms" (Article 2). Signatories agreed "to take all necessary measures to prevent compulsory or forced labour from developing into conditions analogous to slavery" (Article 5).

A remarkable but generally overlooked feature of this early antislavery history was the creation of antislavery courts through a series of British treaties to outlaw slavery (Martinez 2007). Though only active from 1806 to 1817, these courts heard over 600 cases and liberated some 80,000 people from the bonds of slavery (Martinez 2007). These were the first international human rights courts.

Following World War II, the UN General Assembly proposed and states ratified a protocol to the 1926 treaty replacing the League of Nations with the United Nations and replacing the Permanent Court of International Justice with the ICJ. In 1957, a supplementary convention extended prohibitions to "institutions and practices similar to slavery." The focus today is on these "practices," which stem mostly from human trafficking in which children are sold for labor and women and children for sexual exploitation. The US State Department estimated that 800,000 people per year are victims of international trafficking, but this number "does not include millions trafficked within their own countries" (US Department of State 2014:7). The ILO claimed that "almost 21 million people are victims of forced labour—11.4 million women and girls and 9.5 million men and boys" (ILO 2014).

The UN Convention for the Suppression of the Traffic in Persons and of the Exploitation of the Prostitution of Others (1949) entered into force in 1957. It codified four earlier agreements and resolutions addressing the problem previously called "white slavery." The progressive codification of international mechanisms for enforcement is carried out largely through the efforts of the UN Commission on Crime Prevention and Criminal Justice. Commission resolutions on migrant workers, trafficking in children, and violence against women created the foundation for the most recent international agreement. A supplementary protocol on the trafficking of women and children entered into force in 2003. It was drafted with the participation of some 120 countries and numerous NGOs. States ratifying the protocol must (1) criminalize all forms of trafficking, (2) pass legislation or take other measures to prevent the misuse of commercial carriers for the smuggling of migrants, (3) legally require that commercial carriers check passenger travel documents, and (4) prepare travel documents that are difficult to misuse, falsify, alter, or replicate (Articles 11–13). By 2014, 117 states had signed the protocol.

## The International Labour Organization

The Labour Commission created the International Labour Oganization (ILO) in 1919 at the Peace Conference in Paris by incorporating its constitution into the Versailles Treaty. The first ILO convention addressing discrimination in the workplace was Convention No. 111 in 1956. It defines discrimination as "any distinction, exclusion or preference made on the basis of race, colour, sex, religion, political opinion, national extraction or social origin, which has the effect of nullifying or impairing equality of opportunity or treatment in employment or occupation."

A number of other important ILO conventions address discrimination issues, including No. 100 in 1950, the Equal Remuneration Convention, dealing with gender wage equity, and two others dealing with forced labor, the Forced Labour Convention (Convention No. 29 in 1930) and the Abolition of Forced Labour Convention (Convention No. 105 in 1957). The Discrimination (Employment and Occupation) Convention, No. 111, had 172 ratifications as of 2014. The United States is not among them.

In 1989, the ILO revised what was at that time the only international treaty addressing the rights of indigenous peoples—the Indigenous and Tribal Populations Convention (Convention No. 107). The result was Convention No. 169, the Convention Concerning Indigenous and Tribal Peoples in Independent Countries, which entered into force in 1991. The impetus for revision came from an increasingly active international indigenous movement that succeeded in persuading member states that the earlier convention was paternalistic and inadequate to the needs and rights of indigenous peoples from their perspective, in contrast with the perspective of the states' representatives who wrote the earlier convention (Wilmer 1993).

In 2003 and 2007, the ILO issued comprehensive reports on the status of employment discrimination in the world. The first report focused on gender wage discrimination and the distinct circumstances women face in the paid labor force. It also reported on national policies implemented to achieve the goals of Conventions No. 100 and 111, mentioned above. It acknowledged the problem of women's unpaid household labor, calling women "invisible workers." The 2007 report reviewed "long recognized forms of discrimination" such as those based on gender, race, religion, status as a migrant worker, and social origin, as well as "newly recognized forms of discrimination" including those based on age, disability, sexual orientation, and infection with HIV/AIDS, and evaluated changes since 2003 in seven countries, including the United States, Canada, India, Malaysia, South Africa, Namibia, and the United Kingdom, in specific Northern Ireland. Overall, these countries were favorably reviewed, but the ILO also emphasized corporate social responsibility and efforts to bring labor and employer groups together informally.

The most recent and innovative ILO initiative is called Decent Work Country Programmes linking the United Nations, the ILO, and national development programs. The elimination of discrimination is one of the major objectives of the ILO's involvement in UN development programs. These programs assist states in identifying means to achieve four goals of the ILO: (1) guaranteeing workers' rights and international labor standards, (2) creating opportunities for employment, (3) providing for social security, and (4) promoting dialogue among workers, employers, and national governments. The ILO reviews conditions in a country, evaluates strengths and deficiencies in achieving these objectives, and then makes recommendations for addressing the deficiencies.

## Elimination of Racial Discrimination

Through the United Nations, the international community has continued to develop international standards and rights aimed at eliminating racial discrimination. The International Convention on the Elimination of All Forms of Racial Discrimination was adopted by the UN General Assembly in 1965 and entered into force in 1969. By 2014, 177 states were parties to the convention, which established the Committee on the Elimination of Racial Discrimination to monitor its provisions by reviewing country reports every two years.

The convention allows individuals to make complaints against a state if the state accepts the competence of the committee to hear individual complaints under Article 14. Fifty-three states recognize the competence of the committee to hear such complaints. In 1993, the committee adopted procedures allowing preventive measures in situations deemed at risk of escalating into civil conflict involving racial grievances. The committee may also designate a country as in a state of "early warning" for conflict and instability and undertake confidence-building measures to make deescalation and stability more likely. It can also issue urgent measures to respond immediately to "prevent or limit the scale or number of serious violations of the Convention" (Committee on the Elimination of Racial Discrimination 2008).

The United Nations declared 1972–1982 the Decade to Combat Racism and Racial Discrimination and dedicated two more decades to "Action to Combat Racism and Racial Discrimination" from 1983 to 1992 and 1994 to 2003. The first decade (1972–1982) was focused on implementation of international provisions, and the second (1983–1992) on remedies for individual victims of racial discrimination. In 1978, the First World Conference to Combat Racism convened in Geneva, with a second conference in 1983. Both conferences ended without agreement on the two most prominent issues on the agenda: apartheid in South Africa and the conditions of Palestinians in the occupied territories.

After the General Assembly passed a resolution equating Zionism with racism in 1978, Israel and the United States withdrew from the conference. (Ironically, as the Israeli ambassador pointed out during the debate, the resolution passed on the thirty-seventh anniversary of Kristallnacht, when Nazi stormtroopers attacked Jewish homes, businesses, and synagogues all over Germany.) Most of the rest of the first conference was devoted to the

---

## Objectives of the Convention on the Elimination of Racial Discrimination

To review progress made in the fight against racism and racial discrimination, in particular since the adoption of the Universal Declaration of Human Rights, and to reappraise the obstacles to progress in the field and to identify ways to overcome them;

To consider ways and means to better ensure the application of existing standards and their implementation to combat racism and racial discrimination;

To increase the level of awareness about the scourge of racism and racial discrimination;

To formulate concrete recommendations on ways to increase the effectiveness of the activities and mechanisms of the United Nations through programmes aimed at combating racism and racial discrimination;

To review the political, historical, economic, social, cultural and other factors leading to racism and racial discrimination;

To formulate concrete recommendations to further action-oriented national, regional and international measures aimed at combating all forms of racism and racial discrimination; and

To draw up concrete recommendations to ensure that the United Nations has the necessary resources for its activities to combat racism, racial discrimination, xenophobia and related intolerance.

issue of apartheid in South Africa and efforts to isolate South Africa within the international community through embargoes, sanctions, and cutting off of diplomatic ties.

The second conference was plagued by dissent and divisiveness until Germany, acting on behalf of nine members of the European Community, withdrew from the conference (Camponovo 2002–2003). While Western governments expressed strong opposition to apartheid, they objected to statements that affirmed a right of armed resistance to apartheid. In regard to the situation between the Palestinians and the Israelis, the final document of the second conference recalled "with deep regret the practices of racial discrimination against the Palestinians as well as other inhabitants of the Arab occupied territories which have such an impact on all aspects of their daily existence that they prevent the enjoyment of their fundamental rights."

Four blocs formed within the second conference—the Western Europe and other states group, the Africa group, the Latin America and the Caribbean group, and the Asia group. The second conference also took up the question of reparations for slavery, an issue that emerged from the regional and preparatory meetings. The conference became predictably divided over the issue, with the African, Asian, Latin American, and Caribbean members favoring compensation, and the Western Europeans and other states calling for a more limited agenda.

Hopes ran high for the third conference in 2001. Apartheid in South Africa was over and the meeting was to take place in Durban, South Africa. But language equating Zionism with racism—calling Israel a "racist, apartheid state"—derailed US participation. Seventeen states opposed and eleven abstained from voting on the paragraph containing this language. Christopher Camponovo, US delegate to the Durban conference in 2001, would look back on the conference and describe the dissenting opinions:

> Most delegations opposing the paragraph saw this characterization of Israeli practices in the occupied territories as counterproductive to achieving peace in the Middle East. Some asserted that it was arbitrary to single out one member state for condemnation and criticism, particularly by comparing Israel to South Africa. Other delegations characterized the problems in the Middle East as political with no direct relation to the issue of eliminating racial discrimination or saw this issue as one outside the parameters of the Conference. (Camponovo 2002–2003:3)

The third decade (1994–2003) emphasized education, a global perspective, and putting racial discrimination more broadly into the category of basic human rights. The most comprehensive conference yet was planned, the World Conference Against Racism, Racial Discrimination, Xenophobia, and Related Intolerance, to be held in Durban, South Africa, in late summer 2001. Two preparatory meetings were held in Geneva in May 2000 and May 2001 as well as regional meetings of experts in Geneva, Switzerland; Warsaw, Poland; Bangkok, Thailand; Addis Ababa, Ethiopia; and Santiago de Chile to work out what issues were important at a local level.

In 1998, the UN General Assembly declared 2001 as the International Year of Mobilization Against Racism, Racial Discrimination, Xenophobia, and Related Intolerance. However, as the date drew near, that the 2001 world conference would likely end much as the two previous conferences had became increasingly evident: sharply divided and without adopting "concrete measures for securing the full and universal implementation of U.N. decisions and resolutions on racism, racial discrimination, apartheid, de-colonization and self-determination" (Resolution 3507, November 2, 1972).

When delegations met for the Durban conference in late summer of 2001, the first order of business was adopting an agenda and plan of action. After four days of discussions in which the United States tried without success to get the language equating Zionism with racism removed, the United States and Israel withdrew again. Secretary of State Colin Powell expressed regret "because of the importance of the international fight against racism and the contribution that the Conference could have made to it." He also stated,

> I know that you do not combat racism by conferences that produce declarations containing hateful language, some of which is a throwback to the days of "Zionism equals racism;" or supports the idea that we have made too much of the Holocaust; or suggests that apartheid exists in Israel; or that singles out only one country in the world—Israel—for censure and abuse. (Statement of Secretary Colin Powell, September 3, 2001, World Conference Against Racism)

Fliers claiming that a victory for Hitler would have prevented the establishment of Israel and other anti-Semitic propaganda were displayed and distributed at the conference. Some human rights organizations asked Jewish delegates to leave and the Jewish center in Durban closed after receiving threats of violence (Braun 2008). Finally, the Brazilian delegation proposed that issues for which no agreement could be reached be deleted from the final document by a "motion of no action," which was approved by a vote of fifty-one to thirty-eight (Braun 2008).

The conference did condemn slavery as a crime against humanity and affirmed links among colonialism, slavery, and racism. It also specifically included "indigenous peoples" as victims of these practices, as well as people of African and Asian descent. Delegates did take up the question of apologies and reparations, but they neither adopted a common position nor issued an apology. Instead, the final document said,

> We acknowledge and profoundly regret the massive human suffering and the tragic plight of millions of men, women and children caused by slavery, the slave trade, the transatlantic slave trade, apartheid, colonialism and genocide, and call upon States concerned to honour the memory of the victims of past tragedies and affirm that, wherever and whenever these occurred, they must be condemned and their recurrence prevented. We regret that these practices and structures, political, socio-economic, and cultural, have led to racism, racial discrimination, xenophobia and related intolerance.

Conferees acknowledged a link between historical injustices and current social and economic conditions of the African diaspora. They recognized the Palestinians' right to self-determination while affirming the right of all states to security—a balance between the grievances and justifications for violence on both sides of the Israeli-Palestinian conflict.

All three conferences are widely regarded as failures, and the walk-out of the US and Israeli delegations after four days was soon eclipsed by the unprecedented attacks on the World Trade Center in New York City and the Pentagon in Washington, DC, on September 11, 2001 (Camponovo 2002–2003). Enthusiasm for achieving the objectives of the original convention or any of the subsequent conferences and the designated goals of the three decades the United Nations devoted to combatting racism through concrete measures eroded in the face of three failed world conferences. The international community's attention shifted away from eliminating racial intolerance and toward the US-initiated global war on terror.

The most recent, fourth World Conference Against Racism was held in Geneva in 2009; the United States and Israel refused to attend, as did Australia, Canada, Germany, Italy, the Netherlands, New Zealand, and Poland. When Iranian president Ahmadinejad referred to Israel as a racist state and publicly denied its right to exist, nearly forty countries walked out. That same year, the UN General Assembly mandated a meeting of its members in 2011 to commemorate the tenth anniversary of the 2001 conference, but both the United Nations and the process of trying to unite all member states in a common effort to combat racism on a global scale have for now lost much credibility.

## Emerging Rights Issues

Most of the issues discussed in this chapter implicate the social construction of the state—an imagined and naturalized extension of groups defined by national identity (sometimes narrated in ethnic and religious terms) whose self-determination reaches its fullest expression in statehood—as an underlying cause of intergroup conflict and institutionalized discrimination.

As was argued in Chapter 4 and is presented as a recurring theme through-out much of this text, the state holds the capacity to both perpetrate and remedy human rights injuries—the paradox of self-regulation, as Professor Abdullahi Ahmed an-Na'im (2008) called it. The rights of children, dis-abled persons, and lesbian, gay, bisexual, and transgender (LGBT) people are not necessarily new rights issues, but they have recently gained more widespread attention, and advocacy networks have put these rights issues on global and local human rights agendas. In some cases, these issues point to states as perpetrators because states reflect the values and worldviews, including the prejudices, of their leaders and, in democracies, their majori-ties. However, the capacity of the state to take action to end and remedy the injustices, injuries, and discriminatory policies affecting these groups and individuals—the promise of liberalism—also inspires hope for enlarging the spheres of justice through political action.

## The Rights of Children

Children's rights are on the frontier of contemporary global social justice advocacy. Like women a century ago in Western democracies, children enjoy few rights on their own, relying instead on the protection of their rights by those to whom their care is legally entrusted. As victims of vio-lence, abuse, or exploitation within the family, they have few rights and little recourse for direct action. Perhaps the most progressive provisions are found in Scandinavia where, for example, Sweden has outlawed "parental chastise-ment" and South Africa outlawed chastisement or corporal punishment in schools in 1995 in the wave of democratization that ended apartheid. In some countries, children can legally terminate their relationship with their parents before they reach an age of majority. However, not all see this trend in a positive light. The Convention on the Rights of the Child is criticized by some as going too far in eroding parental authority or restricting parental rights. A coalition of 1,600 NGOs formed the Child Rights Information Net-work, whose activism led to the adoption of the previously mentioned con-vention by the UN General Assembly in 1989.

Because the well-being of children is linked to the living conditions of those on whom they rely to meet their basic needs, which generally means that children rely on women, women's economic marginalization has a direct impact on the condition of children, a condition that sometimes is less than perfect. Nearly 1.8 billion children under the age of eighteen die from waterborne diseases each year. More than 3 million children die every year from hunger and related causes—nearly 8,300 a day (The Hunger Project 2014). The UN Children's Fund (UNICEF 2014) estimated that 29,000 children die each day from causes directly related to poverty.

More than 2 million children a year die because they are not immunized; 15 million a year are orphaned by HIV/AIDS (Shah 2013). Anup Shah estimated that of 1.9 billion people eighteen and younger in developing countries, 640 million live without adequate shelter, 400 million have no access to safe water, and 270 million have no access to health services (Shah 2013). According to the Millennium Development Goals report, 72 million primary-school-aged children in the developing countries were not in school in 2005 (United Nations 2007). Basic education, safe water, and sanitation for everyone would, Shah argued, cost less than the amount people in Europe and the United States spend on pet food in one year.

Children's rights appear in the ICESCR in articles on the family, physical and mental health, and education. Article 10, paragraph 3 calls for the protection of children "without any discrimination for reasons of parentage" and says they should be "protected from economic and social exploitation." On child labor, the article states, "Their employment in work harmful to their morals or health or dangerous to life or likely to hamper their normal development should be punishable by law." The convention also prescribes setting a legal age under which children may not work.

Child labor has long been a concern of the ILO as well as labor and child advocacy movements in industrializing countries. UNICEF (2013) estimated that worldwide more than 150 million children—one in six between the ages of five and seventeen—are working. Article 32 of the Convention on the Rights of the Child stipulates that "parties recognize the right of the child to be protected from economic exploitation and from performing any work that is likely to be hazardous or to interfere with the child's education, or to be harmful to the child's health or physical, mental, spiritual, moral or social development." Though some economists argue in defense of child labor (e.g., Friedman 1999), others argue against it, including Nobel Laureate Amartya Sen (1997). Among the strongest objections are that the largest number of employed children are prostitutes and soldiers, that their working conditions are unhealthy, and that work interferes with their access to education and thus in the long run hurts the whole society.

In addition to deprivation and death from structural inequalities and economic marginalization, children's human rights are affected by direct violence too. Abolition of the death penalty has long been on the agenda of Amnesty International. Although all states outlawed or renounced the use of the death penalty for children by 2005, Amnesty International reports that in 2007 fourteen child offenders were executed worldwide; eight were executed in 2008; seven in 2009; and between one and three every year since through 2013 (Amnesty International 2014d). In 2009, Saudi Arabia executed five men by beheading, two of them juveniles (Amnesty International 2009c). The main international instruments prohibiting the execution of children are the ICCPR (1967), the American Convention on Human Rights (1969), the Convention on the Rights of the Child (1989), and the African Charter on the Rights and Welfare of the Child (1990). The UN Economic and Social Council passed a resolution in 1984 that was also endorsed by the General Assembly, providing safeguards for the rights of those facing the death penalty. The resolution declared, "Persons below 18 years of age at the time of the commission of the crime shall not be sentenced to death" (Amnesty International 2014d).

Perhaps the most serious and growing problem of violence against children is the increasing use of child soldiers, especially but not only in sub-Saharan Africa. The problem is most evident in Angola, Burundi, Colombia, the Democratic Republic of Congo, Rwanda, Sierra Leone, Sri Lanka, and Uganda. Human Rights Watch (2009) said that since 2001, the use of children as soldiers has been documented in twenty-one countries, with estimates ranging from 250,000 to 300,000 child soldiers worldwide today. Amnesty International described the children's situation: "Easily manipulated, children are sometimes coerced to commit grave atrocities, including rape and murder of civilians using assault rifles such as AK-47s and G4s. Some are forced to injure or kill members of their own families or other child soldiers. Others serve as porters, cooks, guards, messengers, spies, and sex slaves" (Amnesty International 2014d).

## Minors Executed Between 1990 and 2009

| | |
|---|---|
| China | 2 |
| Democratic Republic of Congo | 1 |
| Iran | 46 |
| Nigeria | 1 |
| Pakistan | 4 |
| Saudi Arabia | 5 |
| Sudan | 2 |
| United States | 22[a] |
| Yemen | 1 |

*Source:* Amnesty International, "Child Soldiers: From Cradle to War," www.amnestyusa.org/our-work/issues/children-s-rights/child-soldiers?id=1021176.

*Note:* a. The number for the United States includes defendants who were under the age of eighteen at the time of the crime, though they were adults when executed. The US Supreme Court outlawed this practice in 2005.

War often separates children from their parents or their entire families and neighbors, leaving them vulnerable to exploitation by whoever provides for their basic needs. The situation is exacerbated when the child is traumatized by the murder of family members. Human Rights Watch (2009) also reported, "Both girls and boys are used as child soldiers. In some countries, like Nepal, Sri Lanka and Uganda, a third or more of the child soldiers were reported to be girls." In some conflicts, girls may be raped or given to military commanders as "wives."

In 1998, a coalition of six international NGOs was formed to stop the use of child soldiers. Their advocacy led to the adoption of the Optional Protocol to the Convention on the Rights of the Child on the involvement of children in armed conflict by the General Assembly and, in turn, the declaration of February 12 as Red Hand Day to raise awareness and mobilize support for the abolition of children in the military. February 12 was chosen because on that day in 2002 the protocol entered into force.

### The Rights of the Disabled

In 1982, the UN General Assembly declared December 3 as the International Day of Disabled People in order to raise public awareness and encourage state action to promote and protect the rights of disabled persons. The WHO estimated the number of disabled persons worldwide at 1 billion in 2011, with 80 percent living in developing countries (WHO and World Bank 2011). The number of disabled people in developing countries is high and continues to grow disproportionately because those countries are more severely affected by war, violence, and inadequate medical and rehabilitation services (Center for International Rehabilitation 2010). Ninety percent of people disabled by landmines are civilians, a third of them children (Center for International Rehabilitation 2010).

The range of problems experienced by people with disabilities includes not only discrimination in employment, education, and public accommodation but also greater vulnerability to physical abuse, mental or criminal manipulation, and sexual exploitation, particularly among mentally disabled people. The UN General Assembly adopted the Declaration on the Rights of Mentally Retarded Persons in 1971 and the Declaration on the Rights of Disabled Persons in 1975. The Convention on the Rights of Persons with Disabilities and its optional protocol, which created a monitoring and implementation committee, were opened for signature in 2007. The convention was the most quickly negotiated treaty in the history of the United Nations, with the most number of signatories on the day it opened for signature. The convention identifies persons with disabilities as "those who have long-term physical, mental, intellectual, or sensory impairments which in interaction with various barriers may hinder their full and effective participation in society on an equal basis with others" (Article 1). Instead of defining "persons with disabilities," the convention remarkably recognizes that "disability is an evolving concept and that disability results from the interaction between persons with impairments and attitudinal and environmental barriers that hinders their full and effective participation in society on an equal basis with others" (Preamble, paragraph e).

The convention and protocol entered into force in March 2008, and in 2014, the convention had 158 signatories and 147 ratifications. Virtually all developed states and even most developing states have signed, including the United States, which signed in 2009 but had not ratified the convention as of 2014. Signatories to the convention met in conference in 2008 and 2009 to establish the committee pursuant to the protocol. The committee reviews reports submitted by state parties on judicial, legislative, and policy efforts to implement the convention. The convention stresses equality and nondiscrimination, accessibility, reasonable accommodation, independent living, full participation in society, and protection against violence including "torture or cruel, inhuman or degrading treatment or punishment" (Article 15); "freedom from exploitation, violence, and abuse" (Article 16); and protection of the "physical and mental integrity" of disabled persons "on an equal basis with others" (Article 17).

## Discrimination and Persecution
## Based on Sexual Identity

Discrimination, harassment, and various kinds of public and private violence against LGBT people are deeply embedded within social, cultural, and even religious norms and beliefs. "Homosexual acts" are completely illegal in about one-fourth of the countries in the world. In countries where homosexual acts have been criminalized, sentences range from several months to life imprisonment (e.g., Tanzania), and in nine countries—all in Africa—homosexual acts are punishable by death. In this way, sexual identity differs from other identities subjected to discrimination. However, not all cultures have a history of discriminating against individuals of non-heterosexual identity or prohibiting nonheterosexual practices. Many indigenous cultures, for example, incorporate respect for a variety of sexual identities and some even hold them in high esteem (Williams 1986; Roscoe 1991; Jacobs, Thomas, and Lang 1997; Gilley 2006).

The International Lesbian, Gay, Bisexual, Trans and Intersex Association (ILGA) reported that in 2013 eighty countries criminalized individuals based on sexual orientation and gender identity (Itaborahy 2013). The climate of criminalization makes people identified as LGBT (or LGBT/two spirit when referring to indigenous sexual identity) more likely to be home-

### Examples of Public and Private Offenses and Abuses Endured by People Whose Sexual Identity Is Not Heterosexual

Raped to "cure" their lesbianism, sometimes at the behest of their parents.

Prosecuted because their private and consensual relationship is deemed to be a social danger.

Denied custody of their children.

Beaten by police.

Attacked, sometimes killed, on the street—a victim of a "hate crime."

Subjected to verbal abuse.

Bullied at school.

Denied employment, housing, or health services.

Raped and otherwise tortured in detention.

Denied asylum when they do manage to flee abuse.

Threatened for campaigning for their human rights.

Driven to suicide.

Executed by the state.

*Source:* Amnesty International 2014e.

less and more vulnerable to human trafficking (US Department of State 2014). The issue of criminalization versus legality is not the only concern to LGBT human rights, but other than private violence, it has the most severe and immediately injurious consequences. The LGBT community faces substantial fears in addition to criminal prosecution, imprisonment, and capital punishment, such as private violence in the form of hate crimes and harassment. For example, of 6,718 hate crimes reported to the Federal Bureau of Investigation (FBI) in 2012, 19.6 percent involved individuals targeted because of sexual orientation (FBI 2013).

Criminalization of homosexuality is most prevalent in Africa, which has become a battleground for religiously conservative attitudes toward the LGBT community (Kaoma 2009; *Herald Sun* 2010). Legislation was proposed in Uganda in 2009 with the Anti-Homosexuality Bill, which targeted gays and lesbians by potentially imposing the death penalty and criminalizing gay rights initiatives, and passed in 2014 after the death penalty was replaced with life imprisonment for conviction. Burundi passed a criminalization law in 2009. In Nigeria male homosexual acts are illegal everywhere, but laws differ between areas controlled by sharia and those not. In areas where sharia reigns, both male and female homosexuality are illegal; male homosexuality punishable by death and lesbianism punishable by lashing and possibly imprisonment. In other areas, homosexuality is legal for women while the penalty for men is up to fourteen years imprisonment. However, Rwanda backed down on criminalization after sustained international and domestic pressure to abandon similar legislation there. The Rwandan case indicates that international pressure can make a difference.

Although discrimination on the basis of sexual identity is not yet specifically prohibited by any international agreements, the European Court of Human Rights applied the European Convention on Human Rights to a series of cases in 1981, 1988, and 1993 involving sexual identity, in particular criminalization of such activity. The court emphasized the "right to private life" provided for in Article 8 of the convention (Human Rights Education Associates 2008). Article 8 was also cited by the European Court of Human Rights as prohibiting a ban on homosexual service in the military. European case law also includes a decision by the European Commission of Human Rights that considered a law designating a higher age of consent for homosexual than for heterosexual acts and concluded that this issue was also one of a right to privacy and constituted discrimination according to Article 14 of the convention. Additionally, Articles 8 and 14 were both cited in a case involving the custodial rights of a homosexual father, citing protection against discrimination in Article 14 and the right to family life in Article 8.

## Conclusion

Discrimination based on identity is pervasive in most societies and across the span of human history. One can think about the political implications in many ways. States, and the people who control them, have often institutionalized different forms of discrimination. Categories of those discriminated against represent identities that have or can be used to mobilize political loyalties—religion, ethnicity, and what some call "race." *Race* is probably one of the most misused terms outside of the fields of sociology and political science because it has historically implied a link between biological attributes and social groups that for the most part do not exist, at least not when painted with the broad brush that is often used to refer to "race." In a political sense, however, the category has significance simply because it has been used as if a self-evident link exists between biological attributes and social groups (Malik 1996). Sociologist Ronald Taylor (2008) commented on "the rather dubious status of the term 'race' as a scientific concept":

Although long embraced as a valid term for sorting and characterizing variations in human populations around the world, the term has been abandoned by a growing number of natural and social scientists who see it as mired in a biological, cultural, and semantic swamp. They have concluded that all attempts to classify Homo sapiens into races have proven a futile exercise. Perhaps the best and latest evidence is presented in *The History and Geography of Human Genes,* a 1,032-page tome published more than a decade ago (1994), which synthesizes more than 50 years of research in population genetics.

The authors of this study (Cavalli-Sforza, Menozzi, and Piazza) conclude that there is no legitimate biological basis for sorting individuals into groups that correspond to races, as they are popularly perceived.

The political logic of discrimination, particularly when such discrimination is the official policy of states, is that ethnic, religious, or communal identities compete for loyalty and the state runs more efficiently (the need for coercive obedience is reduced) when it lays claim to the loyalty of its citizens based on narratives of identity. Since we know the world has far fewer states than communal identities, building an identity on which loyalty to the state may rely and that will trump other forms of identity is not a trivial matter. The creation and dissolution of Yugoslavia illustrates an extreme but not unique case of how state identity can conflict with other forms of identity, and indeed, how national identities were both suppressed in order to create the Yugoslav state and later unleashed by nationalist leaders in order to accelerate and ensure its destruction.

Similarly, religion can be used to mobilize strong loyalties that may be more powerful than nationalism or citizenship since their claims are moral. The relationship between religion and political mobilization raises a number of thorny issues from the religious wars of Christian Europe to the Holocaust and contemporary Islamist movements.

Other kinds of identity exist that are not implicated by efforts to create and sustain loyalty to the state—age, gender, disability, and sexual orientation, for example. While children can be discriminated against on the basis of their not having reached an age of moral maturity that warrants granting them the full privileges and responsibilities of adult citizens, generally children as a class are not targeted for discrimination by state policies. For the same reason they sometimes receive special protection or treatment, for example, in the way they are treated by criminal courts and in sentencing for criminal acts. However, children are often targeted for certain kinds of human rights violations, like being used as soldiers, forced to labor, and exploited sexually.

The same is true for gender discrimination, which primarily affects women, and discrimination because of sexual orientation, which is on the frontier of current efforts to create more just and less violent societies. In this chapter, I have touched on issues of discrimination against women, for

example, the exclusion of women abolitionists from the antislavery conference in 1840, the devaluation of women's unpaid work, and victimization
through human trafficking. However, because the human rights of women
are imperiled primarily because of social norms and structures sometimes
institutionalized in law, women's human rights are taken up in more detail
within the context of human rights as human needs in the next chapter.

# 12

# Women's Rights

If the great moral struggle of the 19th century was slavery and the great moral struggle of the 20th century was the defeat of totalitarian ideologies, then the great moral struggle of the 21st century is ending the worldwide oppression of women.　　　　　　　—US journalist Nicholas Kristof, 2012

We have to start looking at the world through women's eyes. How are human rights, peace, and development defined from the perspective of the lives of women? It's also important to look at the world from the perspective of the lives of diverse women, because there is not a single women's view, any more than there is a single men's view.
　　　　　　　—Charlotte Bunch, founder, Center for
　　　　　　　Women's Global Leadership, 2005

THE HUMAN RIGHTS ISSUES RAISED IN EARLIER CHAPTERS—TORTURE, war crimes, genocide, and racial or religious discrimination—suggest that the state is made up of a set of institutions produced and legitimated by certain normative beliefs and practices that, though also imbued with positive attributes, are often used to rationalize public policies and private behaviors that violate human rights. From this perspective, contemporary international human rights can be viewed as a reaction to or an attempt to correct these negative potentialities of state institutions and norms to at least correct human rights issues at the public level. However, feminists question the distinction between "public" and "private," arguing that such a distinction enables the continuation of practices that discriminate against and marginalize women in so-called private spheres, such as the household or family (Fraser 1990; Romany 1993). A few issues also connected with women's human rights have already been raised in preceding chapters: human trafficking, the exclusion of women abolitionists in the early antislavery movement, rape as a war tactic and war crime, employment discrimination, and the marginalization of women within various religious traditions. In this chapter, I examine these issues in greater depth, survey a broader range of women's human rights, and put them into a political and legal context.

The norms and practices that lead to violations of women's human rights are embedded within, reproduced, and sustained by cultural beliefs and by a broader, overarching ideology of patriarchy. Ideologies that sustain inequalities also operate in other areas of human rights, like racial discrimination and even the prejudices used to mobilize genocides. But the inequalities women suffer, and thus assertion of their rights, are distinct due to the physically and emotionally intimate nature of the relationships between women and men who have formed romantic bonds because these relationships often perpetuate an ideology of sexual domination.

The 2013 annual report from the UN special rapporteur on violence against women was devoted to a study on state responsibility for eliminating such violence through the legal principle of due diligence. Under the due diligence standard, when the private sector fails to protect rights, the state assumes responsibility. Article 4(c) of the UN Declaration on Elimination of Violence Against Women specifically requires the "exercise of due diligence to prevent, investigate and in accordance with national legislation punish acts of violence against women whether those actions are perpetrated by the state or private persons." Nondiscrimination is a central principle in the application of due diligence; that is, preventing, investigating, punishing, and remedying violence against women must be pursued with the same level of rigor as the state would other forms of violence (Manjoo 2012).

## What Is Patriarchy?

"First we should get rid of patriarchy," said 2003 Nobel Peace Prize winner and Iranian judge Shirin Ebadi (2004), "[and] then we will see what problems Islam has with women." "We need to fight patriarchy, not men," she said, separating culture from religion, because any religion can have many interpretations, and culture is the lens through which religion is interpreted. As she saw it, when patriarchy is embedded within culture, religion is interpreted in a patriarchal way.

From an anthropological perspective, patriarchy can be viewed as a family and social structure controlled or dominated by men, masculinity, and values associated with masculinity. The ideology underlying men's control or masculine dominance—that men *ought* to be in control and *ought* to have more or ultimate power and authority in a social system—is especially problematic. This attitude carries over into political systems when that control is institutionalized legally. Since Rayna Reiter and others began to question the social foundations of patriarchy in *Toward an Anthropology of Women* in 1975, patriarchy has been a subject of continuing controversy and debate among anthropologists and feminist scholars. Patriarchy today is pervasive, though evidence can be found of sexually egalitarian, or perhaps even a few matriarchal, societies in the past.

Many assume that the unequal treatment of women is a problem more common and more severe in traditional, as compared to modern, societies. Anthropological studies of nonstate, small-scale cultures, however, show a wide variety of social practices and cultural perspectives on gender roles, as do studies across cultures within the modern system of states. Anthropology is an academic discipline that is itself a product of Western culture, although a critique of its ethnocentrism was already emerging in the 1970s (Douglas 1978). Some caution against ethnocentric biases should be exercised, particularly when interpreting the cultural meanings and social practices of other cultures. Henrietta Moore (1988) described the effect of Western cultural bias on the study of gender roles in anthropology:

> When researchers perceive the asymmetrical relations between men and women in other cultures, they assume such asymmetries to be analogous to their own cultural experience of the unequal and hierarchical nature of gender relations in Western society. A number of feminist anthropologists have now made the point that, even where more egalitarian relationships between men and women exist, researchers are very often unable to understand this potential equality because they insist on interpreting difference and asymmetry as inequality and hierarchy. (2)

While some of the most egregious and violent offenses against women's human rights may be occurring today in non-Western settings, generalization to the broader case of non-Western societies not only understates the lack of protection or even recognition of certain human rights for women in Western societies but also overlooks cases where women's human rights are more respected in some non-Western societies. Equating "Western" with "advanced" and "non-Western" with "backward" produces a fallacy of dichotomous and hierarchical oversimplification so often at the heart of feminist criticism in social theory (Peterson 1992).

Patriarchal ideology rationalizes the diminishment and violation of women's human rights within the broader context of economic and social practices, some of which are not only embedded within the state and its normative foundations but also rooted in social or cultural norms and practices or both. This invasiveness is particularly true, for example, in the case of women's status and treatment. Is female genital mutilation (FGM) a form of torture or a cultural practice? As torture, it is not carried out by the state, but should the state outlaw it as it does other violent acts? As a cultural practice, should it be protected against state intrusion? What about women's reproductive labor, which is unpaid, takes them out of the paid labor force, and imposes on them lifetime economic disadvantages and makes them more likely to be dependent on others? If women did not do this work, society would collapse without any children and without anyone to care for them in their first months or years. Is disregard for women's work inside the home a social practice with which the state ought not interfere or a form of structural inequality sanctioned tacitly by the state's silence?

Issues affecting women's human rights fall roughly into two categories. The first category of issues covers those that structurally affect women's well-being and economic independence because of women's status as women: for example, doing unpaid work like infant and family care and household management in a monetized society makes women economically dependent on those who labor for cash or income. Women's status may actually change from interdependent to dependent when a nonmonetized society becomes monetized, that is, where labor is rewarded with wages paid to particular individuals in contrast with an interdependent household or communal division of labor where status and access to basic needs are not determined by valuing labor in wages. The second category of issues affecting women's human rights covers those resulting from direct violence, such as bride burning, rape, domestic and partner violence, and human trafficking. Some, like domestic and partner violence, along with human trafficking, directly affect men as well, though not in the same high proportion.

## Women and the Economy

Social practices marginalize women economically and politically in many ways. These injurious effects are described as "indirect" because social practices create institutions and norms that marginalize or impair women's rights, often leading to physical deprivations. Women's economic marginalization makes them more vulnerable to a variety of harmful conditions and injustices ranging from economic dependency on men to debt bondage, human trafficking, and even murder (when parents refuse or are unable to pay a dowry to satisfy the groom or his family). This practice is known as "dowry burning," "bride burning," or "honor killings" (UN Development Fund for Women 2010). For example, a recent study of women in Kerala, India, showed a strong link between women's property ownership and vulnerability to domestic violence:

> Despite Kerala's favourable human development indicators, 36% of the women reported long-term physical violence, and 65% reported psychologi-

cal abuse. Physical violence during pregnancy—which can cause miscar-
riages, low birth weight infants, and even fetal and maternal death—was especially high. . . . 49% of the propertyless women reported long-term physical violence compared with 18% and 10% respectively of those who owned
either land or a house, and 7% if they owned both. (Agarwal 2007)

Another study by the UN Commission on Sustainable Development on
women and property ownership found that "alarming numbers of cases are
reported of in-laws having evicted widows upon the death of their husband.
A widow is not considered a part of the clan and is expected to return to her
parents and/or fend for herself" (Benschop 2004).

The same report noted that 70 percent of all squatter households in
Kenya are female-headed and that more than a quarter of women living in
the slums were migrants from rural areas where they had been dispossessed
of their land (Benschop 2004). Other studies show a link between women's
property rights and the spread of HIV/AIDS infection due to the practice of
"widow inheritance," in which a widow is forced to marry a relative of her
deceased husband, who may be infected with HIV/AIDS (Kinoti 2006).

Historically, many cultures have treated women as property. In the past
few centuries, the issue has been more one of women's rights to own property, and not until the eighteenth and nineteenth centuries did British common law and codified or positive law in most Western countries begin to
recognize and expand women's capacity to own and inherit property
(Salmon 1986; Lewis 2009).

Women constitute the largest percentage of those economically marginalized globally. Of the total number of people living in poverty worldwide—about 2 billion by World Bank estimates—approximately 70 percent
are women (World Bank 2014). Women make up three-fourths of the
world's 27 million refugees, a third of the paid labor force in developing
countries, and almost half the paid labor force in industrialized countries.
They spend about twice as much time doing unpaid work as men and produce more than half the food grown in developing countries (United
Nations 2013b; FAO 2013). Their unpaid household and community work
was estimated to be worth around $11 trillion in 1995 (Peterson 2003).
Studies of non-European economies indicate that national incomes would
increase by 25–50 percent if the value of unpaid domestic and household
work were included in calculating national income (Anker 1983).

In the United States, women earn on average 23 percent less than
men with the same level of education, which means that over their average working lives, women with a high school degree will make $700,000
less than their male counterparts, $1.2 million less with a four-year col-
lege degree, and $2 million less with graduate or law degrees (Murphy
2006). The European Commission, the executive body of the European
Union, published figures on gender pay equity in 2009 showing a gap

ranging from 30 percent in Estonia, 25.5 percent in Austria, and 21 percent in the United Kingdom to a low of 4.4 percent in Italy (Metro 2009). The commission also reported that this gap results in higher poverty rates for aging women, with 21 percent of women age sixty-five and older at risk of poverty compared to 16 percent of men. Using data from the ILO, the UN Development Programme, the World Bank, the WHO, and the Inter-Parliamentary Union, the 2013 World Economic Forum evaluated the gender gap by country and region to produce the *Global Gender Gap Report* (Hausmann, Tyson, and Zahidi 2012). The authors of the report evaluated economic participation and opportunity, educational attainment, political empowerment, and health and survival to develop a composite global gender gap index. Using a scale of 1.00 for equality, rankings for economic empowerment and opportunity ranged from 0.27 in Syria to 0.83 in Mongolia. The highest-ranking Western country was Norway at 0.83 in fourth place. The United States was ranked eighth with a score of 0.81 (Hausmann, Tyson, and Zahidi 2012). After one takes into account composite scores based on all variables, the top four countries are all in Scandinavia: Iceland, Finland, Norway, and Sweden. Notably high-ranked non-Western countries include Lesotho (fourteenth), South Africa (sixteenth), and Cuba (nineteenth). The United States comes in at twenty-second place with Mozambique, Burundi, and Australia just below (in twenty-third to twenty-fifth places). In no country are men and women yet entirely equal.

A clear correlation also exists between literacy and economic empowerment. Not only are literate women more qualified for jobs with higher pay, but they are also likely to marry later, have fewer children, maintain better health, and, along with their children, have better housing, clothing, water, and sanitation (SIL International 2014). Two-thirds of all illiterate adults in the world are women (WomenAid International 2010). In twenty-seven countries the rate of illiteracy for women is 50 percent or higher (Nationmaster 2010).

Finally, women's social, political, and economic marginalization has serious consequences for their health. They are increasingly exposed to HIV/AIDS, particularly infected by husbands who have had extramarital sex with infected persons, and they now make up about 42 percent of HIV/AIDS cases globally. The World Health Organization (2014b) reported that approximately 20 million women undergo unsafe abortions each year, 70,000 of them dying as a result. More than a half million women die every year from complications and lack of access to medical care during pregnancy and childbirth, and 51 percent of all pregnant women globally have iron-deficient anemia, a preventable condition that left untreated leads to premature births and underweight babies (United Nations 2008b).

## Women's Legal and Political Equality

One of the earliest impediments to legal equality to be dealt with by international agreement was women's citizenship status when married to someone of a different nationality. The political and legal significance of nationality in the form of citizenship developed when the state was institutionalized with normative reference to nationalism. National identity gave legitimacy to the institutions of popular government, a notion that developed during the seventeenth century and became the normative foundation of the democratic state as a result of the revolutions beginning in the eighteenth century.

As norms outlining the rights and duties attached to citizenship were codified, so was the status of married women, who were historically excluded from direct political participation, ostensibly "represented" within these new democracies by men (husbands or fathers). Thus, women's citizenship status was conferred on them primarily by derivative rights and was not an issue unless they married a foreign national. Between the eighteenth and twentieth centuries, many states formally codified in their laws the status of women who married foreigners (Studer 2002). The United States, for example, passed a law in 1907 clarifying that a woman married to a foreign national assumed the citizenship nationality of her husband. Switzerland did the same in 1941 (Bredbenner 1998). In some countries, a woman marrying a foreign national could retain her native citizenship if she was denied citizenship by her husband's country (Hill 1924). But tying the wife's citizenship to her husband's was obviously not without its complications. For example, the fact that some US-born women who had married German nationals lost possession of their property during World War I strengthened the case for "independent citizenship" and the reversal of the 1907 law in 1922 (Hill 1924). The Convention on the Nationality of Married Women, approved by the UN General Assembly in 1957 and entering into force in 1958, strengthened the provision contained in Article 15 of the Universal Declaration that "everyone has a right to nationality" and "no one shall be arbitrarily denied of his nationality." Its purpose was to resolve conflicts of law brought about by differing laws regarding the effects of women's citizenship through either marriage or divorce and to clarify and secure women's independent rights to citizenship.

The Convention on the Political Rights of Women was ratified in 1953 and entered into force in 1954, so around the same time as the convention previously discussed, and set the international standard for women's rights to political participation, voting, and serving in elected office. In 1869, Wyoming was the first subnational government in a democracy to give women the right to vote; the first country was New Zealand in 1893. Switzerland gave women national suffrage in 1971 and

Liechtenstein in 1986. The Swiss canton of Appenzell Innerrhoden gave women the right to vote in local elections in 1989. Women still cannot vote in Saudi Arabia. In 1995, the first cabinet with an equal number of men and women was formed in Sweden. In 2014 only 13 of 197 states had women heads of state, with five female representative heads of state—primarily governors general. Thirty-six countries have had a woman head of state at some time, but only six have had more than one. The number of women serving in parliamentary offices has steadily increased with the greatest percentage in Nordic countries, as a region, and the smallest percentage in Arab states.

One of the most basic rights for any human being is the right to choose one's marriage partner and to do so at an age of legal competence to consent, eighteen in most countries. The right of marriage by consent is covered in both the ICCPR (Article 23, paragraph 3) and the ICESCR (Article 10, paragraph 1). Both covenants address marriage in relation to the family. The ICCPR guarantees citizens in signatory states the "right to found a family," asserting that the family is "the natural and fundamental group unit of society and is entitled to protection by society and the State" (Article 23, paragraph 1). The ICCPR further calls on parties to the covenant to "take appropriate steps to ensure the rights and responsibilities of spouses" upon entering into, during, and on dissolution of a marriage and, in the case of dissolution, declares that "provisions shall be made for the necessary protection of any children." The ICESCR affirms the fundamental nature of the family as a societal group unit and specifies expectations about the economic and social protection of mothers in paragraph 2 (and then elaborates prohibitions against child labor). The covenant states, "Special protection should be accorded to mothers during a reasonable period before and after childbirth. During such period working mothers should be accorded paid leave or leave with adequate social security benefits."

Most cultures have historically engaged in some form of arranged marriage, although the practice has virtually disappeared in Western societies. "Liberal" or consent marriages are becoming the norm in China, though recent studies indicate "business-deal" arranged marriages still occur. As a consequence, women's high suicide rate in China may correlate with, among other factors, arranged marriage (Allen 2006). Arranged marriages still occur in South Asia and some African and Islamic cultures. Arranged marriages have an impact on not only social and political but also economic rights. As a social norm, this practice often occurs in conjunction with the denial of other economic rights that taken together render women economically dependent on men, a situation that can compromise their physical security.

Arranged marriage is distinguished from forced marriage because in the former case, one or both of the prospective spouses may sometimes refuse the proposed partner, which is not true in forced marriages. Forced marriages also often involve "early" marriage, or marriage before the age of legal majority, particularly for girls. Researchers find obtaining accurate estimates of the problem of forced early marriage difficult both because these marriages are often undocumented and because individuals in these marriages live in very closed societies (The Advocates for Human Rights 2007). The International Center for Research on Women estimated that in 2003 more than 51 million girls under the age of eighteen were married (Rude-Antoine 2005). Forced marriage and "bride-kidnapping" are reportedly becoming more prevalent in Eastern Europe and Central Asia since the dissolution of the Soviet Union (Kleinbach, Ablezova, and Aitieva 2005; The Advocates for Human Rights 2007).

The Convention on Consent to Marriage, Minimum Age for Marriage and Registration of Marriages entered into force in 1964 after eight states acceded to the treaty. As of 2014, there were fifty-five signatories. In a case heralded by some as a precedent for future potential cases in the ICC, the Special Court for Sierra Leone charged and convicted three men who were leaders of the Revolutionary United Front with the crime of forced marriage. Arguing that forced marriage is a crime against humanity, the chief prosecutor said, "Our position is that sexual slavery is a horrendous crime. Victims would be held for days or weeks and forced into sex acts. Forced marriage is all of that plus essentially being consorts to the rebels" (Humanitarian News and Analysis 2010). Although the Sierra Leone case dealt with forced marriages in the context of war and war crimes, the prosecution's argument that forced marriage amounts to sexual slavery may break new ground in legal efforts to end the practice in other contexts. In many of the member states of the Council of Europe, specific acts associated with forced marriage, such as marital rape, can be prosecuted under either criminal or civil law, and Norway has actually defined and outlawed forced marriage (Rude-Antoine 2005). In Western countries, the problem is often perceived as one associated with immigrants and naturalized citizens coming from other countries. In point of fact, however, no religion condones forced marriage, and in no culture is it practiced exclusively, though it is embedded within some cultural traditions.

## Bride Burning, Dowry Burning, and Honor Killing

Dowries are payments in cash or goods or some combination to a new husband by the bride or, more often, the bride's family. In contrast, the husband, or his family, pays a "bride price" to the bride (or her family). Both have historically been practiced throughout the world, and today the focus is on South Asia, in particular India and Pakistan, though these countries are not the only ones where the practice persists. Though these payments were historically intended to provide a degree of initial security to the new-lyweds, the human rights concern today is that the failure to meet the price (primarily dowries) often leads to retributive violence against the bride. Even worse, impoverished families who do not expect to be able to save an adequate dowry for their daughters' marriages sometimes murder infant girls to avoid the cost of a dowry. Sometimes a husband or family will increase the dowry request after an initial agreement has been made or after the marriage has taken place, leading to violent exchanges between families (Ash 2003).

Whether incidences of bride burning are increasing or simply increasingly reported is difficult to tell. "Bride-burning is the practice of dousing a new bride with kerosene and setting her ablaze to die," said Avnita Lakhani (2005), who surveyed the reasons scholars offer for its possible increase in India, including the patriarchal structure of traditional Indian society, growing greed in conjunction with the spread of consumerist culture, as a defense against the spread of Islamic culture in India, and as a remnant of British colonialism and subjugation. Considered the most common form of "dowry death," bride burning occurs primarily in Pakistan, India, Bangladesh, Nepal, Bhutan, and Sri Lanka, with the most reports of bride burning coming from the first two. As a social practice, bride burning was done as retribution for an inadequate dowry or when a promised dowry was not fully paid by the wife's family. The Indian government reported over 8,000 dowry-related deaths in 2012 (Williams 2013). According to *Time* magazine, bride burning increased dramatically between the 1980s and 1990s, from around 400 to 5,800 a year (Pratap 1995). CNN gave a lower figure of 2,500 reported incidents of bride burning per year in India (CNN Interactive 1996). Lakhani (2005) referred to dowry deaths as "gendercide" because they involve mass killing. She provided a similar figure to that given by CNN but noted that the Indian government estimated that as many as 6,500 women a year are murdered in dowry deaths. Andrea Krugman (1998) calculated that from Indian independence in 1947 to 1990 "approximately 72,000 young brides between the ages of 15–20 years old were burned to death" (224). The Indian government enacted the Dowry Prohibition Act in 1961, and dowry murders subsequently became a criminal offense in 1986, though the act is criticized for having a number of technical flaws and being weakly enforced (Lakhani 2005). The Indian Penal Code also prohibits acts of "cruelty" by a woman's husband or relative of her husband, and demanding a dowry is included as such an act (Jobanputra 2008). Pakistan has not outlawed dowries.

## Female Infanticide

Female infanticide, the intentional killing of baby girls for the purpose of gender selection, occurs in societies where girls are regarded primarily as an economic liability and boys as an economic asset. A 1994 article by John-Thor Dahlburg reported this chilling account of probable female infanticide in rural India:

> In the nearly 300 poor hamlets of the Usilampatti area of Tamil Nadu [state], as many as 196 girls died under suspicious circumstances [in 1993]. . . . Some were fed dry, unhulled rice that punctured their windpipes, or were made to swallow poisonous powdered fertilizer. Others were smothered with a wet towel, strangled, or allowed to starve to death. (Dahlburg 1994)

India is also the heartland of sex-selective abortion. According to Malavika Karlekar (1995), after amniocentesis was introduced in India in 1974, initially for early detection of birth defects, it was quickly appropriated by medical entrepreneurs. A spate of sex-selective abortions followed. Says Karlekar, "Those women who undergo sex determination tests and abort on knowing that the fetus is female are actively taking a decision against equality and the right to life for girls. In many cases, of course, the women are not independent agents but merely victims of a dominant family ideology based on preference for male children" (55).

According to Gendercide Watch (2013), India and China are the primary focus of concerns about female infanticide today. It is often viewed as a particular "subset" of infanticide practiced for genetic selection. Being female often leads to a rejection of the child in much the same way that infants who are physically or mentally handicapped are often killed. Expected dowry and wedding expenses, which can add up to around 1 million rupees or US$35,000, associated with having daughters is widely perceived as the most common motive for female infanticide in India. In one study of a community in India, 250 families admitted to having committed female infanticide.

The history of infanticide in China has been shaped by tradition, government population policies, criticism from human rights advocates and Western governments, and improvements in women's economic status and opportunities. Infanticide, neglect, and abandonment of female infants predates the Communist Party takeover in 1949. Under modernization policies, the practice declined in the 1950s, 1960s, and 1970s until the "one-child" policy aimed at stunting population growth was initiated in 1979. Although there were exceptions for ethnic minorities and rural areas (allowing a second child if the first was a girl), the policy in effect led to a sharp increase in the number of "missing" girls in the 1980s and 1990s. The WHO estimated in 1997 that "more than 50 million women were estimated to be 'missing' in China because of the institutionalized killing and neglect of girls" resulting from the one child policy (quoted in Farah 1997).

In the face of widespread international criticism, it is difficult to determine the exact scale of the practice today, although recorded male births outnumber recorded female births 116:100 (Kristof and WuDunn 2009). Many female births are unrecorded, sex-selective abortion is believed to be widely practiced, and infant girls put up for adoption are at risk of ending up in orphanages where they die from neglect. Nicholas Kristof and Sheryl WuDunn, whose work on exposing the global scale and effect of gender inequalities was first inspired by their discovery of the extent of infanticide in the 1980s, offer this hopeful assessment, after recounting the current problems of discrimination, sex-selective abortion, and workplace harassment:

> All that said, no country has made as much progress in improving the status of women as China has. Over the past one hundred years it has become—at least in the cities—one of the best places to grow up female. Urban Chinese men typically involve themselves more in household tasks like cooking and child care than most American men do. Indeed, Chinese women often dominate household decision-making, leading to the expression "qi guan yan" or "the wife rules strictly." And while job discrimination is real, it has less to do with sexism than with employers being wary of China's generous maternity benefits (208).

## Female Genital Mutilation

Female genital mutilation (FGM), sometimes called female circumcision or female genital cutting, involves a range of practices with varying degrees of severity and risk to the health of the infant, girl, or young woman. The term *circumcision* misleadingly equates FGM with the practice of male circumcision. Both involve "cutting" the genitals or genital area, though the degree, severity, and sexual and health consequences for women are generally much more debilitating. In practice, the two have little in common beyond the legal issues raised regarding surgical or cutting procedures that alter the genitalia of children who are not of a legal age of consent. Male circumcision involves the removal of some or all of the foreskin of the penis, and the majority of male circumcisions are performed on infants. Debates are currently taking place about the preventive health benefits of male circumcision and its effects on sexual performance. FGM involves more radical procedures, and most FGM is associated with serious threats to health, with the majority of the procedures performed on girls over the age of ten.

Some critics of FGM also call for an end to male circumcision and condemn all genital cutting of children as offenses against their physical integrity. However, by most accounts, the vast majority of FGM cases involve procedures that fall into one of the first three categories, all going well beyond anything comparable to male circumcision, hence the most common reference to "mutilation" in the cases involving girls. It can be performed on infants as young as a few weeks old, but it is also often considered a rite of passage into womanhood and performed on girls as old as fifteen. The WHO estimated that about 100 million to 140 million girls worldwide, including 92 million on whom the procedure was performed at the age of ten or later, currently live with the consequences of FGM, which include recurrent bladder and urinary tract infections; cysts; infertility; the need for later surgeries (e.g., the FGM procedure that seals or narrows a vaginal opening is surgically changed to allow for sexual intercourse and childbirth and sometimes stitched closed again afterwards); and an increased risk of childbirth complications and newborn deaths (WHO 2014a).

Campaigns to end FGM press governments to outlaw the practice, but some critics argue that laws alone are inadequate both because they are often unenforced or difficult to enforce and because the practice is so deeply embedded within a system of cultural beliefs and local social orders. Nevertheless, under pressure from both the WHO and international human

## The World Health Organization's Four Categories of Female Genital Mutilation

*Clitoridectomy:* partial or total removal of the clitoris (a small, sensitive, and erectile part of the female genitals) and, rarely, the prepuce (the fold of skin surrounding the clitoris) as well.

*Excision:* partial or total removal of the clitoris and the labia minora, with or without excision of the labia majora (the labia are "the lips" that surround the vagina).

*Infibulation:* narrowing of the vaginal opening through the creation of a covering seal. The seal is formed by cutting and repositioning the inner, and sometimes outer, labia, with or without removal of the clitoris.

*Other:* all other harmful procedures to the female genitalia for nonmedical purposes (e.g., pricking, piercing, incising, scraping, and cauterizing the genital area).

*Source:* WHO 2014a.

rights NGOs, a number of states have banned FGM. Sudan outlawed FGM, particularly infibulation, while that area was still under British rule, but the practice resumed following decolonization. Postcolonial efforts to ban the practice by law can become politicized by debates over cultural imperialism both because the pressure often originates from outside a postcolonial society and because during the colonial period Christian missionaries frequently banned genital cutting and mutilation among their adherents and converts. For these reasons, some opponents within countries where FGM is still practiced argue for encouraging communities at the local level to voluntarily abandon and renounce FGM. This strategy has been, to varying degrees, successful in Senegal, Burkina Faso, The Gambia, and Sudan (Tostan 2010). The UN Population Fund has declared February 6 as International Day Against Female Genital Mutilation and regards FGM as a violation of the basic rights of women and girls as defined in the Convention on the Rights of the Child. The African Union has called for an end to FGM with twenty-five member states ratifying the convention.

Although Western countries do not culturally or socially accept FGM, legal issues are still raised by the practice in these countries, because they receive immigrants from states where it is practiced. The US State Department recognizes FGM as a human rights violation (Reymond, Mohamud, and Ali 2010). In 2004 the Ninth Circuit US Court of Appeals ruled in favor of an immigrant plaintiff seeking asylum in the United States on the grounds of having a "well founded fear of future persecution" as a victim of FGM should she be returned to her home country of Somalia (*Mohamed v. Gonzalez* 400 F.3d 785 [2005]). Although this case upheld the argument that past infliction of FGM, in association with other factors, constituted a basis for fear for future persecution, the US Board of Immigration Appeals disagrees, arguing that FGM is a one-time injury and once inflicted cannot be repeated, thus creating no future threat (CRS Report for Congress 2010). Both US courts and the Bureau of Immigration accept FGM as a form of persecution.

## Rape

Though rape is not a new form of violence against women, it has received greater international attention recently both because it seems to be an increasingly prevalent and brutal tactic associated with armed conflict and, therefore, because it has been denounced as a war crime for which perpetrators can be held legally responsible in international courts. UNICEF (2008c) estimated that 20,000 women and girls were raped during the Yugoslav wars in the 1990s, and 15,700 were raped between April 1994 and April 1995 in Rwanda. As a tactic, rape is used to terrorize not only the individual victim but also whole families and communities (Stiglmayer 1994; Wilmer 2002). Raped, then released, the girls, women, and their families will flee, desperate to leave behind the physical scene of the trauma. Thus, it became a tool of ethnic cleansing in the Yugoslav wars.

Until the wars in Yugoslavia and Rwanda, the best-known rape-murder atrocity was the Nanking Massacre, also known as the Rape of Nanking, in which, in 1937, the Japanese army entered the then capital city of China, Nanking (now officially spelled *Nanjing*), and murdered 300,000 people over a six-week period (The History Place 2008). However, the women were not just killed:

> Old women over the age of 70 as well as little girls under the age of 8 were dragged off to be sexually abused. More than 20,000 females (with some estimates as high as 80,000) were gang-raped by Japanese soldiers, then stabbed to death with bayonets or shot so they could never bear witness.
>
> Pregnant women were not spared. In several instances, they were raped, then had their bellies slit open and the fetuses torn out. Sometimes, after storming into a house and encountering a whole family, the Japanese forced Chinese men to rape their own daughters, sons to rape their mothers, and brothers their sisters, while the rest of the family was made to watch. (The History Place 2008)

In a brutal ongoing civil war in the Democratic Republic of Congo, government forces as well as those fighting them are implicated in the rape of hundreds of thousands of women. According to Chris McGreal (2006), "in one province alone, South Kivu, about 42,000 women were treated in health clinics for serious sexual assaults last year, according to statistics collected by the human rights group, Global Rights." Women are raped not only by individuals and in gangs, but also with implements including hot plastic and rifles, with the rapist sometimes firing directly into the vagina (Womenspace 2008). If the women survive, these torture-rapes often destroy the vagina leading to a condition called fistula where fecal material from the colon and urine from the bladder seep into the vagina (Jones 2008). Surgery is often required, though many cannot access medical treatment, and even multiple surgeries are not always successful. Additionally, many women do not receive medical treatment within the seventy-two-hour period when antiretroviral drugs are most effective in preventing HIV infection (McGreal 2006).

Another manifestation of war-related sexual exploitation is the use of so-called comfort women, a term referring to women forced into sexual slavery or prostitution in wartime. The term is particularly associated with the Japanese exploitation of Korean women during World War II. The atrocities associated with these practices came to light in the early 1990s when survivors began to speak out. One reviewer of the book *Comfort*

*Women Speak: Testimony by Sex Slaves of the Japanese Military* described their revelations:

> During World War II, an estimated 200,000 girls and young women were forced into sexual slavery by the Japanese imperial military, which was authorized by the highest levels of Japan's wartime government. This system resulted in the largest, most methodical and most deadly mass rape of women in recorded history.
>
> Japan's Kem pei tai political police and their collaborators tricked or abducted females as young as eleven years old and imprisoned them in military rape camps known as "comfort stations," situated throughout Asia. These "comfort women" were forced to service as many as fifty Japanese soldiers a day. They were often beaten, starved, and made to endure abortions or injections with sterilizing drugs. Only a few of the women survived, and those that did suffered permanent physical and emotional damage. (Schellstede 2000:54)

A more recent example of the exploitation of women for military purposes involved the kidnapping of some 300 girls and women by the Nigerian Islamic terrorist group Boko Haram in April 2014. The girls and women are widely believed to have been kidnapped not only for sexual exploitation but to acquire ransom to fund the group (Johnston 2014). About sixty of those abducted escaped in July 2014. The kidnapping sparked an international "Bring Back Our Girls" campaign supported by many prominent Western political leaders and celebrities. As of November 2014, efforts to obtain their release have been unsuccessful, with Boko Haram leaders claiming 200 of the girls had converted to Islam and been "married off" as the extremists continue to expand their control over territory, including the town where the girls were originally abducted (Smith 2014).

Rape and sexual assault are not just associated with the violence of war, nor are they exclusively perpetrated against women either in war or elsewhere. One out of three women worldwide is a victim of rape or sexual assault (NSRV 2014). While women and girls are by far the largest percentage of victims, men are also raped in prison, and the sexual assault, torture, rape, and degradation of men as captives during war also constitute human rights violations. Two NGOs, Human Rights Watch and Amnesty International, have developed programs on prison reform to end rape and other prison abuses (Human Rights Watch 2010).

## Human Trafficking

Trafficking is another human rights violation that affects mostly, but not exclusively, women and girls. The US Department of State (2014) said that most of the estimated 20 million people internationally trafficked each year are women and children. Because human trafficking is an underground and often an explicitly illegal activity, obtaining accurate figures for the number of victims is difficult. The head of the UN Office on Drugs and Crime estimated that at any given time, as many as 2.4 million people are victims of trafficking, with 80 percent of them exploited as sexual slaves (*USA Today* 2012). According to the UN Population Fund, illegal trafficking, with links to organized crime, generates between $7 billion and $12 billion a year (Alcalá 2006).

Many trafficking victims are "stateless persons" who do not possess proof of citizenship in any state and thus are not protected by any state or international law. Lacking identification, they are vulnerable to kidnapping or extortion and can neither escape from their circumstances nor return to their country of residence. Migrant workers and street children are also more at risk for being exploited by traffickers. Migrant workers are often encouraged or find it necessary to their survival to move across international boundaries on the promise of paid jobs but often must become indebted to do so. The international agreements that allow their migration often provide little or no protection once they leave their home countries. For example, one Nigerian woman was brought to Europe severely beaten, and then forced to work to repay $50,000 worth of debt (US Department of State 2008). Some governments that enter into these agreements impose severe fines on workers who fail to desert overseas jobs (US Department of State 2008). In the 2008 *Trafficking in Persons Report*, the US State Department describes the "myth of the runaway worker" this way:

> "Migrant workers will be imprisoned up to two years and face a $3,205 fine if they are found to have deliberately deserted their contracted jobs when overseas," declares the law of a government of a country that is a major source of migrant laborers. Some governments of destination countries pursue workers who have "run away" with tenacity and harsh penalties. Several are known to offer bounties for each runaway worker found by citizens who deputize themselves as immigration officers. (US Department of State 2008:25)

Individuals can be lured into sex trafficking by promises of a legitimate job, educational opportunity, or a marriage proposal, only to end up kidnapped or in bondage for sexual exploitation. Many are children. Some children are sold into the trade by their parents. As fear of HIV/AIDS infection has grown, so has the demand for children in the sex trade, especially when they are perceived or presented to be virgins (Kershaw 2006).

Human Rights Watch Executive Director of the Women's Rights Division, in testimony before the US Congress in 2000, described a pattern they have documented of the trafficking of women in Asia and eastern and southeastern Europe:

The most common form of coercion Human Rights Watch has documented is debt bondage. Women are told that they must work without wages until they have repaid the purchase price advanced by their employers, an amount far exceeding the cost of their travel expenses. Even for those women who knew they would be in debt, this amount is invariably higher than they expected and is routinely augmented with arbitrary fines and dishonest account keeping. Employers also maintain their power to "resell" indebted women into renewed levels of debt. In some cases, women find that their debts only increase and can never be fully repaid. Other women are eventually released from debt, but only after months or years of coercive and abusive labor. To prevent escape, employers take full advantage of the women's vulnerable position as migrants: they do not speak the local language, are unfamiliar with their surroundings, and fear of arrest and mistreatment by local law enforcement authorities. (Ralph 2000)

The United Nations documented 127 countries of origin for trafficking victims and 137 "countries of destination" (UN Development Fund for Women 2010). Thirty-eight states have laws allowing for the prosecution of their citizens for crimes related to child sex tourism committed in other countries (US Department of State 2007). Ninety-three countries have outlawed trafficking (UN Development Fund for Women 2010). Additionally, a coalition of international tourism NGOs wrote the Code of Conduct for the Protection of Children from Sexual Exploitation in Travel and Tourism in 1999, signed by more than 600 companies from twenty-eight countries (US Department of State 2007). Trafficking is a transnational crime with the main countries of origin in central and southeastern Europe, Asia, and West Africa and the main countries of destination in Western Europe, North America, and Asia (UN Development Fund for Women 2010). A new and disturbing trend in international human trafficking that affects men along with women and children is body-part trafficking; however, women and children are still disproportionately affected because of their higher levels of vulnerability (Ebbe 2006).

## Domestic Violence

Finally, when considering violent offenses against women's human rights, one must include the problem of domestic violence. Though most often directed at women, domestic violence injures the entire family, including children. Although between 14 percent and 16 percent of US victims of domestic violence are men (Futures Without Violence 2009), in the United States alone, between 1,200 and 1,400 women a year—an average of three per day—are killed because of domestic violence (FBI 2005). UN Women, an organization created by the UN in 2010, estimated that in 2013 35 percent of women globally had experienced nonpartner sexual violence or intimate partner violence and that half of all women killed worldwide in 2012 were killed by intimate partners (UN Women 2014). According to the US Centers for Disease Control and Prevention, more than 12 million women and men are victims of intimate partner violence (CDC 2014). Amnesty International regards domestic violence as torture and took up the cause of domestic violence as a human rights issue in the 1990s. Domestic violence is the main cause of death and disability to European women between the ages of sixteen and forty-four (Amnesty International 2008). In 1993, the United Nations passed the Declaration on the Elimination of Violence Against Women declaring that "states should exercise due diligence to prevent, investigate, and in accordance with national legislation, punish acts of violence against women, whether those acts are perpetrated by the State or private persons."

The WHO Multi-Country Study on Women's Health and Domestic Violence Against Women estimated that "ever-partnered [married by statutory or common law] women who had ever experienced physical or sexual violence, or both, by an intimate partner in their lifetime, ranged from 15% to 71% with most sites falling between 29% and 62%" (WHO 2007).

In a breakthrough, if not precedent-setting, case, a US woman appealed to the Inter-American Commission on Human Rights for an investigation and judgment into circumstances leading to the deaths of her three daughters stemming from the failure of the State of Colorado to enforce a restraining

## Treaties and Conventions on Women's Rights

1934: Inter-American Convention on the Nationality of Women (signed by 20 parties)

1949: Inter-American Convention on the Granting of Civil Rights to Women (signed by 21 parties)

1949: Inter-American Convention on the Granting of Political Rights to Women (signed by 24 parties)

1954: UN Convention on Political Rights of Women (signed by 121 parties)

1958: UN Convention on Nationality of Married Women (signed by 70 parties)

1964: UN Convention on Consent to Marriage, Minimum Age for Marriage and Registration of Marriages (signed by 54 parties)

1981: UN Convention on the Elimination of All Forms of Discrimination Against Women (signed by 186 parties)

1995: Inter-American Convention on the Prevention, Punishment, and Eradication of Violence Against Women (signed by 32 parties)

order against her estranged husband. The girls' mother, a victim of domestic violence, took out a restraining order against their father, who subsequently kidnapped his daughters and then died in a shoot-out with local police. The three girls were found dead at the scene (ACLU 2005). The question put to the commission was, what is the state's ultimate responsibility for failing to enforce the restraining order and thus failing to protect the woman and her daughters? In 2011, the commission found that the United States "failed to act with due diligence" to protect the mother and her daughters from domestic violence and therefore failed to provide equal protection of the law (IACHR 2011).

Since the 1990s, scholars and activists have argued that domestic violence has been overlooked as an issue of international human rights because, although all of the activities that constitute domestic violence fall clearly into the category of rights internationally protected, those rights are compromised by the gender bias of domestic law and society (Thomas and Beasley 1993). From a legal perspective, another impediment is the narrowing of the international "doctrine of state responsibility" that allows for prosecution of human rights violations committed by public officials only. Expanding the doctrine to include the acts of private individuals would change the discourse and legal standing surrounding the issue of domestic violence.

## Protecting and Promoting Women's Human Rights

Eight international conventions specifically address women's human rights. In addition to these conventions, three protocols to conventions and one to the African Charter have been written relating to women's rights. Under the Optional Protocol to the UN Convention on Elimination of All Forms of Discrimination Against Women, states may recognize the authority of the committee to oversee implementation of this protocol and convention. So far 104 states have signed the optional protocol. A protocol to the African Charter specifically addresses women's rights in Africa. Among other things, it commits signatories to prohibit "all forms of harmful practices which negatively affect the human rights of women and which are contrary to recognized international standards" and elaborates methods of doing so. Finally, two protocols were added to the UN Convention Against Transnational Organized Crime to address the trafficking and smuggling of migrants.

Many contemporary international conventions began as UN General Assembly declarations, and the Assembly has also issued two declarations pertaining to women's rights not yet codified by international conventions: the Declaration on the Protection of Women and Children in Emergency and Armed Conflict (1974) and the Declaration on the Elimination of Violence Against Women (1993).

The Fourth World Conference on Women was convened in Beijing, China, by the UN Commission on the Status of Women. The three previous conferences were held in 1975 in Mexico City, Mexico, in 1980 in Copenhagen, Denmark, and in 1985 in Nairobi, Kenya. The Beijing conference produced a platform that identified twelve "areas of critical concern" to be reviewed annually. The commission also regularly adopts "action-oriented" recommendations resulting from the annual reviews. At the tenth annual review, the commission reaffirmed the declaration at the Beijing conference and the platform for action. The fifteenth review in 2010 emphasized "good practices, with a view to overcoming remaining obstacles and new challenges, including those related to the Millennium Development Goals" (Division for the Advancement of Women 2010). Action-oriented recom-

---

### The Beijing Conference's Platform for Areas of Critical Concern

1. The persistent and increasing burden of poverty on women.
2. Inequalities and inadequacies in and unequal access to education and training.
3. Inequalities and inadequacies in and unequal access to health care and related services.
4. Violence against women.
5. The effects of armed or other kinds of conflict on women, including those living under foreign occupation.
6. Inequality in economic structures and policies, in all forms of productive activities and in access to resources.
7. Inequality between men and women in the sharing of power and decision-making at all levels.
8. Insufficient mechanisms at all levels to promote the advancement of women.
9. Lack of respect for and inadequate promotion and protection of the human rights of women.
10. Stereotyping of women and inequality in women's access to and participation in all communication systems, especially in the media.
11. Gender inequalities in the management of natural resources and in the safeguarding of the environment.
12. Persistent discrimination against and violation of the rights of the girl child.

mendations have taken the form of conclusions agreed upon following most annual sessions. They have included financing gender equity (2008); equal sharing of responsibilities between men and women, including caregiving (2009); increasing access and participation of women and girls in education, training, and science and technology (2011); and a focus on elimination and prevention of all forms of violence against women and girls (2013).

In 2005, the World Bank issued a report evaluating progress and summarizing initiatives by the World Bank to improve women's conditions since the conference in Beijing. While noting a number of programs aimed at making economic and educational opportunities more available as well as noting some improvement in women's access to political influence and participation, the authors of the report concluded that women's participation in elected political office was still low and that equality had not been realized in any region in the world. The report also contained an acknowledgment that closing the educational gender gap would accelerate economic growth (World Bank 2005b).

---

### The World's Women: Trends and Statistics

There are 57 million more men than women globally, but more women than men concentrated in older age groups.

Fertility declined worldwide to 2.5 births per woman, but women who bear more than five children are still common in countries where women marry early.

Early marriage and high fertility still severely diminish women's chances for advancement in life.

Women live longer than men in all regions, and the proportion of women receiving prenatal care has increased and child mortality has decreased except in Africa.

Seventy-two million children are not in school, 54 percent of them girls.

Women and girls are more likely than men and boys to perform unpaid work within their own households.

In the private sector, women are on most boards of directors in large companies, but their number remains low compared to men.

The largest corporations remain male dominated, and of the 500 largest corporations worldwide, only thirteen have women chief executive officers (CEOs).

*Source:* UN Department of Economic and Social Affairs 2010.

Women's social, economic, and political conditions certainly improved worldwide in the twentieth century. A total of 186 states are party to the Convention on the Elimination of All Forms of Discrimination Against Women and submit annual country reports as required by the convention. The UN Department of Economic and Social Affairs, in the report *The World's Women 2010: Trends and Statistics* of October 2010, found that most countries can and do track women's progress using sex-disaggregated statistics on such variables as population, enrollment in education, and employment. The authors of the report noted progress in the literacy of adult women worldwide and an increase in women entering traditionally male-dominated occupations, while noting "they are still rarely employed in jobs with status" (UN Department of Economic and Social Affairs 2010).

## Conclusion

Feminism is frequently regarded as coming in three historical waves. The first aimed to end women's invisibility. The second aimed to end women's inequality. The third aims to end the exclusion of women's epistemology— ways of knowing. The movement to articulate and protect women's rights reflects all three waves of feminism. Women's lack of visibility and marginalization in public life are still evident in their low level of representation in political and economic institutions and organizations. Being visible is more difficult when you cannot speak for yourself.

Any progress toward ending invisibility can be attributed to the organization and activism of tens of thousands of women and women's groups over the past sixty years, and in no small part to Eleanor Roosevelt's efforts in calling the world's representatives to action at the inaugural meeting of the UN General Assembly in London in 1946. The delegates' response—with just over fifty states represented at the time—was to create the Sub-Commission on the Status of Women under the Commission on Human Rights. The first chair of the subcommission wasted no time pressing for full status as a commission, which was granted immediately, so that it became the UN Commission on the Status of Women. This entity has enabled women and women's organizations from all over the world to focus their efforts and to appeal to an international audience through the United Nations. The commission established strong relationships with NGOs and international treaty bodies early on, concentrating first on ending legal discrimination and inequality following its first meeting in 1947 and working through the early 1960s. Commission members were influential participants in the drafting of the Universal Declaration. During this period the commission also worked to include in the Universal Declaration issues of marriage discrimination (requiring consent, not giving up one's nationality, and establishing a minimum age) and improved political rights for women like voting and holding office and programs to promote women's literacy, including access to education. The commission also worked to get an ILO convention on equal pay drafted in 1951 (WomenWatch 2013).

Between 1963 and 1975, the commission's attention turned to increasing women's participation in drafting the Convention on the Elimination of All Forms of Discrimination Against Women, adopted in 1979. On the twenty-fifth anniversary of the commission's creation, the commission promoted the designation of 1975 as International Women's Year, with the First World Conference on Women being held that year in Mexico City. By then the United Nations had over 150 member states, and 133 of them sent representatives to attend this First World Conference on Women, while NGOs held a parallel conference attended by 6,000 NGO representatives (WomenWatch 2013).

The United Nations declared the next ten years the Decade for Women, Equality, Peace, and Development, and the Second World Conference on Women, attended by representatives of 145 states, was held in Copenhagen, Denmark, in 1980. This time the commission focused on women's health, employment, and education and planned another world conference for 1985 to review progress. The 1985 conference took place in Nairobi, Kenya, where almost 2,000 delegations from 157 states, 17 intergovernmental organizations, and 163 NGOs met to identify obstacles to women's progress and formulate specific strategies to overcome them. Over 12,000 official delegates attended the conference, including many African and especially Kenyan women (WomenWatch 2013).

As the commission's attention shifted to some of the thornier issues including genital cutting and domestic violence, the shield of privatization weakened and the commission began work on the Declaration for the Elimination of Violence Against Women, adopted by the General Assembly in 1993. Gender equality found its way onto the agenda of global and regional development conferences and programs everywhere, setting the stage for the Fourth World Conference on Women in Beijing, where 6,000 delegates from 189 countries, 4,000 NGOs, and another 4,000 journalists met in 1995 and heard these words from keynote speaker Hillary Clinton:

> The great challenge of this conference is to give voice to women everywhere whose experiences go unnoticed, whose words go unheard. Women comprise more than half the world's population, 70% of the world's poor, and two-thirds of those who are not taught to read and write. We are the primary caretakers for most of the world's children and elderly. Yet much of the work we do is not valued—not by economists, not by historians, not by popular culture, not by government leaders. (WomenWatch 2013)

The second wave of feminism—equality—has been the driving force behind worldwide activism, and no one can have any doubt that the United Nations played a critical role in opening a space for mobilized women to speak and act. But the third wave is also evident in efforts to end the shield of privacy that made action on issues like domestic violence, bride burning, forced marriage, and genital cutting so difficult to put on the international agenda. Still, this last wave is where the greatest work needs to be done, that is, in redefining the epistemology of human rights, to put "women's ways of knowing" on equal footing with men's ability to shape the normative foundations of politics and law, as the debate over abortion suggests. Fiona Robinson (2006) argued for a feminist reconceptualization of rights that will change the way human rights discourse functions for diverse groups and individuals by challenging the claim of moral universality so long as it remains tied to an epistemology of difference and the normativity of masculine experience. Instead, a feminist conceptualization of rights begins by recognizing relationships "as a fundamental ontological feature of human social life" (163). Similarly, Gayle Binion (1995) imagined how human rights would be interpreted in light of women's experiences to form "[the] foundation for theorizing and enforcement" (509). Invoking "cultural difference" is, in this view, simply a way of sustaining the public-private boundary that shields violence and injustice against women from scrutiny and enforcement.

Perhaps Atlanta businesswoman Lya Sorano captured best the irony of slow progress for women's economic equality when she said, "When we talk about equal pay for equal work, women in the workplace are beginning to catch up. If we keep going at this current rate, we will achieve full equality in about 475 years. I don't know about you, but I can't wait that long" (quoted in Paludi 2010:163).

# 13

# Economic, Social, and Cultural Rights

We are challenged to rid our nation and the world of poverty. Like a monstrous octopus, poverty spreads its nagging, prehensile tentacles into hamlets and villages all over our world. Two-thirds of the people of the world go to bed hungry tonight. They are ill housed; they are ill nourished; they are shabbily clad. I've seen it in Latin America; I've seen it in Africa; I've seen this poverty in Asia. —Martin Luther King Jr., 1968

What sets worlds in motion is the interplay of differences, their attractions, and repulsions. Life is plurality; death is uniformity. By suppressing differences and peculiarities, by eliminating different civilizations and cultures, progress weakens life and favors death. The ideal of a single civilization for everyone, implicit in the cult of progress and technique, impoverishes and mutilates us. Every view of the world that becomes extinct, every culture that disappears, diminishes a possibility of life. —Octavio Paz, 1984

Affirming further that all doctrines, policies and practices based on or advocating superiority of peoples or individuals on the basis of national origin or racial, religious, ethnic or cultural differences are racist, scientifically false, legally invalid, morally condemnable and socially unjust.
—UN Declaration on the Rights of Indigenous Peoples

ALTHOUGH ONE WAY TO THINK ABOUT HUMAN RIGHTS IS TO SAY that they inhere in us because we are human, a more concrete conception of human rights is linked to basic needs: human rights protect those things that human beings need in order to live a fully human life. The ICESCR affirms these rights, recognizing "the right of everyone to an adequate standard of living for himself and his family, including adequate food, clothing and housing, and to the continuous improvement of living conditions." The Universal Declaration also includes the right to "medical care and necessary social services, and the right to security in the event of unemployment, sickness, disability, widowhood, old age, or other lack of livelihood in circumstances beyond his control" (Article 25, paragraph 1).

## The Basic Rights and Beyond

Human beings need security in the form of safety but also clean water that does not make them ill or kill them, adequate nutrition to lead a healthy life free of undernourishment, shelter from the elements, and basic health care within the resource limits of their society. Lack of access to clean water and inadequate nutrition kill human beings just as surely as torture and extrajudicial execution. UNICEF reported that poor nutrition causes nearly half of child deaths under the age of five (World Food Programme 2014). Every year 3.4 million people die from a waterborne disease (Water.org 2014). Gender is also a factor; since the elderly and children depend more on women, gender inequalities exacerbate the problem. "If women farmers had the same access to resources as men," according to the UN's World Food Programme, "the number of hungry in the world could be reduced by up to 150 million" (World Food Programme 2014).

Controversies arise over what constitutes a basic need and whether inequalities should be addressed by public policy, and if so, how. For example, how much health care is basic, and what kind of shelter is adequate to reasonably protect people from the elements and the worst effects of natural disasters? Should health care be a private good available only to those who have adequate income to purchase it? Should better quality health care be available to the wealthy? Should a basic need like water be privatized? Who should pay the costs of meeting these needs? People who live in rich, industrialized countries are generally better protected against injury, death, and property loss from natural disasters than people in Haiti or the Philippines, but the poor are more vulnerable everywhere. Three-quarters of a billion people—more than a tenth of the entire world population and one third of them in sub-Saharan Africa—lack access to clean water, but who should pay the costs of making clean water accessible to everyone? Do human beings have a basic right to leave a place where their needs cannot be met and move to a place where they can? Does any condition that threatens a human being's ability to survive, such as lacking access to clean water and adequate nutrition, constitute a security need that is just as essential as freedom from arbitrary arrest, detention, torture, and extrajudicial execution?

Economic rights can be considered aspirational rather than litigable because governments aspire to promote and protect them within the limits of their country's economic and social conditions. Monitoring provisions often focus on evidence of progress toward fulfillment of these rights. In contrast, civil liberties and civil rights are more legally actionable: if an individual is denied due process or experiences discrimination, then he or she can make a legal claim against the responsible party. However in the case of some economic rights, like the right to economic development or clean water, governments are expected to make an effort toward the fulfillment of those rights, as indicated in Article 11 of the ICESCR referring to "the continuous improvement of living conditions."

General agreement can be found that economic and social rights include a right to development and access to clean water and adequate nutrition. The UN General Assembly recognized the right to development in the preamble to the Declaration on the Right to Development: "Recognizing that development is a comprehensive economic, social, cultural and political process, which aims at the constant improvement of the well-being of the entire population and of all individuals on the basis of their active, free and meaningful participation in development and in the fair distribution of benefits resulting therefrom."

The declaration invokes the spirit of both the UN Charter and the Universal Declaration through containing provisions linking rights and freedoms to the necessity of a social and international order that enables all individuals the fulfillment of all basic needs, underscoring the claim that civil liberties, civil rights, political rights, and the fulfillment of basic material needs are interdependent. Although the right to development remains a subject of controversy—specifically in debates about what kind of responsibilities or obligations are or can be created by such a right—the Vienna Declaration, adopted with widespread, nearly unanimous support, also affirms this right. A related or corollary claim can be made to a right of education. Although not addressed separately, it is woven throughout the discussion of economic and development issues. If human beings possess a right to their fullest development, then that right includes the right to an education adequate to its achievement.

Less agreement can be found about including rights to a clean environment, peace, sustainability of natural resources, or intergenerational equity. Intergenerational equity is based on the belief that the present generation holds an obligation to future generations to maintain or improve the integrity of the environment and their quality of life. These rights frequently evoke normative debates because they challenge ideological claims that lead to very different conclusions about the proper role of public versus private action. For example, environmental degradation and the depletion of nonrenewable resources are often a consequence of exploitation of fossil fuels by large energy producers, and they resist regulations that threaten to reduce profits and raise consumer prices. Their resistance has been the justification for regulation or oversight of energy production and pricing, in some cases, and, in others, outright public ownership of energy utilities. If private actors (energy producers) would voluntarily incorporate sustainable practices, there would be no demand for public regulation.

Several reasons can be given for mindfulness of the role of the state in creating conditions for the fulfillment of economic rights. First, the state is the primary unit through which values and resources are authoritatively allocated. States manage economic conditions within their jurisdiction and regulate trade and economic relations with other states. Additionally, activities taking place within a state can effect resource depletion and environmental degradation beyond that state's borders. Another reason responsibility for economic rights falls to the state is that the state mediates the movement of people, capital, and resources across state boundaries. The greater mobility of labor and capital has become a driving force behind both international cooperation and conflict. The distribution of and access to natural resources and the benefits of their use are at the heart of a number of contemporary human rights debates. In the 1970s, for example, developing countries sponsored UN resolutions declaring sovereignty over natural resources and calling for rich states to undertake special measures, such as making development grants or low-interest loans available to developing states to help accelerate their industrialization. The justification was that because rich states had benefited from colonialism at the expense of the development of the people and resources in the territories colonized, rich states now had a special responsibility to promote that progress.

Finally, the state also regulates the distribution of and access to the resources necessary to citizens to live lives of basic dignity. It sets the ground rules for the conduct of economic activities, the exploitation of resources, and the distribution of the wealth created within its jurisdiction. For example, childbearing women are often excluded from the paid labor market when they perform reproductive and family care labor without economic compensation, making them vulnerable to exploitation by those on whom they must depend for access to the economic necessities for living a dignified life (in other words, men). The case of arranged and forced marriages in Chapter 12 illustrated this point most vividly.

## An Adequate Food Supply

The ICESCR goes beyond recognition of the right to an "adequate standard of living" and obligates signatory states to take action to end and prevent hunger. Can the current world economic system produce enough food to feed the more than 7 billion people living on the earth now? According to the Food and Agriculture Organization, an affiliated agency of the United Nations, world food production, even adjusted for population growth, averages 17 percent more calories per capita now than thirty years ago and could theoretically provide everyone living on the earth with 2,720 calories per day (World Hunger Education Services 2013). The problem is not supply but access and distribution, which are currently determined by a combination of market and public policy factors that ultimately rely on economic and political decisions.

Complex interactions among social, political, and historical factors combine to create conditions that result in hunger and malnutrition. These factors include imperialism, decolonization, and state making; changes in economic and food production systems under imperialism; demographic changes that increase population and the proportion of population that is made up of children; undemocratic governments that have no incentive to be responsive to human needs; and the absence of sufficient political will overall to end hunger. Social changes brought on by modernization, imperialism, the globalization of markets, and state control of economies have dramatically altered patterns of food production and distribution over the past several centuries. The self-sufficiency of precolonial, small-scale, and culturally cohesive communities with subsistence-oriented economies was radically altered by the globalization of economic production.

Small-scale, precolonial societies are often characterized as subsistence economies, but such a label does not mean that they did not produce a surplus beyond immediate subsistence needs (Chase-Dunn and Hall 1997). Many small-scale societies before they came in contact with capitalism or European explorers/conquerors also produced surpluses to trade, to reserve for leaner years, or to sustain them through drought conditions (Scott 1984). Their economies differed from capitalist economies, however, because the primary organizing principle of their economic practices emphasized sustainable production.

The logic of capitalism, in contrast, aims at maximizing production of surplus for the purpose of accumulating wealth that is then invested in increasing the capacity for producing more surplus and raising the standard of material life. Agricultural goods and commodities derived from natural resource extraction produce less surplus or profit in contrast with manufactured goods. The labor required to produce them generates more surplus wealth than the production of agricultural goods and commodities, and economies with a larger manufacturing sector therefore tend to be relatively richer. The development of transportation technology makes moving agricultural and manufactured goods into global markets possible. Instead of local economies engaged in community-level diversified production, labor and resources are appropriated under capitalism for mass, monocultural production of crops, the resultant product being sold in a global market. Colonization restructured agricultural land use and ownership, leaving many once self-sufficient and diverse local economies dependent on the large-scale production of a few cash crops. Demands for land reform in the aftermath of decolonization are rooted in these historical conditions.

The prevalence of poverty and inadequate food supply in large sectors of many developing countries today stems not only from grossly inequitable land distribution but also from the displacement of diverse local agricultural production by large-scale "plantation-style" production of cash crops exacerbating economic stratification and dualism (extremes of wealth and poverty) in postcolonial states. The decline of local rural economies increases the number of people migrating to urban areas seeking employment and, in turn, increases pressure on the infrastructure to provide food, water, and sanitation and accommodate rapid urbanization. These problems are compounded by demographic changes such as increasing life expectancy and decreasing infant mortality. On their own, these demographic changes are positive trends, but they can also further intensify population pressures created by increasingly crowded and polluted urban areas. If a high percent of a country's population is under the age of fifteen, the problem is exacerbated because children are net consumers of food rather than producers. Germany, Canada, the United Kingdom, China, and the United States, for example, all have less than 20 percent of their total populations under the age of fifteen. In contrast, in Yemen, Tanzania, Ethiopia, and Burundi that age group accounts for between 40 and 45 percent, while India's population under the age of fifteen accounts for 28.5 percent (CIA 2014).

Finally, many poor and less economically developed countries are not only experiencing the negative economic effects of postcolonialism but are also often controlled by undemocratic governments, making them more vulnerable to protracted civil wars and civil unrest and further aggravating and creating conditions that lead to deprivation of basic needs and physical safety. Armed conflict not only kills people directly but also disrupts agricultural production and transportation of food to markets, contributing to food shortages and killing even more people indirectly.

Freedom House (2014) reported that in 2013, 41 percent of countries in sub-Saharan Africa were living under political conditions that were "not free" (in contrast to 35 percent in 2003) and another 39 percent under conditions that were only "partly free." The International Food and Policy Research Institute (2014) developed the Global Hunger Index of 120 countries and found that the ten worst affected were also in sub-Saharan Africa, and "all ten of them were affected either directly or indirectly by war or its repercussions."

## The Case of Tanzania: The Complex Relationship Among Development, Colonialism, and Economic Deprivation

The Human Development Index, created by the UN Development Programme, measures quality of life using factors including wealth, education, and health care. Tanzania ranks 159 out of 177 countries reported on the index—nineteenth from the bottom—with a per capita income of $744, the fourth lowest.

As of 2002, Tanzania was considered a "modest net agricultural importer," bringing in about 11 percent of the cereal consumed by Tanzanians—an important dietary staple, especially for children (Policy Coherence for Development 2008). So why can't Tanzania feed its own population? One reason is because only 4 percent of the total land area of the country is arable, and that land is used to produce cash crops. Export earnings then purchase food needed beyond the food yielded by domestic production. Tanzania's primary agricultural exports are coffee, sisal (a plant from the agave family, the fibers of which are used to make rope), tea, cotton, pyrethrum (a plant in the chrysanthemum family used to make insecticide), cashews, tobacco, and cloves. All are either nonfood crops or luxury crops (cashews and cloves) for export.

Not only do a host of indicators place Tanzania in the "poorest of the poor" category, but the country also has one of the highest HIV/AIDS infection rates in the world (12th), one of the highest infant mortality rates (100 per 1,000 live births), one of the highest cervical cancer rates (5th),[1] and is one of the most densely populated states in Africa (7th). Eighty percent of the workforce is employed in the agricultural sector. Average per capita income is $1,590 annually, about $3.50 per person per day. About 73 percent of Tanzania's population lives on less than $2 a day (World Bank 2014). As elsewhere in sub-Saharan Africa, a child born in Tanzania has a higher risk of HIV/AIDS infection; the adult prevalence of infection is close to 5 percent compared to 1 percent in the Caribbean. Sub-Saharan African children are also more likely to not survive past the age of one (only one in ten), and those that do are more likely to suffer malnutrition and a lifetime of poverty.

*Note:* 1. The risk of cervical cancer is doubled by poverty.

## Access to Clean Water and Sanitation

Many of the conditions contributing to hunger also deprive people of access to clean water and sanitation. UN independent expert Catarina de Albuquerque called sanitation a "taboo topic" in international efforts to promote basic human rights (quoted in UN News Center 2010). Waterborne illness takes up an average of 12 percent of the national health budgets of countries in sub-Saharan Africa, with overall economic costs in that region, including lost work and school days due to sanitation-disease illnesses, at about US$1 billion a year (UN News Center 2010). A report by the World Commission on Water for the 21st Century indicated that in 2000, 1.8 million children died from waterborne diseases—5,000 a day, one every fifteen seconds (BBC News 2000). Although more than twice as many die from those causes today, UN water expert Brian Appleton poignantly talked about the tragedy in these terms in 2000: "That's equivalent to 12 full jumbo jets crashing every day. If 12 full jumbo jets were crashing every day, the world would want to do something about it—they would want to find out why it was happening" (quoted in BBC News 2000).

Waterborne diseases like diarrhea, cholera, malaria, and typhoid kill 700,000 children a year in Africa alone (One Campaign 2008). Since women and girls usually do water collection, female students are 12 percent more likely to attend school if water is available within fifteen minutes of their homes (One Campaign 2008). Millions of people spend hours a day and expend most of their caloric intake hauling water. In one study, researchers calculated that every $1 invested in water would create a return of $10–$12, and that the total cost of reaching that goal would be about $20–$25 per capita (WHO 2009a).

The world's socioeconomic system today is characterized by extremes of access to and deprivations of basic needs. In the case of water, while three-quarters of a billion people lack access to clean water at all, 12 percent of the world's population uses 85 percent of available clean water (Barlow 2001). According to Andrew Posner, "the United States uses, on average, about 345 billion gallons of fresh water per day . . . [and] 136 billion gallons are for irrigation, another 136 billion for cooling electric power plants, 47 billion for public and domestic supply, and roughly 20 billion are for industrial uses" (2008). These conditions contrast sharply with those in developing countries, particularly in Africa. The average US citizen uses 100–176 gallons of water per day while an entire African family uses an average of 5 gallons a day (Water.org 2012). According to the United Nations, in addition to the over 780 million people who lack access to safe drinking water, 2.5 billion people do not have access to basic sanitation (United Nations 2013a).

The World Bank estimated that demand for water is doubling every twenty-one years and reported health-threatening water shortages in eighty countries (Arizona Water Center 2010). To make things worse, the International Business Times reported estimates that by 2100, 2.2 billion people globally will lack adequate water due to the effects of climate change (Osborne 2014).

Increased demand for water is driven not only by a growing population but also by a growing demand for industrial and agricultural use and economic development. Whereas world population has increased fourfold since 1900, water use has increased tenfold (Savewater! 2010). The population of the United States has only doubled since 1900, but the country's residents consume six times more water now (Arizona Water Center 2010). Agriculture accounts for 70 percent of the world's freshwater use with wide regional variations, from 88 percent in Africa to less than 50 percent in Europe. Only 1 percent of all the water on the planet is available for human use (Postel, Daily, and Ehrlich 1996; Gleick 2000).

The countries that consume the most water are the United States, Australia, Italy, Japan, and Mexico. The average annual per capita water footprint (including all direct and indirect uses, that is, water used to produce all things an individual consumes in addition to the water directly consumed) in these countries is 328,500 gallons, but the United States has an annual per capita water footprint of 656,000 gallons with an average daily household use of 151 gallons. In contrast, Yemen's yearly per capita footprint is 163,500 gallons, and Somalia's is 177,500 (Water Footprint 2012). Some highly industrialized countries, like many in Europe, appear to have lower consumption, but much of their demand is externalized through imports, that is, because they import much of the water they consume, it is counted in the consumption of the country of origin rather than country of consumption (Pahlow and Mekonnen 2012).

Meat consumption as a proportion of diet also increases with income, further contributing to increased water use since nearly 2,000 gallons of water are required to produce one pound of beef (Streeter 2009). Both because many developing countries are encouraged to increase agricultural production for export as a path to development, and because many people still lack food security, agricultural production and irrigation will continue to increase. The United Nations reported that "water withdrawals for irrigation have increased over 60 percent since 1960" (Water for Life 2010). A potential water crisis that both affects and results from agricultural irrigation is not limited to developing countries. Recent satellite data monitoring California river basins revealed an alarming drop in underground water, showing "the amount of water lost in the two main Central Valley river basins within the past six years could almost fill the nation's largest reservoir, Lake Mead in Nevada" (G. Burke 2010). The United States as a whole goes through about 345 billion gallons of freshwater daily (G. Burke 2010). Reporting that more than 75 percent of the loss is from agricultural irrigation, the scientist who led the monitoring project said, "All that water has been sucked from these river basins. . . . The data is telling us that this rate of pumping is not sustainable" (quoted in G. Burke 2010).

From the great irrigation and urban sanitation systems of the Aztec and Roman empires to waterborne epidemics during the European Middle Ages after the fall of the Roman empire (Garrison 1999), the management of water in densely populated cities has long been considered one of the most important functions of governments. Governments can collect the funds and make the infrastructure investment necessary to treat and distribute clean water. Government management of water supply reflects the perception that clean water is a public good, what Paul Samuelson (1954) identified as a "collective consumption good" (see also Gleick et al. 2002). In theory, a public good is nonexcludable and noncompetitive, meaning that once it is produced, no one can be excluded from consuming it, and no one's consumption diminishes anyone else's. The individual consuming clean water and using a sanitation system benefits by being healthier, and the society as a whole also benefits from a lower risk of transmitting disease and more healthy people who can be economically productive.

Increased private sector involvement in varying degrees of partnership to produce a clean water supply has generated significant controversy. Although 90 percent of world waterworks are still publicly owned, increasing privatization raises the question of whether water is a public good, best treated as a basic human right, or a commodity, best allocated by market forces (Salina 2008). The International Conference on Water and Environment held in 1992 in Dublin, for example, declared that "water has an economic value in all its competing uses and should be recognized as an economic good" (Gleick et al. 2002:6). Former Nestlé CEO Peter Brabeck-Letmathe denied that access to clean water is a human right (Samson 2013). The trend is in the direction of privatization. For example, whereas well into the 1990s public water monopolies were the norm in South America, "by the end of the millennium Argentina, Chile, and Colombia were among the 93 countries with some form of privatized water or sanitation services" (Gleick et al. 2002:24).

Pressure to privatize often comes as a condition attached to development loans from the World Bank, the International Monetary Fund, and the Inter-American Development Bank, but privatization can have more negative than positive effects. In Bolivia, for example, taking control of the water supply out of public hands led to a 200 percent increase in the price of water, costing many poor families as much as 20 percent of their income for access to clean water. These developments sparked the successful Cochabamba Water Revolt in April of 2007, when thousands of Bolivians filled the streets demanding the return of waterworks to public control (Shultz 2008).

While the trend toward greater involvement of the private sector in water management has gained momentum in the past decade in developed and developing countries, water will not necessarily be completely commodified (Gleick et al. 2002:6). Private sector involvement takes several forms: outsourcing or contracting for various services along with operations and maintenance of supply and sanitation systems; involvement in design, building, and operation partnerships of public and private sectors and agreements on water and sanitation operations; and sale of assets transferring ownership of public water utilities to private companies. The main concerns with privatization are that higher costs will lead to more expensive water, limited services, the exclusion of people unable to afford water and sanitation services, and secondary or spillover effects on the environment if private providers are inadequately regulated.

Water privatization is not limited to countries with a strong capitalist ideological orientation. China and Cuba have also involved private companies in water supply and treatment operations (Gleick et al. 2002:22). The main motivations center on efficiency arguments—that the private sector is more efficient at operations, mobilizing the necessary investment capital, and at bringing investment and capital into poor countries. Theoretically, the result should be that more, not fewer, people will have access to safe and clean water. Private sector involvement may indeed improve supply and delivery in countries where governmental institutions are weak and underfunded. However, the concern with excluding poor people is real. Documentary filmmaker Irena Salina (2008) revealed in her film *Flow: For Love of Water* that 30,000 people in La Paz, Bolivia, did not get water because they could not afford the connection cost of $450—two years' salary for poor families.

Water is also privatized by corporations that buy water rights and then package and market bottled water, claiming it is of better quality than municipal tap water. The Environmental Working Group, a nonprofit organization dedicated to public advocacy, studied the content of bottled water sold in the United States, however, and found that about a quarter of the bottled water is actually just tap water (Dwyer 2009). US consumption increased from 415 million gallons of bottled water in 1978 and to 8.2 billion gallons in 2006 (Pacific Institute 2008). Although the United States is the biggest consumer of bottled water, Mexico, in second place, is not far behind at 5.5 billion gallons. China comes in third at 4.5 billion (World Water.org 2010).

As a final issue, one must consider the social impact associated with efforts to meet growing, dire needs for clean water and sanitation, particularly in that big water projects often require the displacement and relocation of large numbers of people. India's "big dam" projects are a particular case in point. The government of India has been engaged for decades in building hundreds of large dams in order to increase the supply of water to burgeoning cities where half or more of the population lives in "shanty towns" or slums (Menon 2001; Roy 2002). The World Commission on Dams, jointly funded by private and public sector entities, studied the impact of big dams in sixty-eight countries and found that in India two-thirds of the people displaced by these projects were from socially and economically disadvantaged communities (Menon 2001). Additionally, the dams have deforested over 22 million acres of land. Most of the displaced people end up living in city slums in much worse conditions than before their displacement (Wide Angle 2003). The government of India argues that the dams will bring water to 40 million people living in those impoverished urban areas as well as provide much-needed irrigation to Indian farmers. Critics not only challenge the officially estimated number of people who will benefit but argue that the government did not even adequately consider other more sustainable local options with less devastating impacts on the villages flooded by dam projects (Roy 1999; Khagram 2004; Connell 2013).

## The Right to Refuge

People become refugees mostly because they flee from conflicts that threaten their lives. They also leave because of natural disasters like the Indian Ocean tsunami that displaced nearly a million people in 2004, the earthquake in Pakistan that displaced an estimated 3 million people in 2005, or the more recently tragic earthquake that hit Haiti in 2010. The Office of the UN High Commissioner for Refugees (UNHCR) estimated that as of June 2013 the total number of *persons of concern,* a term that includes refugees and internally displaced persons, was 38.7 million and expected to top 40 million by the end of the year. The largest numbers came from Colombia (4.7 million), Syria (4.6 million), the Democratic Republic of Congo (3.3 million), Pakistan (2.6 million), Sudan (2.1 million), and Afghanistan (1.5 million) (UNHCR 2013).

Refugees are primarily a contemporary problem, emerging after World War I with the redrawing of European boundaries and rising significantly as millions fled countries destroyed by Nazi occupation and collaborationist governments. The main refugee populations after World War I were Armenians escaping genocide in Turkey, non-Russian minorities in Russia who were displaced by invading German and Austrian forces, and about a quarter of a million Belgians who immigrated to Great Britain after Germany invaded in October 1914 (Gatrell 2001). World War II created the first international refugee crisis beginning with Hitler's mass expulsion of Jews from annexed Austria in 1938 (Wyman 1985). The UNHCR was established in 1950 in order to deal with the millions of refugees in the aftermath of the war, particularly in Europe. The 1951 Convention Relating to the Status of Refugees defines a refugee as "any person who, owing to a well-founded fear of being persecuted for reason of race, religion, nationality, membership in a social group, or political opinion, is outside the country of their nationality, and is unable to or, owing to such fear, is unwilling to avail him/herself of the protection of that country." Under the 1951 convention, only individuals within Europe who were fleeing from events that occurred before January 1951 could obtain refugee status.

War criminals and other human rights violators do not enjoy protection as refugees. With the horrors of the Holocaust fresh in the memory of its drafters and signatories, the 1951 convention does not apply to any person who has committed a crime against the peace, war crime, or crime against humanity; committed a serious nonpolitical crime outside the country of refuge; or acted in any way contrary to the UN Charter.

These exclusions received little attention until the Rwandan genocide in 1994 when 2 million Hutus, many complicit in the genocide and fearful of Tutsi revenge, fled to neighboring states and the Tutsi Rwandan Patriotic Front took control of the Rwandan government. The refugee camps in what was then known as Zaire (now the Democratic Republic of Congo) notoriously became recruiting grounds for a new generation of Hutu militia and contributed to escalating the current conflict and atrocities in the Democratic Republic of Congo (Solomon 1997). Because the vast majority of Hutus fleeing Rwanda had directly participated in the genocide, their entitlement to protection under the 1951 convention was uncertain.

Concerns following the attacks of September 11, 2001, led some states to take action within the framework of domestic law and policy to prevent terrorists from obtaining refugee status. Though the 1951 convention does not exclude terrorists because the term can be subject to selective application for political purposes, under existing provisions pertaining to the commission of crimes against humanity or acts contrary to the purposes and principles of the United Nations, one could make a legal argument for their exclusion.

A protocol was added in 1967 expanding the geographic scope to all refugees anywhere in the world and eliminating the temporal restriction. A total of 147 states are parties to the convention or the protocol or both. To legally qualify under the UN convention and protocol, refugees must both have the well-founded fear of persecution and have crossed international borders. The UNHCR and the convention do not protect economic migrants. Although not legally covered by the convention, internally displaced persons are often helped by the UNHCR. In a growing number of civil wars people are forced to leave their homes either because they are afraid of the consequences of remaining or because the homes are uninhabitable, but the refugees do not leave the country. About half of the total population the UNHCR designated as "of concern" in 2013 were internally displaced (UNHCR 2013).

The first international border crossed by a refugee is the country of first asylum. Several factors bear on whether the individual will actually be any safer or more secure in the country they flee to first than in the country of origin. First, civil wars can have a transnational dimension: rebel forces may pursue their victims into a neighboring country or even have bases there. For example, women fleeing the Taliban in Afghanistan were often equally at risk in Pakistan (Newland 2002). Second, neighboring countries may be embroiled in conflicts or civil strife themselves, making them only marginally or temporarily safer. Third, the resources of neighboring countries may already be so overstressed that they cannot offer the most basic accommodations for refugees. Even if international agencies set up temporary housing in camps and provide a minimal food supply, the problem of access to clean water and sanitation still exits, a problem the country of first asylum may not even be able to solve for its own citizens. Between 80 percent and 90 percent of refugees are hosted in the regions of their home countries (UNHCR 2014).

Only about 100,000 refugees out of tens of millions of "people of concern" (a category including refugees and internally displaced persons and not including Palestinians in the occupied territories) to the UN Office of the High Commissioner for Refugees are resettled every year (UNHCR 2014). Others are returned to their home countries or remain in refugee camps. Refugee camps are intended to provide temporary, emergency accommodations. The camp conditions create huge stresses on families: parents do not work, children do not go to school, and everyone's aspirations for the future are put on hold. Because the physical conditions and circumstances are so dire, most efforts focus attention on lifesaving or life-sustaining emergency services like food, water, shelter, and, if possible, the provision of minimal health care. Refugee camps are also the perfect environments for airborne, waterborne, and epidemic diseases. Under these circumstances, the deprivation of aspirations and hope for the future is easy to overlook, but the longer people remain in a camp, the more this kind of deprivation can lead to serious psychological problems. Of those resettled in a third country—a country other than their original country of origin or the country of first asylum—about half come to the United States with Australia and Canada accounting for another 21 percent together. The rest go to countries like Sweden, Norway, Denmark, Finland, New Zealand, the Netherlands, and the United Kingdom. All of these countries have policies that limit the number of individuals they will accept for resettlement (Bruno 2014; Patrick 2004; UNHCR 2012).

## The Right to Migrate

Migrants are people who move across international borders to live and work in another country temporarily or permanently. They are often viewed as having left their home countries by choice, though as UNESCO (2005a) noted, "these choices are sometimes extremely constrained." Although there is no internationally recognized legal definition of a migrant, the International Organization for Migration claims that it is "usually understood to cover all cases where the decision to migrate is taken freely by the individual concerned for reasons of 'personal convenience' and without intervention of an external compelling factor" (International Organization for Migration 2014). Migrants' rights conflict with the right of states to regulate immigration. The definition above points to the central concern that migrants are vulnerable to arbitrary treatment and lack the ability to assert any rights because they are outside the territory of their home state, and the legal protection of migrants has been viewed as a matter of domestic jurisdiction within states. The convention, entering into force in 2003, elaborates the rights of migrant workers and covers migrant workers and their families. It provides basic freedoms, due process, privacy, equality with nationals, the right to transfer their earnings, right to information about their rights, and several provisions specifically pertaining to employment conditions and freedom of movement.

The number of migrant workers worldwide reached 232 million in 2013, growing by about 1.2 percent annually. Roughly equal numbers of migrants move South-South and South-North, and half are women (UN Department of Economic and Social Affairs, Population Division 2014). In developing countries, migration is often symptomatic of a "brain drain"— the emigration of a country's most educated people. Brain drain is often a response to a generally repressive human rights climate, because intellectuals are more frequently targeted by repressive regimes or because better educated migrants have little prospect for employment in their home countries. According to the United Nations (2005), 33 percent to 55 percent of highly educated people from Angola, Burundi, Ghana, Kenya, Mauritius, Mozambique, Sierra Leone, Uganda, and Tanzania and about 60 percent of highly educated people from Guyana, Haiti, Jamaica, and Trinidad and Tobago in 2005 were living in OECD countries.

The question of how to maximize the benefits and reduce the negative effects of migration was highlighted when the General Assembly hosted "high-level dialogues" on migration in 2006, 2008, and 2013. A total of 127 states participated in planning interactive roundtables, and 162 state representatives, along with sixteen UN agencies, two UN regional commissions, and twelve NGOs, participated, as they worked to identify key issues related to migration and development. Member states adopted a declaration calling for respect for human rights and international labor standards, reaffirming their commitment to fight human trafficking and condemning racism and intolerance.

The ILO has engaged the issue of migrant workers since its founding in 1919 and has promoted international efforts both by supporting the Migrant Workers Convention of 1975 and by continuing to address migrant workers' rights within the organization's own framework. ILO director-general Guy Ryder called for greater international strategic cooperation on migration issues, saying that misinformation leads to the incorrect perception in host countries that more migrant workers are in their countries than there really are, and that they receive more public services and social protection than they contribute, noting that the reverse is actually true (ILO 2014). In his view, the real problem is the lack of adequate job creation and development in home countries. The ILO maintains databases on migration statistics, antidiscrimination profiles, and good practices in labor migration.

## Health Care

Health care and a clean environment, as discussed in the next section, are two examples of collective rights that belong to people as a whole and not because they are individuals or members of a particular group. These rights place an expectation on governmental institutions to take action in order for a right to be realized. Like other economic and resource issues, claims of rights to health care and a clean environment can be understood both in national and international contexts. If health care is viewed as a public good, that is, a good from which no one ought to be excluded and one more efficiently delivered by governments than by markets, then the ability to deliver it will depend on the resources available to a particular government and the other public goods it is expected to provide. A government might reasonably prioritize clean water and sanitation services over providing medical care, or it might be able to provide adequate clean water and sanitation and minimal health care, for example, prioritizing prenatal care over geriatric care. Most rich industrialized democracies provide some health care through government programs and some access to private market-delivered services.

Health care is often measured as spending relative to the average per capita income in a particular state, but access to health care and a clean environment are also embedded within transnational and international contexts. For example, when international markets priced antiretroviral drugs to treat AIDS at $10,000–$15,000 a year, they were out of reach to most people with AIDS in more than 150 developing countries where that cost exceeds total per capita income. A decline to about $100 per person per year has increased access with over 50 percent of people needing treatment receiving it (UNAIDS 2012).

The Human Development Index was widely adopted in the 1990s to measure the overall quality of life instead of relying exclusively on per capita income for such a measurement because the latter does not take into account distribution of income and access to and delivery of services. The Human Development Index formula includes life expectancy, education, adult literacy, and per capita gross domestic product to produce a composite number. Predictably, rich industrialized countries score high and developing countries rank at the bottom. Of the thirty lowest-ranking countries, twenty-seven are in Africa (Human Development Report 2013). Life expectancy in the thirty-two countries that rank the lowest on the index is between forty-four and fifty-six while in the top thirty-two countries, life expectancy is between seventy-seven and eighty-two. In fact, people in the top seventy countries have a life expectancy of seventy years or more. People in the poorest countries live about two-thirds as long as those in rich countries.

Life expectancy by region ranges from a low in Africa of forty-nine years to a high of seventy-six in the Americas, the western Pacific, and Europe (WHO 2013b). Child mortality—the number of children per 1,000 who die before the age of five—also reflects large disparities between rich and poor countries with only 12 deaths per 1,000 in high-income countries and 40 deaths per 1,000 in low-income countries (WHO 2013b).

Not only do people who lack access to basic health care have much shorter life expectancies, but mothers also have more children with low birth weights and more children who die before their first birthday. Lack of access to health care is costly to the whole society, now and in the future, since people in poor health cannot contribute their full energy and talents to the economic, cultural, and social well-being of their families and communities. Nobel Prize–winning economist Amartya Sen (1990) sparked a debate among policymakers and scholars when he calculated the number of women who had likely died because of unequal access to health care, calling them "missing women." Sen estimated that discriminatory health-care practices accounted for the deaths of 100 million women in China, southern Asia, and northern Africa.

Two indicators often used to evaluate access to quality health care are the number of physicians per 100,000 people and health-care spending, although both of these indicators must be used with some caution. The first figure does not include nonphysician providers like nurse practitioners, physician assistants, and midwives. Furthermore, health-care spending alone does not indicate how efficiently money is used to buy health care, nor does it indicate how spending and services are distributed within a society. The United States, for example, has the highest per capita health-care spending of any country in the OECD, which consists almost entirely of rich industrialized countries (Reinhardt, Hussey, and Anderson 2004), but ranks a disappointing thirty-seventh in the world for overall quality (measured by spending per capita and percent of the population covered) (WHO 2000). Cuba, ranked just behind the United States, is the country that spends the least per capita on health care, but Cubans have a life expectancy also very close to their US counterparts (Access to Health Care 2008).

Wide disparities in both physician-to-patient ratio and health-care spending can be found worldwide. Cuba tops the list of countries with the most physicians per capita at 591 per 100,000 people, Sweden has 328, and

Norway has 313. At the bottom are Tanzania, Malawi, and Niger with 2 physicians per 100,000 people (Human Development Report 2013). Once again, sub-Saharan African countries are concentrated at the bottom. The top 5 percent of world population spends 4,500 times as much as the bottom 20 percent. The WHO's 2008 report showed that average per capita spending on health care from public and private sector expenditures combined averaged $2,672 in rich countries and $16 in poor countries (WHO 2009b). The study also reported that worldwide 47 million pregnant women gave birth without the assistance of any skilled caregivers (including midwives) in 2006 (WHO 2009b). Eight hundred women die every day from pregnancy and childbirth complications (WHO 2014b). A tremendous disparity can be identified in maternity mortality rate, often measured in the number of maternal deaths per 100,000 live births. In developed countries, the rate is 9, compared with 450 in developing countries overall and 900 in sub-Saharan Africa (WHO 2009b).

Large gaps can also be found within countries. The WHO (2009b) defined the coverage gap as "an aggregate index of the difference between observed and 'ideal' or universal coverage in four intervention areas: family planning, maternal and neonatal care, immunization, and treatment of sick children." The organization further reported,

> There are large within-country differences in the coverage gap between the poorest and wealthiest population quintiles. In India and the Philippines, the wealthiest groups are three times more likely to receive care than the poorest. In terms of absolute difference, Nigeria has the largest inequity in coverage: the difference between maximum and actual coverage is 45 percentage points larger for the poorest than for the best-off population quintile. Some countries, including the formerly socialist republics Azerbaijan and Turkmenistan, have remarkably small differences by wealth quintile. . . . Inequalities between population groups are particularly high for maternal and neonatal care, which includes antenatal care and the presence of a skilled attendant at delivery. For these interventions, the coverage gap for the poorest and best-off quintiles differs by 33.9 percent. The difference is smallest for the treatment of sick children and family planning.

The incidence of HIV/AIDS is also dramatically higher in developing countries where access to health care and treatment are much lower, and access to drugs often unaffordable. The Joint United Nations Programme on HIV/AIDS (UNAIDS) reported in 2013 that improved access to treatment has led to a decrease in the number of AIDS deaths from 2.3 million in 2005 to 1.6 million in 2012 (UNAIDS 2013). As of 2008, Africa had 11.6 million AIDS orphans (AVERT 2008). In 2005, Africa had 203 deaths per 100,000 people from HIV/AIDS compared with 9 in Europe, 9 in the Mediterranean region, and 4 in the western Pacific region. The Americas had 13 deaths from HIV/AIDS per 100,000 people (WHO 2009b). The

United Nations estimated that 35.3 million people were living with HIV/AIDS in 2013 and that the number of new infections was reduced by 50 percent (UNAIDS 2013). The number of women as a percentage of those infected has leveled off at 50 percent over the past few years, but children now account for 43 percent of new infections (UNAIDS 2013).

Changes in "high risk" behavior have led to some decrease in the percentage of people infected in sub-Saharan Africa, where the disease was first found in the green monkey population before human infections were detected in Haiti in 1981. In addition to a slightly lower percentage of people infected in sub-Saharan Africa, the affordability of treatment drugs has improved the prognosis for many people in developing countries. The NGO Doctors Without Borders reported a 99 percent cost reduction since 2001 for the combination antiretroviral treatment that is most commonly used today—down to under $100 per person from $10,000 before generically produced drugs, mostly from India, entered the market (Doctors Without Borders 2008).

## A Clean Environment

Exposure to environmental pollution also contributes to health problems. Like health care, the cost of maintaining or reclaiming environmental quality is beyond the reach of most developing countries. Although many environmental problems transcend national boundaries, rich countries have more resources and can more easily afford the cost of environmental regulation, although costs are arguably passed along to consumers in many cases and can make those same goods more expensive in international markets.

Deterioration of environmental conditions and exposure to pollution have an adverse impact on health. Meeting basic needs for an adequate food supply, clean water, and sanitation would prevent deaths, prevent disease, and reduce health risks. Similarly, environmental pollution as a source of health risks is a relatively recent concern that has emerged in connection with industrial development and its negative impact on environmental quality (as well as depletion of nonrenewable resources). For example, the WHO estimated that at least 3 million children a year die from environment-related diseases, including 2 million child deaths from diseases that produce diarrhea as a symptom, 90 percent of which can be traced directly to environmental conditions.

According to the WHO, improvements in the health aspects of the environment could prevent 13 million deaths per year including 40 percent of malaria deaths, 41 percent of deaths due to respiratory infections, and 94 percent of diarrheal deaths (WHO 2008). As many as one-third of child deaths under the age of five can be traced to unsafe water and air pollution. Unhealthy environmental conditions are a factor in 85 of the 102 diseases and injuries listed in *The World Health Report* (WHO 2008). The main health-related trends associated with climate change are changes in the weather and oceans, increasing temperatures and more extreme storms with adverse impact on the elderly and on children; and the movement of ecosystems that spread waterborne and vector-borne diseases such as malaria, Lyme disease, and West Nile virus into areas where they previously did not exist. Environmental degradation contributes to the spread of waterborne diseases as well as an increase in respiratory infections, asthma, allergies, and chronic heart and lung problems.

## The UN Millennium Development Goals

In September 2000, the United Nations hosted the largest gathering of world leaders to date to review the role of that organization in the twenty-first century. Attendees included 160 state representatives and heads of state as well as thousands of experts and representatives of NGOs. At the conclusion of the Millennium Summit, as it was known, 189 members of the United Nations signed a declaration committing themselves to, among other things, eradicating extreme poverty and hunger. The following year, with additional members and over twenty international organizations signing on, the Millennium Development Goals were set with a targeted timeline of 2015 and a targeted and measurable goal of reducing the number of people living on less than $1 a day by half by that date. Eight goals address many of the issues raised in this chapter. Using a start date or baseline of 1990 to measure progress toward goals, and a target date of 2015, the goals and specific targets and indicators include

- Eradicating extreme hunger and poverty by reducing both by half.
- Achieving universal primary education.
- Promoting gender equality and empowerment of women.
- Reducing child mortality by two-thirds and maternal mortality by three-fourths.
- Halting and reversing the spread of HIV/AIDS, malaria, and other diseases.
- Ensuring environmental sustainability and reversing environmental and biodiversity decline.
- Developing a global partnership for development that includes poverty reduction (Millennium Project 2010).

The United Nations commissioned the UN Millennium Project in 2002 and appointed US economist Jeffrey Sachs as its director. Sachs served until 2006, producing a comprehensive report entitled *Investing in Development: A Practical Plan to Achieve the Millennium Development Goals* in 2005. He concluded the report with ten concrete recommendations, including specific targets for development assistance, debt reduction, capacity building, involvement of the private sector, ways to finance strategies-targeted scientific research, and low-cost and easily implemented short-term measures to promote growth and save lives (Sachs 2005b). After an initial assessment and progress report covering the period 1990–2005, yearly progress reports have been made to the United Nations.

The 2013 report pronounced six of the goals achieved or targets within reach: (1) reducing by half the number of people living in extreme poverty; (2) increasing access to clean drinking water for 2 billion people; (3) reducing the mortality rate for malaria by 25 percent and by 50 percent the death rate from tuberculosis; (4) reducing the number of people living in slums and providing access to potable water for more than 200 million who continue to live in slums; (5) lowering the debt burden and increasing exports of the least developed countries; and (6) reducing by 23.2 percent the proportion of people undernourished in developing countries. It further called for accelerated action on seven other targets and for focusing attention on reducing disparities both between rich and poor and rural and urban living conditions (United Nations 2014b).

The UN Millennium Development Goals are laudable for identifying specific targets and strategies for accelerating economic development as an antidote to poverty and economic deprivation. The 2011 report on the program indicated that, after a setback during the 2008–2009 recession, countries are back on track to poverty reduction. Child mortality has also been reduced by half with 12,000 fewer children under the age of five dying each day in 2013 than in 1990. Unfortunately, four out of every five child deaths under the age of five still occur in sub-Saharan Africa (United Nations 2014b). Much of the improvement is due to increased immunization, leading to a 78 percent drop in measles deaths globally, with nearly 14 million child deaths prevented between 2000 and 2012 due to measles vaccination alone (United Nations 2014b).

## The Question and Obligation of Social and Cultural Rights

Do humans have needs beyond those required for physical existence? For example, do human beings have a basic need to participate in and express culture or, as Abraham Maslow and other sociologists and psychologists argued, a need for self-actualization? Is expressing oneself in the first language learned a basic need and a prerequisite for self-actualization? Can self-actualization occur when cultural integrity is not protected? Indeed, is the ability to use one's first language in order to protect one's legal rights a basic need? Is forming loving and committed relationships a basic human need? Do children's needs differ from adult needs, and if so, how? These issues are some of those raised by discussions of social and cultural rights. For all of these, what is the role, or is there a role, for government in promoting or protecting these needs-based rights?

Some rights like self-determination directly implicate the creation of states and state boundaries. Some social and cultural rights, such as children's rights, disability rights, and rights to be free from discrimination and hate crimes because of sexual identity, are relatively new to the international human rights agenda but bear little relationship to state formation and boundaries. Below I examine some social and cultural rights related to the processes of state making and maintenance—self-determination, cultural integrity, and language rights. These rights are also newly emerging on the international human rights agenda and are more deeply embedded within social and cultural systems.

## Self-Determination

Self-determination is the right of a people to determine its own political destiny, assuming that for some significant period in the group's history, that group did have such control. Before the twentieth century, self-determination in Europe was bound up with movements for popular democracy, particularly those aimed at shifting the authoritative basis for governing from hereditary systems to "governments by the people." Self-determination is also associated with a number of colonial revolutions undertaken by former colonists and their descendants, mostly in the Americas. In the twentieth century, the 1917 Bolshevik revolutionaries in Russia declared the right of nations and colonies to self-determination. After World War I, the term was memorialized following Woodrow Wilson's "Fourteen Points" speech on January 8, 1918, although he did not actually use the term. The speech was aimed primarily at governments that asserted imperialistic control over nations and at peoples under imperial rule, specifically in the territories formerly occupied by the Ottoman and Habsburg empires. In "Fourteen Points," President Wilson said, "The peoples of Austria-Hungary, whose place among the nations we wish to see safeguarded and assured, should be accorded the freest opportunity to autonomous development." After Turkey secured its sovereignty, he said, "The other nationalities which are now under Turkish rule should be assured an undoubted security of life and an absolutely unmolested opportunity of autonomous development."

World War I signaled the decline of imperialism as competing empires were increasingly strained in their efforts to maintain control over national subgroups. The borders of the Ottoman and Habsburg empires created a fault line in present-day Bosnia-Herzegovina and Serbia and along the Croatian-Serbian border. Many scholars believe the "spark" that ignited World War I was the assassination of Habsburg archduke Franz Ferdinand, heir to the Austro-Hungarian throne, by a Serbian student nationalist protesting imperialistic control over the Serbian people. Wilson's call for self-determination broadly attempted to put the peoples subjected to imperialism on an equal footing with the colonial powers. He called for "a free, open-minded, and absolutely impartial adjustment of all colonial claims, based upon a strict observance of the principle that in determining all such questions of sovereignty the interests of the populations concerned must have equal weight with the equitable claims of the government whose title is to be determined." This call has yet to be answered.

The redrawing of postwar, postimperial European boundaries still left many nationalities without control of a state, and thus they became minorities within larger states. During the interwar period the League of Nations established a minorities protection system, which was developed with the goal of minorities within the new states having some ability to appeal to the League of Nations for protection of their rights as national minorities. The system did not really materialize as the winds of a second world war gathered in Germany, but when the United Nations was founded in 1945, the Charter declared "respect for the principle of equal rights and self-determination of peoples" among the four purposes for creating the new organization in Article 1.

The Trusteeship Council was created as one of the six major organs of the United Nations. Its role is outlined in Chapters XI and XII of the UN Charter. Chapter XI, the Declaration Regarding Non-Self-Governing Territories, asserts the right of self-determination for people living under colonialism "to develop self-government, to take due account of the political aspirations of the peoples, and to assist them in the progressive development of their free political institutions, according to the particular circumstances of each territory and its peoples and their varying stages of advancement." The declaration, however, fails to acknowledge the harm and violence implicit in imperialist control.

Chapter XII gives the Trusteeship Council responsibility for promoting the "progressive development" of formerly colonized peoples "towards self-government or independence as may be appropriate to the particular circumstances of each territory and its peoples and the freely expressed wishes of the peoples concerned." Between 1945 and 1960, thirty-six new states in Africa and Asia were formed by decolonization. These new states asserted the claim of self-determination within the General Assembly, leading the body to adopt Resolution 1514 in 1960, known as the Declaration on Granting of Independence to Colonial Countries and Peoples, with eighty-nine countries voting in favor, none against, and nine—all formerly colonial powers plus South Africa and the Dominican Republic—abstaining. The declaration was more direct in its criticism of Western colonization, which had persisted over the previous two centuries:

> 1. The subjection of peoples to alien subjugation, domination, and exploitation constitutes a denial of fundamental human rights, is contrary to the Charter of the United Nations and is an impediment to the promotion of world peace and co-operation.
> 2. All peoples have the right to self-determination; by virtue of that right, they freely determine their political status and freely pursue their economic, social and cultural development.

By 1990, nearly 100 countries had declared independence through decolonization and almost two-thirds of the UN membership was made up of non-Western, formerly colonized peoples and territories. Indigenous peoples living in settler states continue to be denied any of the recognition or rights associated with decolonization.

Within the UN framework, the status of self-determination as a right is limited by state sovereignty, though many subnational and indigenous peoples ground their claims to sovereignty in demands for recognition of their right to self-determination. The assertion of self-determination has thus far been confined to the circumstances of formerly colonized people living in "non-self-governing territories" over which European states previously claimed colonial control and subsequently granted independence. In a 1995 case heard by the ICJ involving the people of East Timor the court said, "The principle of self-determination of peoples has been recognized by the United Nations Charter and in the jurisprudence of the Court; it is one of the essential principles of contemporary international law." The declaration does not give "a people" the right to redraw the boundaries of their colonial territories (even though they were drawn by colonial powers) as they become independent and self-governing. It also does not give subnational groups within those boundaries the right to secede from the new states. Neither has it yet been applied to indigenous peoples living as "internal colonies" within settler states (Snipp 1986). Self-determination cannot be asserted against the sovereignty of a state as a basis for secession, a principle that was affirmed in 1970 by General Assembly Resolution 2625, the Declaration on Principles of International Law Concerning Friendly Relations and Co-operation Among States in Accordance with the Charter of the United Nations. That view was reaffirmed when 171 state representatives met and signed the Vienna Declaration and Programme of Action on human rights 1993. The Vienna Declaration, citing Resolution 2625, said that the right to self-determination shall not be construed as authorizing or encouraging any action which would dismember or impair, totally or in part, the territorial integrity or political unity of sovereign and independent States conducting themselves in compliance with the principle of equal rights and self-determination of peoples and thus possessed of a Government representing the whole people belonging to the territory without distinction of any kind.

In addition to these General Assembly resolutions, the right of self-determination appears in both the ICCPR and the ICESCR, which, unlike the resolutions, are legally binding agreements. The African Charter on Human and Peoples' Rights goes the furthest in elaborating the right of self-determination by referring specifically to the rights of "peoples" collectively and not just as individuals. It also elaborates on self-determination in the context of the colonial experience in Article 20:

> 1. All peoples shall have the right to existence. They shall have the unquestionable and inalienable right to self-determination. They shall freely determine their political status and shall pursue their economic and social development according to the policy they have freely chosen.
> 2. Colonized or oppressed peoples shall have the right to free themselves from the bonds of domination by resorting to any means recognized by the international community.
> 3. All peoples shall have the right to the assistance of the States parties to the present Charter in their liberation struggle against foreign domination, be it political, economic, or cultural.

In 1996, the Committee on the Elimination of Racial Discrimination issued a recommendation on the right to self-determination. Noting the link between ethnic or religious groups and minorities and the principle of self-determination, the committee affirmed the obligation of all states to promote and implement the right to self-determination and to distinguish aspects of self-determination that are both internal and external to the state. Within the state, self-determination includes "the rights of all peoples to pursue freely their economic, social and cultural development without outside interference." The committee's recommendation describes the external aspect as implying that "all peoples have the right to freely determine their political status and place in the international community based upon the principle of equal rights and exemplified by the liberation of peoples from colonialism and by the prohibition to subject peoples to alien subjugation, domination, and exploitation." The committee also affirmed that the exercise of self-determination could not be asserted in ways that impair state sovereignty: "None of [the] Committee's actions shall be construed as authorizing or encouraging any action which would dismember or impair, totally or in part, the territorial integrity or political unity of sovereign and independent states" (Committee on the Elimination of Racial Discrimination, General Recommendation 21).

In several recent cases, self-determination was applied to postcolonial areas that fought for independence from a larger postcolonial or Global South state rather than from a European colonial state. Eritrea became independent from Ethiopian rule in 1993, and East Timor became independent from Indonesian rule in 1999. Eritrea came under Italian colonial rule when Italy invaded Ethiopia and Eritrea in 1890. Following independence, Ethiopia gradually took over Eritrea de facto, provoking a violent independence movement that lasted thirty years. The United Nations called for and supervised a referendum, and Eritrea was internationally recognized as a sovereign state in 1993. East Timor's relationship with Indonesia during Portuguese colonial rule was historically similar, though the colonial government generally neglected East Timor. When Indonesia became independent in 1974, the Indonesian military moved quickly to invade and occupy East Timor, though its status remained officially a "non-self-governing territory" under nominal Portuguese control. In reality, the Indonesian occupation was brutal and violently resisted by East Timor guerrilla forces. The United Nations was instrumental in bringing all parties (plus the United States) into talks on peace and independence, and in 1999 a referendum was held, although continuing violence delayed independence for three more years.

Other struggles are still ongoing. Secessionist movements in Cabinda, a noncontiguous territory under Angolan rule, and Aceh, now a "special" or semiautonomous territory in Indonesia, did not lead to recognition of independent states. Both rest their aspirations for independence to some extent on ethnic distinctiveness and, in the case of Aceh, a precolonial history of independence as a sultanate in the fifteenth century. One cannot easily account for the success of some independence movements under the banner of a right to self-determination while others fail. Conflicting interpretations of how that right can be realized by a "people" living as a minority within a sovereign state suggest that the normative conflict between self-determination and sovereignty persists. Other peoples asserting self-determination against domination by a state include the Palestinians and the hundreds of groups that make up the world's more than 370 million indigenous persons.

## Language

"It is the world of words that creates the world of things," said Jacques Lacan (1953[1977]:65). Stephen May (2011) called language rights the "Cinderella of human rights." Language rights, he said, were relegated to the status of stepchild in the family of fundamental human rights, but he saw them as fundamental, and as contentious as ever. Around the time of World War I and in its aftermath, many European minorities, particularly during the Habsburg and Ottoman eras, were defined primarily by their distinct languages, including Serbs, Croats, Slovaks, Czechs, and Romanians. Language was also an important focus for rallying Kosovars (Kosovo Albanians) in Serbia when the Yugoslav state dissolved, and language was used as an instrument of domination when violent nationalism arose in the former Yugoslav republics. Language was used again as an identity marker ostensibly distinguishing Russians from Ukrainians in Ukraine in the crisis still unfolding as of 2014. Language rights are also central to the concerns and identities of indigenous peoples, particularly those living in settler states where they have been subjected to decades of policy aimed at assimilating them and destroying their languages. Finally, language rights are the single most important issue for groups like the Québécois specifically and French Canadians more broadly, particularly those who live outside of Quebec. In New Zealand, the Maoris have their own name for the country, Aotearoa. They have asserted language rights as a mechanism for mobilizing their people and altering their power relations with what they call the Pakehas (non-Maori settlers).

While language is recognized as a marker of identity that can be the basis for discriminatory practice, it is strangely absent from antidiscrimination norms as described in the ICESCR. Article 2, paragraph 2 promises rights without discrimination "as to race, colour, sex, language, religion, political or other opinion, national or social origin, property, birth or other status." Its absence is probably due to the complicated mosaic of European subnational language-based identities. If delineated by language, there are literally thousands of groups living within fewer than 200 states. It may also be a practical matter since recognition of multiple national languages under these circumstances makes it more difficult to establish formally or informally an official language or even several languages in most states.

Language rights evoke many circumstances where, without them, individuals are at risk of unequal, inequitable, or unjust treatment. One example is the designation of official languages, although, as discussed earlier, the choosing of a state language does not necessarily arise from ill will toward language minorities but rather as a necessity in the conduct of institutional processes. However, even though arising from practical needs, holding one language above the rest causes problems for speakers of other languages. When individuals face criminal charges, for instance, they need to understand the charges being made against them. Interpreters must be provided. Can states realistically provide all the interpreters that might be necessary, particularly given the movement of migrants and refugees across national boundaries and establishing permanent or temporary residence in countries where their languages are not spoken? This situation does not necessarily constitute discrimination in itself, but it clearly is when individuals are marginalized when their first or native language is deliberately targeted by policies of forced assimilation, as was the case with indigenous peoples. French Canadians, Basques, and Catalonians find themselves in yet another situation, where language is an important signifier of cultural identity, their history and origins within the state are shared with those whose language is officially recognized, and yet their languages are marginalized. People for whom an official language is not a first language also bear an extra burden in realizing the full benefits of their citizenship because they must learn a second language to read the news, participate in elections, apply for social benefits and government services, and understand how to avail themselves of legal protection.

What language must be spoken in order for a speaker and listener to communicate fundamentally defines the way power is structured between the two. A is privileged and B disadvantaged not only when A requires B to understand A's language but also when A does not have to make any effort to learn B's language. Where there is privilege, there is marginalization on the other side in a power relationship. Marginalization may be unintentional and seem innocuous; nevertheless, it puts the individual who must learn to speak a second language in a relatively disadvantaged position.

Language activism can bring a people together, for better or worse. Maori language activism, for example, shifted power in the Maori-Pakeha relationship, and today many non-Maoris pride themselves in learning Maori language and many of Auckland's city signs are now bilingual. Winning this particular battle by no means indicates that Maoris will prevail in political and legal struggles, but it does demonstrate how language can be used as an instrument of political mobilization. Similarly, the nationalists whose objective was to destroy Yugoslavia deliberately destroyed the combined Serbo-Croatian language that enabled Serb and Croatian Yugoslavs to identify and live both as Serbs/Croats and as Yugoslavs (Wilmer 2002). Language was used to politically mobilize people in the Yugoslav conflict as well, with violent consequences.

Language can also be implicated in cultural destruction when forced assimilation policies include the deliberate killing of languages. Indigenous peoples and the boarding schools in the United States, Canada, and Australia are the most obvious case, but resistance to language assimilation by the Basques and others in Europe also arises from the will of groups to survive as culturally and linguistically distinct. Languages contain meanings specific to particular worldviews, so the destruction of a language includes the destruction of a distinct worldview, as Benjamin Whorf (1941) argued. The trend in many areas today is toward language recovery or revitalization where hegemonic states used forced assimilation to destroy minority languages. James Crawford (1995), a researcher on bilingualism, described the situation:

The threat to linguistic resources is now recognized as a worldwide crisis. . . . [A]s many as half of the estimated 6,000 languages spoken on earth are "moribund"; that is, they are spoken only by adults who no longer teach them to the next generation. An additional 40 percent soon may be threatened because the number of children learning them is declining measurably. In other words, 90 percent of existing languages today are likely to become seriously embattled within the next century. (17)

Some regard the reluctance of the international community to give more serious attention to language rights as a function of the fact that such rights are inherently collective, rather than individual, and that individual rights have been afforded priority since World War II and the emergence of a serious discussion about giving human rights international legal status (May 2011). There is some truth in this claim that individual rights have been prioritized over collective rights, but it is also true that Western-led efforts to articulate and internationalize human rights have made focusing on individual rights, due process, and fundamental freedoms easier. However, as non-Western voices, including those of indigenous peoples, enter the international conversation, they have made clear that language can be as powerful a marker of identity and selfhood as other protected freedoms, like speech and religion.

## Cultural Integrity

Protection of cultural integrity is an issue for minorities within states, majorities dominated by minorities, transnational communal groups, and indigenous peoples asserting a right of self-determination. Cultural integrity rights mean that individuals identified in association with cultural groups have a right to the free expression and continued development of their culture—that individuals not only have a right to a physically secure and safe existence but to live within and securely participate in cultures. The first article of the ICESCR clearly identifies cultural expression as protected by the right of self-determination: "All peoples have the right of self-determination. By virtue of that right, they freely determine their political status and freely pursue their economic, social, and cultural development."

A right to cultural integrity is not limited to groups asserting self-determination. For example, the covenant also says, "States Parties to the present covenant recognize the right of everyone . . . to take part in cultural life." In other words, while a right of self-determination includes protection of cultural integrity, self-determination need not be asserted in order to claim a right to the protection of a group's cultural integrity.

The need to assert a right to cultural integrity arises from the fact that both states and nonstate actors such as churches and multinational corporations have interfered with or impaired the exercise of cultural rights. In addition to the kinds of discrimination discussed in Chapter 11, minorities like indigenous peoples have been or are still subjected to a range of injurious policies including forced assimilation aimed at the destruction of their culture and identity as indigenous peoples. Richard Henry Pratt, who founded the Carlisle Indian Industrial School, a boarding school for Native Americans in Carlisle, Pennsylvania, once said the purpose of his school was to "kill the Indian and save the man" (American Experience 1992). The issue of cultural rights can be stated simply: the individual has a right to exist, and to pursue the fulfillment of basic human needs according to a distinct and freely chosen path of cultural evolution (Wilmer 1993). Proselytizing and evangelical churches are sometimes recruited to assist in assimilation projects. As a result, the Anglican, Roman Catholic, and Presbyterian churches have all been involved in reconciliation efforts, and the United Church of Canada apologized for its role in the abuse of indigenous children in Canadian boarding schools (Anglican Church of Canada 1993; The United Church of Canada 1998).

Although indigenous peoples are not the only groups who have experienced interference with the exercise of cultural rights, their case is instructive. In virtually all European settler states—not only the British settler states of Canada, the United States, New Zealand, and Australia, but also many Spanish and Portuguese settler states in Central and South America—the ideological grounds for colonization rested on a conception of non-European peoples in general and indigenous peoples in particular as "backward." This characterization, in turn, rationalized policies aimed not only at indigenous peoples' physical destruction but also survivors' forced assimilation into the culture of the European settler state, including policies that deliberately attempted to destroy indigenous languages along with religious, spiritual, and even community cultural practices. In the eyes of Western imperialistic ideologies, indigenous peoples, because of their cultures, stood in the way of progress, which was true in light of the way progress was understood then (and often now), as the exploitation of resources in the natural world. Only later did Westerners realize what the indigenous peoples already knew: that this exploitation was destructive and unsustainable.

Even non-Western states frequently draw on the same prejudices about "backwardness" and "progress" to justify discriminatory and assimilationist policies aimed at minority groups that have remained somewhat isolated or remote from the process of state making and "modernization." The Chinese government, for instance, recognizes fifty-five ethnic minority groups living alongside the dominant Han Chinese. The Ainu in Japan are regarded as an indigenous minority, and indigenous groups in India are referred to as "tribal" or "scheduled tribes." In Africa, some groups that had a more sustained and proximate relationship with European colonizing powers now regard minority tribal peoples within their independent post-colonial states as "indigenous" and have the same prejudices about backwardness. The Twa or Batwa people who live mostly in Rwanda, Burundi, Uganda, and the Democratic Republic of Congo are one of these groups that are often seen as "indigenous" by other indigenous peoples. Western anthropologists called these and other African groups "pygmies" because their height is generally less than five feet, though the term has often been used pejoratively.

Indigenous peoples have mobilized on a global scale to protest, arrest, and reverse or repair the effects of policies aimed at their destruction or forcible assimilation (Wilmer 1993). About twenty indigenous NGOs have been granted consultative status at the United Nations (Wilmer 1993). Additionally, hundreds of indigenous and nonindigenous NGOs advocate internationally for indigenous rights, including cultural integrity. These efforts led to the adoption of the Declaration on the Rights of Indigenous Peoples by the General Assembly in September 2007. Several features of the document address cultural integrity and the historical injury resulting from prejudices arising out of ideologies of cultural superiority.

In addition to self-determination, land rights are a central component of indigenous claims in light of a history of forced removal from and dispossession of resources and lands occupied by indigenous peoples, as they say, "since time immemorial." The assertion of land rights implicitly links their ability to strengthen and maintain their institutions, cultures, and traditions with their ability to regain control of land and resources, acknowledging that cultural values underlie conceptions of development. As one indige-

---

### Excerpts from the
### Declaration on the Rights of Indigenous Peoples

*Affirming* further that all doctrines, policies and practices based on or advocating superiority of peoples or individuals on the basis of national origin or racial, religious, ethnic or cultural differences are racist, scientifically false, legally invalid, morally condemnable and socially unjust. . . .

*Recognizing* that respect for Indigenous knowledge, cultures and traditional practices contributes to sustainable and equitable development and proper management of the environment. . . .

*Convinced* that control by Indigenous peoples over developments affecting them and their lands, territories and resources will enable them to maintain and strengthen their institutions, cultures and traditions, and to promote their development in accordance with their aspirations and needs.

nous representative said to the World Bank, "development can have different meanings" (quoted in Wilmer 1993:37). Cultures, as anthropologists and indigenous leaders alike acknowledge, must have a material base. Cultural practices minimally require a physical space free from intervention and restrictions by outside forces; cultural practices are often linked to place, whether a church, community center, or a geographic feature regarded as sacred; cultural practices involve the production of art and narrative; and a people starved out of existence will not long have a culture to practice.

## Conclusion

At the heart of debates about economic rights is this question: If they are rights, then who has an obligation to protect and promote them? The transformation of Western economies by capitalism and industrialization means that fewer people can obtain fewer of their needs through subsistence living, and most must rely on their ability to earn income in order to fulfill their basic needs. The economies of European and settler states were not entirely structured around subsistence systems, that is, local modes of economic production and distribution where people's work and fulfillment of basic needs were closely linked. However, the extent to which individuals could satisfy basic needs through subsistence activities like localized agriculture was much greater before industrialization and much less afterward.

The shift from localized subsistence to cash to large-scale and market-based economies means greater reliance on the public policies and political institutions to manage or referee the private sector. At the same time, industrialization brings urbanization and, with it, the need for infrastructure including sanitation, water distribution, energy, and transportation. These transitions in developing countries today raise the issue of whether private or public production of certain goods and services is necessary and efficient in order to meet basic human needs. If access to clean water, shelter, adequate nutrition, and basic health care are human rights, and if the private sector alone will not adequately meet these needs at a level above putting human beings at risk of severe physical deprivation including death, then these rights place an obligation on public institutions to provide sufficient goods and services.

Henry Shue's (1980) work is a reminder that economic deprivations cause physical suffering and death just as surely as do torture and execution. Both kinds of deprivations are caused by human agency, so they are also preventable with the commitment and political will to do so. The trend toward privatization raises controversies about the efficiency of providing clean water, on one hand, and accessibility to clean water on the other. The same could be said of other basic economic needs like adequate nutrition, sanitation, and shelter. Exposure to injury or health risks from environmental sources also raises controversies about a clean environment not only as a public good but as a transnational one, and therefore one that can only be guaranteed in many cases through international agreements and regimes.

The range of social and cultural issues that have become the subject of international norms and agreements points to the emergence of a global society and the globalization of a moral community. A moral community exists when people share a sense of communal obligation for the well-being of others and a growing awareness of how each of our choices affects the living conditions of people both within and beyond the borders of our own states. One can no longer dismiss extremes of wealth and poverty as the difference between industrious character and "advanced" cultures and backwardness or lack of aspiration. Common sense would suggest that all people are industrious enough to meet their basic needs and all societies have done so. With millions lacking clean water and sanitation and 22,000 children dying every day from causes directly related to living in poverty, oversimplifications of the problem and justifications of relative privilege are morally inadequate responses.

Spending reflects choices and values—the cost of spending more on the military includes the loss of services not provided such as education and health care. All the countries in the world combined spent $1.464 trillion on their militaries in 2009 (Stockholm International Peace Research Institute 2010). At the June 2008 World Summit on the Hunger Crisis, UN secretary-general Ban Ki-moon said that the world's food supply could be doubled in the next two decades at a cost of $15 billion to $20 billion a year—less than 2 percent of annual world military spending (Reuters 2008). Algeria, Angola, Guinea, Kenya, and Mali all spend more of their gross domestic product on the military than on either education or health care. Military spending in Burundi is four times higher than spending on health care and more than twice as high as education. In Eritrea, military expenditures account for 24.4 percent of gross domestic product and are six times higher than expenditures on health care and eight times higher than those on education. In Ethiopia, spending is four and a half times higher for military than for health care, while Liberia spends twice as much on military than health care. These figures contrast sharply with most industrialized countries that spend two, three, and four times more on health care than their militaries.

Many human needs issues highlight the transnational and interdependent nature of the world economy and its effect on distribution of resources to meet basic needs. Water contamination, disease, air pollution, and hunger are all problems that show little respect for national boundaries. Paradoxically, economic development generally does not take into account the cost of depleted nonrenewable resources, air and water pollution, and other environmental or ecological consequences. Yet focusing on the "development" of impoverished and deprived areas of the world will only accelerate these negative externalities.

By some accounts, Western development was subsidized by the transfer of environmental damage to the future. Nineteenth-century Western and settler states did not have to consider whether deforesting an area for agricultural production would have a negative impact on the level of global carbon dioxide (Miller 1995). Energy consumption in North America is six times the rate of consumption in the Middle East and almost ten times that of Africa (US Energy Information Center 2008). Europe and North America together consume twice as much as Central America, South America, Eurasia, the Middle East, and Africa combined. If development is successful in these parts of the world, the rate of energy consumption there will match that of the industrialized rich countries, accelerating the depletion of nonrenewable resources and the production of carbon dioxide. The absence of accelerated technological solutions, in the meantime, will increase the price of energy for all countries. If a common enemy can unite or bring people together, perhaps common problems that both have global roots and require transnational solutions might also for practical reasons lead at least to coordinated responses.

# Part 4

## Where Do We Go from Here?

# 14

# The Future of International Human Rights

Human rights are inscribed in the hearts of people; they were there long before lawmakers drafted their first proclamation.
—Mary Robinson, former UN high commissioner
for human rights, 1997

First, fully acknowledge the particularities of different civilizations and respect the choice of the development path made by countries based on their national conditions and their people's will. Due to differences in historical and cultural tradition, level of economic development and social system, countries face different challenges and priorities in the area of human rights. It is not desirable to impose one single model for human rights promotion and protection.              —Liu Zhenmin, vice-minister in China's
Ministry of Foreign Affairs, 2009

INTERNATIONAL HUMAN RIGHTS ARE TRADITIONALLY THOUGHT TO be grounded in a belief in fundamental human dignity that transcends cultural and historical particularity, as the first quote above indicates. However, the statement from the Chinese ambassador to the United Nations contradicts this belief. Although the concept of human dignity and the idea that human beings are obligated to refrain from behavior that violates the dignity of other human beings are neither new nor unique to any particular cultural tradition; these ideas have been "globalized" in the twentieth century. Nevertheless, globalization also highlights philosophical differences in the ways that various cultural traditions conceive of human dignity, moral authority, and obligations arising out of moral authority. The resulting dialogue challenges contemporary claims that human rights are universal. However, the real issue may not be so much whether they are universal in

349

an ontological sense as whether most people accept them most of the time. Most people agree with the idea that the world would be a better place if everyone had access to clean water, adequate nutrition, shelter, and basic health care; if everyone were free to express, associate, and participate in political processes; and if everyone were protected from the arbitrary use of power. The main impediment is that current economic, social, and political structures do not secure these conditions and rights, and remedies require not only economic resources but also the political will to restructure underlying power relations and current patterns of privilege and deprivation. International relations, relations between states, have become world politics, relations among states, nonstate actors, and individuals. World politics are producing norms, agreements, normative debates, and a narrative of community. Does that community constitute a moral community of shared obligation for the well-being of others, consciousness of the consequences of our choices for the living conditions of others, and in the face of gross violations of human rights, a responsibility to protect?

Some point to misguided priorities. In an article published by the Institute for Policy Studies, Sarah Anderson and John Cavanaugh (2008), criticizing the 2008 bailout of US and European financial institutions, expressed this view: "The approximately $4.1 trillion that the United States and Europe have committed to rescue financial firms is 40 times the money they're spending to fight climate and poverty crises in the developing world." Every decision must take into account "opportunity costs," or the loss incurred by spending money on one thing instead of another—the cost of spending more on military includes the loss of services not provided because of lowered social spending.

In this book, I have examined how the development and globalization of international human rights have historically been shaped in response to the excesses, failures, and shortcomings of the state as well as by the aspirations, ideals, and promises of liberalism. Genocide, torture, and violations of civil and political rights point to state responsibility to refrain from violating physical integrity rights, and to protect individuals from such violations by private actors like the Janjaweed in Darfur. Issues of discrimination and the lack of protection for economic and social rights point to the state as an enabler of deprivations through neglect, by perpetuating or even institutionalizing inequalities, and by failing to manage economic resources and conditions in ways that secure basic human needs. Weak, failing, or failed states lack adequate institutional capacity to carry out basic state functions and are both vulnerable to conflict and undermined by it. Some states at risk of failure are weak because they are politically repressive and thus unable to mobilize and utilize the benefits of citizen support, energy, and talent. Some become more repressive as they weaken, and others collapse altogether into a state of civil strife or civil war. Africa, particularly central Africa and the Great Lakes region, has suffered from seemingly intractable state failure, particularly over the past few decades. National, regional, international, and private efforts to implement human rights offer some hope for strengthening institutional and social protection of human rights standards worldwide.

The contemporary state and interstate system in which 4,000 to 5,000 communal groups are under the jurisdiction of around only 200 states and where state sovereignty often trumps international normative claims raises some concern about the future of human rights. For example, can international human rights be better protected and more secure by reforming the state? That is, if the structure of state power is or has historically been complicit in the violation of human rights, then can it be reformed to make human rights violations and deprivations less likely and, beyond that, to encourage state promotion, protection, and enforcement of human rights? This question leads to a second one: Can the interstate system or world order be democratized, and would (or how would) the democratization of world order strengthen the promotion and protection of international human rights? Finally, the question of enforcement arises. After the Holocaust, the world promised "never again," yet new genocides and other massive human rights violations have taken place in Cambodia, Rwanda, Bosnia, and Darfur, and the world did not respond with decisive intervention. The international community did establish the first war crimes tribunals since World War II for Rwanda and the former Yugoslavia, Cambodia is prosecuting alleged perpetrators under a national war crimes tribunal, and the ICC has indicted Sudanese president Omar al-Bashir for war crimes in Darfur, including charges of genocide. But these actions are all after the fact. The lack of political will to mount an intervention that came sharply into focus in Rwanda and Bosnia now also plagues efforts to stop ongoing violations in Darfur. What are the prospects for developing an effective international enforcement regime that includes the capability of mobilizing an adequate international interventionist military force?

## Reforming the State

The issue of reforming the state has become increasingly salient in light of two relatively recent historical developments. The first was the acknowledgment by international relations theorists in the 1970s and 1980s that states exist within a broader dynamic of changing social and economic conditions. The "billiard ball model" served as a metaphor for interstate relations during the nineteenth century and well into the twentieth—states were solid and impenetrable "things" that bumped into one another, even forcefully. This view is also associated with realists who, even if they might concede that interests are transnational and interpenetrating, would still regard self-sufficiency as desirable to the greatest extent possible and the primacy of national interests over international norms as the best guide to foreign policy.

Theorists began challenging this metaphor in the 1970s, arguing international relations and world politics were instead made up of a mix of state and nonstate actors within a structure of complex interdependent relations. Today's students of international relations should be very familiar with this model. In this account, the people, interests, and ideas in one state can and do cross over state boundaries and spill into other states. With the revolution in communications technology that took place in the 1980s and 1990s, this model is even more valid than it was in the late 1960s when interdependence was first observed by political economist Raymond Vernon (1968), who is sometimes called "the oracle of globalization." From the perspective of those studying how changes in the structure of power relations in world politics affect the way states and those who control them can and do use power internally and project power externally, the issue is less one of intentionally reforming the state than changing the way the state is understood and thought about.

Robert Keohane and Joseph Nye (1977) are best known for the early development of the interdependence model and its implications for theorizing international relations, giving rise to the idea of regimes. Whether or not a single unified and integrated world order was emerging when they wrote their book in the late 1970s was debatable, but evidence of order in specific issue areas was hard to deny. States collaborated in these areas— trade, monetary policy, international finance, and, to some extent, security—in relation to norms, creating rules and making decisions with expectations of compliance with those norms (Krasner 1983). Taken together, the renewed interest in interstate cooperation repositioned liberalism as a practical and even rational response to complex interdependence.

One question for those interested in international human rights is whether interdependence, on balance, contributes more to the promotion and protection of human rights, or whether, by increasing the proximity of states constituted mainly as authoritative institutions rather than as societies, interdependence makes conflict (and thus human rights injuries) and violence more likely and more deadly. Does interdependence brighten the spotlight of world public opinion, or does interdependence create pressures on fragile state institutions that make them vulnerable to takeover by "strongmen" who are not averse to repression and inequality but who will cooperate with corporations and rich powerful states that exploit resources to increase wealth at the expense of protecting and respecting human rights? The contemporary version of this debate centers on the effects of globalization and whether, as a consequence of it, the state as a unit is being displaced by some other form of governance, such as regional international organizations or confederations (Kahler 2002).

A further question is whether or not an international human rights regime can be found, at least in the sense first outlined by Stephen Krasner (1983), that is, a set of "principles, norms, rules, and decision making procedures around which actor expectations converge in a given issue-area" (2). Some kind of human rights regime probably does exist, even if human rights norms are weakly or inconsistently enforced. Regime theory argues that in the absence of an overarching and authoritative world order, states have still developed issue- or function-specific regimes, that is, norms, decisions, and expectations that constitute predictable patterns of state behavior. The most easily recognized regime is an international free trade regime, now embodied in the World Trade Organization as well as numerous regional free trade agreements. Under regimes, in which states participate voluntarily, norms are inclined to be self-enforcing (or in the language of international law, self-executing) since actor expectations "converge" (in Krasner's language) around them. The role of norms has become a subject of both theorizing and empirical examination in the past decade or so. In the area of human rights in particular, Kathryn Sikkink and others have worked on models of norm diffusion that examine how norms are articulated and spread throughout the international system (Risse, Ropp, and Sikkink, 1999; see also Klotz 1995). Are human rights norms articulated authoritatively primarily at the international level and then diffused downward, or are they transmitted by local actors into transnational, regional, and international settings where they become authoritative and then diffused downward, creating expectations regarding the conduct or behavior of governments (Martin and Wilmer 2008)?

The end of the Cold War and efforts by postcommunist states to transition to democracies and market economies have also sparked an interest in state reform. The ideological reductionism of the Cold War led many to surmise that in its aftermath, the transition to democracy and free markets would be relatively peaceful. Instead, in spite of a peaceful transition like that in Czechoslovakia, postcommunist Yugoslavia showed horrific violence and human rights violations not seen in Europe since World War II. Most postcommunist states experienced something in between these extremes. The issue of state reform is still very much on the minds of political leaders and academics as many question whether the model of political and economic institutional development taken from the experience of Western Europe and North America can simply be grafted onto the societies of central and eastern Europe and central Asia (Oleinik 2008). The end of the Cold War similarly unleashed the possibility for reform in Latin America, where the transition from right-wing authoritarian to democratic governments has brought more than a few democratic socialist leaders to power (Lora 2006).

## Democratizing World Order

Whether contemporary human rights have a Western bias or not, respect for human rights is still intricately linked to a vision of the good society, that is, one that respects and protects international human rights. Given its roots in Western culture and experience, the concept of international human rights today is also tied to the way Western societies think about democracy as a classic liberal political order. Liberal states are, ideally, based on majority rule while protecting the rights of minorities to dissent, they ground political authority in the rule of law, and they protect individuals' fundamental freedoms against abuses of state power by respect for due process while maintaining a limited role for government in defense of individual liberty. Does advancing international human rights in national societies move the international system toward a more democratic world order? An answer in the affirmative would be a variation on the "democratic peace" thesis that proposes that the democratization of individual states will eliminate motives for militarized conflict and thus lead to a more peaceful interstate system. The democratic peace proposition anticipates peaceful world order as states across the world democratize. As a contrast, another theory holds that democratizing world order at the top will lead to the spread of international norms that will in turn encourage ipso facto the creation of democratized states. Democratic peace theory does not assert that democracies, in a world of democratic and nondemocratic states, are more peaceful, only that they do not go to war with other democracies. Research on the theory consistently underscores this point (Ray 1995; Weart 1998; Huth and Allee 2002).

One of the most important issues that liberal political theorists grapple with is whether liberalism is so embedded within the cultural and philosophical perspective of Western societies that it cannot be transplanted to societies whose cultural and philosophical perspectives are radically different (I. Young 2000; Benhabib 2002; Connolly 2005). Indeed liberalism, arising within eighteenth- and nineteenth-century European societies that were sharply stratified by economic and social class but otherwise much more homogeneous than today, encounters difficulties on the question of minority rights even in Western societies. These criticisms of liberalism raise issues about the inadequacies of liberalism in pluralistic and non-Western settings. First, "Western" and "non-Western" are cultural rather than geographic spaces. Indigenous peoples, for example, who continue to live in the territories of their ancestors but in spaces where Western settler states have since been established arguably retain philosophical and cultural orientations that contrast sharply with those of the Westerners who created the settler states (Canada, the United States, New Zealand, Australia, and many states in Central and South America). This debate also serves as a reminder that Western versus non-Western is an oversimplification and is often structured as a dichotomous hierarchy where "Western" represents a superior value. The social reality both within and across state boundaries is better described as one of cultural interpenetration, a product of historical and ongoing adaptation and encounter, or acculturation across boundaries of cultural and societal distinctiveness.

That said, questions raised by the extent to which liberalism is a product of Western experience and whether it is adaptable to non-Western societies are important and surface in international human rights debates around the issue of universality versus relativism, an issue that has implications for a global normative order. The rights of minorities, due process as a protection against abuses of authoritative state power, and the effective and independent functioning of the rule of law are all important elements of international human rights. But as of yet, being part of the majority rather than the minority is still preferable in a pluralistic society. The attempt to constitute or reform non-Western societies around principles of liberalism, occurring as it does in the aftermath of several centuries of injustice brought about by Western imperialism, can understandably evoke an anti-Western backlash.

Nevertheless, the Vienna Declaration and Programme of Action at the World Conference on Human Rights in 1993 was supported by 171 states in attendance. States representing people of virtually every religious, cultural, and social tradition agreed to and reaffirmed the same human rights recognized in the original Universal Declaration of Human Rights:

> *Recognizing* and affirming that all human rights derive from the dignity and worth inherent in the human person, and that the human person is the central subject of human rights and fundamental freedoms, and consequently should be the principal beneficiary and should participate actively in the realization of these rights and freedoms,
>
> *Reaffirming* their commitment to the purposes and principles contained in the Charter of the United Nations and the Universal Declaration of Human Rights,
>
> *Reaffirming* the commitment contained in Article 56 of the Charter of the United Nations to take joint and separate action, placing proper emphasis on developing effective international cooperation for the realization of the purposes set out in Article 55.

Perhaps less concern should be given to where ideas come from than whether or not they are good ideas. Whether liberalism can be adapted to non-Western societal contexts or globalized remains debatable, but in the meantime, the globalization of commitments to international human rights standards has become a reality.

The globalization of human rights as a mechanism for democratizing world order is also implicated by the democratic peace proposition discussed above (Elman 1997). From philosopher Immanuel Kant to the rigorous application of empirical analysis and hypothesis testing in the field of international relations today, the proposition that democracies are less likely to go to war with other democracies simply because they are democracies has sustained the imagination of political scientists and policymakers perhaps longer than any other. John Owen argued in a 2005 essay published in *Foreign Affairs* that President George W. Bush was actually following the logic of the democratic peace proposition when he declared his intent to overthrow the undemocratic regime of Saddam Hussein and engage Iraqis in building a democracy. Eliminating Hussein and thereby, in theory, allowing for democracy to take root, the president argued, was the way to eliminate Iraq as a threat to the United States. In addition to making a case for the war, invasion, and occupation, the president appealed secondarily to Saddam Hussein's human rights record, particularly his use of chemical weapons on Kurdish civilians. He was also suspected of continuing a program aimed at developing nuclear weapons, in contravention of numerous UN resolutions, including the one that made the withdrawal of the alliance from Iraq in 1991 conditioned on the dismantling of that country's weapons development program. These legal and political rationales were offered in support of the invasion. However, the moral argument was grounded in Saddam Hussein's human rights violations that he had used chemical weapons to kill "his own people," the Kurds. Owen (2005) pointed out that not only President George W. Bush but his two predecessors, both the elder George H. W. Bush and Bill Clinton, made reference to the democratic peace theory.

Owen (2005) reviewed one of the more recent and rigorously researched books on the democratic peace theory written by Edward Mansfield and Jack Snyder (2005). While taking differences and inequalities in power into consideration, Mansfield and Snyder found that the stability and maturity of a democracy are major factors in predicting how prone to war a state is. New or "transitioning" democracies, they concluded after examining evidence from the Congress of Vienna in 1815 to the present, are the most likely to engage in conflict behavior, particularly when they do not develop democratic institutions and practices in the "right" order, by starting out with free elections with accountable political institutions to restrain those elected (Mansfield and Snyder 2005). Importantly, from the perspective of human rights, the institutions that determine the likelihood of successful transition to democracy are those associated with the protection of human rights, and as discussed in Chapter 5, the contemporary idea of basic human rights was often developed in response to the potential excesses of state power.

## Is an Enforceable International
## Human Rights Regime Possible?

Reforming the state in order to better protect and respect international human rights means not only incorporating international human rights into state legal systems but also holding states accountable for those obligations. This approach has several problems. First, state leaders often have difficulty mobilizing support from their own publics to invest resources in policies aimed at holding other states accountable for their human rights records. The genocides in Bosnia and Rwanda provide examples. In the case of Bosnia, the United Nations declared several areas of eastern Bosnia as "safe areas" where civilians could seek refuge and parties to the conflict were admonished not to engage in armed attack or "any hostile act" in those areas. However, the United Nations stopped short of providing a mechanism for effective enforcement of its declaration. In the Rwandan case, the US government avoided designating the genocide as a genocide because doing so, in the view of some administration officials, would impose a responsibility on the US government to take enforcement action.

Even if state power is reformed, restrained, or moderated by the widespread acceptance of human rights norms, and even if acceptance of human rights norms leads to a more democratic world order, human rights violations will still occur. Violations threatening security and physical integrity rights, particularly those involving direct violence, raise the question of enforcement, including interventions to stop ongoing violations and justice for victims. Recent research on the behavior of rogue states, including their propensity for repressive human rights policies internally, supports the claim that states that violate human rights norms are also more likely to violate other international norms, including the norm of nonaggression toward other states:

> When observance of international human rights norms is used as the standard against which to measure rogue state status, . . . states characterized by more severe violations of those standards are also more likely to engage in a host of aggressive and dangerous international behaviors than states with better performance on human rights. Human rights rogues represent conventional threats to international security through their greater likelihood to engage in aggressive interstate conflict behavior. But they are also more likely to pose unconventional threats to international security through a greater propensity to both support international terrorism and pursue the development and acquisition of weapons of mass destruction than states whose behavior is characterized by closer adherence to the standards of the international human rights regime. . . .
>
> The results of the analysis show that human rights rogues are more likely to become involved in militarized interstate disputes in general, and

violent interstate disputes specifically, than other states during the period 1980–2001, suggesting that policymakers must keep a close watch on serial human rights abusers, while seeking to identify future threats to international security. (Caprioli and Trumbore 2006:32–33)

This work has led to another thesis about international norms known as the normative transfer thesis, for which rigorous examination so far provides support. Subjecting the thesis to a series of statistical tests using alternative hypotheses about the relationship between human rights violations and "rogue" foreign policy behaviors, Leah Graham (2008) concluded,

> The three sets of models illustrate the viability of the normative transfer thesis as an area of further research. Controlling for other theorized factors that contribute to dispute initiation and hostility levels, the statistical significance and robustness of human integrity rights indicate that a state's policy of violence against its own population can be used to explain aggressive behavior in the international realm. (22)

Establishing and confirming a link between repressive domestic government and a propensity for belligerent foreign policies that threaten international peace and stability are important steps toward creating an effective and enforceable international human rights regime, but these steps will also take leadership to mobilize and channel adequate political will in the international community. So far, human rights concerns have been treated as secondary to security threats, including human rights violations as an additional moral justification for taking action against particular regimes when leaders rally public support for military responses to other more conventional notions of security threats. President George H. W. Bush described the US objective in the Gulf War as restoring Kuwaiti sovereignty and expelling Iraqi invasion forces. The offense that warranted the intervention was Iraq's violation of the nonaggression norm, but, he added, military force was needed and sanctions were inadequate to achieve that objective because "while the world waited, Saddam Hussein systematically raped, pillaged, and plundered a tiny nation, no threat to his own. He subjected the people of Kuwait to unspeakable atrocities—and among those maimed and murdered, innocent children" (Bush 1991). President Bill Clinton's call to action in Kosovo drew on both the repressive policies of the Slobodan Milošević government and the potential for destabilizing the region: "Already Macedonia is so threatened. Already Serbian forces have made forays into Albania, which borders Kosovo. If we were to do nothing, eventually our allies and then the United States would be drawn into a larger conflict, at far-greater risks to our people and far-greater costs" (Clinton 1999).

Speaking to human rights advocates critical of such selective intervention, citing, among other failures, the US reluctance to intervene in

Rwanda and his administration's initial refusal to acknowledge the genocide there (instead carefully instructing the State Department to say only, eventually, that "acts of genocide have occurred"), Clinton said, "Now, we can't respond to every tragedy in every corner of the world, but just because we can't do everything for everyone doesn't mean that, for the sake of consistency, we should do nothing for no one" (US Department of State 1994). When President George W. Bush made the case for the invasion of Iraq in March 2003, he cited Saddam Hussein's alleged nuclear weapons program and his threat to the security of the United States and the world as provocation for an invasion and his active removal from power. In press conferences later and upon the execution of Saddam Hussein after his trial by a US-backed Iraqi Special Tribunal, President Bush referred to Hussein's violations against "his own people," citing often the use of chemical weapons against the Kurds. But this argument augmented the primary justifications, which focused on acts of aggression and violations of Security Council resolutions.

So while human rights considerations have been incorporated into decisions about recipients of US foreign and military aid and included as justification for interventions otherwise driven by conventional security concerns, much progress has not yet been made toward the development of an enforceable international human rights regime. Advocates continue to urge US leaders to promote the development of such a regime. Said Harold Hongju Koh (2008), former assistant secretary of state for democracy, human rights, and labor:

> The United States is built on human rights and the rule of law, and our commitments to these ideals define who we are as a nation and a people. . . . A string of well-publicized policies have seriously diminished the United States' global standing as a human rights leader and left our nation less secure and less free. [President Barack Obama] needs to reassert our historic commitments to human rights and the rule of law as major sources of our nation's moral authority. Even before his Inauguration, [Obama] should unambiguously signal his intention to move decisively to restore respect for human rights in national security policy with a package of executive orders, proposed legislation, agency shakeups, and concrete foreign policy actions.

President Clinton was right when he said that the United States cannot possibly intervene everywhere that human rights are being violated, but leadership for multilateral support to develop a more effective and enforceable human rights regime is still important. As was indicated in Chapter 6, numerous enforcement efforts are already under way, and the issue of human rights no longer needs to be thought of strictly as low politics while security is thought of as high politics. International security can be strengthened with the development of an effective international human rights regime. States at risk of failing pose an international threat even as they fail to protect or, worse, actively violate the human rights of those living within their borders.

States do not dispense perfect social justice and many do not manage resources in such a way that people living in them can meet even their basic material needs. Nor do they do an equally good job of protecting and promoting international human rights; indeed states have often been perpetrators of, collaborators in, or enablers of human rights violations. But to the extent that human rights norms are internationalized and strengthened as a mechanism for, at minimum, preventing or substantially restraining the worst excesses of power used arbitrarily and without accountability, hope can be found for what Richard Falk, Samuel Kim, and Saul Mendlovitz (1991) called a "more just world order." Beyond that, however, state uses of power accountable to international human rights standards and developing an effective and enforceable international human rights regime can contribute to creating a more stable and secure international environment with security benefits for all states and the people who live in them (Burke-White 2004).

Since in this chapter, I have tied political theories of realism and liberalism to questions about the future of human rights, a word about insights from constructivism is also in order. Whereas realists view the sovereignty of the state and the cultural and ideological pluralism of the world as obstacles to the development of universal and enforceable norms, and liberals emphasize cooperation as a necessity and normative agreement as a practical consequence, constructivists would point out that the present state of international relations will change because identities and interests change. They would likely be unwilling to conjecture about the direction of change though they may venture to identify several possible futures for human rights and international relations. Anarchy in the realists' sense—the absence of authoritative power above the state—is in the constructivists' view only one kind of structure, while issue-specific regimes organized by states cooperating over common interests (in the case of trade and finance, for example) and common values (in the case of human rights) are another. Agents—social actors making choices—are both constrained by structures and able to change them by making choices or engaging in social action. Individuals, states, intergovernmental organizations, NGOs, and other non-state actors are all social agents whose choices and actions will shape the future structure of world politics, in the constructivists' view. Neither future, the worse (more genocides and no effective enforcement regime) or the better (an enforceable human rights regime that leads to a decline in human rights violations), is inevitable.

## The Future of International Human Rights

Whether and how the state is reformed to strengthen respect for and promotion of human rights, and whether and how the international system develops effective mechanisms for holding states accountable and for acting to stop ongoing atrocities will depend on the political will that emerges from both leaders and the broader publics they serve.

NGOs and other private sector actors can increase awareness of human rights causes through their campaigns and activities. Although the framework of this book has been focused on the state and in Chapter 7 on high-profile nonstate actors and individuals, the greatest hope for the future of human rights may stem from the willingness of ordinary people in their capacity as citizens to place a high value on human rights in their own societies as well as at a global level.

Those who live in societies with responsive democratic governments can use their votes to force their leaders to listen, and those who must struggle against undemocratic institutions need courage, knowledge, and the support of fellow human beings across all national boundaries. This book was written with the hope not only of providing readers with a broad base of knowledge about the many international human rights issues of concern in the world today, but also of offering some understanding of the social, political, and historical context in which these issues arose. It was also written in the hope of cultivating a deep and abiding commitment to the progression of human rights in the soul of the reader. Political theorist Hannah Arendt, who reported on the trial of Adolf Eichmann and wrote extensively about the immorality of totalitarian thinking and the necessity of defeating it, once said, "The sad truth is that most evil is done by people who never make up their minds to be either good or evil" (1978:194).

# 15

# What Can I Do?

The opposite of love is not hate, it's indifference. The opposite of art is not ugliness, it's indifference. The opposite of faith is not heresy, it's indifference. And the opposite of life is not death, it's indifference.
—Elie Wiesel, 2009

You may never know what results come of your actions, but if you do nothing, there will be no results. —Mahatma Gandhi, 1919

HAVING TAUGHT A COURSE ON INTERNATIONAL HUMAN RIGHTS FOR the past twenty-two years, I have obtained the nickname among political science students as "Professor Doom and Gloom." I think it's about the course and not me—but it is still the most popular course I teach, no matter how frequently I teach it. We read, discuss, watch films, write essays, and grapple with all of the disturbing ugliness, all the offenses to everyone's sense of humanity, that the topics raised by this subject entail. Some have made serious life decisions, they later tell me, because of some eye-opening experience that they had while taking the course. They end up going to law school, changing majors and career goals, or joining the military service. During the regular semester, the class meets once a week for three hours. From week to week, we integrate the issues covered in each class and the emotions they arouse.

But inevitably, at the end of the course, many students have both a greater awareness of the state of international human rights and a motive to act on that awareness, on the one hand, and a sense of powerlessness that things will mostly go on as they were before, on the other. Young college students are in an exciting time of life, a time of liberation and young adulthood, greater personal responsibilities, and a seemingly endless road to the future, filled with more promises than disappointments. The subject of international human rights temporarily intervenes in this excitement. Many ask me, at the end of the course, "What can I do to improve respect for human rights?" This chapter—really more of a postscript—is for them.

*Locate a human rights NGO in your community or state and find out what that organization is doing.* There may be citizens' groups in your town or, if not, in your state, that work to promote human rights locally. Sometimes these groups hold proactive programs in the community, bringing in speakers or holding "awareness" events like hosting a beans and rice supper on World Food Day or organizing speakers and participants for marches on Gay Pride Day or Holocaust Memorial Day. They may be working on age-appropriate programs for public schools. Is there a domestic violence shelter in your community? A program to feed and temporarily house the homeless? Remember that rich countries are the most common destinations for sex trafficking, and even troubled, homeless, and runaway kids in the United States are being duped or recruited into sex trafficking schemes today. Trafficking is a human rights issue that affects all countries, rich and poor. You can investigate local efforts to combat trafficking and find out what you can do to advance those efforts. If you do gain an interest in a particular group, find out when the group came into existence and why. Was it created in response to specific events in your community?

*Identify a national or international human rights advocacy group and learn more about that group's projects and campaigns.* This task obviously requires less than becoming involved in establishing a campus or community chapter (see below), but you can still identify some of the national and international groups and just find out what they are doing. The American Association for the Advancement of Science, for example, has a program entitled "Scientific Responsibility, Human Rights, and Law." The Internet makes this kind of research interesting. You can also look into whether civic groups in your area, like the Kiwanis, have international programs and find out whether they are involved in projects that promote human rights.

*Learn more about a topic of special interest to you.* This book is intended to be more comprehensive on the issues of international human rights in order to introduce the reader to the issues and the main debates surrounding them and hopefully to provoke an interest in learning more about some of them. Of course you can pick up on any of these issues and continue learning about it, following it in the news, and so on. You can also use the issues as a springboard for ideas to research for other classes or assignments. If your program of study includes a research capstone, for example, plenty of questions have been raised and theoretical direction offered for the topic as a whole and in relation to some of the specific issues. Human rights research is also cited that can give you ideas about what kinds of methodologies human rights scholars employ.

*Look into your own family's history to find out what experiences in regard to losing or gaining access to human rights your family members or ancestors have had.* The possibilities here are limitless. The United States is often said to be a country of people with "hyphenated identities," which by the beginning of the twentieth century was a derogatory term referring to our immigrant heritage. At least half of us are also women, and researching the history of women in your family can tell a larger story about changing views of and by women over the past century or so.

*Join a human rights advocacy group with college chapters, such as Engineers Without Borders, Doctors Without Borders, or Amnesty International, or start your own on-campus advocacy group or chapter.* Many of the most active organizations are discussed in previous chapters. Amnesty International has campus chapters all over the country. They work on "urgent action" projects aimed at freeing political prisoners and can offer ideas about how to promote education and awareness about international human rights in your community or on your campus.

*Talk about human rights issues with your friends and professors to see if they might be interested in organizing a human rights film festival or arranging for guest speakers to come to your campus.* Whether you are a member of a student social, academic, political, or preprofessional group or not, you can still get together with a couple of friends or work with an existing student group (such as student government) to plan a program around a human rights theme. It could be a full-blown film festival, a single speaker, or even a single film event. You can organize a panel on the death penalty issue with speakers on both sides. The ACLU is usually available to participate, and perhaps you could invite local prosecutors or others in the legal profession who support the death penalty to give another perspective. Your history department might have a scholar who specializes in constitutional history who can moderate or contribute. Local radio stations might be interested in carrying the panel discussion as a broadcast.

*Plan some community or campus events around days like Martin Luther King Jr. Day or International Human Rights Day.* Your college or university probably already invites a guest speaker to commemorate Martin Luther King Jr. Day, but probably not the UN Human Rights Day on December 10 (the day the Universal Declaration was passed in 1948). Another important day to commemorate is November 20, Universal Children's Day, to celebrate the Convention on the Rights of the Child. Research other human rights commemorative days you can use as a platform to plan an event.

*Visit local schools and find out what kinds of human rights activities are going on or whether interest exists in organizing some.* If you have not seen it, the documentary *Paper Clips* is an excellent example of how one high school class left a legacy of learning after studying the Holocaust. The students' journey began when their teacher realized they had no way of imagining how many people 6 million is—and so they began collecting 6 million paper clips. Watch the movie to see what happens after that! You can invite social studies teachers at local schools to watch the film with you and offer to present the film in their classes and lead a class discussion. High school students (and their teachers) usually enjoy having local college or university students take over their class for a day. Many other films that feature human rights issues could be used the same way. Find out what programs or classes in local schools address issues of human rights.

*Consider applying for an internship with a human rights organization.* Nonprofit organizations are always looking for free help. You might find one in your geographic area that would appreciate your coming in a few hours a week to help. You might be trained to work on a hotline with victims of domestic violence, take and investigate complaints of human rights problems, or just answer phones and do whatever the organization needs done. You could also make arrangements for a more extensive internship that, if your school has an academic internship program in place, you could receive college credit or community service credit for doing. These volunteer efforts can be great resume builders even if you are not working for academic credit.

*Research potential graduate programs or law schools that specialize in human rights.* Political science students often go into a graduate program in either political science or public administration, law school, or political fieldwork, the last straight out of undergraduate school. If the last appeals to you, the previous suggestion might be a good stepping stone to finding out where there are job openings and a great way to acquire some relevant experience, if you want to work in the area of human rights. As for graduate, public administration, and law school programs, if you are so motivated, you can find those with an emphasis in or special opportunities for studying human rights.

*Look into study abroad programs available through your college or university.* Many study abroad programs in the United States are linked to institutions in former communist countries and in areas transitioning to democratic governance, from the Middle East to South Africa. Find out what the opportunities are with a specific eye to your interest in having a firsthand encounter with human rights issues on the ground. You can talk to your study abroad coordinator or office, and you can research the human rights conditions in countries available for a study abroad semester or year in advance of going.

This list is by no means exhaustive and talking with your professors and friends might inspire additional ideas. If you have little time but an abundance of interest, several of them really don't take much time; some are even "one time only" commitments like bringing in a guest speaker or showing a single human rights film on campus. You may not agree that all of the issues covered in this book are equally important or even valid. Many of them have no relationship at all to conservative or liberal views, though no doubt some do. Conservative-leaning individuals, for instance, will probably find a greater resonance with issues related to civil liberties, or the question of whether and how the spread of free-market capitalism can be a force for meeting more needs of more people. Liberal-leaning individuals may be more drawn to issues of civil rights and discrimination. But, hopefully there will be debates and dissenting views on some of the controversies raised by the text.

Ending this book on a very positive note is difficult after studying war crimes, rape, sex trafficking, genocide, racial discrimination, women's marginalization, and so on. But not that long ago, taking a broad historical view, little or no attention was given to human rights as an international problem, and not because human rights problems didn't exist. That gains have been made is encouraging.

You may feel helpless in the face of such huge issues, but no act on your part is too small to matter. You will be more comfortable, after reading this book, even just talking with friends or following a news story about human rights issues more closely. Author Alice Walker said, "Activism is the rent I pay for living on this planet." Or, maybe, just the rent we pay for being born in a democracy.

# Acronyms

| | |
|---|---|
| ACLU | American Civil Liberties Union |
| AIDS | acquired immune deficiency syndrome |
| ATCA | Alien Tort Claims Act |
| CEO | chief executive officer |
| CIA | Central Intelligence Agency |
| DEA | Drug Enforcement Agency |
| EU | European Union |
| FBI | Federal Bureau of Investigation |
| FGM | female genital mutilation |
| HIV | human immunodeficiency virus |
| ICC | International Criminal Court |
| ICCPR | International Covenant on Civil and Political Rights |
| ICCR | Interfaith Center on Corporate Responsibility |
| ICESCR | International Covenant on Economic, Social and Cultural Rights |
| ICJ | International Court of Justice |
| ICTR | International Criminal Tribunal for Rwanda |
| ICTY | International Criminal Tribunal for the Former Yugoslavia |
| ILGA | International Lesbian, Gay, Bisexual, Trans, and Intersex Association |
| ILO | International Labour Organization |
| LGBT | lesbian, gay, bisexual, and transgender |
| NATO | North Atlantic Treaty Organization |
| NGO | nongovernmental organization |
| OECD | Organisation for Economic Co-operation and Development |
| OHCHR | Office of the UN High Commissioner for Human Rights |
| OPEC | Organization of the Petroleum Exporting Countries |
| OSCE | Organization for Security and Cooperation in Europe |

| | |
|---|---|
| SS | Schutzstaffel |
| TAN | transnational advocacy network |
| TNB | transnational bank |
| TNC | transnational corporation |
| UN | United Nations |
| UNAIDS | Joint United Nations Programme on HIV/AIDS |
| UNESCO | UN Educational, Scientific, and Cultural Organization |
| UNHCR | UN High Commissioner for Refugees |
| UNICEF | UN Children's Fund |
| WHO | World Health Organization |

# References

Abiew, F. K. 1999. *The Evolution of the Doctrine and Practice of Humanitarian Intervention*. Alphen aan den Rijn, Netherlands: Klewer Law International.

Access to Health Care. 2008. "Disparities in Health Care Spending and Numbers of Doctors." *UC Atlas of Inequality*. http://ucatlas.ucsc.edu.

ACLU (American Civil Liberties Union). 2005. "Mother of Slain Children Takes Case to International Tribunal." December 27. www.aclu.org.

ACLU and Human Rights Watch. 2014. *With Liberty to Monitor All: How Large-Scale US Surveillance Is Harming Journalism, Law, and American Democracy*. New York: Human Rights Watch. www.hrw.org/reports/2014/07/28/liberty-monitor-all-0.

The Advocates for Human Rights. 2007. "Forced Early Marriage." Stop Violence Against Women, October. www.stopvaw.org.

Agarwal, Bina. 2007. "Women and Property: Reducing Domestic Violence, Enhancing Group Rights." *People and Policy*, no. 8 (July–September): 1–4.

Akcam, Taner. 2006. *A Shameful Act: The Armenian Genocide and the Question of Turkish Responsibility*. New York: Metropolitan.

Albert, Mathias, Lothar Brock, and Klaus Dieter Wolf. 2000. *Civilizing World Politics: Society and Community Beyond the State*. Lanham, MD: Rowman and Littlefield.

Alcalá, María José. 2006. *State of World Population 2006. A Passage to Hope: Women and International Migration*. New York: UN Population Fund.

Alford, C. Fred. 1989. *Melanie Klein and Critical Social Theory*. New Haven, CT: Yale University Press.

———. 1997. *What Evil Means to Us*. Ithaca, NY: Cornell University Press.

Algan, Bülent. 2004. "Rethinking 'Third Generation Human Rights.'" *Ankara Law Review* 1, no. 1 (Summer): 121–155.

Al-Jazeera. 2012. "Has the Arab Spring Taken an Islamist Turn?" December 12.

Allen, Christopher. 2006. "Traditions Weigh on China's Women." BBC News, June 19.

Alston, Philip, and Mary Robinson, eds. 2005. *Human Rights and Development: Towards Mutual Reinforcement*. Oxford: Oxford University Press.

American Experience. 1992. "In the White Man's Image." *The American Experience*. Native American Public Broadcasting Consortium and Nebraska Educational Television Network. Christine Lesiak, Director.

Amnesty International. 2008. "Stop Violence Against Women Campaign." www .amnestyusa.org.

———. 2009a. "Enforced Disappearances: Annual Report 2008." London: Amnesty International. www.amnesty.org/en/enforced-disappearances/annual-report-2008.

———. 2009b. "Seeking Justice for Extrajudicial Executions." London: Amnesty International.

———. 2009c. "Juveniles Among Five Men Beheaded in Saudi Arabia." www .amnesty.org/en/news-and-updates/news/juveniles-among-five-men-beheaded -saudi-arabia-20090512.

———. 2010. "UN Norms for Business—Taking Corporate Responsibility for Human Rights to the Next Level!" www.amnestyusa.org.

———. 2011. "Report 2011: Amnesty International at 50 Says History Change on Knife-Edge." London: Amnesty International. www.amnesty.org/en/news-and -updates/report-2011-amnesty-international-50-says-historic-change-knife -edge-2011-05-13.

———. 2013. "History of Amnesty International." www.amnesty.org.

———. 2014a. *Torture in 2014: 30 Years of Broken Promises.* London: Peter Benenson House.

———. 2014b. "Figures on the Death Penalty." www.amnesty.org/en/death-penalty /numbers.

———. 2014c. "Roma Demanding Equality and Human Rights." www.amnesty .org/en/roma.

———. 2014d. "Executions of Juveniles Since 1990." www.amnesty.org.

———. 2014e. "Sexual Orientation and Gender Identity." www.amnesty.org/en /sexual-orientation-and-gender-identity.

Anderson, Benedict. 1991. *Imagined Communities: Reflections on the Origin and Spread of Nationalism.* London: Verso.

Anderson, Sarah, and John Cavanaugh. 2008. "Bailouts Dwarf Spending on Climate and Poverty Crises, Institute for Policy Studies." www.ips-dc.org.

Angle, Stephen. 2002. *Human Rights and Chinese Thought: A Cross-Cultural Inquiry.* Cambridge: Cambridge University Press.

Anglican Church of Canada. 1993. "Anglican Church of Canada's Apology to Native People." www.anglican.ca.

Anker, Richard. 1983. "Female Labour Force Participation in Developing Countries: A Critique of Current Definitions and Data Collection Methods." *International Labour Review* 709 (November–December): 709–723.

An-Na'im, Abdullahi Ahmed, ed. 2002. *Human Rights Under African Constitutions: Realizing the Promise for Ourselves.* Philadelphia: University of Pennsylvania Press.

———. 2008. *Islam and the Secular State.* Cambridge: Harvard University Press.

———. 2011. "Human Rights, Universality, and Sovereignty: Human Rights in Islam." Presentation, March, Duke University Franklin Center for Interdisciplinary and International Studies. www.youtube.com.

Apodaca, Clair, and Michael Stohl. 1999. "United States Human Rights Policy and Foreign Assistance." *International Studies Quarterly*, no. 43: 185–198.

Arendt, Hannah. 1951. *The Origins of Totalitarianism.* New York: Schocken.

———. 1978. *The Life of the Mind.* Mary McCarthy, ed. New York: Harcourt Brace Jovanovich.

Arizona Water Center. 2010. "Global Water Shortage Looms in New Century." http://ag.arizona.edu.

ARKA News Agency. 2009. "Turkey Must Recognize Armenian Genocide; PM." *ARKA News,* October 19.

Artz, Donna E. 1990. "The Application of International Human Rights Law in Islamic States." *Human Rights Quarterly* 11, no. 2 (May): 202–230.

Ash, Lucy. 2003. "India's Dowry Deaths." BBC News, July 17.

Asia-Pacific Human Rights Information Center. 2014. "Final Declaration of the Regional Meeting for Asia of the World Conference on Human Rights." www.hurights.or.jp/archives/other_documents/section1/1993/04/final -declaration-of-the-regional-meeting-for-asia-of-the-world-conference-on -human-rights.html.

Associated Press. 2012. "Report: 338 Killed During Tunisia Revolution." www .sacbee.com.

Austin, John. 1995 [1832]. *The Province of Jurisprudence Determined.* Edited by Wilfrid E. Rumble. Cambridge: Cambridge University Press.

AVERT. 2008. "Worldwide HIV and AIDS Statistics." www.avert.org.

Baek, Buhm-Suk. 2008. "Economic Sanctions Against Human Rights Violations." *Cornell Law School Inter-University Graduate Student Conference Papers*, no. 11. Ithaca, NY: Cornell University.

Balakian, Peter. 2007. "Hrant Dink's Assassination and Genocide's Legacy." Open Democracy, January 29. www.opendemocracy.net.

Bamford, David. 2002. "Rwanda Sets Up Genocide Courts." BBC News, November 25.

Barenblatt, Daniel. 2004. *A Plague upon Humanity.* New York: HarperCollins.

Barlow, Maude. 2001. "Water as Commodity—The Wrong Prescription." *Backgrounder* (Institute for Food and Development Policy) 7, no. 3 (Summer): 1–8.

Barnett, Anthony. 2008. "The Three Faces of the World Social Forum." Open Democracy. www.opendemocracy.net.

Barreiro, Jose. 2010. *Thinking in Indian: A John Mohawk Reader.* Golden, CO: Fulcrum.

Barro, Richard. 1991. "Economic Growth in a Cross Section of Countries." *Quarterly Journal of Economics* 106, no. 2: 407–443.

———. 1997. *Determinants of Economic Growth: A Cross-Country Empirical Study.* Cambridge, MA: MIT Press.

Battle, Michael. 1997. *Reconciliation: The Ubuntu Theology of Desmond Tutu.* Cleveland, OH: Pilgrim.

Bauman, Zygmunt. 1989. *Modernity and the Holocaust.* Ithaca, NY: Cornell University Press.

BBC News. 1999. "South Asia Bride Burning 'Kills Hundreds.'" August 27.

———. 2000. "Billions Without Clean Water." March 14. http://news.bbc.co.uk/2/hi /676064.stm.

———. 2004. "Powell Declares Genocide in Sudan." September 9.

———. 2008 [1942]. "Britain Condemns Massacre of Jews." December 17.

———. 2012. "Rwanda 'Gacaca' Genocide Courts Finish Work." www.bbc.com.

BBC Online. 2008. "EU Hails Turkey Free Speech Move." April 30.

Benedict, Ruth. 1959. *Patterns of Culture.* Boston: Houghton Mifflin.

Benhabib, Seyla, ed. 2002. *The Claims of Culture: Equality and Diversity in the Global Era.* Princeton, NJ: Princeton University Press.

Bennett, Carline. 2003. "Seven Who Change Their Worlds." *Women's E-News*, December 23. www.womensenews.org.

Benschop, Marjolein. 2004. "Women's Rights to Land and Property." Commission on Sustainable Development: Women in Human Settlements Development. www.unhabitat.org.

Bhabha, Homi. 1990. *Nation and Narration.* New York: Routledge.

Binion, Gayle. 1995. "Human Rights: A Feminist Perspective." *Human Rights Quarterly* 17, no. 3: 509–526.

Bix, Herbert. 2000. *Hirohito and the Making of Modern Japan.* New York: Harper-Collins.

Black, Robert, Saul Morris, and Jennifer Bryce. 2010. "Where and Why Are 10 Million Children Dying Every Year?" *Lancet* 361: 2226–2234.

Bloch, Sidney, and Peter B. Reddaway. 1977. *Psychiatric Terror: How Soviet Psychiatry Is Used to Suppress Dissent.* New York: Basic.

Block, Robert. 1994. "Hutus Keep On Killing Tutsi in Goma Camp: Robert Block in Goma Finds Rwanda's Genocidal Conflict Is Being Carried Over to Refugee Camps in Zaire." *The Independent*, July 27.

Bourdieu, Pierre. 1984 [1974]. *Distinction: A Social Critique of the Judgment of Taste.* Trans. Richard Nice. Cambridge: Harvard University Press.

———. 1991. *Language and Symbolic Power.* Cambridge: Harvard University Press.

Bowser-Soder, Brenda. 2013. "Kiobel Ruling Undermines U.S. Leadership on Human Rights." Human Rights First. www.humanrightsfirst.org.

Brackman, Arnold C. 1987. *The Other Nuremberg: The Untold Story of the Tokyo War Crimes Trial.* New York: William Morrow.

Brackney, William H. 2005. *The Christian Tradition.* Vol. 2 in *Human Rights and the World's Major Religions.* New York: Praeger.

Braun, Elihai. 2008. "The UN World Conference Against Racism, Racial Discrimination, Xenophobia and Related Intolerance, Durban, South Africa (August 31–September 8, 2001)." Jewish Virtual Library, American-Israeli Cooperative Enterprise. www.jewishvirtuallibrary.org.

Bredbenner, Candice Lewis. 1998. *A Nationality of Her Own: Women, Marriage, and the Law of Citizenship.* Berkeley: University of California Press.

Brewer, Marilynn B. 1991. "The Social Self: On Being the Same and Different at the Same Time." *Personality and Social Psychology Bulletin* 17, no. 5 (October): 475–482.

Brook, Timothy. 2001. "The Tokyo Judgment and the Rape of Nanking." *Journal of Asian Studies* 60, no. 3 (August): 673–700.

Brown, Chris. 2000. "Cosmopolitanism, World Citizenship and Global Civil Society." *Critical Review of International Social and Political Philosophy* 3, no. 1: 7–26.

Brown, Dee. 1991. *Bury My Heart at Wounded Knee.* New York: Holt.

Bruno, Andorra. 2014. "Refugee Admissions and Resettlement Policy." Washington, DC: Congressional Research Service.

Brysk, Alison. 2009. *Global Good Samaritans: Human Rights as Foreign Policy.* Oxford: Oxford University Press

Brzezinski, Zbigniew. 1993. *Out of Control: Global Turmoil on the Eve of the Twenty-First Century.* New York: Touchstone.

Burke, Edmund. 1905 [1756]. *A Vindication of Natural Society.* Ann Arbor: University of Michigan Press.

———. 2009 [1790]. *Reflections on the Revolution in France.* Edited by L. G. Mitchell. Oxford: Oxford University Press.

Burke, Garance. 2010. "California's Groundwater Shrinking Because of Agricultural Use." *Christian Science Monitor,* January 4.

Burke-White, William W. 2004. "Human Rights and National Security: The Strategic Correlation." *Harvard Human Rights Journal* 17: 249–280.

Burkhalter, Holly. 2004. "Trafficking in Persons: A Global Review." Testimony

Before the 108th Congress, Subcommittee on International Terrorism, Nonproliferation, and Human Rights, House Report 108-809. June 24.

Bush, George H. W. 1991. "Address to the Nation on the Invasion of Iraq." www.americanrhetoric.com.

Bush, George W. 2001. "Address to a Joint Session of Congress and the American People." September 20. www.whitehouse.gov.

Business and Human Rights Resource Centre. 2013. "UN Secretary-General's Special Representative on Business and Human Rights." www.business-human rights.org.

Cambanis, Thanassis. 2011. "Stand Alone: The Case for a New Isolationism." *Boston Globe,* February 6. www.bostonglobe.com.

Cambodian Tribunal Monitor. 2012. "Composite Chronology of the Evolution and Operation of the ECCC." Chicago, IL: Center for International Human Rights, Northwestern University School of Law.

Cammaert, Patrick. 2013. "Issue Brief: The UN Intervention Brigade in the Democratic Republic of the Congo." New York: International Peace Institute.

Camponovo, Christopher. 2002–2003. "Disaster in Durban: The United Nations Conference Against Racism, Racial Discrimination, Xenophobia and Related Intolerance." *George Washington International Law Review* 34, no. 4: 659–699.

Caprioli, Mary, and Peter Trumbore. 2006. "Human Rights Rogues: Aggressive, Dangerous, or Both?" Paper presented at the annual meeting of the International Studies Association, San Diego, CA, March 22.

Carter, Jimmy. 1978. "Human Rights Violations in Cambodia Statement by the President." April 21. The American Presidency Project, University of California, Santa Barbara. www.presidency.ucsb.edu/ws/?pid=30693.

CBC News. 2008. "Civilians Killed in Darfur Refugee Camp: Reports." CBC News online, August 25. www.cbc.ca/news/world/civilians-killed-in-darfur-refugee -camp-reports-1.700871.

CDC (Centers for Disease Control). 2014. "National Intimate Partner and Sexual Violence Survey." www.cdc.gov/violenceprevention/nisvs/.

Center for Constitutional Rights. 2014. "FAQs: Does the U.S. Torture People?" http://ccrjustice.org.

Center for Holocaust and Genocide Studies. 2010. "Gypsies: A Persecuted Race." University of Minnesota. www.chgs.umn.edu.

Center for International Rehabilitation. 2010. "Frequently Asked Questions." www.cirnetwork.org.

Chapman T., and S. Chaudoin. 2012. "Ratification Patterns and the Limits of the International Criminal Court." *International Studies Quarterly* 57, no. 2: 400–409.

Chase-Dunn, Christopher, and Thomas D. Hall. 1997. *Rise and Demise: Comparing World-Systems.* Boulder, CO: Westview.

Châtel, Vincent, and Chuck Ferree. 2001. "Auschwitz-Birkenau: The Death Factory." The Forgotten Camps. www.jewishgen.org.

Chatterjee, Pratap. 2012. "Chiquita Banana to Face Colombian Torture Claim." *Corpwatch.* March 30. www.corpwatch.org.

Chesterman, Simon. 2011. "Leading from Behind: The Responsibility to Protect, the Obama Doctrine, and Intervention After Libya." *Ethics and International Affairs* 25: 279–285.

Chirot, Daniel. 1996. *Modern Tyrants: The Power and Prevalence of Evil in Our Age.* Princeton, NJ: Princeton University Press.

Chomsky, Noam. 2009. "The Unipolar Moment and the Culture of Imperialism." Podcast, *Democracy Now!,* December 17.

CIA (Central Intelligence Agency). 2014. *World Factbook*. Washington, DC: Central Intelligence Agency. www.cia.gov.

Cingranelli, David L., and Thomas E. Pasquarello. 1985. "Human Rights Practices and the Distribution of U.S. Foreign Aid to Latin American Countries." *American Journal of Political Science* 8, no. 1: 539–563.

Clark, Dana L. 2002. "The World Bank and Human Rights: The Need for Greater Accountability." *Harvard Human Rights Journal* 15 (Spring): 205–226.

Claude, Richard Pierre. 1983. "The Case of Joelito Filartiga and the Clinic of Hope." *Human Rights Quarterly* 275: 275–301.

Clinton, William J. 1999. "Crisis in the Balkans, Clinton's Speech on Kosovo: 'We Also Act to Prevent a Wider War.'" *New York Times*, April 2.

CNN. 2000. "400 Sentenced to Death in Rwanda Genocide Trials." July 19. http://archives.cnn.com.

CNN Interactive. 1996. "Bride-Burning Claims Hundreds in India." August 18. www.cnn.com.

Cole, David. 2003. "Are Foreign Nationals Entitled to the Same Constitutional Rights as Citizens?" *Thomas Jefferson Law Review* 25, no. 3: 367–388.

Cole, Wade. 2005. "Sovereignty Relinquished? Explaining Commitment to the International Human Rights Covenants." *American Sociological Review* 70: 472–495.

———. 2009. "Hard and Soft Commitments to Human Rights Treaties, 1966–2000." *Sociological Forum* 24: 563–588.

Committee on the Elimination of Racial Discrimination. 2008. "Concluding Observations of the Committee on Elimination of Racial Discrimination." United Nations Seventy-Second Session, Geneva, February 18–March 7.

Connell, Daniel. 2013. "Large Dams and the 'Risk Society.'" *Global Water Forum*. www.globalwaterforum.org/2013/03/28/international-water-politics-large-dams-and-the-risk-society/.

Connolly, William. 2005. *Pluralism*. Chapel Hill, NC: Duke University Press.

Cookman, Claude. 2007. "An American Atrocity: The My Lai Massacre Concretized in a Victim's Face." *Journal of American History* 94, no. 1: 154–162.

CorpWatch. 2014. "About Corpwatch." http://corpwatch.org/article.php?id=11314.

Council of Europe. 2014. "Framework Convention for the Protection of National Minorities—Summary of the Treaty." http://conventions.coe.int.

Coward, Harold. 2005. *The Hindu Tradition*. Vol. 4 of *Human Rights and the World's Religions*. New York: Praeger.

Crawford, James. 1995. "Endangered Native American Languages: What Is to be Done, and Why?" *Bilingual Research Journal* 19, no. 1 (Winter): 17–38.

Crosby, Alfred. 2003. *The Columbian Exchange: Biological and Cultural Consequences of 1491* (30th Anniversary Edition). New York: Praeger.

Cross, Allison. 2012. "Canada Rejects UN Human Rights Criticism Detailed in Amnesty International Report." *National Post*, December 19.

Crowe, David. 1995. *A History of the Gypsies of Eastern Europe and Russia*. London: I. B Tauris.

———. 2014. *War Crimes, Genocide, and Justice: A Global History*. New York: Palgrave MacMillan.

CRS Report for Congress. 2010. "Asylum Law and Female Genital Mutilation." www.fas.org.

Dadrian, Vahakn N. 1995. *The History of the Armenian Genocide: Ethnic Conflict from the Balkans to Anatolia to the Caucasus*. New York: Berghahn.

Dahlburg, John-Thor. 1994. "The Fight to Save India's Baby Girls." *Los Angeles Times*, February 22.

Dalai Lama. 1999. *Ethics for the New Millennium*. New York: Riverhead.

Davenport, Christian. 2000. *Paths to State Repression: Human Rights Violations and Contentious Politics*. Boulder: Rowman and Littlefield.

Davenport, Christian, and Allan C. Stam. 2009. "What Really Happened in Rwanda?" *Miller-McCune,* October 6.

Davis, Robert C. 2003. *Christian Slaves, Muslim Masters: White Slavery in the Mediterranean, the Barbary Coast and Italy, 1500–1800*. New York: Palgrave MacMillan.

Death Penalty Information Center. 2014a. "The Innocence List." www.deathpenalty info.org.

———. 2014b. "Abolitionist and Retentionist Countries." www.deathpenalty info.org.

de Azcarate, Pedro. 1945. *The League of Nations and National Minorities*. Washington, DC: Carnegie Endowment for International Peace.

de Bary, William Theodore. 1998. *Asian Values and Human Rights: A Confucian Communitarian Perspective*. Cambridge, MA: Harvard University Press.

de Bary, William Theodore, and Tu Weiming, eds. 1998. *Confucianism and Human Rights*. New York: Columbia University Press.

Defeis, Elizabeth F. 1999. "The Treaty of Amsterdam: The Next Step Towards Gender Equality?" *Boston College International and Comparative Law Review* 23, no. 1. http://lawdigitalcommons.bc.edu.

DeLaet, Debra L. 2005. *The Global Struggle for Human Rights: Universal Principles in World Politics*. Belmont, CA: Thomson Higher Education.

Deng, Francis Mading. 2003. *Dilemmas of Self-Determination: A Challenge to African Constitutionalism*. Washington, DC: United States Institute of Peace.

*Detroit News*. 2011. "Labor Movement Drives Egypt, Tunisia Protests." February 10.

Deva, Surya. 2004. "UN's Human Rights Norms for Transnational Corporations and Other Business Enterprises: An Imperfect Step in the Right Direction?" *ISLA Journal of International and Comparative Law* 10: 493–523.

Dippie, Brian W. 1982. *The Vanishing American: White Attitudes and U.S. Indian Policy*. Middleton, CT: Wesleyan University Press.

Direct News National. 2014. "6 Things You Should Know About the World's 50 Million Refugees." http://national.deseretnews.com/article/1775/6-things-you -should-know-about-the-worlds-50-million-refugees.html.

Division for the Advancement of Women. 2010. "Beijing + 15." www.un.org.

Doctors Without Borders. 2008. "Affordability, Availability and Adaptability of AIDS Drugs in Developing Countries: An On-Going Challenge." August 1. www.doctorswithoutborders.org.

Donnelly, Jack. 1986. "International Human Rights: A Regime Analysis." *International Organization* 40, no. 3: 559–642.

———. 2013. *Universal Human Rights in Theory and Practice*. Ithaca, NY: Cornell University Press.

Douglas, Mary. 1978. "Cultural Bias." Occasional paper. London: Royal Anthropological Institute.

Dower, John. 1999. *Embracing Defeat*. New York: W. W. Norton.

Drinan, Robert F. 1980. "The Christian Response to the Holocaust." *Annals of the American Academy of Political and Social Science* 450: 179–189.

———. 2002. *The Mobilization of Shame: A World View of Human Rights*. New Haven, CT: Yale University Press.

Duran, Eduardo, and Bonnie Duran. 1995. *Native American Postcolonial Psychology*. Albany: State University of New York Press.

Dwyer, Devin. 2009. "Water Wars: Is Bottled Water Better Than Tap?" ABC News, July 8.

Easton, David. 1965. *A Framework for Political Analysis*. Englewood Cliffs, NJ: Prentice Hall.

Ebadi, Shirin. 2004. Speech at the 2004 World Social Forum, Mumbai, India, January 16.

Ebbe, O. N. 2006. "Domestic and International Trafficking in Human Beings: Sex and Body Part Trades." Paper presented at the annual meeting of the American Society of Criminology, Los Angeles, November 1.

*The Economist*. 2013. "The International Criminal Court on Screen: Ready for Its Close Up." June 24.

———. 2014. "The Lesson of Algeria." April 19.

Efron, Sonni. 2014. "Rise of Neo-Fascism: In Parts of Europe the Far Right Is Gaining Ground." *News Tribune* (Tacoma), May 11.

Egeland, Jan. 2008. *A Billion Lives: An Eyewitness Report from the Frontlines of Humanity*. New York: Simon and Schuster.

Eide, Asbjorn, Wenche Barthe Eide, Susantha Goonatilake, Joan Gussow, and Omawale, eds. 1984. *Food as a Human Right*. Tokyo: United Nations University Press.

Elman, Miriam Fendius. 1997. *Paths to Power: Is Democracy the Answer?* Cambridge, MA: MIT Press.

Elsea, Jennifer. 2008. "U.S. Policy Regarding the International Criminal Court." In *Law and Law Enforcement Issues*, edited by Gerald M. Kessler. New York: Nova Science Publishers.

Elshtain, Jean Bethke. 1987. *Women and War*. Chicago: University of Chicago Press.

Emerick, Yahiya. 2001. *The Complete Idiot's Guide to Understanding Islam*. Exton, PA: Alpha.

Englehart, Neil. 2009. "State Capacity, State Failure, and Human Rights." *Journal of Peace Research* 46, no. 2: 163–180.

Erman, Michael. 2008. "Watchdog Group Says Chevron Complicit in Myanmar," Reuters, April 29.

Ernst, Jasminka Z., Branka Vukicevic, Tatjana Jakulj, and Wilma Ilich. 2003. "Sarajevo Paradox: Survival Throughout History and Life After the Balkan War." *Intermarium* (Columbia University, East Central European Center) 6, no. 3: 1–15.

Ertuna, Can. 2011. "The Regime Is Overthrown, What Now?" *Huriyet Daily News*, February 15.

Esposito, John L., and John O. Voll. 2001. "Islam and Democracy." *Humanities* 22, no. 6 (November–December). www.neh.gov.

EU Agency for Fundamental Rights. 2010. "National Human Rights Institutions in the EU Member States: Strengthening the Fundamental Rights Architecture in the EU I." Luxembourg Publications Office, European Union, May 7.

European Concerted Research Action. 2004. "Memorandum of Understanding for the Implementation of a European Concerted Research Action Designated as COST A28 Human Rights, Peace and Security in EU Foreign Policy. www.timeshighereducation.co.uk/news/mou-for-the-implementation-of-a-european-concerted-research-action-human-rights-peace-and-security-in-eu-foreign-policy-link/188150.article.

European Court of Human Rights. 2014a. "Analysis of Statistics." March. www.echr.coe.int.

———. 2014b. *Statistics 2013*. www.echr.coe.int.

Evans, Gareth, and Mohamed Sahnoun. 2001. *The Responsibility to Protect: Report of the International Commission on Intervention and State Sovereignty.* Ottawa: International Development Research Centre.

Falk, Richard, Samuel S. Kim, and Saul H. Mendlovitz. 1991. *The United Nations and a Just World Order.* Boulder, CO: Westview.

Fanon, Frantz. 1952. *Black Skin, White Masks.* New York: Grove.

———. 1961. *Wretched of the Earth.* Paris: François Maspero.

FAO (Food and Agricultural Organization). 2013. "Women Feed the World." www.fao.org/docrep/x0262e/x0262e16.htm.

Farah, Joseph. 1997. "Cover-Up of China's Gender-cide." *WND Commentary.* September 29. www.wnd.com.

FBI (Federal Bureau of Investigation). 2005. *Supplementary Homicide Reports, 1976–2004.* Washington, DC: Federal Bureau of Investigation.

———. 2013. "2012 Hate Crime Statistics." http://gaylife.about.com.

Fink, Carole. 1995. "The League of Nations and the Minorities Question." *World Affairs* 157 (Spring): 197–205.

Finnemore, Martha. 1996. "Constructing Norms of Humanitarian Intervention." In *The Culture of National Security,* edited by Peter J. Katzenstein, pp. 153–185. New York: Columbia University Press.

Finnemore, Martha, and Kathryn Sikkink. 1998. "International Norm Dynamics and Political Change." *International Organization* 52, no. 4 (Autumn): 887–917.

Fischer, David Hackett. 2004. *Washington's Crossing.* Oxford: Oxford University Press.

Florida, Robert E. 2005. *The Buddhist Tradition.* Vol. 5 of *Human Rights and the World's Major Religions.* New York: Praeger.

Foer, Franklin. 1997. "War Crimes." *Slate,* July 20.

Forsythe, David. 2000. *Human Rights in International Relations.* New York: Cambridge University Press.

Francisco, Ronald A. 1996. "Coercion and Protest: An Empirical Test in Two Democratic States." *American Journal of Political Science* 40, no 4: 1179–1204.

Fraser, Nancy. 1990. "Rethinking the Public Sphere: A Contribution to the Critique of Actually Existing Democracy." *Social Text,* no. 25/26: 56–80.

Freedom House. 2014. "Freedom in the World 2014." www.freedomhouse.org.

———. 2012. "Methodology." *Freedom in the World 2012.* www.freedomhouse.org.

Freeman, Michael. 2004. "Human Rights and Force: Revisiting the Question of Intervention." Paper presented at the annual convention of the International Studies Association, Montreal, Canada, March 17–20.

Friedman, Milton. 1999. "Take It to the Limits: Milton Friedman on Libertarianism." Interview, February 10. www.uncommonknowledge.org.

Fund for Peace. 2014. "Failed States Index Scores 2012." www.fundforpeace.org.

Futures Without Violence. 2009. "The Facts on Domestic, Dating, and Sexual Violence." www.futureswithoutviolence.org.

Garrison, Ervan G. 1999. *A History of Engineering and Technology: Artful Methods.* Boca Raton, FL: CRC.

Gascoigne, Bamber. 2001. "History of Rwanda." In *History World.* www.historyworld.net/wrldhis/PlainTextHistories.asp?historyid=ad24.

Gatrell, Peter. 2001. *A Whole Empire Walking: Refugees in Russia During World War I.* Chicago: University of Chicago Press.

Gendercide Watch. 2013. "Case Study: Female Infanticide." www.gendercide.org.

George Mason University Sexual Assault Services. 2010. "Worldwide Sexual Assault Statistics." www2.gmu.edu.

Giddens, Anthony. 1991. *Modernity and Self-Identity: Self and Society in the Late-Modern Age.* Stanford, CA: Stanford University Press.

Gilley, Brian Joseph. 2006. *Becoming Two-Spirit: Gay Identity and Social Acceptance in Indian Country.* Lincoln: University of Nebraska Press.

Gilligan, Carol, and David A. Richards. 2009. *The Deepening Darkness: Patriarchy, Resistance, and Democracy's Future.* New York: Cambridge University Press.

Glassman, Ronald M. 1995. *The Middle Class and Democracy in Socio-Historical Perspective.* Boston: Brill Academic.

Gleick, Peter. 2000. *The World's Water.* Washington, DC: Island.

Gleick, Peter H., Gary Wolff, Elizabeth L. Chalecki, and Rachel Reyes. 2002. *The New Economy of Water: The Risks and Benefits of Globalization and Privatization of Fresh Water.* Oakland, CA: Pacific Institute.

Glennie, John. 2011. "NGOs Criticize World Bank's New Lending Plan for Poorer Countries." *The Guardian,* October 21.

Global Exchange. 2007. "Boycotts." www.thirdworldtraveler.com.

Goldhagen, Daniel Jonah. 1997. *Hitler's Willing Executioners.* New York: Random House.

Goodland, Robert. 1984. *Tribal Peoples and Economic Development: Human Ecologic Considerations.* Washington, DC: World Bank.

Goodliffe, Jay, and Darren G. Hawkins. 2006. "Explaining Commitment: States and the Convention Against Torture." *Journal of Politics* 68, no. 2: 358–371.

Goodwin, Matthew. 2013. "Europe and the Ongoing Challenge of Right-Wing Extremism." *World Politics Review,* January 22.

Gourevitch, Philip. 1999. *We Wish to Inform You That Tomorrow We Will Be Killed with Our Families.* New York: Picador.

Graham, Leah. 2008. "A Test of the Normative Transfer Thesis: Clarifying the Association Between Domestic and International Behaviors." Paper presented at the annual meeting of the Southern Political Science Association, New Orleans, January 9.

Greenberg, Karen J., and Joshua L. Dratel. 2005. *The Torture Papers: The Road to Abu Ghraib.* Cambridge: Cambridge University Press.

Greenhouse, Steven. 2013. "Obama to Suspend Trade Privileges with Bangladesh." *New York Times,* June 26.

Greenwald, Glenn. 2012. "America's Drone Sickness." Salon.com, April 19.

Greer, Jed, and Kavaljit Singh. 2000. "A Brief History of Transnational Corporations." CorpWatch. www.globalpolicy.org.

Grinde, Donald A., Jr., and Bruce E. Johansen. 1991. *Exemplar of Liberty: Native America and the Evolution of Democracy.* Berkeley: University of California Press.

Grossman, David. 1996. *On Killing.* Boston: Back Bay.

Grotius, Hugo. 2012 [1625]. *The Law of War and Peace.* Edited by Stephen C. Neff. Cambridge: Cambridge University Press.

Grumm, Christine. 2008. "Help Eliminate Poverty—Invest in Women: When a Woman Prospers, a Family Prospers." *Christian Science Monitor,* October 17.

Gurr, Ted Robert. 1970. *Why Men Rebel.* Princeton, NJ: Princeton University Press.

Gürün, Kamuran. 1985. *The Armenian File: The Myth of Innocence Exposed in 1985.* New York: Palgrave MacMillan.

Haas, Peter J. 2005. *The Jewish Tradition.* Vol. 1 of *Human Rights and the World's Major Religions.* New York: Praeger.

Habermas, Jürgen. 1984. *Reason and the Rationalization of Society.* Vol. 1 of *The Theory of Communicative Action.* Boston: Beacon.

Hafner-Burton, Emilie Marie, Edward Mansfield, and Jon C. Pevehouse. 2008. "Democratization and Human Rights Regimes." http://ssrn.com/1123771.

Hafner-Burton, Emilie M., and Kiyoteru Tsutsui. 2007. "Justice Lost! The Failure of International Human Rights Law to Matter Where Needed Most." *Journal of Peace Research* 44, no. 4: 407–442.

Handicap International. 2007. "International Day of Disabled People." www.handi cap-international.org.

Handwerk, Brian. 2003. "Can Islam and Democracy Coexist?" *National Geographic News,* October 24.

Harff, Barbara, and Ted Robert Gurr. 1988. "Toward Empirical Theory of Genocides and Politicides: Identification and Measurement of Cases Since 1945." *International Studies Quarterly* 32, no. 3 (September): 359–371.

———. 1994. *Ethnic Conflict in World Politics.* Boulder, CO: Westview Press.

Harris, Whitney R. 1954. *Tyranny on Trial: The Trial of the Major German War Criminals at the End of World War II at Nuremberg, Germany, 1945–1946.* Dallas: Southern Methodist University Press.

Hathaway, O. 2002. "Do Human Rights Treaties Make a Difference?" *Yale Law Journal* 111, no. 8: 1935–2042.

Hausmann, Ricardo, Laura D. Tyson, and Saadia Zahidi. 2012. *Global Gender Gap Report.* Geneva: World Economic Forum.

Hayes, J. P. 1988. "Divided Opinions on Sanctions Against South Africa." *World Economy* 11, no. 2: 267–280.

Hayner, Priscilla. 2001. *Unspeakable Truths: Transitional Justice and the Challenge of Truth Commissions.* Sussex, UK: Psychology Press.

*Herald Sun.* 2010. "Anti-Gay Pastor Screens Porn in Ugandan Church to Garner Support for Laws Dubbed 'Odious' by Barack Obama." February 18.

Hersh, Seymour M. 2004. *Chain of Command: The Road from 9/11 to Abu Ghraib.* New York: HarperCollins.

Hildebrandt, Timothy, Courtney Hillebrecht, Peter M. Holm, and Jon Pevehouse. 2013. "The Domestic Politics of Humanitarian Intervention: Public Opinion, Partisanship, and Ideology." *Foreign Policy Analysis* 9, no. 3: 243–266.

Hill, Cyrill D. 1924. "Citizenship of Married Women." *American Journal of International Law* 18, no. 4 (October): 720–736.

Hilpold, Peter. 2002. "Humanitarian Intervention: Is There a Need for a Legal Reappraisal?" *European Journal of International Law* 12: 437–467.

The History Place. 1997. "The Holocaust Timeline." www.historyplace.com.

———. 2008. "The Rape of Nanking 1937–1938 300,000 Deaths." www.history place.com.

———. 2010. "Nazis Burn Books in Germany." http://www.historyplace.com.

Hobson, John A. 1902. *Imperialism: A Study.* New York: James Pott and Co.

Hoge, Warren. 2004. "U.N. Threatens Sanctions Against Sudan." *New York Times,* September 18.

Holocaust Museum. 2008a. "Jewish Population of Europe in 1933: Population Date by Country." www.ushmm.org.

———. 2008b. "American Jewish Yearbook." www.jewishvirtuallibrary.org.

The Holocaust\Shoah Page. 1997. "Chronology of the Holocaust 1930–1945." http://frank.mtsu.edu.

Holzgrefe, J. L., and Robert O. Keohane, eds. 2003. *Humanitarian Intervention: Ethical, Legal, and Political Dilemmas.* Cambridge: Cambridge University Press.

Honig, Jan Wilhelm, and Norbert Both. 1997. *Srebrenica: Record of a War Crime.* New York: Penguin.

Horton, Scott. 2007. "Scott Horton on George Washington, for His Birthday." Brad DeLong, weblog, February 20. http://delong.typepad.com/sdj/2007/02/scott _horton_on.htm.

Hovannisian, Richard G. 1998. *Remembrance and Denial: The Case of the Armenian Genocide*. Detroit, MI: Wayne State University Press.

Howard, Rhoda E. 1993. "Cultural Absolutism and the Nostalgia for Community." *Human Rights Quarterly* 15, no. 2: 315–338.

Howard, Rhoda, and Jack Donnelly. 1986. "Human Dignity, Human Rights, and Political Regimes." *American Political Science Review* 80, no. 3 (September): 801–817.

Human Development Report. 2013. "Human Development Indicators and Thematic Tables: Statistical Tables from the 2013 Human Development Report." http:// hdr.undp.org.

Humanitarian News and Analysis. 2010. "Sierra Leone: 'Forced Marriage' Conviction a First." *IRIN*, January 13.

Human Rights Education Associates. 2008. "Sexual Orientation and Human Rights." www.hrea.org.

Human Rights Watch. 1997. "Bosnia-Herzegovina/The Unindicted: Reaping the Rewards of 'Ethnic Cleansing.'" www.hrw.org.

———. 2007. "2007 World Report: Cuba." www.hrw.org.

———. 2009. "Child Soldiers." www.hrw.org.

———. 2010. "US: Prevent Prison Rape." www.hrw.org.

———. 2013a. "World Report 2013." www.hrw.org.

———. 2013b. "World Report 2013: Challenges for Rights After Arab Spring." February 1. www.hrw.org

The Hunger Project. 2014. "Know Your World: Facts About Hunger and Poverty." www.thp.org.

Huth, Paul K., and Todd L. Allee. 2002. *The Democratic Peace and Territorial Conflict in the Twentieth Century*. Cambridge: Cambridge University Press.

IACHR (Inter-American Commission of Human Rights). 2011. "Report No. 80/11 case 12. 626 on merits of Jessica Lenahan (Gonzalez) et al." July 21.

ICC (International Criminal Court ). 2014. "About the Court." www.icc-cpi.int.

ICJ (International Court of Justice). 1993. "Application of the Convention on the Prevention and Punishment of the Crime of Genocide. Further Requests for the Indication of Provisional Measures, Separate Opinion of Judge Lauterpacht [1993]," ICJ Reports 440, paragraph 100 (September 13). The Hague, Netherlands: International Court of Justice.

ICTR (International Criminal Tribunal for Rwanda). 2014. "Status of Cases." www.unictr.org.

ICTY (International Criminal Tribunal for the Former Yugoslavia). 1999. "President Milosevic and Four Other Senior FRY Officials Indicted for Murder, Persecution and Deportation in Kosovo." Press release, May 27. www.icty.org.

———. 2010. Press Advisory. June 3. www.icty.org/sid/10413.

———. 2014. "The Cases." www.icty.org

Ignatieff, Michael. 1993. *Blood and Belonging: Journeys into the New Nationalism*. New York: Farrar, Straus and Giroux.

ILO (International Labour Organization). 1998. "Report of the Commission of Inquiry Appointed Under Article 26 of the Constitution of the International Labour Organization to Examine the Observance by Myanmar of the Forced Labour Convention, 1930." July. Document GB.267/16/2, GB.268/14/8, GB.268/15/1. Geneva: International Labour Organization.

———. 2013. "Complaints/Commissions of Inquiry." www.ilo.org.

———. 2014. "ILO Head Calls for Fair Migration Agenda." www.ilo.org.

Indian Residential Schools. 2008. "Truth and Reconciliation Commission." www .trc-cvr.ca.

Institute for Indigenous Sciences and Cultures. 2001. "The World Bank and the Prodepine Project: Towards an Ethnic Neoliberalism?" Editorial. *Boletin* 3, no. 25 (April). http://icci.nativeweb.org.

Inter-American Commission on Human Rights. 2013. "Precautionary Measures." www.cidh.org.

Inter-American Court of Human Rights. 2001. Barrios Altos Case (*Chumbipuma Aguirre et al. vs. Peru*), Series C No. 75 [2001] IACHR 5 (Judgment March 14).

International Food and Policy Research Institute. 2012. "The Challenge of Hunger." www.welthungerhilfe.de.

———. 2014. "Global Hunger Index: The Challenge of Hunger." www.ifpri.org.

International Labor Rights Forum. 2009. "Organizations Question Nestlé's Commitment to Fair Trade Cocoa." December 7. www.laborrights.org.

International Migrants Rights Watch Committee. 1999. "Feature Report: ILO Reviews Instruments on Protection of Migrant Workers Rights." Supplement to pilot issue of *Migrants Rights Bulletin*, October–November. www.migrants rights.org.

International Monetary Fund. 2014. "Report for Selected Countries and Subjects." *World Economic Outlook*, April.

International Organization for Migration. 2014. "Key Migration Terms." www.iom .int/cms/en/sites/iom/home/about-migration/key-migration-terms-1 .html#Migrant.

Inter Press Service. 2008. "Unchecked Arms Trade Fuelling Conflict, Poverty." October 9. http://www.ipsnews.net/2008/10/politics-unchecked-arms-trade -fuelling-conflict-poverty/.

Ispahani, Laleh. 2009. "Voting Rights and Human Rights: A Comparative Analysis of Criminal Disenfranchisement Laws." In *Criminal Disenfranchisement in an International Perspective,* edited by Alec Ewald and Brandon Rottinghaus, pp. 25–58. Cambridge: Cambridge University Press.

Itaborahy, Lucas Paoli. 2013. "State-Sponsored Homophobia: A World Survey of Laws Criminalising Same-Sex Sexual Acts Between Consenting Adults." *IGLA Annual Report.* www.igla.org.

Jackson, Helen Hunt. 1995 [1881]. *A Century of Dishonor.* Norman: University of Oklahoma Press.

Jackson, Robert. 2007. *Sovereignty: The Evolution of an Idea.* Cambridge, UK: Polity.

Jacobs, S., W. Thomas, and S. Lang, eds. 1997. *Two-Spirit People: Native American Gender Identity, Sexuality, and Spirituality.* Urbana: University of Illinois Press.

Jacobsen, Michael, and Ole Bruun, eds. 2000. *Human Rights and Asian Values: Contesting National Identities and Cultural Representations in Asia.* Surrey, UK: Curzon.

Jayantunge, Ruwan M. 2010. "Psychological Effects of Torture." *Sri Lankan Guardian*, February 15. www.srilankaguardian.org.

Jefferson, Thomas. 1782. "Notes on Virginia." http://etext.virginia.edu.

Johansen, Bruce E. 1982. *Forgotten Founders: How the American Indian Helped Shape Democracy.* Boston: Harvard Common.

Johansen, Bruce E., Donald A. Grinde, and Barbara A. Mann. 1998. *Debating Democracy: Native American Legacy of Freedom.* Sante Fe, NM: Clear Light.

Johnston, Ian. 2014. "Kidnapped Nigerian Girls 'Escape from Boko Haram Abductors.'" *The Independent,* July 16.

Jones, Ann. 2008. "Mass Rape in the Congo: A Crime Against Society." Truthout, December 24. www.truth-out.org.

Joyner, Christopher. 2005. *International Law in the 21st Century: Rules for Global Governance.* Landham, MD: Rowman and Littlefield.

Kagan, Robert. 2004. *Of Paradise and Power.* New York: Vintage.

Kahler, Miles. 2002. "Bretton Woods and Its Competitors: The Political Economy of Institutional Choice." In *Organizing the World Economy,* edited by David Andrews, Randall Henning, and Louis Pauly, pp. 38–59. Ithaca, NY: Cornell University Press.

Kaoma, Kapya. 2009. *Globalizing the Culture Wars: U.S. Conservatives, African Churches, and Homophobia.* Somerville, MA: Political Research Associates.

Karlekar, Malavika. 1995. "The Girl Child in India: Does She Have Any Rights?" *Canadian Woman Studies* 15, nos. 2–3: 55–57.

Kasinof, Laura. 2012. "Yemen Legislators Approve Immunity for the President." *New York Times,* January 21.

Keck, Margaret E., and Kathryn Sikkink. 1998. *Activists Beyond Borders: Advocacy Networks in International Politics.* Ithaca, NY: Cornell University Press.

Keen, Sam, Bill Jersey, and Jeffrey Friedman, producers. 1985. *Faces of the Enemy.* Video. Catticus Corporation. Berkeley, CA: Quest Productions.

Keene, David. 2008. "Making Famine in Sudan." Emergency Nutrition Network. www.ennonline.net.

Kegley, Charles J., Jr., and Shannon Blanton. 2014. *World Politics: Trend and Transformation.* New York: Wadsworth.

Keith L. 1999. "The United Nations International Covenant on Civil and Political Rights: Does It Make a Difference in Human Rights Behavior?" *Journal of Peace Research* 36, no. 1: 95–118.

Keohane, Robert, and Joseph Nye. 1977. *Power and Interdependence.* Boston: Little, Brown.

Keppler, Elise, Shirley Jean, and J. Paxton Marshall. 2008. "First Prosecution in the United States for Torture Committed Abroad: The Trial of Charles 'Chuckie' Taylor, Jr." *Human Rights Brief Volume* 15, no. 3: 18–23.

Kershaw, Stuart. 2006. *The Virgin Trade: Sex, Lies, and Trafficking.* In the Dark Productions. Distributed by Electric Sky.

Khadduri, Majid. 1984. *The Islamic Concept of Justice.* Baltimore, MD: Johns Hopkins University Press.

Khagram, Sanjeev. 2004. *Dams and Development: Transnational Struggles for Water and Power.* Ithaca, NY: Cornell University Press.

King, Martin Luther, Jr. 1990. *A Testament of Hope: The Essential Writings and Speeches of Martin Luther King, Jr.* San Francisco: Harper.

Kinoti, Kathambi. 2006. "The Nexus Between Women's Land Ownership Rights and Their Vulnerability to HIV Infection." Association for Women's Rights in Development, August. www.awid.org.

Kirk, Russell, and James McClellan, eds. 1967. *The Political Principles of Robert A. Taft.* New York: Fleet Press.

Kirkpatrick, Jeane. 1982. *Dictatorships and Double Standards: Rationalism and Reason in Politics.* New York: Simon and Schuster.

Klein, Melanie. 1975. *The Writings of Melanie Klein III: Envy and Gratitude and Other Works, 1946–1963.* New York: Free Press.

Klein, Robert A. 1974. *Sovereign Equality Among States: The History of an Idea.* Toronto: University of Toronto Press.

Kleinbach, Russell, Mehrigiut Ablezova, and Medine Aitieva. 2005. "Kidnapping for Marriage (ala kachuu) in a Kyrgyz Village." *Central Asian Survey* 6, no. 1: 191–202.

Klempner, Mark. 2006. *The Heart Has Reasons: Holocaust Rescuers and Their Stories of Courage.* New York: Pilgrim.

Klotz, Audie. 1995. *Norms in International Relations: The Struggle Against Apartheid.* Ithaca, NY: Cornell University Press.

Knell, Yolanda. 2013. "Reconsidering the Two-State Solution." BBC News, March 21.

Koh, Harold Hongju. 2008. "National Security, Human Rights, and the Rule of Law." www.americanprogressaction.org.

Koh, Tommy. 1993. "The 10 Values Which Undergird East Asian Strength and Success." *International Herald Tribune* (Paris), December 11–12.

Kowalewski, David. 1983. "Transnational Banks and the Trilateral Commission." *Journal of Cotemporary Asia* 13, no. 3: 303–313.

Krasner, Stephen, ed. 1983. *International Regimes.* Ithaca, NY: Cornell University Press.

———. 1999. *Sovereignty.* Princeton, NJ: Princeton University Press.

Kristof, Nicholas D., and Sheryl WuDunn. 2009. *Half the Sky: Turning Oppression into Opportunity for Women Worldwide.* New York: Alfred A. Knopf.

Krugman, Andrea. 1998. "Being Female Can Be Fatal: An Examination of India's Ban on Pre-Natal Gender Testing." *Cardozo Journal of International and Comparative Law* 6: 215–237.

Lacan, Jacques. 1977 [1953]. "The Function and Field of Speech and Language in Psychoanalysis." *Écrits: A Selection.* Translated by Alan Sheridan. London: Tavistock.

Lakhani, Avnita. 2005. "Bride-Burning: The 'Elephant in the Room' Is Out of Control." *Rutgers Conflict Resolution Law Journal* 3, no. 2 (Spring): 2–71.

Landes, Joan B. 1988. *Women and the Public Sphere in the Age of the French Revolution.* Ithaca, NY: Cornell University Press.

Landman, Todd. 2005. *Protecting Human Rights: A Comparative Study.* Washington, DC: Georgetown University Press.

Lee, Chris, Sandra Maline, and Will H. Moore. 2000. "Coercion and Protest: An Empirical Test Revisited." In *Paths to State Repression: Human Rights and Contentious Politics in Comparative Perspective,* edited by C. Davenport, pp. 127–147. Boulder: Rowman and Littlefield.

Lenin, Vladimir. 2010 [1916]. *Imperialism: The Highest Stage of Capitalism.* New York: Penguin Classics.

Leporini, Christopher M. 1998. "Affirmative Action: A Dialogue on Race, Gender, Equality and Law in America." *Affirmative Action in the Workplace* 13, no. 2 (Spring). www.americanbar.org.

Lewis, Jone Johnson. 2009. "Property Rights of Women." http://womenshistory .about.com.

Lichbach, Mark Irving, and Ted Robert Gurr. 1981. "The Conflict Process: A Formal Model. *Journal of Conflict Resolution* 25, no. 1: 3–29.

Lifton, Robert Jay. 1993. *The Protean Self: Human Resilience in an Age of Fragmentation.* New York: Basic Books.

Little, David. 2005. "Religion and Peacemaking: Human Rights, East and West." Washington, DC: US Institute for Peace.

Lora, Eduardo. 2006. *The State of State Reform*. Stanford, CA: Stanford Economics and Finance.

Lutz, Ellen L., and Caitlin Reiger, eds. 2009. *Prosecuting Heads of State*. Cambridge: Cambridge University Press.

Lynch, Owen, and Greg Maggio. 1997. "Human Rights, Environment, and Economic Development: Existing Emerging Standards in International Law and Global Society." www.ciel.org/Publications/olp3i.html.

Lyons, Scott. 2006. "The African Court on Human and Peoples' Rights." *American Society for International Law Insights* 10, no. 24 (September 19). www.asil.org.

Malik, Kenan. 1996. *The Meaning of Race: Race History and Culture in Western Society*. New York: New York University Press.

Malouf, Amin. 2012. *In the Name of Identity: Violence and the Need to Belong*. New York: Skyhorse Publishing.

Manik, Julfikar, and Jim Yardley. 2013. "Building Collapse in Bangladesh Leaves Scores Dead." *New York Times*, April 24.

Manirabona, Amissi M., and François Crépeau. 2012. "Enhancing the Implementation of Human Rights Treaties in Canadian Law: The Need for a National Monitoring Body." *Canadian Journal of Human Rights* 1, no 1: 25–59.

Manjoo, Rashida. 2012. "Summary Paper on the State Responsibility for Eliminating Violence Against Women." www.ohchr.org.

Mann, Charles C. 2005. *1491: New Revelations of the Americas Before Columbus*. New York: Knopf.

Mansfield, Edward D., and Jack Snyder. 2005. *Electing to Fight: Why Emerging Democracies Go to War*. Cambridge, MA: MIT Press.

Marcuse, Herbert. 1964. *One Dimensional Man*. Boston: Beacon.

Martin, Pam, and Franke Wilmer. 2008. "Transnational Normative Struggles and Globalization: The Case of Indigenous Peoples in Bolivia and Ecuador." *Globalizations* 5, no. 4: 583–598.

Martinez, Jennifer S. 2007. "Antislavery Courts and the Dawn of International Human Rights Law." *Yale Law Review*, no. 117 (Fall): 550–642.

Maslow, Abraham H. 1943. "A Theory of Human Motivation." *Psychological Review* 50: 370–396.

Masterson, James F. 1988. *The Search for the Real Self: Unmasking the Personality Disorders of Our Age*. New York: Collier Macmillan.

Matas, David, and David Kilgour. 2007. *Revised Report into Allegations of Organ Harvesting of Falun Gong Practitioners in China*. January 31. Ottawa: Coalition to Investigate the Persecution of the Falun Gong in China.

Mattei, Ugo. 1999. "Patterns of African Constitution in the Making." *Cardozo Law Bulletin*. www.jus.unitn.it.

May, Stephen. 2011. "Language Rights: The 'Cinderella' Human Right." *Journal of Human Rights* 10, no. 3: 265–289.

Mayer, Jane. 2008. *The Dark Side: The Inside Story of How the War on Terror Turned into a War on American Ideals*. New York: Doubleday.

Maynard, Douglas H. 1960. "The World's Anti-Slavery Convention of 1840." *Mississippi Valley Historical Review* 47, no. 3 (December): 452–471.

McGreal, Chris. 2006. "Hundreds of Thousands Raped in Congo Wars: Scale of Attacks Emerges as Fighting Decreases. Rights Groups Say Militias See It as Weapon of War." *The Guardian*, November 14.

Mearsheimer, John. 2011. "Imperial by Design." *The National Interest,* January–February.

Meijer, Cecile, and Amardeep Singh. 2001. "News from the International Criminal Tribunal." *Human Rights Brief* 8, no. 2: 1–27.

Menon, Meena. 2001. "Development-India: Poor Pay Social Costs of Big Dams Without Gain, Says Global Report." Paper presented at the World Social Forum, Porto Alegre, Brazil, January 25–30. www.ips.org/socialforum/0122/devindia.htm.

Metro. 2009. "UK Gender Pay Gap 'Among Europe's Highest.'" March 3. http://metro.co.uk.

Milgram, Stanley. 1963. "Behavioral Study of Obedience." *Journal of Abnormal and Social Psychology* 67: 371–378.

———. 1974. *Obedience to Authority: An Experimental View.* New York: Harper-Collins.

Millennium Project. 2010. "Goals, Targets, and Indicators." www.unmillennium project.org.

Miller, Marian L. 1995. *The Third World in Global Environmental Politics.* Boulder, CO: Lynne Rienner.

Minorities at Risk Project. 2008. "Minorities at Risk: Overview." www.cidcm.umd.edu.

Mohawk, John. 1977. *Basic Call to Consciousness.* Akwesasne, NY: Akwesasne Notes.

———. 1997. "The Myth of Progress." Public lecture, City University of New York, March 16.

Moore, Barrington. 1966. *The Social Origins of Dictatorship and Democracy: Lord and Peasant in the Making of the Modern World.* Boston: Beacon.

Moore, Henrietta L. 1988. *Feminist Anthropology.* Minneapolis: University of Minnesota Press.

Morris, Roy, Jr. 1991. *Sheridan: The Life and Wars of General Phil Sheridan.* New York: Crown Publishing.

Morsnik, Johannes. 2009. *Inherent Human Rights: Philosophical Roots of the Universal Declaration.* Philadelphia: University of Pennsylvania Press.

Mowbray, Alastair. 2004. *The Development of Positive Obligations Under the European Convention on Human Rights by the European Court of Human Rights.* Oxford: Hart.

Moxon-Browne, Edward. 1991. "National Identity in Northern Ireland." In *Social Attitudes in Northern Ireland: The First Report,* edited by Peter Stringer and Gillian Robinson, pp. 23–30. Belfast: Blackstrap Press.

Murphy, Evelyn F. 2006. *Getting Even: Why Women Don't Get Paid Like Men—And What to Do About It.* New York: Touchstone.

Nationmaster. 2010. "Education Statistics." www.nationmaster.com.

Neumayer, Eric. 2003a. "Is Respect for Human Rights Rewarded? An Analysis of Total Bilateral and Multilateral Aid Flows." *Human Rights Quarterly* 25, no. 2: 510–527.

———. 2003b. "Do Human Rights Matter in Bilateral Aid Allocation? A Quantitative Analysis of 21 Donor Countries." *Social Science Quarterly* 84, no. 3: 650–666.

———. 2007. "Qualified Ratification: Explaining Reservations to International Human Rights Treaties." *Journal of Legal Studies* 36, no. 2: 397–430.

———. 2008. "Death Penalty: The Political Foundations of the Global Trend Toward Abolition." *Human Rights Review* 9, no. 2: 241–268.

Newland, Kathleen. 2002. "Refugee Resettlement in Transition." Migration Policy Institute. www.migrationinformation.org.

*New York Times.* 1915a. "800,000 Armenians Counted Destroyed." October 7.

———. 1915b. "Million Armenians Killed or in Exile." December 15.

Nijman, Janne Elisabeth. 2004. *The Concept of Legal Personality: An Inquiry into the History and Theory of International Law.* The Hague, Netherlands: T.M.C. Asser.

Nobel Peace Prize. n.d. "Alfred Nobel's Will." Norwegian Nobel Committee. www.nobelpeaceprize.org.

Norris, Pippa, and Ronald Ingelhart. 2004. *Sacred and Secular: Religion and Politics Worldwide.* Cambridge: Cambridge University Press.

Novak, Michael, and Jana Novak. 2006. *Washington's God: Religion, Liberty, and the Father of Our Country.* New York: Basic Books.

NSRV (National Sexual Violence Resource Center). 2014. "Worldwide Sexual Assault Statistics." www.nsvrc.org/publications/fact-sheets/worldwide-sexual-assault-statistics.

OHCHR (Office of the UN High Commissioner for Human Rights). 2008. "Human Rights Bodies." www.ohchr.org/EN/HRBodies/Pages/HumanRightsBodies.aspx.

———. 2010. "Business and Human Rights." www.ohchr.org/EN/Issues/Business/Pages/BusinessIndex.aspx.

Oleinik, Anton, ed. 2008. *Reforming the State Without Changing the Model of Power? On Administrative Reform in Post-Socialist Countries.* New York: Routledge.

One Campaign. 2008. "Debt, AIDS, Trade, Africa: The Data Report 2008." www.one.org/us/policy/data-report-2008/.

Onishe, Norimitsu. 2007. "Decades After War Trials, Japan Still Honors a Dissenting Judge." *New York Times,* August 31.

Osborne, Hannah. 2014. "Climate Change Water Shortage Threatens US and Mediterranean Countries." *International Business Times,* January 2.

Ouguergouz, Fatsah. 2003. *The African Charter of Human and People's Rights: A Comprehensive Agenda for Human Dignity and Sustainable Democracy in Africa.* Amsterdam: Martinus Nijhoff.

Owen, John M., IV. 2005. "Iraq and the Democratic Peace: Who Says Democracies Don't Fight?" *Foreign Affairs* 84, no. 6 (November–December): 122–127.

Oxfam. 2007. "Africa's Missing Billions." Briefing Paper 107. www.oxfam.org.

Pacific Institute. 2008. "The World's Water." www.worldwater.org.

Pahlow, Markus, and Mesfin M. Mekonnen. 2012. "Using the Water Footprint as a Tool for Sustainable Appropriation of Freshwater Resources." Johns Hopkins Water Institute, November 20. http://globalwater.jhu.edu.

Paludi, Michele A. 2010. *Feminism and Women's Rights Worldwide.* Santa Barbara, CA: Praeger.

Pateman, Carole. 1988. *The Sexual Contract.* Palo Alto, CA: Stanford University Press.

Patrick, Erin. 2004. "The U.S. Refugee Resettlement Program." Washington, DC: Migration Policy Institute.

Pearlstein, Deborah. 2008. "Testimony Before Congress." *Bill Moyers Journal,* PBS. July 25.

Peterson, V. Spike. 1992. *Gendered States: (Re)Visions of International Relations Theory.* Boulder, CO: Lynne Rienner.

———. 2003. *A Critical Rewriting of Global Political Economy: Integrating Reproductive, Productive and Virtual Economies.* London: Routledge.

Peterson, V. Spike, and Anne Sisson Runyan. 1993. *Global Gender Issues.* Boulder, CO: Westview Press.

Philpott, Daniel. 2001. *Revolutions in Sovereignty: How Ideas Shaped Modern International Relations*. Princeton, NJ: Princeton University Press.

Plitnick, Michael. 2014. "Poll Shows Diminishing Support for Two-State Solution." Inter-Press Service, June 9.

Poe, Steven C. 1992. "Human Rights and Economic Aid Allocation Under Ronald Reagan and Jimmy Carter." *American Journal of Political Science* 36, no. 1: 147–167.

Poe, Steven C., and Rangsima Sirirangsi. 1993. "Human Rights and US Economic Aid to Africa." *International Interactions* 18, no. 4: 309–322.

Poe, Steven C., and C. Neal Tate. 1994. "Repression of Human Rights to Personal Integrity in the 1980s: A Global Analysis. *American Political Science Reivew* 88, no. 4: 853–872.

Poe, Steven, C. Neal Tate, and Linda Camp Keith. 1999. "Repression of the Human Right to Personal Integrity Revisited: A Global Cross-National Study Covering the Years 1976–1993." *International Studies Quarterly* 43, no. 2: 291–313.

Polaris Project. 2010. "Human Trafficking Statistics." National Human Trafficking Resource Center. www.polarisproject.org.

Policy Coherence for Development. 2008. "Impact of CAP Reform on Sub-Saharan African Case Study Countries." Trinity College Dublin. www.tcd.ie/iiis/policy coherence.

Posner, Andrew. 2008. "Pop Quiz: Water Consumption in the U.S." March 13. www.treehugger.com/culture/pop-quiz-water-consumption-in-the-us.html.

Postel, S. L., G. C. Daily, and P. R. Ehrlich. 1996. "Human Appropriation of Renewable Fresh Water." *Science* 271: 785.

Potobsky, Geraldo von. 1998. *Freedom of Association: The Impact of Convention No. 87 and ILO Action*. Washington, DC: International Labour Organization.

Power, Samantha. 2002. *The Problem from Hell: America and the Age of Genocide*. New York: HarperCollins.

Power, Samantha, and Graham Allison. 2000. *Realizing Human Rights*. New York: Cambridge University Press.

Pratap, Anita. 1995. "Killed by Greed and Oppression." *Time*, September 11.

Prunier, Gerard. 2005. *Darfur: The Ambiguous Genocide*. New York: Hurst.

Radelet, Michael L., Hugo Adam Bedau, and Constance E. Putnam. 1992. *In Spite of Innocence*. Boston: Northeastern University Press.

Ralph, Regan E. 2000. "Testimony Before the Senate Committee on Foreign Relations Subcommittee on Near Eastern and South Asian Affairs." February 22. www.hrw.org/legacy/backgrounder/wrd/trafficking.htm.

Rasheed, Kameelah. 2008. "A Critical Review of the World Social Forum." Global Policy Forum, January 17. www.globalpolicy.org.

Ray, James Lee. 1995. *Democracy and International Conflict: An Evaluation of the Democratic Peace Proposition*. Columbia: University of South Carolina Press.

Raymont, Peter. 2002. *Shake Hands with the Devil: The Journey of Romeo Dallaire*. DVD. Directed by Peter Raymont. Toronto: Investigative Productions, Inc.

Read, Richard. 2008. "Nike's Focus on Keeping Costs Low Causes Poor Working Conditions, Critics Say." *Oregon Business News*, August 5.

Reinhardt, Uwe E., Peter S. Hussey, and Gerard F. Anderson. 2004. "U.S. Health Care Spending in An International Context: Why Is U.S. Spending So High, and Can We Afford It?" *Health Affairs* 23, no. 3: 10–25.

Reiter, Rayna R., ed. 1975. *Toward an Anthropology of Women*. New York: Monthly Review.

Renan, Ernest. 1990. "What Is a Nation?" In *Nation and Narration*, edited by Homi Bhabha, pp. 8–22. New York: Routledge.

Reuters. 2008. "Food Summit Draws Up Plan to Eliminate Hunger." Reuters, June 3.

———. 2013. "Turkey's Secularists Alarmed over the Rise of 'Islamic Moralism.'" *Jerusalem Post*, November 18.

Reymond, Laura, Asha Mohamud, and Nancy Ali. 2010. "Female Genital Mutilation—The Facts." www.path.org.

Risse, Thomas, Stephen Ropp, and Kathryn Sikkink, eds. 1999. *The Power of Principles: International Human Rights Norms and Domestic Change*. Cambridge: Cambridge University Press.

Ritenauer, Chase. 2009. "The Clinton Administration and the Rwandan Genocide: Analyses of Calculated Inaction from Realist and Neo-Liberal Perspectives." Paper presented at the annual meeting of the Midwest Political Science Association, Chicago, April 2.

Robinson, B. A. 2009. "The Roma: Their History, Names, and Ancient Persecution." Ontario Consultants on Religious Tolerance, August 29. www.religious tolerance.org.

Robinson, Fiona. 2006. "Care, Gender, and Global Social Justice: Rethinking 'Ethical Globalization.'" *Journal of Global Ethics* 2, no. 1: 5–25.

Roggio, Bill. 2013. "Female Suicide Bomber Kills 4 Outside Pakistani Hospital." *Threat Matrix*, April 21.

Romany, Celina. 1993. "Women as Aliens: A Feminist Critique of the Public/Private Distinction in International Human Rights Law." *Harvard Human Rights Journal* 6: 87–259.

Rosandić, Rosa, and Vesna Pešić. 1994. *Warfare, Patriotism, and Patriarchy: An Analysis of Elementary School Textbooks*. Belgrade, Yugoslavia: Centre for Antiwar Action.

Roscoe, Will. 1991. *The Zuni Man-Woman*. Albuquerque: University of New Mexico Press.

Rosenau, James. 1990. *Turbulence in World Politics: A Theory of Change and Continuity*. Princeton, NJ: Princeton University Press.

Roy, Arundhati. 1999. *The Cost of Living*. New York: Modern Library.

———. 2002. *Power Politics*. Cambridge, MA: South End.

———. 2004. *The Ordinary Person's Guide to Empire*. Minneapolis, MN: Consortium.

Royal, Robert. 1992. *1492 and All That: Political Manipulations of History*. Washington, DC: Ethics and Public Policy Center.

Rozenberg, Joshua. 2013. "Never Mind Human Rights Law, EU Law Is Much More Powerful." *The Guardian*, October 9.

Rude-Antoine, Edwige. 2005. *Forced Marriages in Council of Europe Member States*. Strasbourg, France: Directorate of Council of Europe.

Rummel, R. J. 1992. *Democide: Nazi Genocide and Mass Murder*. New Brunswick, NJ: Transaction.

Rusbridger, Alan, and Ewen MacAskill. 2014. "Edward Snowden Interview: The Edited Transcript." *The Guardian*, July 18.

Sachs, Jeffrey. 2005a. *The End of Poverty: Economic Possibilities for Our Time*. New York: Penguin.

———. 2005b. *Investing in Development: A Practical Plan to Achieve the Millennium Development Goals*. New York: United Nations.

Said, Abdul Aziz. 1979. "Precept and Practice of Human Rights in Islam" *Universal Human Rights* 1, no. 1 (January–March): 63–79.

Said, Edward. 1977. *Orientalism*. London: Penguin Press.

Salina, Irena, director. 2008. *Flow: For Love of Water*. DVD. Produced by Steven Starr, Gill Holland, and Yvette Tomlinson. Distributed by Oscilloscope Laboratories, New York.

Salmon, Marylynn. 1986. *Women and the Law of Property in Early America*. Chapel Hill: University of North Carolina Press.

Samson, Kevin. 2013. "The Privatization of Water: Nestlé Denies That Water Is a Fundamental Human Right." Global Research, December 14. www.global research.ca.

Samuelson, Paul. 1954. "The Pure Theory of Public Expenditure." *Review of Economics and Statistics* 36, no. 4 (November): 387–389.

*San Francisco Sentinel*. 2014. "Chevron Ecuador Lawsuit Blows Up for Amazon Defense Coalition—Watergate-Tyle Scandal over Faked Data Derails Amazon Pollution Lawsuit." October 29.

Sarfaty, Galit. 2005. "The World Bank and the Internalization of Indigenous Rights Norms." *Yale Law Journal* 114, no. 7 (May): 179–208.

Sato, Masayuki. 2003. *Confucian Quest for Order: The Origin and Formation of the Political Thought of Xun Zi*. New York: Brill.

Savage, Charlie. 2013. "Drone Strikes Turn Allies into Enemies." *New York Times*, April 23.

Savewater! 2010. "Global Water Situation." http://savewater.com.

Schellstede, Sangmie Choi. 2000. *Comfort Women Speak: Testimony by Sex Slaves of the Japanese Military*. New York: Holmes and Meier.

Schiller, Herbert. 1976. *Communication and Cultural Domination*. White Plains, NY: International Arts and Sciences.

Scott, Earl. 1984. *Life Before the Drought*. Boston: Unwin Hyman.

Searle, John. 1995. *Construction of Social Reality*. New York: Free Press.

Segal, Hanna. 1981. *The Work of Hanna Segal: A Kleinian Approach to Clinical Practice*. Northvale, NJ: Aronson.

Segal, Ronald. 2001. *Islam's Black Slaves: The Other Black Diaspora*. New York: Farrar, Straus and Giroux.

Sen, Amartya. 1990. "More than 100 Million Women Are Missing." *New York Review of Books* 37, no. 20 (December 20).

———. 1997. "Human Rights and Asian Values." Sixteenth Annual Morgenthau Memorial Lecture on Ethics and Foreign Policy on May 25, 1997. Washington, DC: Carnegie Council.

Shah, Anup. 2013. "Poverty Facts and Stats." www.globalissues.org.

Shah, Sudhir. 2008. "Dowry & The Law." http://sudhirlaw.com/qhEyy146vb/articles/dowry-the-law.

Shawcross, William. 1985. *The Quality of Mercy: Cambodia, Holocaust and Modern Conscience*. New York: Touchstone.

Shue, Henry. 1980. *Basic Rights: Subsistence, Affluence, and U.S. Foreign Policy*. Princeton NJ: Princeton University Press.

Shultz, Jim. 2008. "The Cochabamba Water Revolt and Its Aftermath." In *Dignity and Defiance: Stories from Bolivia's Challenge to Globalization*, edited by Jim Shultz and Melissa Draper. Berkeley: University of California Press.

SIL International. 2014. "Women and Literacy." www.sil.org.

Silver, Steven, director. 2002. *The Last Just Man*. DVD. Ontario: Bara Alper Productions.

Simmons, Beth A. 2009. *Mobilizing Human Rights: International Law in Domestic Politics*. Cambridge: Cambridge University Press.

Simons, Marlise. 1999. "Crisis in the Balkans: World Court; Yugoslavia Seeks a Legal Order to Halt the NATO Bombing." *New York Times*, May 12.

Sitaraman, Srini. 2009. *State Participation in International Treaty Regimes*. Burlington, VT: Ashgate.

Smith, Anthony. 1991. *National Identity*. London: Penguin.

Smith-Cannoy, Heather. 2012. *Insincere Commitments: Human Rights Treaties, Abusive States and Citizen Activism*. Washington, DC: Georgetown University Press.

Smith, David. 2014. "Nigeria's Boko Haram Seizes Hometown of Kidnapped Girls." *The Guardian,* November 14.

Snipp, Matthew. 1986. "The Changing Economic and Political Status of the American Indian: From Captive Nations to Internal Colonies." *American Journal of Economics and Sociology* (April): 145–157.

Snyder, David, and Charles Tilly. 1972. "Hardship and Collective Violence in France 1830–1960." *American Sociological Review* 87, no. 5: 520–532.

Solis, Gary. 2010. *The Law of Armed Conflict: International Humanitarian Law in War*. New York: Cambridge University Press.

Solomon, Hussein. 1997. "Some Reflections on the Crisis in Zaire." Regional Security, Occasional Paper no. 15, February. Addis Ababa, Ethopia: Institute for Security Studies.

Spender, Dale. 1981. *Men's Studies Modified: The Impact of Feminism on Academic Disciplines*. New York: Pergamon Press.

Stannard, David E. 1992. *American Holocaust: The Conquest of the New World*. Oxford: Oxford University Press.

Stea, Carla. 2013. "Syria: UN Mission Report Confirms That 'Opposition' Rebels Used Chemical Weapons Against Civilians and Government Forces." *Global Research*, December 31.

Steiner, N. D. 2014. "Testing for a Political Bias in Freedom House: Are U.S. Friendly States Judged to Be More Democratic?" *Journal of Comparative Policy Analysis* (May): 1–21.

Stephens, John, and Robyn McCallum. 1998. *Retelling Stories, Framing Culture: Traditional Story and Metanarratives in Children's Literature*. New York: Routledge.

Stiglmayer, Alexandra. 1994. *Mass Rape: The War Against Women in Bosnia-Herzegovina*. Lincoln: University of Nebraska Press.

Stockholm International Peace Research Institute. 2010. *SIPRI Yearbook 2009*. Stockholm: Stockholm International Peace Research Institute.

Stork, Joe. 1999. "Human Rights and U.S. Policy." *Human Rights Watch Policy in Focus* 4, no. 8 (March).

*St. Petersburg Times*. 2006. "Darfur: A Chronology of the Crisis." May 10.

Streeter, April. 2009. "We Use How Much Water? Scary Water Footprints, Country by Country." Treehugger, June 24. www.treehugger.com.

Studer, Brigitte. 2002. "Citizenship as Contingent National Belonging: Married Women and Foreigners in Twentieth-Century Switzerland." *Gender and History* 13, no. 3: 622–654.

Taylor, Ronald L. 2008. "The Changing Meaning of Race in the Social Sciences: Some Implications for Research and Policy." Keynote address at Statewide Meeting on Health Disparities, Hartford, CT, September 19.

Tesón, Fernando R. 1984. "International Human Rights and Cultural Relativism." *Virginia Journal of International Law* 25, no. 4: 869–898.

Thomas, Dorothy Q., and Michelle E. Beasley. 1993. "Domestic Violence as a Human Rights Issue." *Human Rights Quarterly* 15, no. 1 (February): 36–62.

Thornton, Russell. 1987. *American Indian Holocaust and Survival: A Population History Since 1492*. Norman: University of Oklahoma Press.

Tilly, Charles. 2002. *Stories, Identities and Political Change*. Lanham, MD: Rowman and Littlefield.

*Time*. 1966. "Sanctions Against Rhodesia." Time/CNN Online, December 23.

Tostan. 2010. "Abandoning Female Genital Cutting." http://tostan.org.

Totten, Samuel, ed. 2004. *Century of Genocide*. New York: Routledge.

Tran, Mark. 2011. "World Bank Suspends New Lending to Cambodia over Eviction of Landowners." *The Guardian*, August 10.

Treakle, Kay. 1998. "The World Bank's Indigenous Policy." NACLA Report on the Americas, April 18. www.hartford-hwp.com.

Treaty Database Online. 2006. "Treaty Categories." Trade and Global Governance, Institute for Agriculture and Trade Policy. www.iatp.org.

Twahirwa, Amiable. 2007. "Death Penalty—Rwanda: Abolition Spurs Quest for Justice." Inter-Press Service News Agency, September 6. www.ipsnews.net /2007/08/death-penalty-rwanda-abolition-spurs-quest-for-justice.

Ulgen, Fatma. 2010. "Reading Mustafa Kemal Ataturk on the Armenian Genocide of 1915." *Patterns of Prejudice* 44, no. 4: 369–391.

Umozurike, Oji. 1997. *The African Charter on Human and Peoples' Rights*. Boston: Brill Academic.

UNAIDS. 2012. "HIV Treatment Now Reaching More Than 6 Million People in Sub-Saharan Africa." www.unaids.org/en/resources/presscentre/pressrelease andstatementarchive/2012/july/20120706prafricatreatment.

———. 2013. "Global Report." www.unaids.org/en/media/unaids/contentassets /documents/epidemiology/2013/gr2013/UNAIDS_Global_Report_2013_en.pd.

UN Department of Economic and Social Affairs. 2010. *The World's Women 2010*. New York: United Nations.

UN Department of Economic and Social Affairs, Population Division. 2014. "Population Facts." http://esa.un.org/unmigration/documents/The_number_of _international_migrants.pdf.

UN Development Fund for Women. 2010. "Violence Against Women—Facts and Figures." www.unifem.org/attachments/gender_issues/violence_against_women /facts_figures_violence_against_women_2007.pdf.

UNESCO (UN Educational, Scientific, and Cultural Organization). 2005a. "Migration—Glossary—Migrant." Food for Thought, Thought for Action. http:// portal.unesco.org/shs/en/ev.php-URL_ID=3020&URL_DO=DO_TOPIC &URL_SECTION=201.html.

———. 2005b. "Trafficking Project." www.unescobkk.org/fileadmin/user_upload /culture/Trafficking/project/Graph_Worldwide_Sept_2004.pdf.

UNHCR (UN High Commissioner for Refugees). 2008a. *Global Trends: Refugees, Asylum-Seekers, Returnees, Internally Displaced and Stateless Persons*. June. New York: United Nations.

———. 2008b. "The 1951 Refugee Convention: Questions and Answers." www.unhcr.org/basics/BASICS/3c0f495f4.pdf.

———. 2012. "FAQ About Resettlement." www.unhcr.org/4ac0873d6.pdf.

———. 2013. "Mid-Year Trends 2013." http://unhcr.org/52af08d26.html.

———. 2014. "Facts and Figures About Refugees." www.unhcr.org.uk/about-us /key-facts-and-figures.html.

UN Human Rights Council. 2014. "Report of the Special Rapporteur on Extrajudicial, Summary or Arbitrary Executions, Christof Hayns." A/HRC/26/36, April 1. New York: United Nations.

UNICEF (UN Children's Fund). 2006. "State of the World's Children, 2005." January. New York: United Nations.

———. 2008a. "Child Protection from Violence, Exploitation and Abuse." www .unicef.org/protection/index_childlabour.html.

————. 2008b. "State of the World's Children 2008—Child Survival." January. www.unicef.org.

————. 2008c. "War Hits Home When It Hits Women and Girls." www.unicef .org/graca/women.htm.

————. 2013. "Child Protection from Violence, Exploitation and Abuse: Child Labour." www.unicef.org

————. 2014. "Goal: Reduce Child Mortality." www.unicef.org/mdg/childmortality .html.

United Church of Canada. 1998. "United Church Apologizes to First Nations Peoples." www.united-church.ca/aboriginal/relationships/apologies.

United Nations. 1999. *UNGA Res. 52/135. Report of the Group of Experts for Cambodia Established Pursuant to General Assembly Resolution 52/135.* New York: United Nations.

————. 2005. "International Migration Facts and Figures." www.un.org/esa /population/migration/hld/Text/Migration_factsheet.pdf.

————. 2007. "Millennium Development Goals Report 2006." www.un.org /millenniumgoals/pdf/MDGReport2006.pdf.

————. 2008a. "United Nations Transitional Authority in Cambodia: Background (Summary)." www.un.org/Depts/dpko/dpko/co_mission/untacbackgr1.html.

————. 2008b. "Women at a Glance." www.un.org/ecosocdev/geninfo/women /women96.htm.

————. 2013a. "2013: International Year of Water Cooperation." www.unwater.org /water-cooperation-2013/water-cooperation/facts-and-figures/en/.

————. 2013b. "Burden of Unpaid Work Must Be Valued, Formal Sectors Opened to Women, Delegates Urge as Second Committee Takes Up Poverty Reduction." Press release, October 17. www.un.org/press/en/2013/gaef3372.doc.htm.

————. 2014a. "Millennium Development Goals 2014." www.un.org/millennium goals/2014%20MDG%20report/MDG%202014%20English%20web.pdf.

————. 2014b. *Millennium Goals Report 2013.* New York: United Nations.

UN News Center. 2004. "World Court Says It Has No Jurisdiction in Serbia and Montenegro Case Against NATO Members." December 15. www.mail -archive.com/news@antic.org/msg06840.html.

————. 2010. "Better Sanitation Is a Matter of Basic Human Dignity, UN Expert Says." www.un.org.

UN Security Council. 2013. "Reports of the Security Council Missions." www .un.org/en/sc/documents/missions/.

UN Women. 2014. "Facts and Figures: Ending Violence Against Women." www .unwomen.org/en/what-we-do/ending-violence-against-women/facts-and-figures.

*USA Today.* 2007. "U.S. Doesn't Sign U.N. Ban on Forced Disappearances." June 6.

————. 2012. "U.N.: 2.4 Million Human Trafficking Victims." April 4.

————. 2013. "Libyan Militias Promise Wealth in an Unstable Nation." March 13.

US Department of Justice. 1998. *Violence by Intimates: Analysis of Data on Crimes by Current or Former Spouses, Boyfriends, and Girlfriends.* Washington, DC: US Department of Justice, 1998.

US Department of State. 1994. "Disaster Relief for Rwandan Refugees and Displaced Persons." Unclassified memorandum from Francis Cook, Deputy Assistant Secretary, Bureau of Political-Military Affairs, Department of State, to Greg Touma, Director of Logistics and Operations, Department of Defense.

————. 2007. *Facts About Child Sex Tourism.* March 15. Washington, DC: US Department of State.

———. 2008. *Trafficking in Persons Report 2008*. Washington, DC: US Department of State.

———. 2013. *Human Trafficking Defined*. Washington, DC: US Department of State.

———. 2014. *Trafficking in Persons Report 2014*. Washington, DC: US Department of State.

US Energy Information Center. 2008. *Annual Energy Outlook 2008*. Washington, DC: US Energy Information Administration.

van Maarseveen, Henc, and Ger van der Tang. 1978. *Written Constitutions: A Computerized Comparative Study*. New York: Oceana.

Velasquez, Manuel G. 2002. *Business Ethics: Concepts and Cases*. Upper Saddle River, NJ: Prentice Hall.

Vernon, Raymond. 1968. "Economic Sovereignty at Bay." *Foreign Affairs* 47, no. 1: 110–122.

Vilayet Adana. 1909. "30,000 Killed in Massacres." *New York Times*, April 25.

von Glahn, Gerhard. 2012. *Law Among Nations: An Introduction to Public International Law*. 10th ed. Boston: Pearson Publishing.

Vries, Lauren. 2009. "Islam: Governing Under Sharia." Council on Foreign Relations, March 23. www.cfr.org.

Vulliamy, Ed. 1994. *Seasons in Hell*. New London: St. Martin's.

Wæver, Ole, Barry Buzan, and Jaape de Wilde. 1998. *Security: A New Framework for Analysis*. Boulder, CO: Lynne Rienner.

Wafula, Evans. 2008. "Killers Operate Like the Interahamwe." *Africa News*, January 30.

Wallerstein, Immanuel. 1974. *The Modern World-System I: Capitalist Agriculture and the Origins of the European World-Economy in the Sixteenth Century*. New York: Academic Press.

———. 1980. *The Modern World-System II: Mercantilism and the Consolidation of the European World-Economy, 1600–1750*. Cambridge: MIT Press.

———. 1995. *After Liberalism*. New York: New Press.

———. 2004. *World-System Analysis: An Introduction*. Chapel Hill, NC: Duke University Press.

———. 2007. "The After-Globalists' Hit Their Stride." *Civil Society Observer* 4, no. 1 (January–February).

———. 2013. "Upsurge in Movements Around the Globe: 1958 Redux?" Video lecture online. www.iwallerstein.com/upsurge-movements-globe-1968-redux /#more-1417.

Waltz, Susan. 2001. "Universalizing Human Rights: The Role of Small States in the Construction of the Universal Declaration of Human Rights." *Human Rights Quarterly* 23: 44–72.

———. 2004. "Universal Human Rights: The Contribution of Muslim States." *Human Rights Quarterly* 26: 799–844.

Walzer, Michael. 1977. *Just and Unjust Wars: A Moral Argument with Historical Illustrations*. New York: Basic Books.

Water Footprint. 2012. "Water Footprint: Introduction." www.waterfootprint.org.

Water for Life. 2010. "Fact Sheet on Water and Sanitation." www.un.org.

Water.org. 2012. "Data from the U.S. Geological Survey and the World Resources Institute." www.water.org/waterpartners.aspx?pgID=916#Ref_6.

———. 2014. "Water Facts." http://water.org/water-crisis/water-facts/water/.

Weart, Spencer R. 1998. *Never at War: Why Democracies Will Never Fight One Another*. New Haven, CT: Yale University Press.

Weber, Cynthia. 1994. *Simulating Sovereignty: Intervention, the State, and Symbolic Exchange.* Cambridge: Cambridge University Press.

Weiniger, Gabriella. 2012. "Poll: Majority of Israelis Prefer Two-State Solution." *Jerusalem Post,* December 18.

Welch, Matt. 2007. "The Politics of Saying 'Genocide.'" *Los Angeles Times,* April 22.

Welsh, Jennifer, ed. 2004. *Humanitarian Intervention and International Relations.* Oxford: Oxford University Press.

Wendt, Alexander E. 1987. "The Agent-Structure Problem in International Relations Theory." *International Organization* 41, no. 3 (Summer): 335–370.

———. 1999. *Social Theory of International Politics.* Cambridge: Cambridge University Press.

Western, Jon. 2009. "Humanitarian Intervention, American Public Opinion, and the Future of R2P." *Global Responsibility to Protect* 1, no. 3 (June): 324–345.

Wheeler, Nicholas. 2001. *Saving Strangers: Humanitarian Intervention in International Society.* Oxford: Oxford University Press.

WHO (World Health Organization). 2000. "World Health Organization Assesses World's Health Systems." Press release, June 21. www.who.int/whr.

———. 2007. "Summary Report: WHO Multi-Country Study on Women's Health and Domestic Violence Against Women." www.who.int/gender/violence/who _multicountry_study/summary_report/summary_report_English2.pdf.

———. 2008. "10 Facts on Preventing Disease Through Healthy Environments." www.who.int/features/factfiles/environmental_health/en/index.html.

———. 2009a. "Health in Water Resources Development." www.who.int/docstore /water_sanitation_health/vector/water_resources.htm.

———. 2009b. "World Health Statistics 2008." www.who.int/whosis/whostat /EN_WHS08_Part1.pdf.

———. 2013a. "Life Expectancy: Life Expectancy Data by WHO Region." Global Health Observatory Data Repository. http://apps.who.int/gho/data/view .main.690?lang=en.

———. 2013b. "Disability and Health: Fact Sheet No. 352." Geneva: World Health Organization.

———. 2014a. "Female Genital Mutilation." www.who.int/mediacentre/factsheets /fs241/en/index.html.

———. 2014b. "World Health Statistics 2013." http://apps.who.int/iris/bitstream /10665/82058/1/WHO_HIS_HSI_13.1_eng.pdf.

WHO and World Bank. 2011. "World Report on Disability." Malta: World Health Organization.

Whorf, Benjamin. 1956 [1941]. *Language, Thought and Reality.* Reprinted in *Language, Thought and Reality: Selected Writings of Benjamin Lee Whorf,* edited by John B. Carroll. Cambridge, MA: MIT Press.

*Wide Angle.* 2003. "The Damned." PBS, September 18.

Wilkinson, Tracy. 2007. "A Jumble of Realities in Bosnia's Sarajevo." *Los Angeles Times,* September 4. http://articles.latimes.com/print/2007/sep/04/world/fg -history4.

Williams, Carol J. "India's 'Dowry Deaths' Still Rising Despite Modernization." *Los Angeles Times,* September 5. http://articles.latimes.com.

Williams, W. 1986. *The Spirit and the Flesh: Sexual Diversity in American Indian Cultures.* Boston: Beacon.

Wilmer, Franke. 1993. *The Indigenous Voice in World Politics: Since Time Immemorial.* Thousand Oaks, CA: Sage.

———. 2002. *The Social Construction of Man, the State, and War: Identity, Conflict and Violence in Former Yugoslavia.* New York: Routledge.

———. Forthcoming. "Gender, Violence, and Dehumanization: No Peace with Patriarchy." In *Gender and Peacebuilding: All Hands Required,* edited by Maureen Flaherty, Sean Byrne, Thomas Matyok, Jessica Senehi, and Hamdesa Tuso. Lanham, MD: Lexington.

Wilson, Richard J. 2010. "Prosecuting Pinochet in Spain." www.wcl.american.edu /hrbrief/v6i3/pinochet.htm.

Wisotsky, Alexandra L. 2001. "News from the International Criminal Tribunals." *Human Rights Brief* 8, no. 3: Brief 18. www.wcl.american.edu.

Wolters, Stephanie. 2005. "The Gacaca Process." *African Security Review* 14, no. 3: 67–68.

WomenAid International. 2010. "Literacy for Women: A Development Priority." www.womenaid.org.

Womenspace. 2008. "The Padlocked Vagina—Rape as Torture in the Congo." January 24. womenspace/wordpress.com.

WomenWatch. 2013. "Short History on the Commission on the Status of Women." www.un.org.

World Bank. 1991. *Operational Directive 4.20.* September. Washington, DC: World Bank.

———. 1998. *Development and Human Rights: The Role of the World Bank.* Washington, DC: World Bank.

———. 2003. *Implementation of Operational Directive 4.20 on Indigenous Peoples: An Independent Desk Review.* Report No. 25332, January 10. Washington, DC: World Bank.

———. 2005a. *World Development Report 2006: Equity and Development.* Washington, DC: World Bank and Oxford University Press.

———. 2005b. *Improving Women's Lives: World Bank Actions Since Beijing.* Washington, DC: World Bank.

———. 2013. "Defining Civil Society." http://web.worldbank.org/.

———. 2014. "Poverty Headcount Ratio at $2 a Day (PPP) (% of population)." http://data.worldbank.org/indicator/SI.POV.2DAY.

World Food Programme. 2014. "Hunger Statistics." www.wfp.org.

World Hunger Education Services. 2013. "2013 World Hunger and Poverty Facts and Statistics." www.worldhunger.org/articles/Learn/world%20hunger%20facts %202002.htm.

World Social Forum. 2014. "What the World Social Forum Is." www.forumsocial mondial.org.

World Social Forum India. 2006. "About WSF." http://www.wsfindia.org/?q=node/2.

World War II Database. 2014. "Tokyo Trial and Other Trials Against Japan." http://ww2db.com/battle_spec.php?battle_id=221.

World Water.org. 2010. "Data Table 19: Per Capita Bottled Water Consumption, by Country 1999 to 2010." Pacific Institute. http://worldwater.org/wp-content /uploads/sites/22/2013/07/data_table_19_per_capita_bottled_water_by _country.pdf.

Wotipka, Christine Min, and Kiyoteru Tsutsui. 2008. "Global Human Rights and State Sovereignty: State Ratification of International Human Rights Treaties, 1965–2001." *Sociological Forum* 23, no. 4: 724–754.

Wyman, David. 1985. *Paper Walls: America and the Refugee Crisis, 1938–1941.* New York: Pantheon.

Young, Iris Marion. 2000. *Inclusion and Democracy.* Oxford: Oxford University Press.

———. 2003. "The Logic of Masculinist Protection: Reflections on the Current Security State." *Signs: Journal of Women in Culture and Society* 29, no. 1: 1–25.

Young, Joseph. 2009. "State Capacity, Democracy, and the Violation of Personal Integrity Rights." *Journal of Human Rights* 8, no. 4: 283–300.

Young, Oran. 1972. "The Actors in World Politics." In *The Analysis of International Politics,* edited by J. N. Rosenau and M. A. East, 15–144. New York: Free Press.

Zahavi, Dan, Thor Grünbaum, and Josef Parnas. 2004. *The Structure and Development of Self-Consciousness: Interdisciplinary Perspectives.* Philadelphia: John Benjamins.

Zakaria, Fareed. 1994. "Culture Is Destiny: A Conversation with Lee Kuan Yew." *Foreign Affairs* 73, no. 2: 109–126.

———. 2002. "Asian Values." *Foreign Policy*, November–December.

Zimbardo, Philip. 1972. *The Psychology of Imprisonment: Privation, Power, and Pathology.* Palo Alto, CA: Stanford University Press.

———. 2007. *The Lucifer Effect: Understanding How Good People Turn Evil.* New York: Random House.

———. 2008. "Our Inner Heroes Could Stop Another Abu Ghraib." *The Guardian*, February 28. www.theguardian.com.

Zinn, Howard. 1980. *A People's History of the United States.* New York: Harper and Row.

# Index

# About the Book

THIS COMPREHENSIVE INTRODUCTION TO THE STUDY OF HUMAN rights in international politics blends concrete developments with theoretical inquiry, illuminating both in the process.

Franke Wilmer presents the nuts and bolts of human rights concepts, actors, and implementation before grappling with issues ranging from war and genocide to social and economic needs to racial and religious discrimination. Two themes—the tension between values and interests and the role of the state as both a protector of human rights and a perpetrator of human rights violations—are reflected throughout the text. The result is a clear, accessible exposition of the evolution of international human rights, as well as the challenges that those rights pose, in the context of the state system.

**Franke Wilmer** is professor of political science and international relations at Montana State University.